ALLE·ZEIT·WACH
1842

Eckart R. Straube Kurt Hahlweg (Eds.)

Schizophrenia

Concepts, Vulnerability, and Intervention

With 32 Figures

Springer-Verlag Berlin Heidelberg New York
London Paris Tokyo Hong Kong

Prof. Dr. Dipl.-Psych. Eckart R. Straube
Department of Psychiatry, University of Tübingen
Osianderstraße 22, D-7400 Tübingen
Federal Republic of Germany

Prof. Dr. Dipl.-Psych. Kurt Hahlweg
Department of Psychology
Technical University of Braunschweig
Spielmannstraße 12A, D-3300 Braunschweig
Federal Republic of Germany

ISBN 3-540-50573-3 Springer-Verlag Berlin Heidelberg New York
ISBN 0-387-50573-3 Springer-Verlag New York Berlin Heidelberg

Library of Congress Cataloging-in-Publication Data
Schizophrenia: concepts, vulnerability, and intervention/Eckart R.
Straube, Kurt Hahlweg, (eds.). p. cm.
ISBN 0-387-50573-3 (U.S.: alk. paper)
1. Schizophrenia—Pathophysiology. I. Straube, Eckart R., 1939- II. Hahlweg, Kurt.
[DNLM: 1. Schizophrenia. 2. Schizophrenic Psychology. WM 203 S33775] RC514.S3348
1989 616.89′82—dc20 DNLM/DLC for Library of Congress 89-21989

Typesetting: Macmillan India Ltd., Bangalore 25; Printing: Weihert-Druck GmbH, Darmstadt;
Binding: J. Schäffer GmbH & Co. KG, Grünstadt
2119/3140-543210 – Printed on acid-free paper

Table of Contents

List of Contributors

Hans D. Brenner
Psychiatrische Universitätsklinik Bern, Abteilung für Theoretische und Evaluative Psychiatrie, Bolligenstrasse 111, CH-3072 Bern, Switzerland

Connie C. Duncan
Unit on Psychophysiology, Laboratory of Psychology and Psychopathology, National Institute of Mental Health, NIH, Building 10, Room 4C110, Bethesda, Maryland 20892, USA

Thad Eckman
Camarillo/UCLA Research Center, Box 'A', Camarillo, California 93011, USA

Ian R.H. Falloon
Buckingham Mental Health Service, High Street, Buckingham, MK18 1NU, United Kingdom

Paul Fergeson
Department of Psychology, Texas Tech University, Box 4100, Lubbock, Texas 79409, USA

Kurt Hahlweg
Technische Universität Braunschweig, Institut für Psychologie, Spielmannstrasse 12A, D-3300 Braunschweig, Federal Republic of Germany

David Hemsley
Institute of Psychiatry, University of London, De Crespigny Park, Denmark Hill, London SE5 8AF, United Kingdom

Max Hermanutz
Krankenhaus Rottenmünster, Abt. Psychiatrie II, Schwenninger Str. 55, D-7210 Rottweil, Federal Republic of Germany

Bettina Hodel
Psychiatrische Universitätsklinik Bern, Abteilung für Theoretische und Evaluative Psychiatrie, Bolligenstrasse 111, CH-3072 Bern, Switzerland

HARVEY E. JACOBS
Camarillo/UCLA Research Center, Box 'A', Camarillo, California 93011, USA

SIBYLLE KRAEMER
Psychiatrische Klinik und Poliklinik der Technischen Universität München, Klinikum rechts der Isar, Ismaninger Straße 22, D-8000 München 80, Federal Republic of Germany

MARTIN LEMON
Department of Psychology, Texas Tech University, Box 4100, Lubbock, Texas 79409, USA

ROBERT P. LIBERMAN
Camarillo/UCLA Research Center, Box 'A', Camarillo, California 93011, USA

H. KEITH MASSEL
Camarillo/UCLA Research Center, Box 'A', Camarillo, California 93011, USA

SARNOFF A. MEDNICK
University of Southern California, Social Science Research Institute, University Park, Los Angeles, CA 90089-MC-1111, USA

KIM T. MUESER
Camarillo/UCLA Research Center, Box 'A', Camarillo, California 93011, USA

KEITH H. NUECHTERLEIN
University of California, Los Angeles, Department of Psychiatry and Biobehavioral Sciences, Neuropsychiatric Institute, Box 18, 760 Westwood Plaza, Los Angeles, CA 90024, USA

ARNE ÖHMAN
Uppsala Universitet, Psykologiska Institutionen, Box 1854, S-751 48 Uppsala, Sweden

JOSEF PARNAS
Psychological Institute, University Department of Psychiatry Kommunehospitalet, DK-1399 København K, Denmark

HANS-WERNER SCHIED
Krankenhaus Rottenmünster, Abt. Psychiatrie I, Schwenninger Str. 55, D-7210 Rottweil, Federal Republic of Germany

FINI SCHULSINGER
University Department of Psychiatry, DK-1399 København K, Denmark

BONNIE J. SPRING
Department of Psychology, Texas Tech University, Box 4100, Lubbock, Texas 79409, USA

ECKART R. STRAUBE
Eberhard-Karls-Universität Tübingen, Zentrum für Psychiatrie und Neurologie, Nervenklinik, Osianderstraße 22, D-7400 Tübingen, Federal Republic of Germany

NICHOLAS TARRIER
Prestwich Hospital, Bury New Road, Prestwich, Manchester, M25 7BL, United Kingdom

CHARLES J. WALLACE
Camarillo/UCLA Research Center, Box 'A', Camarillo, California 93011, USA

KENNETH M. ZAUCHA
University of California, Los Angeles, Department of Psychiatry and Biobehavioral Sciences, Neuropsychiatric Institute, Box 18, 760. Westwood Plaza, Los Angeles, CA 90024, USA

Introduction

Schizophrenia remains the most complex, puzzling, and because of its tendency towards chronicity, the most severe of the mental disorders. It is a very heterogeneous disorder characterized by extreme disruptions of thought, perception, behavior, and emotion. About 1% of the population worldwide will experience at least one schizophrenic episode. Most of the patients will have a number of exacerbations leading in about 30% of cases to a chronic residual state, due either to the illness itself or to psychosocial environmental factors, or – most likely – to the interaction of both.

Given the enormous personal hardship for patients and their relatives as well as the staggering costs of the illness for our societies, research in schizophrenia has become the number one priority in many countries, especially in the United States. However, research on the etiology of schizophrenia has failed to establish a single causal factor, and it is nowadays accepted to be multifactorial. A combination of biological predisposition and environmental circumstances is assumed to be necessary for the manifestation of the illness. This shift in orientation away from an either/or (biological or environmental, e.g., family interaction) point of view, as evident in the work of the 1950s and 1960s, was certainly desirable to encourage research.

A model has emerged to guide this new type of research, the so-called vulnerability-stress model, a model originally articulated by Rosenthal in 1970 as the diathesis-stress model and more recently modified by Zubin and Spring (1977). According to this model, a predisposition to schizophrenia is inherited or acquired developmentally and forms the basis for indices of vulnerability to the disorder. This vulnerability is modified by all life events that increase or decrease the likelihood that schizophrenia will emerge in early adulthood. In an effort to specify this rather global model, Nuechterlein and Dawson (1984) reviewed the literature and put forward a heuristic vulnerability-stress model for the development and course of schizophrenic psychotic episodes.

The model comprises three major categories (Fig. 1): (a) enduring vulnerability characteristics; (b) external environmental stressors; and (c) development of psychotic symptoms. The enduring characteristics are assumed to be disturbance of information processing, psychophysiological response anomalies, and social competence deficits. These dysfunctions (vulnerability markers) are assumed to be present before, during, and after a schizophrenic episode. External environmental stimuli comprise social stressors (discrete life events) and a

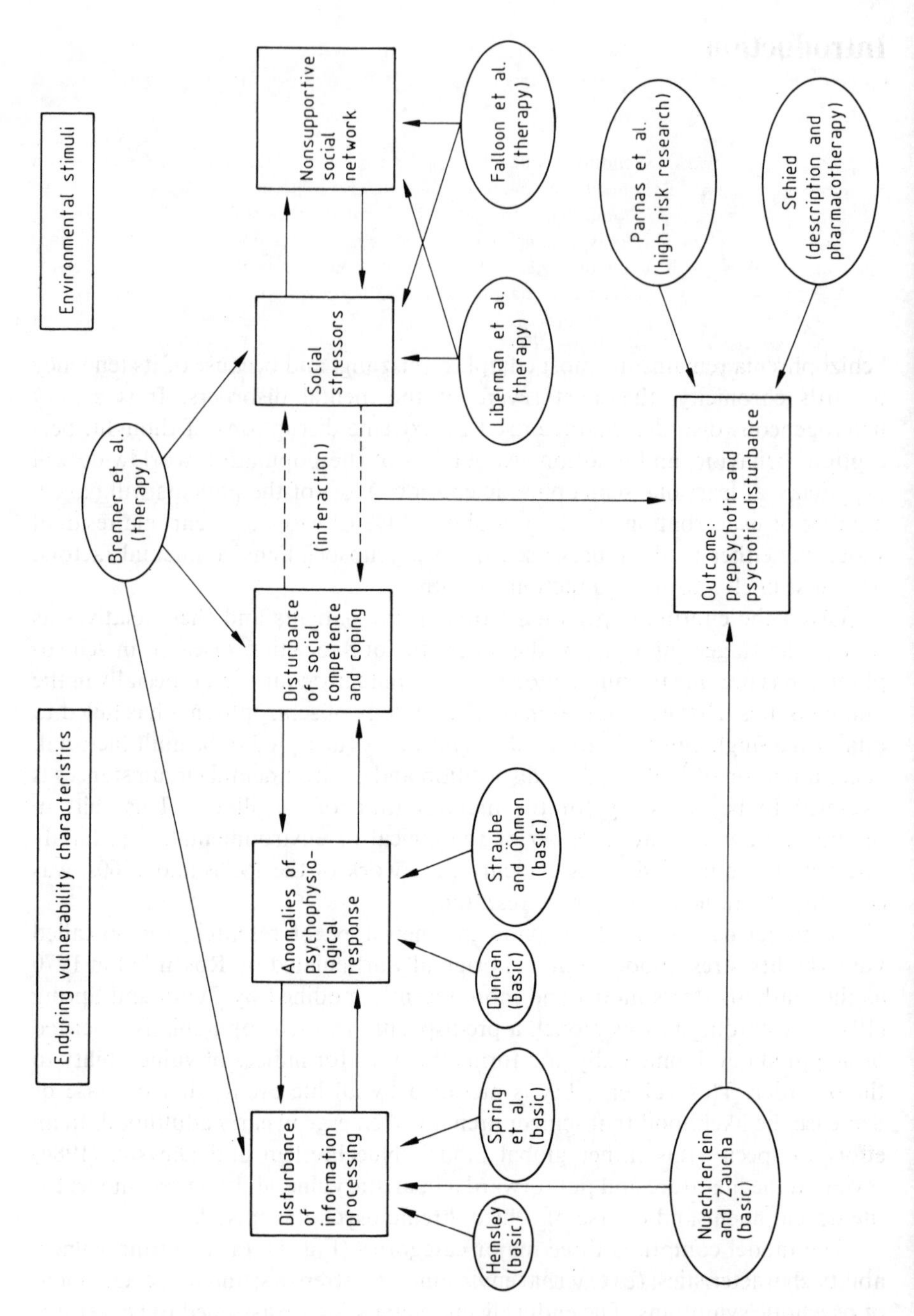

Fig. 1. Vulnerability-stress model: modified and simplified version of the model proposed by Nuechterlein and Dawson (1984). Names of authors who make contributions to components of the model are included

nonsupportive social network, especially a family with high levels of critical and overinvolved attitudes ("expressed emotion," EE). Nuechterlein and Dawson (1984, p. 305) assume that

> . . . certain preexisting, enduring vulnerability characteristics of the individual interact with stressful external environmental stimuli to produce transient intermediate states of processing capacity overload, autonomic hyperarousal, and impaired processing of stimuli before the development of psychotic symptoms. These intermediate states and their behavioral concomitants tend to increase the level and frequency of environmental stressors by causing disruptions in the individual's immediate social and family environment. The feedback loop, in turn, leads to more extreme processing capacity overload, autonomic hyperarousal, and deficient processing of social stimuli. The vicious cycle is viewed as continuing, unless successfully broken, until the transient intermediate states reach an individual's threshold point for the development of schizophrenic reality-distorting, psychotic symptoms.

The vulnerability-stress model is essentially pragmatic to guide research and, as witnessed by the increasing number of publications following this model, has been widely adopted for that purpose. The empirical validity of some components of this model are better established than others; especially the research on EE has resulted in a number of replicated findings showing that the chance of relapse increases four-fold whenever the patient returns to a high-EE household. Unfortunately, despite efforts to identify reliable vulnerability characteristics, none has a secure status as yet.

The model has not only stimulated research, it has also influenced, and to a greater extent, the development of new and efficient psychosocial treatment approaches in schizophrenia. As shown in Fig.1, psychological treatments have been developed which aim at modifying either vulnerability characteristics (cognitive therapy, Brenner et al.; social skills training, Liberman et al.) or family factors (family care, Falloon et al.). Again, in accordance with the biopsychosocial nature of the model, these therapies are nearly always conducted in combination with pharmacological (neuroleptic) treatment as a prerequisite for effective psychological interventions.

The goal of this volume was to bring together experts on basic research in schizophrenia and on the application of results stemming from this research in order to stimulate a dialogue between basic and applied researchers and – even more importantly – inform interested but nonspecialized colleagues about the rather exciting new developments in both areas. Given the latter, the contributions are presented, as far as possible, in nontechnical language. Each contribution refers to one or several components of the vulnerability-stress model as depicted in Fig. 1.

Psychopathology and Vulnerability

The model of Nuechterlein and Dawson predicts overt psychotic behavior as the result of an interaction between vulnerability factors and environmental stress. The chapter by *Schied* describes the different facets of the overt psychotic behavior of schizophrenics. The chapter commences with the development of psychiatric concepts related to a group of behavior disorders first considered to be a clinical entity by Kraepelin. Modern diagnostic concepts and diagnostic criteria are then described in detail. Issues of neuroleptic therapy are discussed as well as the factors involved in success and failure of relapse prevention. It is pointed out that the results of controlled trials with neuroleptic maintenance therapy show that additional therapeutic interventions (e.g., aiming at social stressors) are necessary to reduce relapse rates further. These new intervention methods are described in the therapy section of this volume in detail.

Most important for early intervention and the question of the etiology of schizophrenia are high-risk studies. *Parnas, Schulsinger, and Mednick* report new findings from their Copenhagen project. The authors examined 207 children of schizophrenic women together with a matched control group. In a reanalysis 10 years later, a high proportion of schizophrenics appeared in the group of offspring of schizophrenic mothers, but, interestingly enough, also a high proportion of individuals with schizotypal personality disorder. A detailed analysis revealed differences in the amount of environmental insult (perinatal complications, institutional rearing) between schizophrenics and schizotypals, the former group having a higher incidence of environmental insult. The authors conclude that schizophrenics and schizotypals share comparable genetic liability to schizophrenia (vulnerability or diathesis), but that the development of severe disturbances (schizophrenia) may be a result of additional environmental stressors.

Information Processing and Vulnerability

The contributions of *Hemsley*, of *Nuechterlein and Zaucha*, and of *Spring, Lemon, and Fergeson* deal with different aspects of disturbances of information processing. *Hemsley* demonstrates that schizophrenics perform "better" than normals in experiments where the normal subject "sees" nonexistent structures due to expectations of order. The author explains this by an absence of organizing cognitive factors in schizophrenics. These kinds of experiments are important since they refute the argument that a lack of motivation to collaborate explains the deviant performance of schizophrenics. The author hypothesizes that the vulnerability of schizophrenics can be interpreted as a failure to make use of the redundancies in the environment.

Both *Hemsley* and *Spring* et al. emphasize, however, that the information-processing style within subgroups of schizophrenics is different. Spring et al., therefore, question the widely held assumption that there is only one diathesis for schizophrenia. After reviewing their own findings and results from the literature, the authors conclude that at least two different types of diathesis exist: one type is characterized mainly by distractability, which should be considered as a positive symptom-linked marker, and the other type is mainly characterized by deficits in sustained attention, which should be considered as a negative symptom-linked marker. *Nuechterlein and Zaucha* also consider deficiencies in information processing – according to the model depicted in Fig. 1 – as an underlying vulnerability characteristic since the work of *Spring* and of others shows that such deficits are already present in a high percentage of first-degree relatives and of children who are genetically at risk of developing schizophrenia. The authors assume that information-processing deficiencies interact with social stressors (and/or with a lack of social support) to produce high autonomic arousal and deficient social behavior. Negative feedback loops then intensify the deficiencies, and psychotic symptomatology will appear as a result of this interaction.

Psychophysiology and Vulnerability

Duncan describes the similarities between disturbed attention and reduced late component (P300) of the evoked potential in schizophrenics. She concludes, however, after reviewing her own findings and those reported in the literature, that P300 reduction cannot be considered a genetic marker or a trait characteristic of schizophrenia, since the P300 amplitude changes with symptomatology and P300 reduction can be found in other psychiatric disturbances as well. Studies on relatives of schizophrenics (including a high-risk sample) have yielded mixed results.

Straube and Öhman explain the heterogeneity of the autonomic nervous system (ANS) responsivity, e.g., skin conductance nonresponding and hyper-responding, as different indicators with respect to differences in vulnerability and differences in the developmental course of the illness. The literature concerning the ANS in high-risk children and in actively symptomatic schizophrenics is reviewed. The authors assume that ANS deviations in schizophrenia indicate different states of the illness as the result of an interaction with environmental challenges and coping attempts.

Treatment Approaches

Impairments in information processing are regarded as vulnerability characteristics. However, older treatment/rehabilitation programs rarely took into account the specifics of the basic cognitive deficiencies. Therapeutic recommendations remained general and vague, e.g., avoid overstimulation or reduce the quantity of information. Recently a much more specific treatment program which focuses on directly changing cognitive dysfunctions has been developed and is described by *Brenner, Kraemer, Hermanutz, and Hodel.* The program consists of a number of subprograms aimed at, for example, improving the patient's ability to differentiate cognitively or to foster his/her social perception. This program has been extensively tested using acute and chronic populations. In their paper the authors describe the program in detail and present data on its effectiveness.

Social skills training methods represent another major strategy in the rehabilitation of schizophrenic patients. Building skills is based on the assumption that coping and competence can override stress and vulnerability in reducing relapses and improving psychosocial functioning. *Liberman, Mueser, Wallace, Jacobs, Eckman, and Massel* stress in their paper the fact that skills training needs to incorporate procedures and principles of human learning and information processing. They describe a "problem-solving" model of training which provides general strategies for dealing with a variety of social situations based on behavioral principles. In their opinion, it is essential that social skills training is embedded in a comprehensive program of rehabilitation that features continuity of care, supportive community services, therapeutic relationships, and judicious prescription of psychotropic drugs.

The past decade has witnessed renewed efforts to support the role of family caregivers in the community rehabilitation of schizophrenic patients. *Falloon, Hahlweg, and Tarrier* describe the major family treatment approaches which have been successfully developed over the past few years. Taking the EE findings into account and using the vulnerability-stress model as a framework, all approaches emphasize more effective problem solving to cope with life stressors, provide information about schizophrenia and medication, and encourage more active family participation in the long-term management of schizophrenic patients. The results of controlled outcome studies are very encouraging, demonstrating long-lasting positive effects.

The hope of the editors – in bringing together basic research and therapeutic applications – is that this volume will stimulate research to uncover the complex interactional components which cause the schizophrenic breakdown. The further hope is to stimulate new therapeutic approaches which could provide the much-needed contributions to the amelioration of the life conditions of schizophrenics, since the number of patients who improve only slightly and/or deteriorate after discharge – even when optimal psychopharmacotherapy is guaranteed – is still too high.

References

Nuechterlein, K.H., & Dawson, M.E. (1984). A heuristic vulnerability/stress model of schizophrenic episodes. *Schizophrenia Bulletin*, *10*, 300–312.

Rosenthal, D. (1970). Genetic theory and abnormal behavior. New York: McGraw-Hill.

Zubin, J., & Spring, B. (1977). Vulnerability – a new view of schizophrenia. *Journal of Abnormal Psychology*, *86*, 103-126.

Acknowledgment. The authors would like to thank Dr. Margaret Campbell for her valuable help in the preparation of the manuscripts in this volume.

E.R. Straube

Tübingen and Munich, 1988 K. Hahlweg

Part I
Psychopathology and Vulnerability

Psychiatric Concepts and Therapy

H.-W. Schied

Introduction and Historical Background

The symptoms of what today is known as schizophrenia were described at least 2000 years ago. In Roman times Aretaeus described some of his patients as "stupid, absent, musing, with a stupefaction of the senses of reason and other faculties of the mind" (quoted by Cutting, 1980). From his descriptions of individual mental disabilities and general personality impairments, one can recognise what today would be believed to be schizophrenia. Even in the patients whom he called "melancholic" he described a clear syndrome of paranoia (e.g. illusions of being poisoned, autistic withdrawal and pseudo-religious ideas). Celsus, another Roman physician, classified insanity into several subtypes. In one, he says, the mind is deceived by false images but the intellect is intact. Soranus described the delusions of grandeur of patients such as those who "believed they were God" (quoted by Lehmann, 1975a).

Lehmann (1975a) states that after this early era of clinical interest and of serious attempts to treat schizophrenic disturbances, the concept of schizophrenia subsided into 1000 years of darkness and religious superstition. Innumerable schizophrenics were burnt at the stake for being possessed by the devil or were cast out from society, incarcerated or delivered to brutal asylums. The schizophrenic was banned from the public eye and thus was unavailable to the would-be scientist or clinician.

Treatment

Only in the eighteenth century did one begin once again to *treat* people with mental illness, rather than just keeping them somewhere out of the way. Indeed, the "moral treatment" used at the beginning of the nineteenth century resembles in many ways the "milieu therapy" and other sociotherapeutic procedures widely practised today. "Moral therapy" perhaps represents the first effective attempt at a therapeutic approach to schizophrenia. Alas, once again schizophrenic treatment went through a period of stagnation for over 50 years. Only in the 1930s did Sakel's approach of inducing coma through hypoglycaemia and Meduna's approach of inducing convulsions make an appearance.

But it was not until the 1950s that the decisive step was made with the introduction of the neuroleptic treatment of schizophrenia.

Classification and Diagnosis

Indicative of the difficulties facing investigators of schizophrenia is the fact that what is known as schizophrenia today was only defined as an illness in 1896 by Emil Kraepelin. He collected a range of psychotic syndromes together under the rubric of "dementia praecox".

In fact, already before Kraepelin's influential work, Kahlbaum had made thorough clinical observations of a collection of symptoms – characterised by pathologically increased muscle tone – that made up the syndrome he described in 1868 as "catatonia". Hecker, a student of Kahlbaum, went on to describe a syndrome he called "hebephrenia". In introducing this term in 1871, he emphasised that this illness occurred especially in young adults or adolescents and usually progressed to dementia (Fig. 1).

In 1896 Kraepelin supposed that dementia praecox and hebephrenia were identical, whereas catatonia and dementia paranoides represented separate illnesses. The true breakthrough that brought a new conceptualisation to this group of illnesses occurred with the lecture he gave at the historic conference in Heidelberg in 1898. Here he announced that he considered the different syndromes to belong to one and the same disease which he called "dementia praecox". This illness was, according to Kraepelin, characterised by the absence of external causes, the high incidence among young and previously healthy people and "most importantly" by the eventual development of dementia.

This assessment of schizophrenia necessarily progressing to dementia did not accord with the observations of Eugen Bleuler (1911). He therefore suggested another term – "schizophrenia". In fact, by this time Kraepelin had already reported in a later edition of his book that 13% of his dementia praecox patients remitted. That is, not all of his patients ended up later as demented. In retrospect even this figure has proved to be too low an estimate. The wide-ranging and carefully run long-term investigations of Manfred Bleuler (the son of Eugen Bleuler; 1972), Ciompi and Müller (1976), Huber, Gross and Schüttler (1979) in Europe and Tsuang (1972) in the United States show that approximately a quarter of all schizophrenics have a good long-term prognosis.

Classification Schemes at the Beginning of the Twentieth Century

E. Bleuler saw the central feature of the illness in the splitting of the mind – "schizophrenia". In his major work *Dementia Praecox or the Group of Schizophrenias* (1911/1950) he pointed out that an incurable end was not the most characteristic clinical feature of schizophrenia. Another important contribution of E. Bleuler was the introduction of the concept of a hierarchy of symptoms to

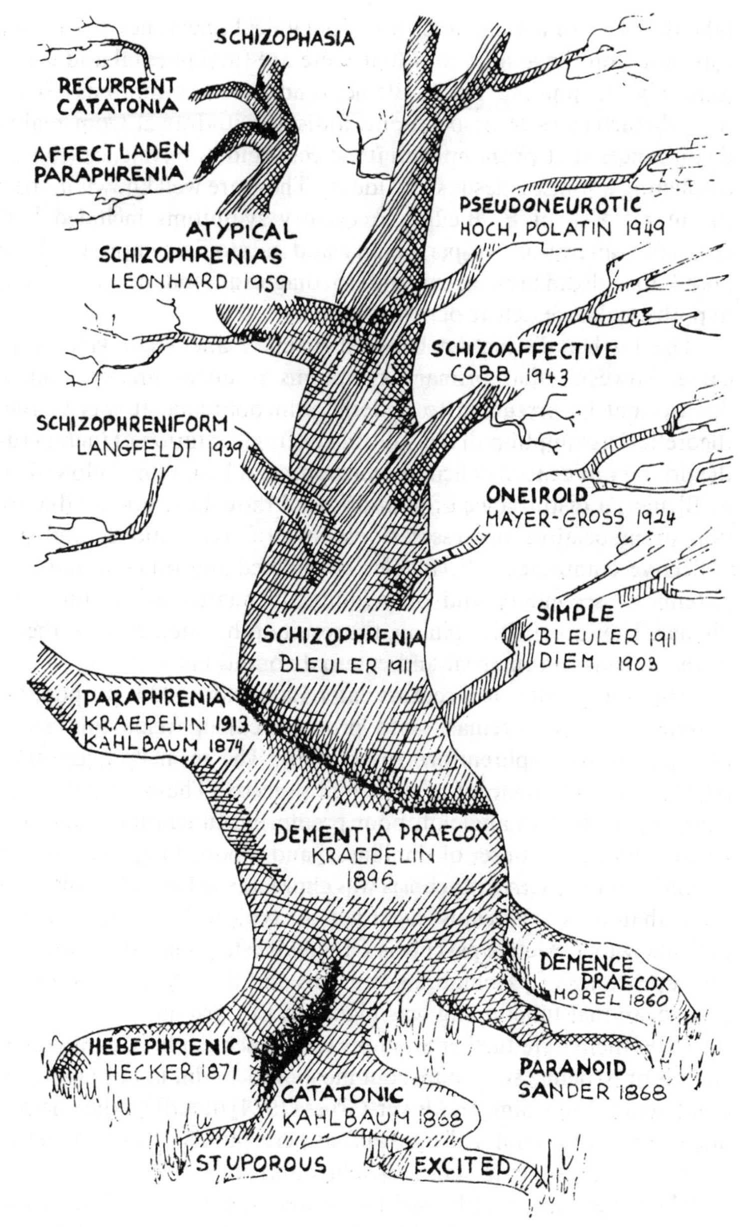

Fig 1. Historical growth and varieties of classification of the schizophrenia concept (after Lehmann, 1975a)

take the place of a mere description of clinical phenomena. This new hierarchy was based on the assumption that there are fundamental and accessory symptoms of schizophrenia. For E. Bleuler fundamental symptoms (*Grundsymptome*) were disturbances of associations, autism (withdrawal from reality), affective disturbances (flat or inappropriate affect), and ambivalence (the experience of conflicting impulses, desires and ideas). These are well known in the literature as the four "A's" of E. Bleuler. Accessory symptoms included hallucinations, delusions, alterations in personality and catatonic symptoms. E. Bleuler proposed this distinction as an aid to diagnosis and not as a reference to a hypothetical core deficit of schizophrenia.

The further distinction between primary and secondary symptoms indicated, however, that primary symptoms resulted directly from the organic disease that he presumed to underlie schizophrenia. It was E. Bleuler's basic theoretical assumption that a splitting or fragmentation of mental functions was the primary or central deficit in schizophrenia. From this followed, according to E. Bleuler, a disturbance of goal-oriented thought processes due to a dysfunction of associative processes (loosening of associations) and a splitting of "affective complexes". E. Bleuler considered the other symptoms of schizophrenia as secondary and only indirectly related to the underlying organic disease. They are, in his opinion, the result of the interaction of the basic process of the illness with internal and external conditions.

About a quarter of a century later Langfeldt (1939) proposed splitting the "group of schizophrenias" into process schizophrenia and reactive schizophrenia (or schizophreniform psychoses). The term "process schizophrenia" relates to the old concept of dementia praecox. These were the schizophrenics with, according to Langfeldt, poor premorbid functioning, an odd or schizoid personality before onset of the illness, and a poor long-term outcome. Schizophreniform or reactive psychosis was characterised by schizophrenia-like symptoms that most clinicians regarded as typical for acute schizophrenia. In patients with a reactive psychosis Langfeldt established that life events preceded the appearance of psychiatric symptoms and that the premorbid level of social and vocational functioning was higher in this group.

Later there were further attempts to split schizophrenia into different disease entities or to define subgroups, but most of these did not obtain the same degree of influence. For example, Mayer-Gross (1924) described the oneiroid, a dreamlike experience stimulated by external perceptions. This can sometimes occur during extremely acute stages of schizophrenia.

The subgroupings still used today were described by Kraepelin: catatonia, hebephrenia and paranoid schizophrenia; to which Diem (1903) and E. Bleuler (1911) added a fourth type, schizophrenia simplex.

Others attempted to define subgroups on the "borderline" of schizophrenia (e.g. schizoaffective (Cobb, 1943) and pseudoneurotic schizophrenia (Hoch & Polatin, 1949) (see Fig. 1). The latter group was later called "borderline schizophrenia". We will discuss this last issue in more detail in "Subgroups of Schizophrenia", p. 18.

Current Concepts of Symptoms and Syndromes

Cognitive Symptoms

Perceptual Disturbances

Reports of sensory disturbances by schizophrenics mostly relate to auditory *hallucinations*. These can be observed in about two-thirds of schizophrenic patients (Sartorius, Shapiro & Jablensky, 1974). Rarer are hallucinations in visual, olfactory, gustatory, and tactile modalities. The *International Pilot Study of Schizophrenia* (IPSS) reported an incidence of approximately 15% for the latter group of perceptual disturbances (Sartorius et al., 1974).

Auditory hallucinations often consist of voices talking about the patient in a short and often insulting way, e.g. "That nasty pig! We know what he is up to!"; or sometimes directly to him: "Why don't you go to church?". Typically the patient hears running commentaries on his behaviour, e.g. "Now he is going to the toilet. He will probably masturbate". The patient often hallucinates the voices of people he knows, who discuss him among themselves, conversing in the third person about him. One voice might say, for example: "Shall we kill him now?"; the other voice, a patient reported to us, then answered, "No, wait. We will lure him into a trap". Sometimes it is the voice of God or the devil.

Some auditory hallucinations are described as thoughts heard aloud, but they have an intermediate quality between thoughts and what the patient normally hears with his own ears. The patient has difficulty in describing the exact nature of what he perceives to the examiner since no common experience exists. Some thoughts are described as being spoken out loud. The patient feels, therefore, that other people can listen to his thoughts. Hallucinations are usually interpreted as representing a dangerous power which the patient cannot influence.

Visual hallucinations are unusual. About 10% of schizophrenics report visual hallucinations (Sartorius et al., 1974). They are more typical of patients with organic psychoses. Besides frequency, some other features help to distinguish visual hallucinations in schizophrenia from those in organic states, and from those in alcoholics or substance abusers. Visual hallucinations of schizophrenics appear, according to an investigation by Frieske and Wilson (1966), less often at night, are less often experienced as moving and are nearly always accompanied by hallucinations in another modality, usually the auditory modality.

Olfactory, gustatory and tactile hallucinations may be observed, but they are even less common. Again, they are usually accompanied by auditory hallucinations in schizophrenia. Sometimes schizophrenics experience coenesthetic hallucinations: these are somatic disturbances without any relevant sensory stimulation (e.g. a sensation of constant pulling of the inner organs or burning of certain parts within the body). Besides these false perceptions, schizophrenics sometimes complain of a general *perceptual hypersensitivity*. Lights, sounds and colours change their intensity, especially in acute phases of the illness.

Disturbances in the processes of *selective attention* are often reported by schizophrenics. McGhie and Chapman (1961) quote the following description from their systematic interviews of patients:

> Everything seems to grip my attention although I am not particularly interested in anything. I am speaking to you just now but I can hear noises going on next door and in the corridor. I find it difficult to shut these out and it makes it more difficult for me to concentrate on what I am saying to you. Often the silliest little things that are going on seem to interest me. That's not even true; they don't interest me but I find myself attending to them and wasting a lot of time this way . . . (Patient 23, p. 104).

Such patients have difficulty in attending to relevant stimuli and ignoring the irrelevant. They are unable to direct their attention at will and feel themselves increasingly determined by outside conditions. McGhie and Chapman (1961) state: "To this extent the patient feels 'open', vulnerable and in danger of having his personal identity swamped by the incoming tide of impressions which he cannot control". Much experimental research in schizophrenia centres on this aspect of the schizophrenic disturbance.

Disorders of Thought, Language and Communication

From the psychiatric point of view, disordered thinking has long been viewed as one of the major features of schizophrenia. E. Bleuler (1911) emphasised the "loosening of associations" that he believed to be one of the primary symptoms. Accordingly, schizophrenic thinking or reasoning is characterised by the loss of the ability to pursue a goal. Thus, associations which are only tangentially related to the subject of a process of reasoning or a conversation insert themselves into the thought process. Harrow and Quinlan (1985) asked their patients to interpret proverbs. One patient explained the proverb "One swallow does not make a summer", as follows: "When you swallow something, it could be all right, but the next minute you could be coughing, and dreariness and all kind of miserable things coming out of your throat". Although the linguistic structure is not affected here, the patient is unable to refer to the overall coherent contextual meaning of the words. Instead he responds to tangential themes associated with the dominant meaning of the word "swallow" (p. 436). The patient treats the sentence as if it were composed of incoherent single parts. The connection between question and response is lost. In some schizophrenics, communication can show a more severe disorganisation of formal thought processes. In such cases the listener is unable to discover the associative connections. An example is the response to the following question: "Why are people who are born deaf usually unable to talk?"; answer of the patient: "When you swallow in your throat like a key it comes out, but not as scissors. A robin, too, it means spring" Harrow and Quinlan, 1985 (p. 429).

The thought-disturbed patient is often incapable of directing his communications in a manner appropriate to the current situation. Even when the content of a conversation is more or less ordered, very often the necessary additional hints about the way in which remarks were meant are missing. Thought-disordered schizophrenics show a typical lack of cohesive links between sentences. The following is an example from Rochester and Martin (1979): "A commuter and a skier are on a lift and *he* looks very cold" (p. 146). Here the listener has no indication as to who is being referred to – the commuter, the skier or another person on the lift? The schizophrenic appears either incapable of viewing the conversation from the point of view of the listener, or indifferent to this. The line of thought appears to follow an idiosyncratic and autistic logic. It is often vague and indefinite. According to the analysis of Andreasen and Grove (1986), derailment (associative loosening), tangentiality, incoherence, loss of goal and illogicality are the most common forms of language and thought disturbances in schizophrenia. However, patients with mania may also display these abnormalities.

Not all schizophrenics show thought disorder. Even clearly thought-disordered patients are disorganised only occasionally and, here again, gross anomalies are rare. Kendell (1987) therefore states: "More commonly there is a gradual slippage in which a sequence of minor shifts eventually produces a major change of theme" (p. 10). Rochester and Martin (1979) found massive impairment in less than a third of patients.

Not only may schizophrenic thought be broken up or vague, but sometimes the patient may also remain completely silent (mutism) or show poverty of speech, symptoms which belong, according to the investigation of Andreasen (1982), to the so-called negative symptoms of schizophrenia. A rare symptom is echolalia, a stereotyped repetition of questions, words or phrases, which sometimes appears in chronic schizophrenics. Finally, one sometimes encounters neologisms, self-invented words.

Delusional Ideation

Persecutory ideation is the most prominent feature of the delusional syndrome. Schizophrenics, especially acute patients, can – for example – be convinced that a certain car belongs to a foreign intelligence agency, and follows him each day on his way home; that psychedelic drugs are added to his food to make him crazy; that he is spied on at his work place by colleagues who are paid by this agency, etc. Closely linked to this are delusions of reference: the news on the radio is somehow altered by certain messages to give him a hint, people on the street cough in a certain unusual way to warn him, etc.

The content of the delusional ideas often deals with hostile and malevolent forces which try to gain power over the patient. Sometimes these delusions develop the form of a delusion of grandeur. The patient is again the centre of interest, but this time he is chosen to become the king or president, or he feels he is selected by God and has to fulfil the will of God. These delusions cannot be corrected by reasoning or facing the patient with reality. Kendell (1987) points out that the presence of delusions is in itself of little diagnostic value, unless their content is obviously bizarre or more elaborate.

The feeling of passivity is a characteristic feature of delusional ideation and hallucinations. The patient may believe that some alien powers are trying to impose their will on him, that he is no longer in control of his own will, of his own thoughts and feelings. He feels that thoughts which are not his own are inserted into his head. These delusions of being controlled and influenced belong to the so-called *passivity phenomena* of schizophrenia.

Psychomotor Symptoms

Quantitative and qualitative behavioural changes are possible in schizophrenia, such as reduction in spontaneous movements, activity and initiative. In rare but extreme cases, as in the stuporous state of catatonia, patients may stop moving altogether, becoming mute and stiff. In some cases they may then maintain strange postures for hours or even days. The "normal" reduction in activity consists, however, in withdrawal from contact with other people, patients stay in bed all day, sit around seemingly without interest in what is going on around them.

The other extreme, especially in acute phases, consists of extremely excited motor activity without obvious cause. In this state patients can be a danger to themselves or their environment.

Qualitative changes express themselves in the form of situationally inappropriate, unpredictable, poorly coordinated behavioural patterns. The movements of schizophrenics sometimes show a characteristic awkwardness. Indeed, in young schizophrenics just such a loss of natural gracefulness of movement is often the first sign of the beginning illness, as Lehmann (1975a) points out.

Affective Changes

Affect is nearly always disturbed in schizophrenia. Just as with psychomotor changes one may observe quantitative and qualitative changes of affective control. A characteristic quantitative change consists in a "flattening" or "blunting" of the emotional response in situations where people normally react with signs of emotional involvement. A schizophrenic might be approached, for example, by his former best friend who has brought the favourite pastry and sweets of the patient with him, but the friend does not get any response from him. Thus many schizophrenics give the impression of being indifferent, if not completely apathetic – at least they sometimes do not express their feelings to other people. Other schizophrenics may still show a certain emotional resonance, happiness, fear and irritation; but often real emotional warmth is lacking. Often the patients themselves admit that their ability to show empathy is reduced.

Emotional reactions that are inappropriate to the situation (parathymia) are a typical qualitative change seen in schizophrenia. A schizophrenic patient might, for example, take the news of the death of one of his children with a slight smile on his lips. Or, in contrast, react with rage to the question as to whether he slept well the previous night.

In chronic stages of the illness the extent of emotional blunting and inappropriateness of emotional reactions indicates how far the course of the illness has changed the essence of the patient's personality. On the other hand, the degree of appropriateness and the depth of feelings expressed represent a good prognostic measure in schizophrenia.

In spite of the frequently observed flattening of affect, many schizophrenics are very much *more sensitive* than most people during the early or *pre-schizophrenic* stages of their illness. This can be easily observed in the acute phase when patients first present themselves at the clinic. They are easily hurt, even by the mildest criticism. This may partially explain the finding of Leff and Vaughn (1985) in London that early relapse is associated with critical, highly emotional or intrusive interactions in the family of the schizophrenic (cf. Falloon, Hahlweg & Tarries, this volume). The same situation may lead to the first appearance of the schizophrenic at the clinic. Huber et al. (1979) found in their systematic investigation that friends and relatives of schizophrenics described the patients as having been sensitive and inhibited before becoming ill. Along with the presence of a schizoid ("cold") personality, this was one of the most frequently noted features in the patients before the illness appeared.

Social Withdrawal

The affective changes described above are closely linked to problems experienced in the patients' social life. Typically they withdraw from friendships, a partnership or from professional activity and they are incapable of developing new and lasting relationships. In some schizophrenics, especially in those with a poor long-term outcome (Strauss, Carpenter & Bartko, 1974), this social deficit is already present a long time before the first breakdown. Whether the social problems are part of the core of the illness or reflect an attempt by the patient to overcome an increase of sensitivity (coping attempts) remains controversial.

Altered Sense of Self

Scharfetter (1983) found five categories of ego dysfunction to be characteristic for schizophrenia: disturbance of identity, loss of ego boundaries, loss of ego consistency, loss of ego activity, and loss of ego vitality. All of these dysfunctions are closely linked to delusions and hallucinations.

The most prominent of these symptoms is the *disturbance of identity*. The patient feels that he has changed identity, for example that he is the son of God or the king of England. Other patients feel uncertainty about their gender. Most patients show, however, less dramatic changes. Rapid fluctuation between the real and the other identity is typical.

A patient who complains that he is without protection, since every sound and every external event penetrates into his inside, that he cannot discern inside from outside any more (etc.), suffers, according to Scharfetter, from a *loss of ego boundaries*. McGhie and Chapman (1961) state: "... the patient feels 'open', vulnerable and in danger of having his personal identity swamped by the incoming tide of impressions which he cannot control" (p. 105). The patient has the feeling that he has no private sphere any more. People can read his thoughts: his suffering is the suffering of all people. It also leads to the patient becoming especially sensitive to all external events. Sometimes patients fuse their identity with that of an external object.

Loss of ego consistency refers to the schism or splitting of functions which led E. Bleuler to coin the term "schizo-phrenia". Rollin (1980) quotes a former patient who describes the loss of consistency by a dream he had:

> To be schizophrenic is best summed up in a repeating dream I have had since childhood. In this dream I am lying on a beautiful sunlit beach but my body is in pieces. This fact causes me no concern since I realize that the tide is coming in and that I am unable to gather the parts of my dismembered body together to run away. . . . This to me is what schizophrenia feels like; being fragmented in one's personality and constantly afraid that the tide of illness will completely cover me (p.165).

Psychological functions as well as parts of the body can be experienced as being disconnected. The patient feels his psyche, as well as his body, is falling apart.

Disturbance of ego activity refers to the feeling that the patient is no longer master of his own will. He has the delusion that an outside force rules his thoughts and behaviour.

In some severe cases the patient is no longer sure whether he is alive or dead. Scharfetter calls this a *loss of ego vitality*.

Subgroups of Schizophrenia

Catatonia

Catatonic schizophrenia appears in two distinct forms. One is characterised by stupor and inhibition, the other by high arousal. Both subtypes show clear anomalies of motor behaviour [e.g. stupor, negativism, posturing, mannerisms, automatic reaction to commands or compulsive repetition of the movements of others (echopraxia)]. Both forms of catatonia need careful supervision.

In the excited form of catatonia patients show extreme psychomotor agitation. They are continually talking or shouting. Language is usually incoherent. Behaviour is almost exclusively controlled by inner experiences. Such patients require particularly intensive care and must be watched in case they do themselves or others injury or collapse through exhaustion.

Stauder (1934) coined the term "pernicious catatonia" for an extremely excited form of catatonia which could not be controlled by the types of sedative treatment then available and could prove life threatening. These types of patients often died after 1 or 2 weeks. The syndrome is characterised by extreme stupor and extreme variations in sympathetic function [e.g. vasoconstriction, hyperthermia (>40°C) and tachycardia]. The danger arises when the patients no longer eat or drink. Thus electrolyte changes in the body fluids lead to somatic deterioration. In some such cases death can only be prevented by electroconvulsive treatment.

Catatonia has become much rarer. The reasons for this are poorly understood. It is possible that early drug treatment – e.g. with tranquillisers before the first full psychotic episode – may play a role in the decrease in incidence.

Hebephrenia

Above all, the hebephrenic type is characterised by disorganisation of behaviour. Thus this subgroup is currently recognised by the *Diagnostic and Statistical Manual of Mental Disorders*, 3rd revised edition (DSM-IIIR; 1987) as schizophrenia of the disorganised type. The essential features are, according to DSM-IIIR, incoherence, marked loosening of associations, grossly disorganised behaviour and flat or grossly inappropriate affect (e.g. laughing without any apparent cause). The absence of *systematised* delusions characterises this subgroup. Delusions or hallucinations are only present as fragments. According to the IPSS (Sartorius et al., 1974), the incidence of hebephrenia among schizophrenics is about 11%.

Paranoid Hallucinatory Schizophrenia

This subtype of schizophrenia is characterised principally by the dominance of delusions. The essential themes are of persecution or of grandeur. The patient is preoccupied, especially in later chronic stages of the illness, with a very elaborate system of delusions. Auditory hallucinations are nearly always present and are related to the content of the delusions. First presentations for paranoid schizophrenia are on average in subjects who are older (e.g. 25–40 years) than those presenting with catatonia or hebephrenia. Patients who have remained healthy up to this age have usually acquired some sort of role and position in society. Consequently their ego is stronger than in the other two groups, and their mental abilities, emotional stability and general behaviour have not deteriorated as much (Lehmann, 1975a).

The typical paranoid is reserved, cautious, tense and suspicious. Not unusually, the paranoid may also be hostile and aggressive. According to the IPSS, paranoid hallucinatory schizophrenia is the subgroup of schizophrenia that appears with the greatest frequency (approximately 40%).

Schizophrenia Simplex

Schizophrenia simplex no longer appears in DSM-IIIR (1987). The closest match in the current manual is with what is called the "schizotypal personality disturbance". However, the *International Classification of Diseases*, 9th edition (ICD-9) continues to describe the "simple" form of schizophrenia, despite the recommendation of the World Health Organization not to use or rarely to use this diagnosis.

In this subgroup the illness starts in a barely noticeable way and develops undramatically. There are no acute phases with paranoid-hallucinatory or catatonic symptoms. Gradually, schizophrenic-like symptoms appear in a weak and unremarkable form. The main disturbance is a gradual yet progressive decline in activity, initiative and interests. The first signs often appear many years before the patient first visits the doctor. Relationships with other people and with reality have then diminished. The patient no longer goes to work, stays in bed all day or gets up very late. The patient becomes autistic, completely withdrawing from social and vocational demands. Only approximately 4% of schizophrenics belong to this subgroup (Sartorius et al., 1974).

There exists, however, no evidence that these subtypes represent independent groups within schizophrenia. Yet it is common to place patients in different subgroups on the basis of the development of their illness. Subtyping means, therefore, that in a certain patient at a certain time, a certain syndrome is prominent. Some patients do, however, stay within one subgroup during their entire illness.

Positive and Negative Symptoms

Cutting across the conventional subtyping of schizophrenia over the last few years, many researchers have divided schizophrenics into two main subgroups – those with positive and those with negative symptoms (Strauss et al., 1974). Crow, Cross, Johnstone and Owen (1982) have expressed the opinion that this division reflects two types of schizophrenia that can be differentiated on prognostic and aetiological grounds. However, Crow et al. have also pointed out that there exists a considerable overlap between the two types.

As a result of this development, Andreasen (1983, 1984) has proposed a scale for the assessment of negative symptoms (SANS). According to this, negative symptoms are defined as affective flattening, alogia, avolition-apathy, anhedonia, asociality and a lack of attention. The scale for the assessment of positive symptoms includes hallucinations, delusions, bizarre behaviour and positive formal thought disorder.

Interest in these two subdivisions goes beyond mere intentions of improving the description or definition. Crow et al. (1982) and Andreasen (1982) have claimed that negative symptoms derive from structural neurological changes in the brain, whereas positive symptoms reflect functional neurochemical changes. During the course of the illness the latter may regress into the negative symptom picture. It has also been suggested that patients with negative symptoms show a less favourable premorbid course and do not respond well to neuroleptic therapy.

Results of recent investigations, however, show that this concept requires refining. Bilder, Mukherjee, Rieder and Pandurangi (1985) could not confirm the existence of the two syndromes with factor analysis. In contrast, this analysis yielded *three* groups, each with some negative and positive symptoms. Furthermore, patients with negative symptoms do respond to neuroleptic treatment (Carpenter, Heinrichs & Alphs, 1985; Straube, Wagner, Foerster & Heimann, 1989). Finally, the independence of the two so-called different types of schizophrenia is called into question by the reported development of a positive symptom group into one with negative symptoms (cf. Andreasen, 1987; Janzarik, 1968).

Carpenter et al. (1985) have argued that certain negative symptoms such as emotional withdrawal, and reduction of initiative and interpersonal social involvement can be regarded as coping strategies and thus may represent secondary aspects of the psychosis. These symptoms can indeed be affected by neuroleptic treatment. Yet other secondary symptoms are themselves effects of neuroleptic treatment (see Hirsch, 1986). This does not exclude the possibility that there are negative symptoms which reflect structural changes in the CNS. To differentiate these symptoms and the relevant subgroup of schizophrenics is a task for further research.

The Borderline Syndrome and Spectrum Schizophrenia (Schizotypal, Schizoid and Borderline Personality Disturbances)

In 1949 Hoch and Polatin described a special clinical type of schizophrenia which they called "pseudoneurotic schizophrenia" (see Fig. 1). As early as in the seventh edition of his textbook, in a chapter on psychopathy, Kraepelin (1903) had spoken of a grey zone between true schizophrenia and certain kinds of personality disorders. Kraepelin used the word *Zwischengebiet* which gave rise, through the translation, to the use of the term "borderline state" in English (Janzarik, 1968).

According to Hoch and Polatin (1949), this condition concerned patients with mainly neurotic symptoms and who were naturally treated for years as neurotics. Yet on closer study, one could find schizophrenic disturbances in these patients in their thought processes and affect. However, these features are often so hidden among their neurotic characteristics that it is very difficult to demonstrate them in a clinical investigation or in psychological tests.

In spite of extraordinary efforts by researchers such as Knight (1953) and Grinker, Werble and Drye (1968), who made very careful studies in this area, in general the literature on borderline states has been characterised for a long time by considerable conceptual confusion.

In DSM-IIIR (1987) borderline schizophrenia no longer exists as a separate entity, but rather in the form of a borderline personality disorder. As such it is included alongside other so-called spectrum schizophrenias as one of several personality disorders. The major part of the spectrum schizophrenias is taken up – in addition to schizophrenia – by, first, the schizotypal and, secondly, the schizoid personality disorders. Some authors would add the paranoid personality disturbance.

The term "spectrum schizophrenia" has its origin in the adoption study of Kety, Rosenthal, Wender, Schulsinger and Jacobsen (1978). They observed personality features reminiscent of mild schizophrenia in children of schizophrenics who had been given for adoption. These observations were later confirmed by Lowing, Mirsky and Pereira (1983) and Kendler, Masterson, Ungaro and Davis (1984). Similarly, Baron et al. (1983) found an increased incidence of schizotypal personality disturbances among blood relatives of schizophrenics. Thus it was assumed that at least schizotypal personality disorder (and probably schizoid personality disorder too) is genetically linked to schizophrenia. However, this does not hold true for the borderline personality disorder (cf. Gottesman, 1987).

The division of the global borderline concept into borderline and schizotypal personality disorders was finally brought about by the large study of

Table 1. Diagnostic criteria for borderline personality disorder (DSM-IIIR, 1987).

A pervasive pattern of instability of mood, interpersonal relationships, and self-image, beginning by early adulthood and present in a variety of contexts, as indicated by at least *five* of the following:

1. A pattern of unstable and intense interpersonal relationships characterised by alternating between extremes of overidealisation and devaluation
2. Impulsiveness in at least two areas that are potentially self-damaging, e.g. spending, sex, substance use, shoplifting, reckless driving, binge eating (do not include suicidal or self-mutilating behaviour covered in 5.)
3. Affective instability: marked shifts from baseline mood to depression, irritability, or anxiety, usually lasting a few hours and only rarely more than a few days
4. Inappropriate, intense anger or lack of control of anger, e.g. frequent displays of temper, constant anger, recurrent physical fights
5. Recurrent suicidal threats, gestures, or behaviour, or self-multilating behaviour
6. Marked and persistent identity disturbance manifested by uncertainty about at least two of the following: self-image, sexual orientation, long-term goals or career choice, type of friends desired, preferred values.
7. Chronic feelings of emptiness or boredom
8. Frantic efforts to avoid real or imagined abandonment (do not include suicidal or self-mutilating behaviour covered in 5.)

Spitzer, Endicott and Gibbin (1979). Here a discriminant analysis based on 808 cases presented by experienced psychiatrists demonstrated the presence of the two subgroups. The most important characteristics of these two groups in comparison with the schizoid personality disorder are shown in abbreviated form in Tables 1–3.

Table 2. Diagnostic criteria for schizotypal personality disorder (DSM-IIIR, 1987)

A. A pervasive pattern of deficits in interpersonal relatedness and peculiarities of ideation, appearance and behaviour, beginning by early adulthood and present in a variety of contexts, as indicated by at least *five* of the following:
1. Ideas of reference (excluding delusions of reference)
2. Excessive social anxiety, e.g. extreme discomfort in social situations involving unfamiliar people
3. Odd beliefs or magical thinking, influencing behaviour and inconsistent with subcultural norms, e.g. superstitiousness, belief in clairvoyance, telepathy, or "sixth sense", "others can feel my felings" (in children and adolescents, bizarre fantasies or preoccupations)
4. Unusual perceptual experiences, e.g. illusions, sensing the presence of a force or person not actually present (e.g. "I felt as if my dead mother were in the room with me")
5. Odd or eccentric behaviour or appearance, e.g. unkempt, unusual mannerisms, talks to self
6. No close friends or confidants (or only one) other than first-degree relatives
7. Odd speech (without loosening of associations or incoherence), e.g. speech that is impoverished, digressive, vague, or inappropriately abstract
8. Inappropriate or constricted affect, e.g. silly, aloof, rarely reciprocates gestures or facial expressions, such as smiles or nods
9. Suspiciousness or paranoid ideation

B. Occurrence not exclusively during the course of schizophrenia or a pervasive developmental disorder

Table 3. Diagnostic criteria for schizoid personality disorder (DSM-IIIR, 1987)

A. A pervasive pattern of indifference to social relationships and a restricted range of emotional experience and expression, beginning by early adulthood and present in a variety of contexts, as indicated by at least *four* of the following:
1. Neither desires nor enjoys close relationships, including being part of a family
2. Almost always chooses solitary activities
3. Rarely, if ever, claims or appears to experience strong emotions, such as anger and joy
4. Indicates little, if any, desire to have sexual experiences with another person (age being taken into account)
5. Is indifferent to the praise and criticism of others.
6. Has no close friends or confidants (or only one) other than first-degree relatives
7. Displays constricted affect, e.g. is aloof, cold, rarely reciprocates gestures or facial expressions, such as smiles or nods

B. Occurrence not exclusively during the course of schizophrenia or a delusional disorder

Diagnostic Concepts

There are no objective characteristics for the diagnosis of schizophrenia, such as characteristic morphological changes in the brain, specific neurochemical findings in the laboratory, specific premorbid development or a predictable course and prognosis. There is no known single cause of schizophrenia. (The mildly increased ventricle size shown with computerised tomography, indicating cerebral atrophy, appears in only 30% of schizophrenics studied and is nosologically nonspecific).

On the other hand, there are a number of symptoms which may be regarded as characteristic of the illness and used to define schizophrenia. Certain medications are able to selectively reduce some of these symptoms. But one cannot define schizophrenia in terms of the type of treatment. Indeed, there are numerous patients described by experienced psychiatrists as schizophrenic who barely respond to neuroleptic therapy.

Two of the major problems are that the symptoms can vary markedly over time and that there can be a large area of overlap with other psychiatric groups (e.g. the affective disorders, Huntington's chorea and temporal lobe epilepsy). Considerable attempts, therefore, have been made to sharpen the discriminative power of the diagnostic process in defining operationalised descriptions based on the consensus of experienced clinicians.

The effort has been particularly marked in the United States since it became evident from the study of Cooper et al. (1972) that the concept of schizophrenia was, compared to the practice in Europe, too widely applied. This effort gave rise to diagnostic criteria in the form of symptom lists such as the well-known Research Diagnostic Criteria (RDC) of Spitzer et al. (1978) and the often cited DSM of the American Psychiatric Association (1987). The application of these and other criteria has led to a noticeable rise in the reliability and precision of the diagnosis. No longer does any reputable scientific journal accept studies on schizophrenics unless the schizophrenia is defined by diagnostic criteria.

The major difference between the RDC of Spitzer et al. and DSM-IIIR (1987) lies in the latter requiring the symptoms to have been present for at least 6 months. Thus with DSM-IIIR acute schizophrenics, who respond well to neuroleptics, are merely given the diagnosis of schizophreniform psychosis. Clearly this means a selection of subjects with chronic features and a poorer prognosis. Leaving out such a large proportion of schizophrenics is controversial among psychiatrists and clinical psychologists, especially as this leads to an under-representation of the acute patients in the make-up of groups for investigation. One presumes that future revisions of the DSM will remove the 6-month requirement.

Diagnostic Studies of the World Health Organization (WHO IPSS)

One of the intentions of the IPSS (Sartorius et al., 1974) run by the World Health Organization (WHO) was to reduce the large discrepancies that had arisen in diagnostic practice. The aim of this investigation was to bring out reliable methods for the diagnosis of schizophrenia which would become standardised and would have a good prospect of being widely recognised. The investigation centred on 1202 patients selected from specific institutions in nine countries (Columbia, Czechoslovakia, Denmark, India, Nigeria, Taiwan, USSR, UK and USA).

All psychiatrists used a standard investigative method, the Present State Examination (PSE) of Wing (1970), in order to arrive at their diagnosis. Data were collected on the symptoms diagnosed and on the psychiatric and social background of the patients. From the 1202 patients, 811 were rated as probably schizophrenic, and 306 of these were selected as a nuclear group – i.e. regarded as certainly schizophrenic according to several methods of evaluation. (In the remaining 505 patients the diagnosis of schizophrenia was considered to be probable but not certain.) The relative frequency of the symptoms of the project patients is shown in Table 4.

This list includes 12 symptoms and has been proposed by Carpenter, Strauss and Bartko (1973) as a diagnostic instrument under the name WHO Pilot Study Criteria, or Carpenter et al. – Flexible Checklist. Carpenter et al. recommend five symptoms to be present for probable and six symptoms for definite schizophrenia (waking early, depressed facies and elation are counted if they are *absent*). The WHO criteria have, compared to other prominent criteria, the advantage of being based directly on the results of an empirical investigation. But like all sets of criteria now in use, they select only a section of those patients who, according to current clinical concepts, can be considered as schizophrenic. The reader who is specially interested in a comparative evaluation of the

Table 4. Relative frequency of symptoms. Results of WHO International Pilot Study of Schizophrenia; only those symptoms occurring in at least 50% of schizophrenics are listed (also used as a "symptom checklist" as proposed by Carpenter, Strauss & Bartko, 1974).

Symptom	Schizophrenics (%)
Lack of insight	97
Auditory hallucinations	74
Verbal hallucinations	70
Ideas of reference	70
Delusions of reference	70
Suspiciousness	66
Flat affect	66
Voices speaking to patient	65
Delusional mood	64
Delusions of persecution	64
Inadequate description of problem	64
Thought alienation	52
Thoughts spoken aloud	50

advantages and disadvantages of the several criteria in use is referred to Overall and Hollister (1979) and to Brockington (1986).

A Review of Different Methods of Treatment

Pharmacotherapy

There can remain little doubt about the general efficacy of the neuroleptic treatment of schizophrenic psychoses following a remarkable number of large and methodologically sound, controlled investigations.

In reviewing 207 double-blind studies of phenothiazines, Davis and Garver (1978) concluded that their effect was markedly greater than any seen under placebo conditions. In 1964 Cole, Klerman and Goldberg showed that of 338 acute and hospitalised schizophrenics treated with four neuroleptics over a 6-week period, 70% showed a clear improvement. Only a few showed no change or some worsening of their symptoms. Nonetheless, 20% showed only a minimal response to neuroleptic treatment. Most patients deteriorated on placebo. But it should not be overlooked that 20% improved spontaneously on placebo treatment.

Clinically speaking, the effect of neuroleptics is marked by a reduction of arousal and tension, a slowing of psychomotor function and, in general, a lowering of drive. Emotionality is attenuated but anxiolytic effects are variable. There is no material impairment of the level of consciousness. Intellectual abilities are either not impaired or are only indirectly affected.

The primary pharmacological effect is a blockade of postsynaptic dopamine receptors. In this way neuroleptics reduce the efficacy of dopaminergic neurotransmission. But neuroleptics can have direct and indirect effects on other neurotransmitter systems too (e.g. noradrenaline; Ackenheil, 1985).

Whilst it is not certain that all neuroleptics affect all dopaminergic pathways to the same extent, it is well known that classical neuroleptics such as haloperidol and chlorpromazine affect the function of the substantia nigra, neostriatum and nucleus accumbens (which is part of the mesolimbic system). They may well affect other areas such as the frontal cortex, but the effects in these areas have been less thoroughly investigated (cf. Spokes, 1980).

The neuroleptic effect on neostriatal function offers a partial explanation for the frequent occurrence of extrapyramidal motor symptoms. The pathways of the basal ganglia are important for motor control, and disruption of their function can lead to anomalous movements such as are seen in parkinsonism, dystonia and akinesis. To some extent, these problems can be controlled by additional anticholinergic medication.

More problematic are the dyskinesias that appear in some patients after long-term treatment (e.g. oral dyskinesias involving involuntary movements of the tongue, lips and the lower part of the face). They are resistant to anticholinergic medication. It remains controversial whether these movements are a result of treatment or not. There is some evidence that they were observed in patients before neuroleptic treatment was introduced.

An important question is whether one type of neuroleptic medication is more appropriate for one type of patient than the other. Most authors still agree, more or less, with the conclusion of May and Goldberg (1978) that clinicians possess neither the experience nor the research results on which to judge whether a particular patient should or should not be given a particular neuroleptic (cf. Donaldson, Gelenberg & Baldessarini, 1983). This matches the result obtained earlier by Cole et al. (1964). In retrospect the authors were unable to say that the different neuroleptics used (chlorpromazine, fluphenazine, thioridazine) exerted differential effects on the different symptoms and syndromes shown in their patients. In other words, the range of effects of neuroleptics shown between individuals is extraordinarily broad.

Even when one takes into account the different minimal doses required by neuroleptics to achieve an antipsychotic effect, it is not possible to establish differential effects, at least in acute schizophrenia. (Table 6 shows the recommended daily doses of a range of neuroleptics.) For example, double-blind comparisons of the effect of haloperidol versus perazine (Schmidt, Schüssler, Kappes, Mühlbauer & Müller-Oerlinghausen, 1982) and haloperidol versus pimozide (Haas, Emrich & Beckmann, 1982) show that these neuroleptics are equally effective on acute schizophrenia (cf. review, Kane, 1987).

Individual studies continually appear in the literature claiming that one neuroleptic is better than another, but in most cases the results cannot be replicated (see Donaldson et al., 1983; Murphy, Shilling & Murray, 1978). This means that decisions in clinical practice can only be made according to rather rough and nonspecific criteria. Just such a scheme is shown in Table 5. From this it can be seen that the degree of antipsychotic or sedative effect can be used as a therapeutic guideline. In turn, this means that for all groups of neuroleptics the stronger their antipsychotic effect, the weaker is their sedative effect (and vice versa).

To estimate the comparative efficacy of doses of different neuroleptics, one must calculate the so-called chlorpromazine equivalence. Such a calculation is not as unproblematical in clinical practice as it might seem since for a given degree of potency the range of side effects of different agents varies enormously.

The equivalent doses of several neuroleptics are shown in Table 6. It should be emphasised that the figures given represent averages. The dosage range used by different authors varies quite considerably. For example, Davis, Schaffer, Killian, Kinard and Chan (1980) administered 500–1000 mg chlorpromazine units to achieve the mean optimal response. Hirsch (1986) called for a lower working range, namely 300–600 mg chlorpromazine equivalents (see also Davis & Gierl, 1984). Hirsch (1986) has suggested that doses in excess of 600 mg chlorpromazine units bring about no extra therapeutic advantage.

The double-blind study of Ericksen, Hurth and Chang (1978) found no therapeutic advantage for acute schizophrenics when starting with 60 mg per day haloperidol compared with 15 mg per day. Indeed there were more side effects at the higher dose. Neborsky, Janowsky, Munson and Depry (1981)

Table 5. Target syndromes of differential therapy with neuroleptic drugs of different types of effect (Schied, 1983)

Schizophrenic target syndromes	Type of neuroleptic drug recommended I	II	III	IV
Acute florid paranoid-hallucinatory syndromes with marked thought disorders	×			
Paranoid-schizophrenic syndromes with predominantly psychomotor agitation and high tension, restlessness, often combined with anxiety and/or hostility.		×		
Acute schizophrenic disorders predominantly with manic-type affective disturbance and loosening of associations, increased psychomotor activity.	×	×		
Schizophrenic syndromes of withdrawal associated with apathy, reduction of energy and activity, psychomotor retardation without marked florid symptoms.			×	
Subacute or subchronic schizophrenic syndromes with predominantly depressive symptoms.				×

Type I: high-potency antipsychotic neuroleptic agent from the group of butyrophenones (e.g. *haloperidol*) or from the piperazine-phenothiazine group (e.g. *fluphenazine*).
Type II: medium- to high-potency, but also sedative neuroleptic agent, e.g. *perphenazine* from the group of piperazine-phenothiazines or *clozapine* from the group of dibenzoepines.
Type III: antipsychotic agent of medium potency with (probably) an activity-increasing effect such as for example *pimozide* (one of the butyrophenones) or *thiothixene* (one of the thioxanthenes).
Type IV: low-potency neuroleptic agent with (probably) antidepressant and activity-increasing effect, as, for example, *thioridazine* from the piperidine-phenothiazines, *trifluoperazine* from the piperazine-phenothiazines, *chlorprothixene* from the thioxanthene group or *clozapine* from the dibenzoepine group.

compared, in a double-blind study, the effects of a mean dose of haloperidol of 48 mg per day over one of 12.5 mg per day in the initial treatment of acutely psychotic young men. They found no differences with respect to antipsychotic or side effects.

The review by Hirsch (1986) of controlled studies of the effects of high or so-called mega-doses of neuroleptics shows that such treatment brings very little therapeutic advantage, as the dose-effect curve has usually flattened out at such doses.

Table 6 relates to the treatment of acutely ill schizophrenics but does not take into account the doses necessary during states of high excitement in acute schizophrenics on the one hand, or the long-term treatment of partially or fully remitted patients on the other.

This does not mean that *very* low doses are advocated here: the earlier an antipsychotic effect is achieved, the more the patient is spared much psychotic

Table 6. Dosage equivalents of the most usual neuroleptics (modified from Davis & Cole, 1975)

Generic name	Equivalent dosage (CPZ = 100) (mg)	Average total daily dosage (mg)	Chlorpromazine equivalents (CPZ = 1)
Chlorpromazine	100	734.00	1:1
Thioridazine	95.3 ± 8.2	700.00	1:1
Perphenazine	8.9 ± 0.6	65.10	1:10
Fluphenazine	1.2 ± 0.1	8.80	1:50
Trifluoperazine	2.8 ± 0.4	20.60	1:20
Chlorprothixene	43.9 ± 13.9	322.00	1:1
Thiothixene	5.2 ± 1.3	38.00	1:20
Haloperidol	1.6 ± 0.4	11.45	1:50

CPZ, Chlorpromazine.

excitation and fear. The longer psychotic experiences last, the greater is the chance that they become permanent. This pertains just as much to the psychotherapeutic approach to psychoses. The sooner one starts to achieve an antipsychotic effect through medication, the sooner one can start with the psychotherapy. Too often, as Davis and Cole (1975) point out, the doses administered are below the necessary antipsychotic level to reach this goal.

The possibility of achieving an *early and favourable influence* on acute psychoses with neuroleptic medication is supported by the literature. For example, the studies of Nedopil, Rüther and Strauss (1980) and Woggon (1980) show that in patients who respond to neuroleptics, 50% of the eventual therapeutic effect has already been achieved by the 5th day of treatment. Similar results have been reported using perazine (Helmchen & Hippius, 1974; van Putten & May, 1978), but such a rapid take-off in neuroleptic efficacy is not seen in all patients. Thus one might suppose that a rapid helpful effect of neuroleptic therapy might be useful for the prediction of therapeutic success in the long term. Van Putten and May (1978) confirm just this point in so far as they found a high correlation between subjective (dysphoric) effects after a single test dose and the improvement observed after 4 weeks.

Although the response to a test dose can indicate the eventual global response quite early on, one cannot recommend changing the type of neuroleptic immediately in the absence of a response to a test dose or shortly thereafter, since certain patients only achieve a good response after a relatively long period of treatment. The recommended period varies between 4 and 12 weeks in the case of acute psychosis. Benkert and Hippius (1986) suggest waiting 4–6 weeks if the initial medication brings about no notable improvement. Mason (1975) found that 6–8 weeks were necessary. In some patients the improvement does not start for 6 months. In the case of chronic patients one should wait considerably longer before changing the medication; Mason recommended a waiting period of 12–24 weeks.

Long-Term Neuroleptic (Maintenance) Treatment and Relapse Prevention

Helmchen (1979) suggested that there were three reasons for long-term neuroleptic treatment – the *suppression* of persistent symptoms, *stabilisation* on remission of acute episodes, and *prophylaxis* against potential relapse during remission. As Heimann (1982) emphasised, there is a nebulous border between the notion of symptom suppression and prophylactic protection against relapse. The two can only be differentiated retrospectively. Stopping medication would, in the prophylactic case, lead to relapse after a relatively long latent period; in the case of symptom suppression, the relapse would be likely to occur with a

Table 7. Maintenance pharmacotherapy in schizophrenia (abbreviated and adapted version[a] of a table originally compiled by Kane, 1987)

Reference	(*n*)	Treatment	Relapse %	Dropout rate%
Treatment period: 9 or 12 months				
Hirsch et al. (1973)	81	FD	8	9
		PBO	66	
Hogarty and Goldberg (1973)	347	Drug	31	8
		PBO	68	
Odejide and Aderounmu (1982)	70	FD	19	25
		PBO	56	
Kane et al. (1986)	163	FD dose		
		Low	56	10
		Intermediate	24	
		Standard	14	
Rifkin et al. (1977)	73	FD+oral	5	11
		PBO	75	
Schooler et al. (1980)	214	FHCL	38	25
		FD	46	
Treatment period: 2 years				
Hogarty et al. (1974)	347	Drug	48	8
		PBO	80	
Crow et al. (1986)	120	Drug	58	11
		PBO	70	
Hogarty et al. (1979)	105	Oral	65	13
		FD	40	
Treatment period: 4 years				
Engelhardt et al. (1963, 1964, 1967)	446	CPZ	20	36
		PBO	31	

[a] Only studies with $n \geq 70$.
Daily administration: CPZ, drug.
Long-acting injection: FD, FHCL.
Long-acting oral medication: Oral.
FD, fluphenazine decanoate; PBO, placebo; Drug, different drugs given; FHCL, fluphenazine hydrochloride; CPZ, chlorpromazine.

short latent period, perhaps immediately following the withdrawal of medication.

In his review Kane (1987) cited 21 double-blind controlled studies that compared the effects of placebo versus long-term antipsychotic medication. The result so clearly favoured the effect of long-term neuroleptic medication (Table 7) that, as Heimann (1982) pointed out, one can no longer ethically carry out a long-term placebo controlled study. Nonetheless, the number of relapses after withdrawing medication vary considerably. As one can see in Table 7, the relapse rate during the 9–12 month placebo phase varied from 56% to 75%. This refers only to the studies with a relatively low drop-out rate (25% and less) and where the population under study was relatively large (ten of 21 studies cited by Kane, 1987). The relapse rate over a 2-year period was similar. But, of course, there were not many studies over such a period that also had a reasonably high number of cases ($n = 70$ and more). One can see from Table 7 that for most types of treatment the relapse rate was lower than that recorded for the placebo groups. The relapse rate varied between 5% and 65%. The variations were largely due to whether or not the neuroleptic was administered in depot form. In a setting where long-acting i.v. drugs were administered, the compliance was considerably higher. Consequently, in these studies the relapse rate was generally low (5%–19%), with the exception of two studies.

Prediction of Outcome of Long-Term Neuroleptic Treatment

As we have shown above, in all the controlled studies of long-term treatment there is a group of patients who do not relapse – of the order of 10%–30% after a year (cf. Hirsch, Gaind, Rhode, Stevens & Wing, 1973; Kane, 1987; Leff and Wing, 1971). In reality this proportion should be set somewhat higher as subjects with a so-called reactive psychosis are under-represented in controlled long-term studies (Davis, 1975).

The following features taken from a number of studies may be regarded as indicating a good long-term prognosis: an emotionally and intellectually well-developed premorbid personality, good social integration, demonstrable causal life events, an acute start to the illness, psychopathological symptoms that include manic-depressive characteristics and an accepting, not overstimulating familial or professional environment before and after the psychotic breakdown (review by Stephens, 1978). From this Ciompi (1981) deduced that patients who have just had an acute psychotic episode and who come from a favourable social and familial environment should not be put on long-term medication. Similarly, Davis (1975) came to the conclusion that a patient who has just experienced a brief reactive psychosis for the first time should be the last to go on long-term medication.

Recently Fenton and McGlashan (1987) showed that even a group of chronic schizophrenics (*n*.23; DSM-III, 1980) did not need long-term maintenance medication if they showed the following features: "better premorbid social and occupational adjustment, higher levels of accrued psychosocial competence and acquired skills, fewer hebephrenic traits and the preservation of affect (depressed mood)" (Fenton & McGlashon, 1987, p. 1306).

Continually a matter for discussion is how far one should go and risk a patient relapsing when the prognostic signs are good. Lehmann (1975b) has emphasised that even patients in full remission will experience a continually deteriorating mental and social situation after every relapse. Furthermore, a relapse can have social consequences, such as the loss of a job, which bring with them further negative psychosocial consequences. As a result Helmchen (1979) offered the following advice when one is weighing up the risks of relapse against those associated with long-term neuroleptic therapy. Long-term medication is indicated:

- After a *first psychotic episode* followed by remission if there is a typical reduction of the amount of emotional and vocational stress that can be tolerated (Helmchen recommends 3–12-month long-term medication to stabilise remission).
- In cases of *relapse,* particularly if the episodes occur at short intervals (e.g. three times in 5 years), even if the patient is currently in remission (Helmchen advises in this case 5 years or more of maintenance therapy).
- Where *symptoms persist* associated with a marked impairment of function, long-term medication will be necessary, possibly for an unlimited period.

Similarly, Lehmann (1975b) recommends medication for 2–3 years even in cases where only the first psychotic episode has occurred. In the case of a relapse he suggests at least 5 years of medication but, if relapses persist, he suggests that neuroleptic treatment should be continued for an unlimited period.

However, in contrast to the opinion of Lehmann (1975b), if a favourable psychosocial development has been reached, many clinicians try to reduce the dose or try to give neuroleptics only at intervals to reduce the unfavourable sedative and motor effects on further psychosocial and vocational development. A study by Pietzcker (1978) demonstrates, however, how difficult it is to assess prognosis and how it necessarily depends on long-term observation of the patient. The author reports on studies that show that precisely those patients who were free of relapses under long-term medication were the ones to relapse (65%) when the treatment was withdrawn.

For such reasons, various maintenance programmes try to reduce neuroleptic treatment in patients who do not appear to be severely disturbed only after a considerable period of close observation as outpatients. Since, as may be seen in Table 7, the relapse rate in such a programme is higher than when using standard doses, a carefully planned psychosocial therapeutic programme is absolutely essential. Such an outpatient programme can (a) by therapeutic measures, preferably including members of the family, reduce the likelihood of factors arising that would increase the stress for the patient; (b) train the patient to notice early signs of symptom deterioration and to seek professional help in order to increase medication to intercept the developing relapse. These programmes will be described briefly in the following sections.

Complementary Psychological Treatment

Modern complementary psychological forms of treatment are presented in the last part of this volume. Therefore we shall restrict ourselves here to the historical background and attempt to integrate the most important new themes and directions in this type of therapy.

Psychodynamic and Other Individual Forms of Therapy

The question of the usefulness of psychodynamically oriented psychotherapy in schizophrenia is still very controversial. A rather sceptical point of view derives to a large extent from the results of controlled studies carried out in the 1960s. In particular, major studies comparing the effects of psychotherapy and other forms of treatment on hospitalised patients were carried out by Rogers, Gendlin, Kiesler and Truax (1967), Grinspoon, Ewalt, and Shader (1968), May (1968) and Karon and O'Grady (1969). Since then there have also been a number of thorough and critical reviews (e.g. Feinsilver & Gunderson, 1972; Gomes-Schwartz, 1984; May, 1974).

Despite this, the psychoanalytical treatment of psychotic individuals has lost much of its original attraction in recent years. Although procedures directly aimed at uncovering psychological mechanisms are contraindicated in psychotic patients, and the investment involved is disproportionate to success compared to other treatment methods, an adapted approach is advocated by some (Furlan & Benedetti, 1985; Müller, 1984). The former authors caution, however, against uncritical use of psychoanalytical techniques in the therapy of schizophrenia and against exaggerated expectations derived solely from successful case reports.

These contradictory views on the value of psychoanalytic treatment were the starting point for a recent large project. The results have recently been reported in *Schizophrenia Bulletin* by Stanton, Gunderson, Knapp, Frank, Vannicelli, Schnitzer and Rosenthal (1984) and Gunderson et al. (1984). The report is based on chronic schizophrenic patients at three clinics in Boston. The authors compared a nonintensive form of psychoanalytic therapy with the routine procedures of the clinic. Both groups continued to receive neuroleptic treatment. Despite the considerable investment of time involved – three times as much contact – psychoanalytic treatment showed no greater overall success. Certainly the follow-up study showed improvements in some areas, such as the handling of psychotic ideas and the amelioration in the area of ego strength, but the group receiving the traditional treatment showed marked improvement too, especially in the area of vocational function.

Milieu Therapy

Thorough analyses of the clinical efficacy of milieu therapy were carried out in the 1970s by Elsworth, Marony, Klett, Gordon and Gunn (1971) and Moos (1975). From the clinical point of view, these studies were successful in showing which type of institutional environment has proven favourable, especially for acute patients. The acutely ill patient appears to improve best in a situation that is staff–intensive, tolerant, supportive and protective, and which offers psychosocial interventions for relatively long periods (3–6 months.)

Several investigations have been able to describe further important characteristics of the milieu. These refer in particular to features that correlate with improved psychosocial adaptive qualities shown by acute patients on discharge (Carpenter, Gunderson & Strauss, 1977; Elsworth, 1980; Elsworth et al., 1971; Kellam, 1980; Moos, 1975; Mosher, Menn & Matthews 1975; Price, 1980; Rappaport, Hopkins, Hall, Bolleza & Silverman, 1978; Smith & King, 1975). The features which these authors report concern the therapeutic team. The members of the therapeutic team should change less than usual on a ward, they should have positive expectations, be actively involved in the decision and treatment processes and should show a practical approach towards the solving of real problems. These features of the milieu have only been appreciated relatively recently. For many years it was maintained that there was hardly, if any, relationship between the characteristics of the milieu and the eventual psychosocial adaptation of formerly acutely ill patients.

Three further clinical investigations have attempted to show that a proportion of acute patients can have a better course, and indeed a better outcome, without neuroleptic treatment than those on medication. In these cases "a better course" refers to better adaptation to the social environment on discharge and a lower relapse rate (Carpenter et al., 1977; Mosher & Menn, 1978; Rappaport et al., 1978). The results of these investigations contradict earlier reports (e.g. May, 1968; Grinspoon, Ewalt & Shader, 1972) of the relative inefficiency of milieu therapy for acute patients without neuroleptic treatment or for chronic patients in combination with medication. But in relation to this one should not overlook two points regarding the study of Carpenter et al. (1977). First, neuroleptics were given "if necessary", albeit not regularly or prophylactically. Secondly, such a programme requires an enormous investment of time and of personnel – to a degree that would not be commonly possible elsewhere. [The study of Carpenter et al. took place on a National Institute of Mental Health (NIMH) research ward. Such wards are not directly comparable to those in other hospitals as the patients are brought together on the basis of their common illness for the purposes of the proposed research.] Nonetheless, these studies demonstrate that it may be possible to gather a particular group of acutely ill schizophrenics along with a large and highly motivated team of therapists and to develop a programme for milieu therapy in which the treatment with neuroleptics can be kept to a minimum. But it will still take a lot of research to make such a programme applicable for routine use in wards elsewhere.

May and colleagues (May, Tuma & Dixon, 1976a; May, Tuma, Ylae, Potepan & Dixon, 1976b) studied the effect of social therapy in a group of inpatients. They found that social therapy had no effect on the course or the discharge rate. However, it is interesting that in the follow-up study they found that if social therapy was combined with neuroleptic treatment, then this brought about a better outcome than medication alone. In other words, the programme helped these patients to show improved psychosocial integration after discharge.

Intervention Programmes for Relapse Prevention

It is important that programmes started while patients are institutionalised should be continued after discharge, or at least be offered to them after discharge. In general, it seems to be very important that inpatients should receive some form of psychological intervention in addition to neuroleptic maintenance therapy (Fairweather, Sanders, Cressler & Maynard, 1969; Paul & Lentz, 1977). In their study of the efficacy of behaviourally oriented treatment continued after release, Paul and Lentz (1977) report that 90% of their chronic schizophrenics showed considerable improvement (change from inpatient to outpatient status) and that the relapse rate over the following 2 years was less then 5%. However, it should be noted that only 10% of the outpatients were actually capable of living completely independently, even if they were able to organise their basic needs for food, accommodation, social contact and recreation themselves.

The result of another controlled study (Hogarty & Goldberg, 1973; Hogarty, Goldberg, Schooler & Ulrich, 1974) showed that as a result of sociotherapy the patients felt a sense of relief and satisfaction in their interpersonal relationships as long as the therapy was combined with medication. However, they also reported that sociotherapy did not reduce the chance of a relapse over the following 2 years.

Hogarty, Goldberg and Schooler (1975) suspect that certain factors which they did not assess, such as the family situation, had an important influence. Thus a negative family environment could, despite social therapy, have brought about an early relapse. The authors point to the results of Brown, Vaughn and Leff at the Institute of Psychiatry in London showing a connection between early relapse and the type of familial interactions (e.g. Leff & Vaughn, 1985).

From this one must once again suggest that specific factors that clearly influence the vulnerability of schizophrenics should be included in the therapy used. This means that friends, relatives or others living with the patient should be brought into the therapeutic process. (See Falloon, et al., this volume, for further details on this type of therapy.)

Well-replicated results show that a particular style of interaction between patients and those with whom they live after their discharge from the clinic can provoke an early relapse. This style can be recorded by the Camberwell Family

Interview. It is defined by the frequency of critical comments and emotional over-involvement and is called "high-expressed emotion" (high EE).

We should emphasise at this point that none of these EE researchers maintains that schizophrenia as such is set off by the experience of high EE. But it does represent a noxious experience, along with other contributory stressful events, which promotes the reappearance of psychotic symptoms. In the meantime, for example Hogarty's group in the United States and Leff, Vaughn and Tarrier in the United Kingdom and other groups in other countries (including a group in our clinic) have set up so-called psychoeducative programmes. These programmes "teach" relatives and friends who live with the patient what is understood about the illness and offer suggestions to reduce stress factors for the relatives and friends as well as for the patient. These programmes try to counteract the frequent occurrence of false reactions to the patient which arise simply through a poor understanding of the situation. As controlled studies have shown, such an information programme can lead to a certain emotional relief in the home atmosphere and a stabilisation of family relationships. In this way, an early relapse can be avoided, as long as continued neuroleptic therapy can also be assured. This means that the relapse rate can fall to a rate comparable to that of patients who live with a low-EE relative and take medication continuously (Hogarty et al., 1986; Leff & Vaughn, 1985; review, Schooler, 1986).

Concluding Remarks on the Role of Neuroleptic Therapy and Complementary Procedures

Although neuroleptics have been used for over 30 years we are only now, in the light of more recent research into the vulnerability for schizophrenia (e.g. studies of relapse), gradually coming to understand their functional importance for the clinical treatment of schizophrenic patients. Neuroleptics show their usefulness in protecting against the recurrence of psychotic symptoms by shielding the patient from the perception of stimuli as noxious (e.g. emotional overstimulation) or the consequences of damaging life events.

In a prospective study Straube, Wagner, Foerster and Heimann (1989) were able to show that patients with limited protection from environmental stimuli profited greatly from neuroleptic treatment. On the other hand, it was this type of patient who tended to have a relapse over the following 2 years. Over this period none of the patients studied was still taking medication regularly.

Thus we are led to suppose that neuroleptics must be responsible for erecting a protective mechanism in the sense of an increased threshold for the perception of noxious events. This idea is illustrated in Fig. 2. The proposal derives from a version of the model put forward by Leff (see Cutting, 1985). However, this model makes it clear that if two factors combine (e.g. emotional interactions and a threatening life event), then the increase in threshold induced by neuroleptic treatment is no longer high enough to prevent a recurrence of psychotic

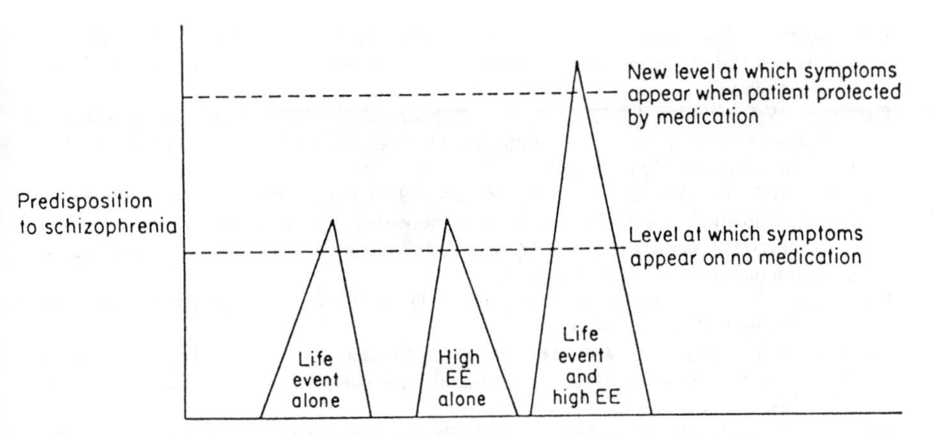

Fig 2. Predisposition to schizophrenia from life events and expressed emotion with and without medication. (After Leff, in Cutting, 1985)

symptoms. The model also makes it clear why psychotherapeutic interventions should be added to neuroleptic treatment in order to raise the threshold further.

Perhaps the principle mode of effect of neuroleptics and additional intervention programmes is realised by just such a buffering action, by raising the threshold against potential noxious stimulation in a vulnerable person.

References

Ackenheil, M. (1985). Neurobiologische Aspekte der Schizophrenie unter Berücksichtigung neuerer biochemischer Forschungsergebnisse. In B. Pflug, K. Foerster, & E. Straube (Eds.), *Perspektiven der Schizophrenieforschung*. Stuttgart:Fischer.

Andreasen, N.C. (1982). Negative symptoms in schizophrenia: Definition and reliability. *Archives of General Psychiatry, 39*, 784–788.

Andreasen, N.C. (1983). *The scale for assessment of negative symptoms (SANS)*. Iowa: The University of Iowa.

Andreasen, N.C. (1984). *The scale for the assessment of positive symptoms (SAPS)*. Iowa: The University of Iowa.

Andreasen, N.C. (1987). The diagnosis of schizophrenia. *Schizophrenia Bulletin, 13*, 9–22.

Andreasen, N.C., & Grove, W.M. (1986). Thought, language, and communication in schizophrenia: Diagnosis and prognosis. *Schizophrenia Bulletin, 12*, 348–359.

Baron, M., Gruen, R., Asnis, L., & Kane, J. (1983). Familial relatedness of schizophrenia and schizotypal states. *American Journal of Psychiatry, 140*, 1437–1442.

Benkert, O., & Hippius, H. (1986). *Psychiatrische Pharmakotherapie* (3rd ed.). Berlin, Heidelberg, New York: Springer.

Bilder, R.M., Mukherjee, S., Rieder, R.O., & Pandurangi, A.K. (1985). Symptomatic and neuropsychological components of defect states. *Schizophrenia Bulletin, 11*, 409–419.

Bleuler, E., (1950). *Dementia praecox or the group of schizophrenias* (J. Zinken, Trans.). New York: International Universities Press. (Original work published 1911).

Bleuler, M, (1972). *Die schizophrenen Geistesstörungen im Lichte langjähriger Kranken- und Familiengeschichten*. Stuttgart: Thieme.

Brockington, I. (1986). Diagnosis of schizophrenia and schizoaffective psychoses. In P.B. Bradley & S.R. Hirsch (Eds.), *The psychopharmacology and treatment of schizophrenia.* Oxford: Oxford University Press.

Carpenter, W.T., Bartko, J.J., Strauss, J.S., & Hawk, A.B. (1978). Signs and symptoms as predictors of outcome: A report from the international pilot study of schizophrenia. *American Journal of Psychiatry, 135*, 940–945.

Carpenter, W.T., Gunderson, J.G., & Strauss, J.S. (1977). Consideration of the borderline syndrome: A logitudinal comparative study of borderline and schizophrenic patients. In P. Hartocollis (Ed.), *Borderline personality disorders: The concept, the syndrome, the patient.* New York: International Universities Press.

Carpenter, W.T., Jr., Heinrichs, D.W., & Alphs, L.D. (1985). Treatment of negative symptoms. *Schizophrenia Bulletin, 11*, 440–452.

Carpenter, W.T., Strauss, J.S., & Bartko, J.J. (1973). Flexible system for the diagnosis of schizophrenia: Report from the WHO international pilot study of schizophrenia. *Science, 182*, 1275–1278.

Carpenter, W.T., Strauss, J.S., & Bartko, J.J. (1974). Use of signs and symptoms for the identification of schizophrenic patients. *Schizophrenia Bulletin, 11*, 37–49.

Ciompi, L. (1981). Wie können wir die schizophrenen besser behandeln? – Eine Synthese neuer Krankheits- und Therapiekonzepte. *Nervenarzt, 52*, 506–515.

Ciompi, L., & Müller, C. (1976). *Lebensweg und Alter der Schizophrenen. Eine katamnestische Langzeitstudie bis ins Senium.* Berlin, Heidelberg, New York: Springer.

Cobb, S. (1943). *Borderland of psychiatry.* Cambridge: Harvard University Press.

Cole, J.O., Klerman, G.L., & Goldberg, S.C. (1964). Phenothiazine treatment in acute schizophrenia. *Archives of General Psychiatry, 10*, 246–261.

Cooper, J.E., Kendell, R.E., Gurland, B.J., Sharp, L., Copland, J.R.M., & Simon, R. (1972), *Psychiatric diagnosis in New York and London: A comparative study of mental hospital admissions.* London: Oxford University Press.

Crow, T.J., Cross, A.J., Johnstone, E.C., & Owen, F. (1982). Two syndromes in schizophrenia and their pathogenesis. In F.A. Henn & H.A. Nasrallah (Eds.), *Schizophrenia as a brain disease.* New York: Oxford University Press.

Crow, T.J., McMillan, J.F., Johnson, A.L., & Johnstone, E.C. (1986). The Northwick Park study of first episodes of schizophrenia: II. A randomized controlled trial of prophylactic neuroleptic treatment. *British Journal of Psychiatry, 148*, 120–127.

Cutting, J. (1985). *The psychology of schizophrenia.* Edinburgh: Churchill Livingstone.

Davis, J.M. (1975). Overview: Maintenance therapy in psychiatry. I. Schizophrenia. *American Journal of Psychiatry, 132*, 1237–1250.

Davis, J.M., & Cole, J.O. (1975). Antipsychotic drugs. In A.M. Freedman, H.Kaplan & B. Sadock (Eds.), *Comprehensive textbook of psychiatry.* II (Vol. 2, pp 1921–1941). Baltimore: Williams and Wilkins.

Davis, J.M., & Garver, D.L. (1978). Neuroleptics: Clinical use in psychiatry. In L.L. Iverson, S.D. Iverson, & S.H. Snyder (Eds.), *Handbook of psychopharmocology.* New York: Plenum.

Davis, J.M., & Gierl, B. (1984). Pharmacological treatment in the care of schizophrenic patients. In A.S. Bellack (Ed.), *Schizophrenia. Treatment, management, and rehabilitation.* Orlando: Grune and Stratton.

Davis, J.M., Schaffer, C.B., Killian, G.A., Kinard, C., & Chan, C. (1980). Important issues in the drug treatment of schizophrenia. *Schizophrenia Bulletin, 6*, 70–87.

Diagnostic and statistical manual of mental disorders (3rd ed. rev.) (DSM-IIIR) (1987). Washington, DC: American Psychiatric Association.

Diem, O. (1903). Die einfach demente Form der Dementia praecox (Dementia simplex). *Archiv für Psychiatrie, 37*, 111–187.

Donaldson, S.R., Gelenberg, A.J., & Baldessarini, R.J. (1983). The pharmacologic treatment of schizophrenia: A progress report. *Schizophrenia Bulletin, 9*, 504–527.

Elsworth, R. (1980). Characteristics of effective treatment settings: a research review. In J.G.

Gunderson, L.R. Mosher, O.A. Will Jr. (Eds.), *Principals and practices of milieu therapy*. New York: Aronson.

Elsworth, R., Marony, R., Klett, W., Gordon, H., & Gunn, R. (1971). Milieu characteristics of successful psychiatric treatment programs. *American Journal of Orthopsychiatry*, *41*, 427–434.

Engelhardt, D.M., Rosen, B., Freedman, N., Mann, D, & Margolis, R. (1963). Phenothiazines in the prevention of psychiatric hospitalization: II. Duration of treatment exposure. *Journal of the American Medical Association*, *186*, 981–983.

Engelhardt, D.M., Freedman, M., Rosen, B., Mann, D., & Margolis, R. (1964). Phenothiazines in the prevention of psychiatric hospitalization: III. Delay or prevention of hospitalization. *Archives of General Psychiatry*, *11*, 162–169.

Engelhardt, D.M., Rosen, B., Freedman, N. & Margolis, R. (1967). Phenothiazines in the prevention of psychiatric hospitalization: IV. Delay or prevention of hospitalization – a reevaluation. *Archives of General Psychiatry*, *16*, 98–101.

Ericksen, S.E., Hurth, S.W., & Chang, S. (1978). Haloperidol dose, plasma levels, and clinical response: A double-blind study. *Psychopharmacological Bulletin*, *14*, 15.

Fairweather, G., Sanders, D., Cressler, D., & Maynard, H. (1969). *Community life for the mentally ill: an alternative to institutional care*. Chicago: Aldine.

Feinsilver, D.B., & Gunderson, J.G. (1972). Psychotherapy for schizophrenics: is it indicated? A review of the relevant literature. *Schizophrenia Bulletin*, *6*, 11–23.

Fenton, W.S., & McGlashan, T.H. (1987). Sustained remission in drug-free schizophrenic patients. *American Journal of Psychiatry*, *144*, 1306–1309.

Frieske, D.A., & Wilson, W.P. (1966). Formal qualities of hallucinations in patients with schizophrenic, organic and affective psychoses. In P.H. Hoch & J. Zubin (Eds.), *Psychopathology of schizophrenia* (pp. 49–62). New York: Grune and Stratton.

Furlan, P.M., & Benedetti, G. (1985). The individual psychoanalytic psychotherapy of schizophrenia: Scientific and clinical approach through a clinical discussion group. *Yale Journal of Biology and Medicine*, *58*, 337–348.

Gomes-Schwartz, B. (1984). Individual psychotherapy of schizophrenia. In A.S. Bellack (Ed.), *Schizophrenia. Treatment, management, and rehabilitation*. New York: Grune and Stratton.

Gottesman, I.I. (1987). The psychotic hinterlands or, the fringes of lunacy. *British Medical Bulletin*, *43*, 1–13.

Grinker, R.R., Werble, B., & Drye, T. (1968). *The borderline syndrome: A behavioral study of ego functions*. New York: Basic Books.

Grinspoon, L., Ewalt, J.R. & Shader, R. (1968). Psychotherapy and pharmacotherapy in chronic schizophrenia. *American Journal of Psychiatry*, *124*, 1945–1952.

Grinspoon, L., Ewalt, J.R., & Shader, R.I (1972). *Schizophrenia: Pharmacotherapy and psychotherapy*. Baltimore: Williams and Wilkins.

Gunderson, J.G., Frank, A.F., Katz, H.M., Vannicelli, M.L., Frosch, J.P., & Knapp, P.H. (1984). Effects of psychotherapy in schizophrenia. II. Comparative outcome of two forms of treatment. *Schizophrenia Bulletin*, *10*, 564–598.

Haas, S., Emrich, H.M., & Beckmann, H. (1982). Analgesic and euphoric effects of high dose diazepam in schizophrenia. *Neuropsychobiology*, *8*, 123–128.

Harrow, M., & Quinlan, D.M. (1985). Disordered thinking and schizophrenic psychopathology. New York: Gardner.

Hecker, E. (1871). Die Hebephrenie. Ein Beitrag zur klinischen Psychiatrie. *Archiv für Pathologie und Anatomie Berlin*, *52*, 394–429.

Heimann, H. (1982). *Methodische Probleme der Wirksamkeitsprüfung von Neuroleptika im Rahmen der Langzeittherapie*. Lecture at Janssen Symposium *Bestandaufnahme der Psychopharmakotherapie*, February 26, Neuss-Rosellen, FRG.

Helmchen, H. (1979). Neuroleptische Langzeitmedikation in der Praxis. *Ärztliche Fortbildung*, *29*, 800–801.

Helmchen, H., & Hippius, H. (1974). Multidimensionale pharmakopsychiatrische Untersuchungen mit dem Neuroleptikum Perazin. 1–7.Mitteilung. *Pharmacopsychiatry*, *7*, 1–64.

Hirsch, S.R. (1986). Clinical treatment of schizophrenia. In P.B. Bradley & S.R. Hirsch (Eds.), *The psychopharmacology and treatment of schizophrenia.* Oxford: Oxford University Press.

Hirsch, S.R., Gaind, R., Rhode, P.D., Stevens, B., & Wing, J.K. (1973). Outpatient maintenance of chronic schizophrenic patients with long acting fluphenazine: A double-blind placebo trial. *British Medical Journal, 1*, 633–637.

Hoch, P.H., & Polatin, P. (1949). Pseudoneurotic forms of schizophreia. *Psychiatric Quarterly, 23*, 248–276.

Hogarty, G.E., & Goldberg, S.C. (1973). Drug and sociotherapy in the aftercare of schizophrenic patients. One year relapse rates. *Archives of General Psychiatry, 28*, 54–64.

Hogarty, G.E., Goldberg, S.C., Schooler, N.R., & Ulrich, R.F. (1974). Drug and sociotherapy in the aftercare of schizophrenic patients. II. Two-year relapse rates. *Archives of General Psychiatry, 31*, 603–608.

Hogarty, G.E., Goldberg, S.C., & Schooler, N.R. (1975). Drug and sociotherapy in the aftercare of schizophrenia: A review. In M.Greenblatt (Ed.), *Drugs in combination with other therapies.* New York: Grune and Stratton.

Hogarty, G.E., Anderson, C.M., Reiss, D.J., Kornblith, S.J., Greenwald, D.P., Javna, C.D., & Madonia, M.J. (1986). Family psycho-education, social skills training and maintenance chemotherapy in the aftercare treatment of schizophrenia. I. One year effects of a controlled study on relapse and expressed emotion. *Archives of General Psychiatry, 43*, 633–642.

Hogarty, G.E., Schooler, N.R., Ulrich, R.F., Mussare, F., Ferro, P, & Herron, E. (1979). Fluphenazine and social therapy in the aftercare of schizophrenic patients: relapse analyses of a two-year controlled study of fluphenazine hydrochloride. *Archives of General Psychiatry, 36*, 1283–1294.

Holzman, P.S., Shenton, M.E., & Solovay, M.R. (1986). Quality of thought disorder in differential diagnosis. *Schizophrenia Bulletin, 12*, 360–372.

Huber, G., Gross, G. & Schüttler, R. (1979). *Schizophrenie. Eine verlaufs- und sozialpsychiatrische Langzeitstudie.* Berlin, Heidelberg, New York: Springer.

Janzarik, W. (1968). *Schizophrene Verläufe.* Berlin, Heidelberg, New York: Springer.

Kane, J.M. (1987). Treatment of schizophrenia. *Schizophrenia Bulletin, 13*, 133–156.

Kane, J.M., Rifkin, A., Woerner, M., & Sarantakos, S. (1986). Dose response relationships in maintenance drug treatment for schizophrenia. *Psychopharmacology Bulletin, 6*, 205–235.

Karon, B. & O'Grady, P. (1969). Intellectual test changes in schizophrenic patients in the first six months of treatment. *Psychotherapy, Theory, Research, and Practice, 6*, 88.

Kellam, S.G. (1980). Ward atmosphere, continuity of therapy, and the mental health system. In J.G. Gunderson, L.R. Mosher, O.A. Will Jr. (Eds.), *Principles and practices of milieu therapy.* New York: Aronson.

Kendell, R.E. (1987). Schizophrenia: Clinical features. In R. Michels, J.O. Cavenar, Jr., A.M. Cooper, S.B. Guze, L.L. Judd, G.L. Klerman, & A.J. Solnit (Eds.), *Psychiatry* (Vol 1). New York: Basic Books.

Kendler, K.S., Masterson, C.C., Ungaro, R., & Davis, K.L. (1984). A family history study of schizophrenia-related personality disorders. *American Journal of Psychiatry, 141*, 424–427.

Kety, S.S., Rosenthal, D., Wender, P.H., Schulsinger, F., & Jacobsen, B. (1978). The biological and adoptive families of adopted individuals who become schizophrenic: prevalence of mental illness and other characteristics. In L.C. Wynne, R.L. Cromwell, S. Matthysse (Eds.), *The nature of schizophrenia: new approaches to research and treatment.* New York: Wiley.

Knight, R. (1953). Borderline states. *Bulletin of the Menninger Clinic, 17*, 1–12.

Kraepelin, E. (1896). *Psychiatrie: Ein Lehrbuch für Studierende und Ärzte (5th ed.).* Leipzig: Barth.

Kraepelin, E. (1913). *Psychiatrie* (Vol. 3) Part 2, 8th edn. Leipzig: Barth. (Translation: *Dementia praecox and paraphrenia.* Edinburgh: Livingstone (1919).

Langfeldt, G. (1939). *The Schizophreniform states.* Kopenhagen: Munksgard.

Leff, J.P., & Wing, J.K. (1971). Trial of maintenance therapy in schizophrenia. *British Medical Journal, 3*, 599–604.

Leff, J., & Vaughn, C. (1985). *Expressed emotion in families. Its significance for mental illness*. New York: Guilford.
Lehmann, H.E. (1975a). Schizophrenia: Introduction and history. In A.M. Freedman et al. (Eds.), *Comprehensive textbook of psychiatry*. II (Vol. 1, 2nd ed. pp. 851–859). Baltimore: Williams and Wilkins.
Lehmann, H.E. (1975b). Psychopharmacological treatment of schizophrenia. *Schizophrenia Bulletin, 13*, 27–45.
Leonhard, K. (1959). *Aufteilung der endogenen Psychosen*. Berlin: Akademie.
Lowing, P.A., Mirsky, A.F., & Pereira, R. (1983). The inheritance of schizophrenia spectrum disorders: A reanalysis of the Danish adoptee study data. *American Journal of Psychiatry, 140*, 1167–1171.
Mason, A.S. (1975). Basic principles in the use of antipsychotic agents. In J.H. Masserman (Ed.), Current psychiatric therapies (Vol. 15, pp. 135–145). New York: Grune and Stratton.
May, P.R.A. (1968). *Treatment of schizophrenia: A comparative study of five treatment methods*. New York: Science House.
May, P.R.A. (1974). A Brave New World revisited: Alphas, betas and treatment outcome. *Comprehensive Psychiatry, 15*, 1–17.
May, P.R.A., & Goldberg, S.C. (1978). Prediction of schizophrenic patients' response to pharmacotherapy. In M.A. Lipton, A. DiMascio, & K.F. Killam (Eds.), *Psychopharmacology – a generation of progress*. New York: Raven.
May, P.R.A., Tuma, H., & Dixon, W.J. (1976a). Schizophrenia – A follow-up study of results of treatment. I. Design and other problems. *Archives of General Psychiatry, 33*, 474–478.
May, P.R.A., Tuma, H., Ylae, C., Potepan, P. & Dixon, W.J. (1976b). Schizophrenia – A follow-up study of results of treatment. II. Hospital stay over two to five years. *Archives of General Psychiatry, 33*, 481–486.
Mayer-Gross, W. (1924). *Selbstschilderungen der Verwirrtheit (Die oneiroide Erlebnisform)*. Berlin, Heidelberg, New York: Springer.
McGhie, A., & Chapman, J. (1961). Disorders of attention and perception in early schizophrenia. *British Journal of Medical Psychology, 34*, 103–116.
Moos, R.H. (1975). *Evaluating correctional and community settings*. New York: Wiley.
Morel, B.A. (1860). *Traité des maladies mentales*. Paris: Masson.
Mosher, L.R. & Menn, A.Z. (1978). Community residential treatment for schizophrenia: Two-year follow-up data. *Hospital and Community Psychiatry, 29*, 715–723.
Mosher, L.R., Menn, A.Z., & Matthews, S.M. (1975). Soteria: evaluation of a homebased treatment for schizophrenia. *American Journal of Orthopsychiatry, 45*, 455–463.
Müller, C. (1984). Psychotherapy in schizophrenia: The end of the pioneers' period. *Schizophrenia Bulletin, 10*, 618–620.
Murphy, E.L., Shilling, D.J., & Murray, R.M. (1978). Psychoactive drug responder subgoups: possible contributions to psychiatric classification. In N.A. Lipton, A. DiMascio, & K.S. Killam (Eds.), *Psychopharmacology – A generation of progress* (pp. 807–820). New York: Raven.
Neborsky, R., Janowsky, D. Munson, E., & Depry, D. (1981). Rapid treatment of acute psychotic symptoms with high- and low-dose haloperidol. *Archives of General Psychiatry, 38*, 195–199.
Nedopil, N., Rüther, E., & Strauss, A. (1980). Zum Zeitverlauf der antipsychotischen Wirkung von Neuroleptika bei akuten Psychosen. In K. Krypsin-Exner, H. Hinterhuber & H. Schubert (Eds.), *Therapie akuter psychiatrischer Syndrome. II. Alpenländisches Psychiatrie-Symposium Stuttgart*: (pp. 139–148), Schattauer.
Odejide, O.A. & Aderounmu, A.F. (1982). Double-blind placebo substitution: withdrawal of fluphenazine decanoate in schizophrenic patients. *Journal of Clinical Psychiatry, 43*, 195–196.
Overall, J.E., & Hollister, L.E. (1979). Comparative evaluation of research diagnostic criteria for schizophrenia. *Archives of General Psychiatry, 36*, 1198–1205.
Paul, G.L. & Lentz, R.J. (1977). *Psychosocial treatment of chronic mental patients: milieu vs. social-learning programs*. Cambridge, Mass.: Harvard University Press.

Pietzcker, A. (1978). Langzeitmedikation bei schizophrenen Kranken. *Nervenarzt, 49*, 518–533.

Price, R.H. (1980). Knowledge into practice: assessment and change in treatment environments. In J.G. Gunderson, L.R. Mosher, O.A. Will Jr. (Eds.), *Principles and practices of milieu therapy*. New York: Aronson.

Rappaport, M., Hopkins, H.K., Hall, K., Bolleza, T., & Silverman, J. (1978). Are there schizophrenics for whom drugs may be contraindicated or unnecesary? *International Pharmacopsychiatry, 13*, 100–111.

Rifkin, A., Quitkin, F., Rabiner, C.J., & Klein, D.F. (1977). Fluphenazine decanoate, fluphenazine hydrochloride given orally, and placebo in remitted schizophrenics. *Archives of General Psychiatry, 34*, 43–47

Rochester, S. & Martin, J.R. (1979). *Crazy talk. A study of the discourse of schizophrenic speakers.* New York: Plenum.

Rogers, C.R., Gendlin, E.G., Kiesler, D.J., & Truax, C.B. (1967). *The therapeutic relationship and its impact.* Madison: University of Wisconsin Press.

Rollin, H.R. (Ed.), (1980). *Coping with schizophrenia.* London: Burnett Books.

Sander, W. (1868). Über eine spezielle Form der primären Verrücktheit. *Archiv für Psychiatrie und Nervenkrankheiten, 1*, 387–419.

Sartorius, N., Shapiro, R., & Jablensky, A. (1974). The International Pilot Study of Schizophrenia. *Schizophrenia Bulletin, 1*, 21–34.

Scharfetter, C. (1983). Schizophrene Menschen. Munich: Urban and Schwarzenberg.

Schied, H.W. (1983). Durchführung der Therapie mit Neuroleptika. In G. Langer, H. Heimann (Eds.), *Psyschopharmaka. Grundlagen und Therapie.* Wien, New York: Springer.

Schmidt, L.E., Schüssler, G., Kappes, V., Mühlbauer, H., & Müller-Oerlinghausen, B. (1982). A double-blind study of the antipsychotic efficacy of perazine compared to haloperidol. *Drug Reserach, 32*, 910–911.

Schooler, N.R. (1986). The efficacy of antipsychotic drugs and family therapies in the maintenance treatment of schizophrenia. *Journal of Clinical Psychopharmacology, 6*, 11–19.

Schooler, N.R., Levine, J., Severe, J.B., Brauzer, B., DiMascio, A., Klerman, G.L., & Tuason, V.B. (1980). Prevention of relapse in schizophrenia: an evaluation of fluphenazine decanoate. *Archives of General Psychiatry, 37*, 16–24.

Smith, C.G., & King, J.A. (1975). *Mental hospitals: a study in organizational effectiveness.* Lexington, Mass.: Lexington Books.

Spitzer, R.L., Endicott, J., & Robins, E. (1978). *Research Diagnostic Criteria (RDC). Biometric research.* New York: NY State Psychiatric Institute.

Spitzer, R.L., Endicott, J., & Gibbin, M. (1979). Crossing the border into borderline personality and borderline schizophrenia: The development of criteria. *Archives of General Psychiatry, 36*, 17–24.

Spokes, E.G.S. (1980). Biochemical abnormalities in schizophrenia: The dopamine hypothesis. In G. Curzon (Ed.), *The biochemistry of psychiatric disturbances.* Chichester: Wiley.

Stanton, A.H., Gunderson, J.G., Knapp, P.H., Frank, A.F., Vannicelli, M.L., Schnitzer, R., & Rosenthal, R. (1984). Effects of psychotherapy in schizophrenia. I. Design and implementation of a controlled study, *Schizophrenia Bulletin, 10*, 520–551.

Stauder, K.H.(1934). Die tödliche Katatonie. *Archiv für Psychiatrie, 102*, 614–634.

Stephens, J.H. (1978). Long-term prognosis and follow-up in schizophrenia. *Schizophrenia Bulletin, 4*, 25–47.

Straube, E.R., Wagner, W., Foerster, K., & Heimann, H. (1989). Findings significant with respect to short- and medium-term outcome in schizophrenia – A preliminary report. *Progress in Neuropsychopharmacology and Biological Psychiatry, 12*, 185–197.

Strauss, J.S., Carpenter, W.T., Jr., & Bartko, J.J. (1974). The diagnosis and understanding of schizophrenia. III. Speculations on the processes that underlie schizophrenic symptoms and signs. *Schizophrenia Bulletin, 11*, 61–69.

Tsuang, M.T., (1982). Long-term outcome in schizophrenia. *Trends in Neuro science, 7*(5), 203–207.

van Putten, T., & May. P.R.A. (1978). Subjective response as a predictor of outcome in pharmacotherapy. *Archives of General Psychiatry, 35*, 477–480.

Wing, J.K. (1970). A standard form of psychiatric Present State Examination (PSE) and a method for standardising the classification of symptoms. In E.H. Hare & J.K. Wing (Eds.), *Psychiatric epidemiology: An international symposium*. London: Oxford University Press.
Woggon, B. (1980) Veränderungen der psychopathologischen Symptomatik während 20-tägiger antidepressiver oder neuroleptischer Behandlung. *Psychiatria Clinica, 13*, 150–164.
Zahn, T.P., Carpenter, W.T., & McGlashan, T.H. (1981). Autonomic nervous system activity in acute schizophrenia. I. Method and comparison with normal controls. *Archives of General Psychiatry, 38*. 251–258.

The Copenhagen High-Risk Study: Major Psychopathological and Etiological Findings

J. Parnas, F. Schulsinger, and A. Mednick

Introduction

The purpose of this presentation is to review major psychopathological and etiological findings from a prospective, longitudinal study of children of schizophrenic mothers. This study, which is still ongoing, was initiated by Mednick and Schulsinger in 1962.

Methodological Advantages and Design of the Studies

The typical research approach to the etiology of schizophrenia has been to compare diagnosed schizophrenic patients with other psychiatric patients or normal controls on biological or social characteristics of theoretical interest. The flaw inherent in such an approach is that one cannot differentiate between characteristics unique to schizophrenics which may have played a causal role in their illness and characteristics which may only be consequences or concomitants of their illness, or be the result of biased retrospective reporting. Consequently, in the 1950s a prospective longitudinal high-risk design was advocated (Mednick & McNeil, 1968). It implies that schizophrenics are initially studied as children, i.e., before they become ill. Eventual adult diagnostic outcomes can be related to data of interest which have been collected premorbidly. Because having a schizophrenic parent increases the risk of developing schizophrenia by at least ten-fold, samples of children can be chosen on the criterion of their having a schizophrenic parent. The following advantages of the described high-risk prospective design can be delineated: (a) the researchers and the relatives of the subject do not know whether he or she will become schizophrenic, which implies that the collected data are unbiased; (b) the information gathered is mainly current, not retrospective; (c) the premorbid and follow-up data are uniformly and systematically obtained, and the subjects are diagnosed independently of their possible hospitalizations; (d) in addition, in the high-risk design, one operates with two groups: one genetically predisposed by having a schizophrenic mother, and the other selected on the criterion that its members do not have a schizophrenic parent, the low-risk group. Consequently, it is possible to study the effect of the same putative environmental stressor, such as parental separation, on two different levels of genetic vulnerability. In other words, the high-risk design allows for longitudinal explorations into the possible gene–environment interactions.

The model of data analyses presented below is based on the paradigm that schizophrenics and borderline schizophrenics (i.e., schizotypes) show comparable genetic vulnerability to schizophrenia. Consequently, possible differences in environmental backgrounds between these two groups may identify factors causally relevant for the schizophrenic breakdown. This approach is in accordance with the theorizing of Meehl (1962, 1972), who postulated that what was inherited in schizophrenia was a "subtle neuro-integrative defect," which he termed schizotaxia. The imposition of social learning history upon schizotaxic individuals results in a personality organization called schizotype. He postulated that schizotypal characteristics are universally learned by schizotaxic individuals; however, the fate of the schizotype, that is whether he or she remains a schizotype or decompensates towards overt schizophrenia, depends upon environmental influences and other genetic influences.

The Course of This Study

As already mentioned, this study began in 1962 with the examination of 207 children of severely schizophrenic mothers [84% of the mothers fulfilled the current criteria for schizophrenia of the *Diagnostic and Statistical Manual of Mental Disorders*, 3rd edition (DSM-III; 1980)], and a control group of children (so-called low-risk children) whose parents had not been hospitalized for schizophrenia. The children were matched for age, sex, parental social class, urban/rural residence, and amount of time spent in public child care institutions in their childhood.

An outline of this study is given in Table 1. As can be seen, in 1972–1974, when the mean age of the children was 25 years, both the index and the control group underwent a diagnostic assessment using the Present State Examination (PSE; Wing, Cooper, & Sartorius, 1974), the Current and Past Psychopathology Scales (CAPPS; Endicott & Spitzer, 1972), and the *International Classification of Diseases*, 8th edition (ICD-8; World Health Organization, 1967). The interviewer was blind with respect to premorbid data on the children and, as far as possible, to the status of the interviewed subject, i.e., whether a member of the high- or low-risk group. The diagnostic status of the children at the age of 25 years is shown in Table 2.

In the studies described in the subsequent sections we have utilized the ICD-8 clinical diagnosis. Since "borderline schizophrenia" in this diagnostic system is very close to the current revised DSM-III (DSM-IIIR; 1987) concept of schizotypal personality disorder (Spitzer & Endicott, 1979), we will utilize the term "schizotypal personality disorder" instead of the term "borderline schizophrenia" originally used.

As already stated, we have been especially interested in the comparison of schizophrenics and schizotypes on the assumption of their comparable genetic

Table 1. Outline of the Copenhagen high-risk study

1962	1967	1972–1974	1980	1980–1983
Initial assessment	5-Year follow-up	10-Year diagnostic interview follow-up	Subsample follow-up	
Children of schizophrenic mothers ($n=207$)	Social worker interview		Diagnostic reexamination CT scan examination	
Children of nonschizophrenic mothers ($n=104$) age 15.1 years	Preliminary comparison of "sick," "well," and control groups			
Psychological examination				Diagnostic interview study of the children's fathers
Psychiatric examination				
Rearing environment				
Parent interview				
Psychophysiological examination				
Perinatal history				
School behavior				

vulnerability to schizophrenia. The *high-risk* mentally healthy group will be used as a kind of control group, in that we assume that high-risk healthy individuals do not possess a schizophrenic genotype.

Inspection of Table 2 reveals that the frequency of schizophrenia-related conditions among high-risk subjects is dramatically higher than among low-risk controls. Although the high-risk design does not enable disentangling genetic and nongenetic familial influences, these results are highly suggestive. In addition, the fact that children born to schizophrenic mothers have an increased risk of developing schizophrenia and schizotypal personality disorders supports the notion of a genetic relationship between these two disorders. Such a genetic relationship has been definitely demonstrated in adoption studies (Kendler, Gruenberg, & Strauss, 1981).

Premorbid Behavioral Data

Evaluation of schizophrenics and schizotypes on the basis of *premorbid* behavioral data may provide insight into the relationship between the two disorders. It may be postulated that premorbid psychopathological traits of a

Table 2. Diagnostic status of high-risk and low-risk groups in 1972

	High-risk group		Low-risk group	
	M (*n*)	F (*n*)	M (*n*)	F (*n*)
Schizophrenia	7	6	1	0
"Schizotypal" personality disorder	17	12	1	0
Other diagnoses				
Schizoid and paranoid personlity disorders	26	16	1	3
Psychopathy	4	1	4	0
Other personality disorders	14	12	6	4
Other conditions	1	0	0	0
Neuroses (symptom and character), high IDS	2	0	6	5
	47	29	17	12
No mental illness	7	16	13	14
Neuroses (character), low IDS	19	13	21	12
	26	29	34	26

IDS, Index Definition of Syndromes.

schizophrenia spectrum disorder relate to more essential features of such a disorder and assist us in the identification of characteristics unique to schizotypes and central or primary to schizophrenic symptomatology. We have performed analyses relevant to this issue (Parnas, Schulsinger, Schulsinger, Mednick, & Teasdale, 1982a). At the initial premorbid assessment children were rated by a psychiatrist on a number of scales evaluating mental status. Retrospective data concerning early childhood behavior were collected by interviewing parents or other guardians. Finally, school teachers completed structured questionnaires concerning school behavior. The results of our analyses are shown in Table 3, which lists characteristics that discriminated schizophrenia spectrum individuals (i.e., schizophrenics and schizotypes) from *high-risk* children who remained mentally healthy.

As can be seen, both the schizophrenics and the schizotypes exhibited premorbidly subtle signs of formal thought disorder and defective emotional contact. It may therefore be concluded that such traits are central to the schizophrenic symptomatology. As babies, they were described as being passive, which is consistent with some anecdotal clinical observations and with the findings of intensive follow-up studies of children of schizophrenic mothers performed by Fish (1977). She considered such passive behavior to be an expression of schizotaxia, i.e., a subtle neurointegrative deficit.

Table 3. Behavioral precursors of schizophrenia spectrum

Early childhood	Passivity
	Poor concentration
School behavior	Rejected by others
	Poor affect control[a]
Clinical assessment (15 years of age)	Formal thought disorder
	Defective emotional rapport

[a] This item discriminated schizophrenics from schizotypes.

The only premorbid behavior which consistently discriminated between schizophrenics and schizotypes was poor impulse control, characteristic of the former and perhaps indicative of minimal brain damage suffered by pre-schizophrenics.

In summary, the results of this study point towards a continuum of psychopathology from childhood to adulthood; i.e., schizophrenia is not to be considered an unexpected disease, but a gradual development due to biological and psychosocial influences.

Perinatal Factors

Quite early in the course of the project it was noticed that the high-risk children who showed evidence of a psychiatric disturbance had suffered a large number of birth difficulties. Consistent with our interest in possible differences between schizophrenics and schizotypes, we explored the frequency and the severity of perinatal complications experienced by these two groups as compared to the high-risk individuals who remained mentally healthy.

The main results appear in Table 4. This comparison (Parnas, Schulsinger, Teasdale, Schulsinger, Feldman, & Mednick, 1982b) revealed that schizophrenics had suffered the most, and the severest obstetric complications, and schizotypes the fewest and least severe complications, whereas the mentally healthy group occupied an intermediate position. We interpreted this distribution in the following way: because preschizophrenics and preschizotypes have comparable genetic liability towards schizophrenia, a perinatal neurological insult will possess a critical effect with respect to whether a person remains schizotypal or develops schizophrenia. In order to remain schizotypal, one has to be free of perinatal complications. The intermediate position of the high-risk mentally healthy individuals can be explained by the assumption that they do not have high genetic liability and consequently the perinatal complications will not produce schizophrenia in these individuals. Although there have been no other studies concerned with perinatal stress and schizotypal personality disorder, indirect support for this reasoning may be derived from studies showing a positive correlation between perinatal stress and the severity of schizophrenic disorder (McNeil & Kaij, 1978).

Table 4. Mean scale scores in the three diagnostic groups.

Perinatal complications	Schizophrenia		Schizotypal personality disorder		No mental illness		Mann Whitney's *U* test *P* value: schizophrenia vs. borderline
	Mean	SD	Mean	SD	Mean	SD	
Frequency score	1.50	1.38	0.40	0.76	0.85	1.09	0.009
Severity score	1.08	0.90	0.40	0.71	0.72	0.83	0.019
Total score	3.17	2.82	0.76	1.67	1.92	2.85	0.008

Cerebral Morphology

In order to test our hypothesis on schizophrenic/schizotypal differences, we undertook a study of three groups of high-risk subjects diagnosed in 1972 as schizophrenic, schizotypal, or mentally healthy (Schulsinger et al., 1984). All subjects underwent diagnostic reassessment, and a computed tomographic (CT) scan provided measures of the ventricle-brain ratio (VBR) and the width of the third ventricle. The 1980 diagnostic groups differed in the predicted direction, in that schizophrenics had the largest ventricles, schizotypes the smallest, and high-risk mentally healthy individuals exhibited intermediate values. Thus, we obtained the same distribution as was the case with obstetric complications. The results appear in Table 5 and Fig. 1. We interpret our findings along the lines described for obstetric complications: for an individual having a schizophrenic diathesis it is critical to avoid neurological insult in order for him or her to remain schizotypal. Again, the intermediate position of healthy high-risk individuals may be explained by their lack of schizophrenic genotype. We have some indication that ventricular enlargement is a precursor rather than a consequence of the disease. We found a positive correlation between low birth weight and subsequent brain atrophy.

Furthermore, a preliminary analysis of correlations between ventricular measures and concurrent mental status description from the PSE (behavior, affect, and speech), indicated that the so-called negative symptoms such as poverty of speech, blunted affect, and organic impairment correlated positively with brain atrophy. Although based on a small sample size, these correlations may support the notion of type 1 and type 2 schizophrenia.

Psychosocial Factors

Psychosocial factors have been the focus of an impressive amount of literature on schizophrenia, particularly inspired by psychoanalytic investigations.

Table 5. CT group means (±SD) for 1980 diagnoses

	Schizophrenic ($n=7$)[a]	Schizotype ($n=11$)	No mental illness ($n=13$)[a]	P[b]
Third ventricle (mm)	4.4±2.1	2.7±1.1	3.2±0.8	.028 (S/ST)
Ventricle-brain ratio (%)	11.4±6.7	5.5±1.9	6.8±1.9	.004 (S/ST) .012 (S/NMI) .066 (B/NMI)

[a] One schizophrenic and one subject in the mentally healthy group refused to undergo CT scanning.

[b] Mann-Whitney *U* test (two-tailed probability). Values are for between-group comparisons; groups being compared are indicated in parantheses. S, schizophrenic; ST, schizotype; NMI, no mental illness.

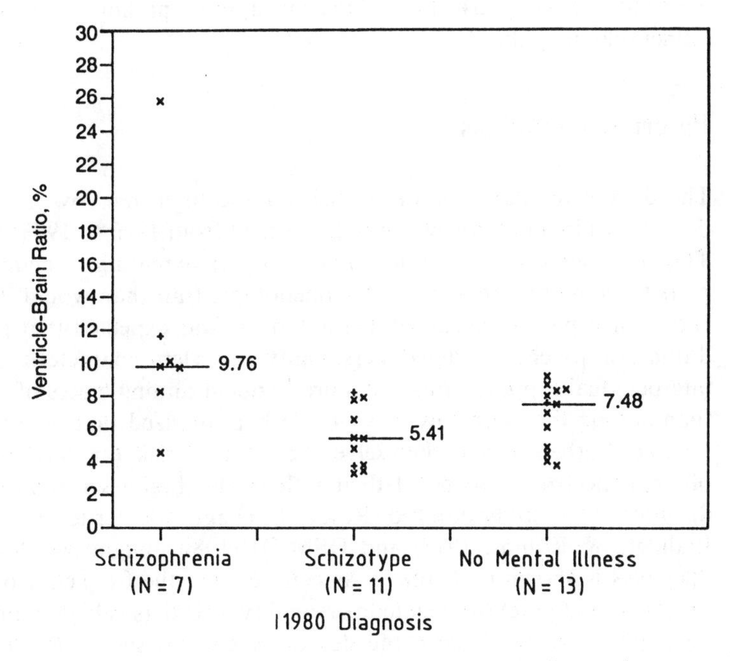

Fig. 1. Distribution of ventricle-brain ratios as function of 1980 diagnostic group (*horizontal line*, median).

Another early finding of this project (at 5-year follow-up) was the association of negative outcomes in the high-risk children with separation from their parents. Since we suspected that prolonged contact with a severely schizophrenic mother is unlikely to improve mental health, we reasoned that perhaps the bad consequences of separation were actually resulting from some influences associated with the parent's absence. For most of the high-risk children separation from parents resulted in prolonged rearing in a public child care institution. In line with our interest in schizophrenic/schizotypal differences, we were interested in examining the amount of institutionalization in the childhood of the high-risk children (Parnas, Teasdale, & Schuslinger, 1985). The main result appears in Table 6, which shows that schizophrenics experienced the most institutionalization during their first 10 years of life. This analysis was performed using a multivariate analysis of covariance, where possible effects of the amount of parental separation and the age of onset of maternal schizophrenia (the latter being regarded as a putative measure of genetic loading) were partialled out. As can be seen, schizophrenics had experienced the highest levels of institutionalization in their childhood. The low-risk controls were matched to the high-risk group for the amount of institutional rearing. We were, however, unable to detect any psychopathogenic effect of institutionalization in the low-risk group. This is impressive support for the diathesis-stress model: that stress, exemplified here by institutional rearing, appears pathogenic only in genetically vulnerable individuals.

Paternal Diagnosis

The diagnostic status of the fathers of the high and low-risk children was determined in an interview study performed from 1980 to 1983 (Parnas, 1985). This study focuses on the question of assortative mating, a tendency for mated pairs to be more similar for some phenotypic trait than would be the case if a choice of a partner occurred at random. It was expected that psychotic conditions or psychosis-related personality disorders characterized by deficient interpersonal rapport would be more frequent among mates of schizophrenics than among their controls. It was also hypothesized that offspring of schizophrenic mothers would themselves be more at risk for developing a schizophrenia spectrum disorder if their fathers also had a schizophrenia spectrum disorder. Our study utilized Research Diagnostic Criteria (RDC; Spitzer, Endicott, & Robins, 1978) and DSM-III (1980) diagnoses. Paternal lifetime diagnosis is shown in Table 7. As can be seen, the frequency of nonaffective psychosis and psychosis-related personality disorders is higher among mates of schizophrenics. In Table 8 the degree of concordance between the paternal diagnosis and the offspring diagnosis is presented. The presence of a schizophrenia spectrum disorder in the father significantly increased the offspring's risk of developing a schizophrenia spectrum disorder.

The degree of assortative mating was significantly higher among mates of schizophrenic women with earlier disease onset. This was interpreted as indicating that women with early onset schizophrenia were more deviant premorbidly and consequently attracted more deviant mates. This finding provides further evidence that assortative mating really takes place. The study suggests

Table 6. Adjusted means for institutionalization[a] as a function of diagnosis and sex (high-risk group only).

	Adjusted group means				ANCOVA[b]			
	Schizophrenia	"Schizotypal" personality disorder	Other diagnoses	No mental illness	Diagnosis	Sex	Diagnosis × sex	Age of offspring
Male	42.4	15.1	21.9	15.4	...	...	...	...
Female	27.0	32.2	17.5	16.5	...	...	...	...
Male + female	35.3	22.1	20.2	16.0	...	...	...	...
F ratio	...	...	...	...	3.0	<1	2.4	2.1
P	...	...	...	...	.033	NS	.068	.024

[a] Institutionalization in months (corrected for mother's age at first hospitalization, contact with mother in months, and contact with father in months).
[b] ANCOVA, analysis of covariance.

Table 7 Paternal lifetime diagnosis

	Mates of schizophrenics		Mates of non-schizophrenics	
	(*n*)	(%)	(*n*)	(%)
Nonaffective psychosis	7	7	1	1.5
Schizotype	4	4	1	1.5
Schizoid, paranoid, narcissistic, borderline	11	11	0	0
Affective disorder	10	10	14	22
Other diagnosis	6	6	4	6
Antisocial/alcoholic	26	27	11	17
No mental illness	33	34	32	50
	97		63	

Table 8. Concordance of father-child diagnosis (high-risk group only)

		At least one child in a sibship with a schizophrenia spectrum diagnosis[b]		
		Yes	No	Total
Father's diagnosis within schizophrenia spectrum[a]	Yes	11	1	12
	No	45	31	76
	Total	56	32	88

[a] Refers to any functional nonaffective psychosis, schizotypal, schizoid, and paranoid personality disorder (DSM-III; 1980).
[b] Refers to ICD-8 diagnosis of schizophrenia, borderline schizophrenia (schizotypal personality disorder), schizoid, and paranoid personality disorder.
$P = .02$ (Fisher's exact test).

that the phenotypic traits which promote assortative mating in schizophrenia include deficient interpersonal rapport.

Summary and Conclusions

The Copenhagen high-risk study illustrates an epidemiological design where, in a genetically defined population, determinants of psychopathology are identified prior to the outcome of interest. Such assertion of temporal sequences of events promotes causal inferences. In addition, inclusion of the low-risk control group provides the possibility of testing gene-environment interactions; i.e., the effect of the same putative environmental agent can be examined within the context of different levels of genetic risk. It is, however, important to realize that the study presented is correlational and nonmanipulative. Thus, the inferences of causality stated below should be viewed with caution.

Data analyses in the study were anchored in a diathesis-stress model of schizophrenic etiology, with special emphasis on the paradigm positing that schizophrenics and schizotypes share comparable genetic liability to schizophrenia, but that the former, in addition, suffer environmental insult. The results of the project demonstrate that schizophrenia and schizotypy are genetically related in that prevalence of both disorders among offspring of schizophrenic mothers is highly elevated as compared to the low-risk control group. Future schizophrenia spectrum individuals exhibit premorbidly subtle signs of formal thought disorder and defective emotional rapport.

This finding may have implications for the psychopathological conceptualization of schizophrenia; i.e., that Bleulerian fundamental symptoms are central to the psychopathology of schizophrenia, and, secondly, that schizophrenia develops through gradually increasing pathology and is not a sudden unexpected affliction.

Development of a schizophrenia spectrum disorder in the high-risk offspring was predicted by assortative mating, i.e., paternal diagnosis of schizophrenia spectrum disorder increased the offspring's risk for such a disturbance.

Environmental factors which discriminated between schizophrenics and schizotypes fell within two domains. First, schizophrenics suffered more perinatal complications, and, secondly, schizophrenics experienced more early psychosocial stress in the form of institutional rearing.

Suggestive evidence was found that perinatal complications in schizophrenics may result in later brain atrophy as measured by the CT scans.

In conclusion, one may conceptualize schizophrenia as an environmentally complicated schizotypal personality disorder. In other words, schizotypy is what is genetically transmitted in schizophrenia, and whether the schizophrenic phenotype attains expression depends on environmental influences. In order to remain on a schizotypal level, one has to experience a favorable environment.

We are currently reexamining the entire sample. On the basis of our own and other genetic calculations we expect to detect a further 17 schizophrenics. This final follow-up will enable us to extend and replicate the analyses presented above.

References

Diagnostic and statistical manual of mental disorders (3rd ed.) (DSM-III). (1980). Washington, DC: American Psychiatric Association.

Diagnostic and statistical manual of mental disorders (3rd ed.-rev.) (DSM-IIIR). (1987). Washington, DC: American Psychiatric Association.

Endicott, J., & Spitzer, R. (1972). Current and Past Psychopathology Scales (CAPPS), *Archives of General Psychiatry*, *27*, 678–687.

Fish, B. (1977). Neurobiologic antecedents of schizophrenia in children: Evidence for an inherited congenital neurointegrative defect. *Archives of General Psychiatry*, *34*, 1297–1313.

Kendler, K.S, Gruenberg, A.M., & Strauss, J.S. (1981). An independent analysis of the Copenhagen sample of the Danish adoption study. II. The relationship between schizotypal personality disorder and schizophrenia. *Archives of General Psychiatry, 38*, 982–984.

McNeil, T.F., & Kaij, L. (1978). Obstetric factors in the development of schizophrenia: Complications in the birth of preschizophrenics and in the reproduction by schizophrenic parents. In L.C. Wynne, R.L. Cromwell, & S. Mattysse (Eds.), *The nature of schizophrenia* (pp. 401–429). New York: Wiley.

Mednick, S.A, & McNeil, T.F. (1968). Current methodology in research on the etiology of schizophrenia: Serious difficulties which suggest the use of the high-risk group method. *Psychological Bulletin, 70*, 681–693.

Mednick, S.A, & Schulsinger, F. (1965). A longitudinal study of children with a high risk for schizophrenia: A preliminary report. In S. Vandenberg (Ed.), *Methods and goals in human behavior genetics* (pp. 255–296). New York: Academic.

Meehl, P.E. (1962). Schizotaxia, schizotypy, schizophrenia. *American Psychologist, 17*, 827–838.

Meehl, P.E. (1972). A critical afterword. In I.I. Gottesmann & J. Shields (Eds.), *Schizophrenia and genetics: A twin study vantage point*, (pp. 367–415). New York: Academic.

Parnas, J. (1985). Mates of schizophrenic mothers. A study of assortative mating from the American-Danish high risk project. *British Journal of Psychiatry, 140*, 602–606.

Parnas, J., Schulsinger, F., Schulsinger, H., Mednick, S.A, & Teasdale, T.W. (1982a). Behavioral precursors of schizophrenia spectrum. A prospective study. *Archives of General Psychiatry, 39*, 658–664.

Parnas, J., Schulsinger, F., Teasdale, T.W., Schulsinger, H., Feldman, P.M., & Mednick, S.A. (1982b). Perinatal complications and clinical outcome within the schizophrenia spectrum. *British Journal of Psychiatry, 140*, 416–420.

Parnas, J., Teasdale, T.W., & Schulsinger, H. (1985). Institutional rearing and diagnostic outcome in the offspring of schizophrenic mothers: A prospective high risk study. *Archives of General Psychiatry, 42*, 762–769.

Schulsinger, F., Parnas, J., Petersen, E.T., Schulsinger, H., Teasdale, T.W., Mednick, S.A., Møller, L., & Silverton, L. (1984). Cerebral ventricular size in the offspring of schizophrenic mothers: A preliminary study. *Archives of General Psychiatry, 41*, 602–606.

Spitzer, R.L., & Endicott, J. (1979). Justification for separating schizotypal and borderline personality disorders. *Schizophrenia Bulletin, 5*, 95–104.

Spitzer, R.L., Endicott, J., & Robins, E. (1978). Research diagnostic criteria: Rationale and reliability. *Archives of General Psychiatry, 35*, 773–782.

Wing, J.K., Cooper, J.E., & Sartorius, N. (1974). *The measurement and classification of psychiatric syndromes*. Cambridge: Cambridge University Press.

World Health Organization. (1967). *Manual of the international statistical classification of diseases, injuries and causes of death* (8th ed.). Geneva.

Part II
Information Processing and Vulnerability

Information Processing and Schizophrenia

D.R. Hemsley

Introduction

This paper will consider the relevance of studies of abnormalities of perception and cognition for an understanding of schizophrenia. It will present a model of the disorder, based on a disturbance of information processing, and will argue that schizophrenic breakdown/relapse may be understood in terms of the interaction of the cognitively impaired individual with his or her environment. Thus, in addition to formulating a model of schizophrenics' cognitive abnormalities, it will be necessary to speculate on the characteristics of environments which may lead to the exacerbation of schizophrenic symptoms. This has obvious implications for therapeutic intervention. Although the considerable intra- and intersubject variability in symptomatology has led some psychologists to question the usefulness of the concept of schizophrenia, the present approach aims to specify, in terms of current models of normal functioning, the form of perceptual/cognitive abnormality in such patients that might account for the range of disturbances of schizophrenics' behaviour and experience.

Why Study Cognitive Abnormalities?

Disordered thinking has long been viewed as one of the most distinguishing features of schizophrenia. Thus Kraepelin (1913/1919) observed: "the patients lose in a most striking way the faculty of logical ordering of their trains of thought" (p. 19). On attention he wrote: "It is quite common for them to lose both inclination and ability on their own initiative to keep their attention fixed for any length of time . . . . there is occasionally noticed a kind of irresistible attraction of the attention to casual external impressions" (pp. 6–7). More generally he noted: "Mental efficiency is always diminished to a considerable extent" (p. 23). These clinical observations are a necessary beginning to the understanding of schizophrenics' cognitive impairment.

Bleuler (1911/1950) was the first to attempt to specify a single underlying psychological defect that would account for all the symptoms of the disorder. In his view, they resulted from a disruption of the associative processes, these being the connections between ideas which enable normals to organize and interrelate many single thoughts and exclude irrelevant thoughts. It will be seen below that this has many intriguing similarities to more recent formulations of the nature of schizophrenic disorganization, based on experimental findings. Bleuler also made the important distinction between primary and secondary symptoms, the former being those resulting directly from the organic disease that he presumed to underlie schizophrenia. The disturbance of association was considered a primary symptom. In contrast, secondary symptoms reflect the normal psychic processes or attempts at adaptation to the primary disturbance. As will be discussed below, more recent investigator (e.g. Hemsley, 1977) have also viewed aspects of schizophrenic symptomatology as resulting from the interaction of the cognitively impaired individual with his or her environment.

While clinical observations have played an important role in stimulating research on schizophrenics' disturbances of perception and cognition, also influential have been the reports of patients themselves. McGhie and Chapman (1961) carried out an extended interview study of newly admitted schizophrenics. This concentrated on recent changes in the patients' subjective experiences, the findings being presented in the form of selected quotations. Typical were the following: "My thoughts get all jumbled up. I start thinking or talking about something but I never get there". "Things are coming in too fast. I lose my grip of it and get lost. I am attending to everything at once and as a result I do not attend to anything". McGhie and Chapman argued that such reports indicated that the primary disorder in schizophrenia is a decrease in the selective and inhibitory functions of attention. It was suggested that many other cognitive, perceptual, affective and behavioural abnormalities could be seen as resulting from this primary *attentional deficit*. A later study (Freedman & Chapman, 1973) employed a standardized questionnaire to interview groups of schizophrenic and non-schizophrenic patients at intake. The former group more frequently reported inability to focus attention, impaired perception of speech, and thought blocking which disrupts speech. About half of the schizophrenics reported an awareness of having an increased difficulty in ignoring irrelevant stimuli.

The study of *cognitive impairment* is therefore important for our understanding of schizophrenia. There are, however, several distinct aims to such research. Most prominent is the attempt to specify a single cognitive dysfunction, or pattern of dysfunction, from which the various abnormalities resulting in a diagnosis of schizophrenia might be derived. There has been a massive research effort directed at demonstrating psychological deficits in schizophrenics which are not present in other subject populations. "Psychological deficit" was defined by Hunt and Cofer (1944) as the loss of efficiency or decrement in performance exhibited by psychiatric patients relative to normals on intellectual and laboratory tasks. However, the results of such research are often theoretically elaborated in two ways. Oltmanns and Neale (1978) write:

> "First, the single empirical measure which has been assessed is assumed to index a more general construct ... . Second, it is then postulated that the construct which is implicated in the deficit is causally related to schizophrenia and can account for a variety of schizophrenic behaviours. In other words it is held to be a primary symptom of schizophrenia (p. 198).

The first stage of this elaboration is dependent on an agreed model of normal cognitive functioning. Much of the early research on cognitive deficits employed tasks which, although ostensibly tapping one cognitive function, were frequently open to alternative explanations.

Several further aims of research on schizophrenics' cognitive impairment may be identified:

- Cognitive measures have been employed in the search for subgroupings of schizophrenia, since it is possible that the relatively crude concept of schizophrenia may be redefinable in terms of the differing cognitive abnormalities shown by such patients. The utility of any such definition would, of course, be dependent on the extent of the external correlates of the classification. For example, Magaro (1980) has argued that there are important differences in the cognitive abnormalities shown by paranoid and non-paranoid schizophrenics.
- The study of residual cognitive impairment in remitted, or partially remitted, schizophrenics is receiving increased attention. It has been argued that this is important in determining rehabilitation outcome (Hemsley, 1978).
- Cognitive measures have been prominent in studies of relatives of schizophrenics, including those of high-risk children, that is, children having one or both parents diagnosed as schizophrenic (e.g. Garmezy, 1978).
- Assessments of cognitive functioning have been employed to monitor change in response to pharmacological treatment (e.g. Spohn, Lacoursiere, Thompson, & Coyne, 1977).

Problems in the Study of Schizophrenics' Cognitive Abnormalities

Two classes of problem may be distinguished. First, there are the methodological difficulties common to much schizophrenia research. These include the selection of schizophrenic subjects, the use of appropriate control groups, the effects of anti-psychotic medication, and finally the question of the stage of the disorder at which measures are taken. As Cromwell (1984) points out: "the premorbid ("high risk"), prodromal, acute, and chronic phases of the disorder reveal themselves in different ways" (p. 16). They may therefore be expected to show different psychological correlates.

In addition, there are particular problems in the specification of schizophrenics' cognitive abnormalities. As noted above, it is partially dependent on agreement on a model of normal cognitive functioning. Although current models of human cognition share many important features, it cannot be claimed that there is an agreed model. Indeed, if there were, several journals would become redundant.

There is increased awareness of the need to demonstrate a differential deficit, that is, a greater deficit on one task than on another. Such research helps to clarify the specific nature of schizophrenics' impairment. However, such studies can pose problems of interpretation. It has been argued by Chapman and Chapman (1973) that a differential deficit may result for purely psychometric reasons, namely the discriminating power of the tests employed. These, in turn, are dependent on their reliability and difficulty level. Chapman and Chapman claim that, unless tasks are matched on these variables, the attribution of a differential deficit to the diagnostic variable may not be justified. However, Carbotte (1978) suggests that when studying cognitive processes, the level of difficulty of a task is often an inherent feature which must change as some particular independent variable is manipulated. An attempt to match two conditions on "discriminative power" could confound two independent variables. Strauss (1978) points out that the matching of tasks "may remove the variance that must be studied in order to make valid inferences about the nature of the psychological processes that are involved in task performance" (p. 318). Both Strauss and Carbotte claim that it is preferable to employ an experimental approach to eliminate alternative hypotheses about the specific processes which could account for an observed deficit in schizophrenics.

Finally, there is the question of schizophrenics' motivation to perform the tasks with which they are presented. In discussing the problem of subject cooperation in studies of schizophrenia Shakow (1962) wrote:

> "The argument may be offered that this poverty in co-operativeness is intrinsic to the psychosis and that therefore any attempt at the separation of its effects is at best academic. This thesis has validity to the extent that poor co-operation is intrinsic. The argument, however, runs into the difficulty of not making a distinction between the intrinsic effects of attitude and other, temporary, or superficial effects (pp. 3–4).

Possible Solutions to (or Evasions of) the Above Problems

1. One may attempt to construct tasks on which schizophrenics would be expected to perform better than normal subjects. A model able to predict such findings successfully would be in a strong position. As Meehl (1978) points out: "A theory is corroborated to the extent that we have subjected it to such risky tests; the more dangerous tests it has survived, the better corroborated it is" (p. 817). Results of this kind are not easily explained in terms of a generalized deficit, "lowered motivation" or "drug effects". A weaker version of this approach attempts to demonstrate qualitatively different patterns of performance in schizophrenic and control groups. Again, Meehl (1978) puts it clearly: "It is always more valuable to show approximate agreement of observations with a theoretically predicted . . . function form, than it is to compute a "precise probability" that something merely differs from something else" (p. 825). Examples of this approach will be presented below.

2. One may examine non-symptomatic correlates of cognitive abnormalities. A good example is provided by Straube's (1979) study concerning the relationship between performance on a dichotic listening task and different patterns of

skin conductance orienting responses to auditory stimuli. There is also recent interest in the measurement of cortical event-related potentials in schizophrenics, carried out while they are performing a cognitive task on which they are known to show a deficit (e.g. Pass, Klorman, Salzman, Klein, & Koskey, 1980).

3. One may examine disturbances of perception and cognition in the relatives of schizophrenics, both offspring who have yet to reach the age of risk for the disorder and healthy adults. As Cromwell (1984) writes: "When deviant factors are identified they serve as candidate hypotheses for either environmental or genetic vulnerability in schizophrenia" (p. 28).

4. One may attempt to relate experimental measures of abnormalities of perceptual and cognitive functioning to questionnaire measures purporting to assess proneness to psychosis. Examples of the latter include Claridge and Broks' (1984) Schizotypal Scale and Eysenck and Eysenck's (1975) Psychoticism Scale. This is perhaps the least powerful of the alternatives since it makes assumptions about the continuity of schizophrenia with normality. Although vigorously defended by Claridge (1985), others have expressed serious reservations about this approach (e.g. Bishop, 1977). Nevertheless, some interesting findings have begun to emerge, and one such will be presented below.

The Information Processing Approach to Schizophrenics' Cognitive Abnormalities

It is generally agreed that psychopathology is most usefully considered within the framework of models of normal functioning. Information-processing psychology has in recent years become dominant in research into adult cognitive processes. The major assumption of such approaches is that perceptual and cognitive activities can be construed or represented as a series of transformations of information. It aims to "make explicit the operations, stages or processes that occur in the time between stimulation and the observed response" (Haber & Hershensen, 1973, p. 158) and "to describe the limits and characteristics of these processes" (Underwood, 1978, p. 2). These stages of processing are not directly observable, and their existence must be inferred from performance on a number of tasks. Inherent in this approach is the need for selectivity within the system, and attention may be viewed as the major control process in the passage of information through the system as a whole. It was noted above that cognitive deficits in schizophrenia remained difficult to interpret. The adoption of the information-processing approach was expected to enable a precise specification of the disturbance, since a feature of such models is the more specific relationship between observed task performance and inferred function. More particularly, it was felt ideally suited to the study of the disturbances of selective attention prominent in clinical observations and patients' reports.

Particularly influential in early studies of schizophrenics' cognitive disturbance was Broadbent's (1958) model. In this, a hypothetical *filter* mechanism screens irrelevant stimuli from a limited-capacity decision channel. The filter was seen as acting in an all-or-nothing fashion on the basis of physical attributes of classes of stimuli. In Broadbent's (1971, 1977) later probabilistic model of the methods by which the systematic selection of information may take place, an important distinction is made between stimulus set (filtering) and response set (pigeonholing). Its application to the study of schizophrenics' cognitive impairment was reviewed by Hemsley (1975). The *pigeonholing* mechanism is considered to operate not solely within tasks aimed at assessing selectivity, but across the range of cognitive functioning. It acts as a bias towards certain categories of response, increasing the probability of certain responses at the expense of others by allocating larger or smaller numbers of "states of evidence" to each category state. An example may make this clearer. Consider a subject who is required to shadow a lengthy series of numbers against a white noise background – 7, 9, 1, 4, etc. If then the sound "ee" is presented, this "evidence" may be sufficient to produce the category state "3". The organism is biased towards perception of digits rather than letters. Thus when the actual stimulus is unexpected, normal biases may act to impair performance. It may be seen as a way of making use of the redundancy and patterning in environmental input to reduce information-processing demands. As Broadbent (1977) writes: "this kind of attention selects some of the possible interpretations that a man may hold about the world and eliminates others as candidates to use in the particular situation" (p. 110).

Studies of defective "filtering" in schizophrenia have been inconclusive. Although schizophrenics are generally inferior to normals on tasks aimed to assess this function, few have found differences when appropriate psychiatric control groups are employed (e.g. Hemsley & Zawada, 1976). The literature on defective pigeonholing in schizophrenia, although limited, is of potentially greater interest. An example is provided by Hemsley and Richardson (1980). The task was based on an experimental paradigm devised by Treisman (1964) which required subjects to shadow one of two simultaneously presented prose passages. The messages were both presented binaurally, in the same voice, at the same volume, and at the same rate of presentation. The passage to be shadowed was presented briefly, then the second passage was superimposed. There is no possibility of the filter mechanism operating to distinguish between the passages. Instead, successful performance of the task requires subjects to use contextual variables in determining selection of the appropriate response. It is thus dependent on the pigeonholing mechanism, whereby category state thresholds may be raised or lowered according to the nature of the evidence derived from the preceding context. The passages to be shadowed were narrative extracts from a novel, and the irrelevant material consisted of technical extracts. Normals, depressives and schizophrenics were tested; these groups did not differ on verbal IQ or shadowing ability without distraction. Two rates of presentation were employed, 60 words per minute and 100 words per minute. The schizophrenics performed significantly worse than both the other groups, at both rates, consistent with a defect at the pigeonholing stage. However, the study is a conventional "deficit" approach to schizophrenics' disturbances of cognition; as such it is subject to some of the problems discussed above.

A Working Hypothesis

I should like to put forward the following tentative hypothesis as to the nature of schizophrenics' cognitive abnormalities. I suggest that schizophrenics are less able to make use of the redundancy and patterning of sensory input to reduce information-processing demands. That is, each stimulus is treated by the system relatively independently of its context (both temporal and spatial), is therefore not predicted and, in information theory terms, "carries" more information. It is thus a variant of the *information overload* approach to schizophrenia (cf. Hemsley, 1977), but is not based on a breakdown in a hypothesized "filter" mechanism, but rather an inefficiency in what Broadbent (1971) refers to as pigeonholing. As Michon (1978) has argued, the temporal patterning of stimuli helps to reduce the class of possible stimuli to be expected, and thus to decrease the likelihood of overload of the processing channels.

In a general sense, most models of normal functioning accept that perception is dependent on an interaction between the stimulus presented and stored memories of regularities in previous input which result in expectancies or response biases. It is also clear that at different times for the same individual, and to differing extents across individuals, either the stimulus or the expectation may exert the greater influence on perception. Thus Norman and Bobrow (1976) make a distinction between "data-driven" processing and "conceptually driven" processing.

If schizophrenics are indeed less able to make use of the redundancy and patterning of sensory input, it should be possible to construct tasks where schizophrenics would be predicted to perform better than normals, due to the latter forming inappropriate expectancies. However, it is unlikely to be a straightforward endeavour, since any such effect must be great enough to counteract the generally lowered performance of schizophrenics resulting from such factors as lowered motivation.

It should be noted at this point that the formulation is not inconsistent with Frith's (1979) suggestion that the primary disturbance in schizophrenia is a breakdown in the system that controls and limits the contents of consciousness. One factor influencing awareness of a stimulus is its predictability, highly predictable stimuli being less likely to reach awareness. If schizophrenics are less able to make use of the regularities of sensory input, one might expect inappropriate intrusions into conscious experiences, as reported by the patients studied by McGhie and Chapman (1961).

Superior Performance by Schizophrenic Subjects

An early finding of this kind was reported by Polyakov (1969). He demonstrated that, in both visual and auditory modalities, an ambiguous signal is identified by normals according to the probabilistic constraints of context more so than by schizophrenics. For example, in the spoken sentence: "The photographer made a pretty . . . .", normals most frequently identify the ambiguous (partially masked by noise) term as "picture". When it is in fact presented, their performance is superior to that of schizophrenics. However, when the ambiguous term is unlikely, schizophrenics are correct significantly more often than normals, presumably because they are relying to a greater extent on the stimulus qualities of the signal, rather than prior expectations. This is consistent with a disturbance in pigeonholing.

A similar explanation is possible for the results of a more recent study (Brennan & Hemsley, 1984) which made use of the phenomenon of "illusory correlation" (Chapman, 1967). This refers to the report by observers of a correlation between two events which in reality are not correlated. It can be demonstrated by repeatedly presenting pairs of words in a random order, some of these pairs having strong associative connections. The form of the task is illustrated in Fig. 1. Each pairing is presented an equal number of times. When normal subjects were required to report how frequently the pairs were presented they overestimated the co-occurrence of pairs having a strong associative connection. It may be viewed as a demonstration of the way in which prior expectations influence, and in this case mislead, subjects. It was therefore predicted that non-paranoid schizophrenics would produce weaker illusory correlations than normals. Magaro (1980) has argued that the nature of the cognitive abnormality shown by such subjects is quite distinct from that of the paranoid. The latter is seen as relying on a rigid conceptual guiding of information processing, hence Magaro would predict stronger illusory correlations in paranoid subjects.

Brennan and Hemsley (1984) assessed 19 schizophrenic subjects and ten normals on three tasks designed to demonstrate the illusory correlation

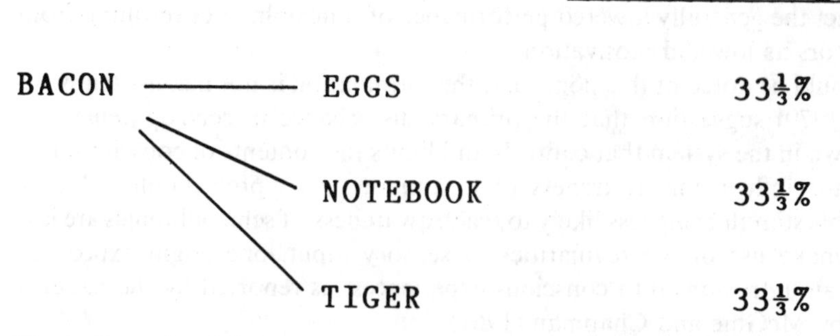

Fig 1. Example of illusory correlation task. (From Brennan & Hemsley, 1984).

phenomenon. The patients were divided into paranoid and non-paranoid groups using the Maine Paranoid Schizophrenic Rating Scale (Magaro, 1980). Scoring was modified so as to reflect a hierarchical model (Foulds & Bedford, 1975) whereby paranoids are not expected to show the more disintegrated features of the non-paranoid (e.g. thought disorder), while non-paranoids may or may not show such paranoid features as delusions. Across tasks the mean frequency estimate for the associated pairs was 34.1% for the non-paranoid group, a figure close to the 33.3% which represents reality. The paranoids showed the strongest overall tendency to report illusory correlation, 43.5%. The normals' mean frequency estimate, 39.9%, fell, as predicted, between those of the other groups. Such a pattern of results is not easily interpretable in terms of either a generalized deficit or lowered motivation.

An important study by Schwartz Place and Gilmore (1980), later replicated by Wells and Leventhal (1984), may also be linked to the present formulation. They employed a numerosity task in which process schizophrenics and normal subjects were to report the number of lines presented in a tachistoscopic display. In their second and most interesting experiment, the experimenter manipulated the perceptual organization, or regularity, of the arrays by varying the similarity and proximity of the line elements. The performance of the controls deteriorated as the organization of the arrays become more complex. The schizophrenics were not affected by the organization variable. Indeed, their average performance was significantly better than that of controls. The authors argue that this is consistent with schizophrenics' failure to organize the information presented. It may also be viewed as a situation where normal subjects' attempts to detect and make use of the minimal regularities present in the most complex array interfere with the counting of the lines. In contrast, the schizophrenics make little use of any spatial regularities present, thus performing worse when these might aid counting, but better when no such regularities are present in the display.

Finally, I should like to suggest an experiment where, with appropriate manipulation of the parameters of the task, one might expect a superior performance from non-paranoid schizophrenics. It is illustrated in Fig. 2. With the appropriate duration of display, many normal subjects fail to notice the repeated "THE". It is an example of where normal biases, based on the previous non-occurrence of a repeated "THE", act to impair performance. On tasks such as this, schizophrenics might be expected to be less easily misled by the context.

Implications for Treatment

1. It is necessary to consider the possibility that certain of the behavioural abnormalities shown by schizophrenics represent "adaptive strategies" to cope with the disorganization resulting from the cognitive abnormality. The model presented continues to view the schizophrenic as in a state of "information overload", although the reason for this differs from the earlier formulation

Fig 2. Example of a "response bias" leading normal subjects to make an error.

(Hemsley, 1977). Hence, the strategies of processing employed by normal subjects in situations of experimenter-induced overload may be relevant to an understanding of schizophrenic behaviour, in particular the negative symptoms such as poverty of speech, social withdrawal and retardation. A similar point was made by Wing (1975) who suggested that "it could be argued that social withdrawal and flatness of affect are in fact a means of coping with severe thought disorder" (p. 241). Thus it might be expected that for those in whom cognitive impairment remains prominent and who have reacted by withdrawing from situations requiring complex decision making, any attempt to increase social interaction may result solely in an increase in florid symptomatology. In contrast, for those patients in whom the cognitive disturbance has largely remitted or has been successfully treated, certain abnormalities of behaviour resulting from previously *adaptive strategies* may no longer be serving a useful function. This brings us to the second point.

2. There is a need to take into account the level of *residual cognitive impairment* when planning *rehabilitation* programmes. The assessment should be carried out once optimal levels of medication have been achieved. It is of interest that both Cancro, Sutton, Kerr and Sugerman (1971) and Zahn and Carpenter (1978) report significant relationships between simple reaction time and prognosis. More recently, Wykes (1985) has demonstrated a significantly greater level of cognitive impairment in chronic schizophrenics requiring continuous hospital care in a long-stay ward than those able to function more independently.

3. It is of interest to consider the *predictability* of the environment in which the schizophrenic is expected to function. This is difficult to quantify, but it is clear that a long-stay ward is more regular and predictable than life outside

hospital. It is also apparent, and expected on the basis of the present formulation, that those in whom cognitive abnormalities remain prominent will function best in a highly predictable setting.

Recently we have attempted to assess the predictability of relatives' behaviour towards schizophrenic patients who are discharged from hospital to live at home (MacCarthy, Hemsley, Schrank-Fernandez, Kuipers, & Katz, 1986). It is clear that the family environment has an important effect on the prognosis of such patients. The *expressed emotion* (EE) rating technique is a reliable method of assessing certain aspects of the family atmosphere (Vaughn & Leff, 1976). If relatives are highly critical or too emotionally involved, the patient is more likely to relapse within 9 months; this is particularly true if the relative and patient spend a high proportion of their day in face-to-face contact or the patient fails to take medication regularly. However, it is not clear how the EE measure relates to actual communication patterns within the home, nor do we understand the mechanism by which the behaviour of relatives precipitates relapse. The main hypothesis of the study was that high-EE relatives provide a more complex home environment by responding to problem behaviours in a more unpredictable way. As a result, they provide more ambiguous information about their own feelings and the kind of behaviour they expect from the patient. A questionnaire was developed to assess the frequency of ten problems in daily living and to assess how relatives coped with these problems. Three common coping responses were listed for each of the ten problems, reflecting either a warm and adaptive (1), a critical (2) or an overinvolved (3) style of coping. A fourth style, labelled "variable", and crucial to our hypothesis, was scored when respondents reported that any of the three above were used in combination, or alternatively "sometimes did one thing, sometimes another". A fifth category was used to code passive coping responses, as when a problem evoked no response or was carefully ignored by relatives. An example is the following question:

Does R sometimes spend time in bed during the day? YES/NO
When this happens do you:
- a Get upset about it? . . . . (3)
- b Go and tell R what time it is? . . . . (1)
- c Keep shouting at R to get up? . . . . (2)
- d Sometimes one thing, sometimes another . . . . (4)
- e None of these (please briefly describe what you do)

The study involved 28 schizophrenic patients who lived permanently with a relative or close friend. Half were recovering from an acute episode, the remaining subjects being long-stay patients who had attended hospital on a daily basis for over a year.

The number of problems relatives reported was significantly negatively correlated with the amount of warmth expressed during the EE interview, but was not related to the number of critical comments. There was a significant correlation in the expected direction between the number of critical comments and the extent to which relatives responded variably to problems. Thus highly critical relatives tended to deal with problems in a variable or unpredictable fashion. No relationship was found between ratings of overinvolvement and the tendency to use variable responses.

Variable responses to individual problems were significantly more likely in the relatives of chronic patients. The relatives of the chronic subgroup also varied their coping style more from problem to problem. While six of the acute subgroup's relatives employed only one style across all ten problems, none of the chronic patients' relatives showed this degree of consistency. These differences are intriguing. The prolonged effect of an unpredictable home environment might operate to maintain the chronically ill status of some patients, but it is equally tenable that chronicity may induce unpredictability as relatives try differing strategies to deal with intractable problems.

The Effect of Short-Term Manipulations of the Patterning of Sensory Input

The present formulation has not, as yet, attempted to relate the hypothesized cognitive abnormality to one of the most prominent features of schizophrenia, *hallucinatory experiences*, although mention was made of possible links with Frith's (1979) model. This will now be attempted.

There has been extensive research on sensory and/or *perceptual deprivation* in normal subjects. Leff (1968) noted that the perceptual experiences reported by subjects in such experiments were of several kinds but that they "overlap considerably with those of mentally ill patients" (p. 1507), and that a proportion of reports appear to satisfy the usual criteria for a true hallucination. It appears that it is the lack of structured input, rather than the absolute level of stimulation that is of major importance. Garner (1962) suggests that "Amount of *structure* can be identified with the amount of correlation between events" (p. 143). He went on to identify "meaning" with "the amount of structure which exists, and is perceived, in a system of variables" (p. 145). Rosenzweig and Gardner (1966) demonstrated that the introduction of meaningful auditory stimulation into a perceptual deprivation experiment reduced the incidence both of intense auditory imagery and hallucinatory-like auditory experiences. Two further factors appear likely to influence the occurrence of abnormal perceptual experiences, the extent to which the input engages the attention of the subject, and whether or not an overt response is required.

Margo, Hemsley and Slade (1981) investigated the short-term manipulation of auditory hallucinations in a group of schizophrenic patients by means of variation in auditory input. Ten conditions were employed, each of 2-min duration; seven involved the presentation of auditory stimuli via stereo headphones and these inputs varied in terms of their structure and the extent to which they were expected to engage the attention of the subject. For example, two conditions were of regular and irregular electronic blips. Two further conditions were of sensory restriction and a resting phase. One condition required the subject to read a prose passage aloud. Immediately following each condition, the earphones were removed and the patient rated his or her hallucinatory experiences for duration, loudness and clarity. Seven chronically hallucinating patients were assessed. The single condition requiring an overt response of the subject produced the most marked reduction in hallucinatory experiences. For the passive conditions, the changes were as predicted, both increasing structure and the attention-commanding properties of the input resulting in a decrease in hallucinations. Consistent with Frith's (1979) model, the experiences appear dependent on the meaningfulness of auditory input. As noted above, Garner's (1962) definition of meaning includes both the objective structure possessed by the input, and the extent to which this is perceived by the subject; the latter is obviously dependent on the attention-commanding properties of the input.

These findings offer no direct explanation of the occurrence of schizophrenic hallucinations, only of the extent to which they may vary under short-term manipulations of sensory input. However, it is tempting to speculate, following Hartmann (1975, p. 73), that "possibly something in the realm of ability to pattern sensory input or interact with it may be involved in the inhibitory factor" (for hallucinatory experience). Since the present formulation suggests that schizophrenics are less able to make use of the structure in presented material, one might argue that hallucinations are related to a cognitive impairment which, even under normal conditions of sensory input, results in ambiguous messages reaching awareness. Feinberg (1962) suggested that a possible explanation for the excess of auditory over visual hallucinations in schizophrenia is that "the visual background is one of patterned stimuli, the auditory background is in general less structured. Thus the latter may be considered more ambiguous, hence more open to interpretation or reconstruction in the direction of affective need" (p. 72).

More recently, Jakes and Hemsley (1986) have examined individual differences in reaction to brief exposure to unpatterned visual stimulation within the normal population. Subjects were seated alone in a dimly lit room in front of a visual display screen. A changing random pattern of dots was presented for 10 min, and subjects were informed that at certain points patterns had been programmed to appear on the screen and that they were to try to detect these patterns. None were in fact so programmed. Subjects were instructed to report at once any patterns detected and their responses were tape recorded. The study followed Zuckerman (1969) in classifying reports as of A or B type. The former includes simple reports of geometric shapes; more complex type B reports are of meaningful objects or integrated scenes. It was predicted that the report of complex visual sensations would be related to a questionnaire measure purporting to assess hallucinatory predisposition (Launay & Slade, 1981), and to the *Psychoticism* scale of the Eysenck Personality Questionnaire (EPQ; Eysenck & Eysenck, 1975). A correlational analysis confirmed both these predictions. The relationship between psychoticism and the report of complex visual sensations is perhaps of greater interest since there is no obvious link between the content of items of the Psychoticism scale and the dependent variables in our experiment. Although both might conceivably be viewed as representing a willingness to acknowledge "socially unacceptable" beliefs or experiences, one might then have expected a negative relationship between the Lie scale of the EPQ and such reports; this was not obtained. In addition, such an explanation would have predicted a relationship between psychoticism and type A reports; again this was not apparent.

Possible Links with Biochemical Models of Schizophrenia

In recent years biochemical theories of schizophrenia have been primarily orientated towards the dopamine system. Two strands of research have been influential. First, the demonstration that amphetamine, which stimulates dopamine release in the brain, can, in chronic abusers, induce symptoms similar to those encountered in schizophrenia (see for example, Angrist, Sathananthan, Wilk, & Gershon, 1974). Second, the effective antischizophrenic drugs have in common the ability to block dopamine receptors in the brain. Although the *dopamine theory* is not without its critics, several authors have attempted to relate it to research on cognitive impairment. For example, Joseph, Frith and Waddington (1979) present a model which links dysfunctions in brain amine systems with abnormalities in the control of attention. More recently, there has been a growth of interest in the effects of amphetamine on attention and their possible implications for models of schizophrenia. Lubow, Weiner and Feldon (1982) have argued that the *latent inhibition* (LI) paradigm is an effective way of manipulating attention in animals. The LI paradigm is as follows. In the first stage a stimulus is repeatedly presented, by itself, to the organism. In the second stage, the pre-exposed stimulus is paired with reinforcement in any of the standard learning procedures, classical or instrumental. When the amount of learning is measured, relative to a group that did not receive the first stage of stimulus pre-exposure, it is found that the stimulus-pre-exposed group learns the new association much more slowly. This is interpreted as indicating a reduction in the deployment of attention to a predictable, redundant stimulus. Lubow et al. (1982) have demonstrated that LI is disrupted if amphetamine is administered in both the pre-exposure and the test phases. They suggest that animals under the influence of amphetamine may be viewed as unable to utilize previously acquired knowledge in newly encountered situations. They write: "Not having the capacity to 'use' old stimuli, all stimuli are novel. Therefore such an organism will find itself endlessly bombarded with novel stimulation, resulting perhaps in the perceptual inundation phenomena described in schizophrenia" (p. 104). There are intriguing similarities to the present suggestion that schizophrenics fail to make use of the redundancy and patterning of sensory input to reduce information processing demands. In more recent work we have been able to demonstrate a reduction in LI in acute schizophrenia (Baruch, Hemsley, & Gray, 1988).

Summary

This paper has attempted to bring together several areas of research relevant to our understanding of the psychological aspects of schizophrenia. While based on the study of disturbances of information processing, it has aimed to go beyond this to a consideration of how symptoms might emerge and the way in which environmental factors may interact with the level of cognitive impairment.

As a working hypothesis it has been suggested that schizophrenics are less able to make use of the redundancy and patterning of sensory input to reduce information-processing demands. It is inevitably at best an oversimplification. For example, the relationship between paranoid and non-paranoid forms of the disorder remains unclear. The distinction may reflect (a) different cognitive disorders; (b) differing methods of adaptation to a similar disorder; or (c) differences in severity of disorganization. The present author tends to favour an interaction of (b) and (c), but much research needs to be carried out to clarify this.

The evidence relevant to the present formulation may be somewhat arbitrarily classified as direct, indirect and very indirect.

Direct Evidence

1. Schizophrenics' performance deficits (e.g. Hemsley & Richardson, 1980).
2. Lack of "illusory correlations" in non-paranoid schizophrenics (Brennan & Hemsley, 1984).

Indirect Evidence

Unstructured (i.e. low redundancy) sensory input leads to: (a) increased hallucinatory experiences in chronically hallucinating schizophrenics (Margo et al., 1981); and (b) "hallucinatory" experiences in normal subjects, the extent of which is related to the dimension of psychoticism (Jakes & Hemsley, 1986).

Very Indirect Evidence

1. A known correlate of relapse (critical comments) is related to unpredictable key relatives' behaviour (MacCarthy et al., 1986).
2. Animals under amphetamine behave as if "all stimuli are novel" (Lubow et al., 1982)

It is clear that what might be termed the "information-processing approach" to schizophrenia can be extended to a consideration of environmental factors leading to relapse, individual differences in proneness to psychosis and possible biological bases of the disorder.

References

Angrist, B.M., Sathananthan, G., Wilk, S., & Gershon, S. (1974). Amphetamine psychosis: Behavioural and biochemical aspects. *Journal of Psychiatric Research, 11*, 13–23.

Baruch, I., Hemsley, D.R., & Gray, J.A. (1988). Differential performance of acute and chronic schizophrenics in a latent inhibition task. *Journal of Nervous and Mental Disease, 176*, 598–606.

Bishop, D.V.M. (1977). The P scale and psychosis. *Journal of Abnormal Psychology, 86*, 127–134.

Bleuler, E. (1950). *Dementia praecox or the group of schizophrenias* (J. Zinkin, Trans.). New York: International University Press. (Original work published 1911).

Brennan, J.H., & Hemsley, D.R. (1984). Illusory correlations in paranoid and non paranoid schizophrenia. *British Journal of Clinical Psychology, 23*, 225–226.

Broadbent, D.E. (1958). *Perception and communication*. London: Pergamon.

Broadbent, D.E. (1971). *Decision and stress*. London: Academic.

Broadbent, D.E. (1977). The hidden preattentive processes. *American Psychologist, 32*, 109–118.

Cancro, R., Sutton, S., Kerr, J., & Sugerman, A.A. (1971). Reaction time and prognosis in acute schizophrenia. *Journal of Nervous and Mental Disease, 153*, 351–359.

Carbotte, R.M. (1978). Converging operations or matched control tasks? *Journal of Psychiatric Research, 14*, 313–316.

Chapman, L.J. (1967). Illusory correlation in observational report. *Journal of Learning and Verbal Behaviour, 6*, 151–155.

Chapman, L.J., & Chapman, J.P. (1973). *Disordered thought in schizophrenia*. New York: Appleton-Century-Crofts.

Claridge, G.S. (1985). *Origins of mental illness*. Oxford: Blackwell.

Claridge, G.S., & Broks, P. (1984). Schizotypy and hemisphere function. I. Theoretical considerations and the measurement of schizotypy. *Personality and Individual Differences, 5*, 633–648.

Cromwell, R.L. (1984). Preemptive thinking and schizophrenia research. In W.D. Spaulding & J.K. Cole (Eds.), *Theories of schizophrenia and psychosis* (pp 1–46). Lincoln: University of Nebraska Press.

Eysenck, H.J., & Eysenck, S.B.G. (1975). *Manual of the Eysenck Personality Questionnaire*. London: Hodder and Stoughton.

Feinberg, I. (1962). A comparison of the visual hallucinations in schizophrenia with those induced by mescaline and LSD-25. In L.J. West (Ed.), *Hallucinations*. New York: Grune and Stratton.

Foulds, G.A., & Bedford, A. (1975). Hierarchy of classes of personal illness. *Psychological Medicine, 5*, 181–192.

Freedman, B., & Chapman, L.J. (1973). Early subjective experience in schizophrenic episodes. *Journal of Abnormal Psychology. 82*, 46–54.

Frith, C.D. (1979). Consciousness, information processing and schizophrenia. *British Journal of Psychiatry, 134*, 225–235.

Garmezy, N. (1978). Attentional processes in adult schizophrenia and in children at risk. *Journal of Psychiatric Research, 14*, 3–34.

Garner, W.R. (1962). *Uncertainty and structure as psychological concepts*. New York: Wiley.

Haber, R.N., & Hershenson, N.E. (1973). *The psychology of visual perception*. New York: Holt, Rinehart and Winston.

Hartmann, E. (1975). Dreams and other hallucinations: an approach to the underlying mechanism. In R.K. Siegel & L.J. West (Eds.), *Hallucinations: Behavior, experience and theory*. New York: Wiley.

Hemsley, D.R. (1975). A two stage model of attention in schizophrenia research. *British Journal of Social and Clinical Psychology, 14*, 81–89.

Hemsley, D.R. (1977). What have cognitive deficits to do with schizophrenic symptoms? *British Journal of Psychiatry, 130*, 167–173.

Hemsley, D.R. (1978). Limitations of operant procedures in the modification of schizophrenic functioning: The possible relevance of studies of cognitive disturbance. *Behavioural Analysis and Modification, 3*, 165–173.
Hemsley, D.R., & Richardson, P.H. (1980). Shadowing by context in schizophrenia. *Journal of Nervous and Mental Disease, 168*, 141–145.
Hemsley, D.R. & Zawada, S.L. (1976). 'Filtering' and the cognitive deficit in schizophrenia. *British Journal of Psychiatry, 128*, 456–461.
Hunt, J. McV., & Cofer, C. (1944). Psychological deficit in schizophrenia. In J. McV. Hunt (Ed.), *Personality and the behaviour disorders* (Vol. 2). New York: Ronald.
Jakes, S. & Hemsley, D.R. (1986). Individual differences in reaction to brief exposure to unpatterned visual stimulation. *Personality and Individual Differences, 7*, 121–123.
Joseph, M.H., Frith, C.D., & Waddington, J.L. (1979). Dopaminergic mechanisms and cognitive deficit in schizophrenia: A neurobiological model. *Psychopharmacology, 63*, 273–280.
Kraepelin, E. (1919). *Dementia praecox and paraphrenia* (R.M. Barclay, Trans.). Edinburgh: Livingstone. (Original work published 1913).
Launay, G., & Slade, P.D. (1981). The measurement of hallucinatory predisposition in male and female prisoners. *Personality and Individual Differences, 2*, 221–234.
Leff, J.P. (1968). Perceptual phenomena and personality in sensory deprivation. *British Journal of Psychiatry*, 114, 1499–1508.
Lubow, R.E., Weiner, J., & Feldon, J. (1982). An animal model of attention. In M.Y. Spiegelstein & A. Levy (Eds.), *Behavioural models and the analysis of drug action*. Amsterdam: Elsevier.
MacCarthy, B., Hemsley, D.R., Sahrank-Fernandez, C., Kuipers, E., & Katz, R. (1986). Unpredictability as a correlate of expressed emotion in the relatives of schizoprenics. *British Journal of Psychiatry, 148*, 727–731.
Magaro, P.A. (1980). *Cognition in schizophrenia and paranoia*. Hillside, NJ : Erlbaum.
Margo, A., Hemsley, D.R., & Slade, P.D. (1981). The effects of varying auditory input on schizophrenic hallucinations. *British Journal of Psychiatry, 139*, 122–127.
McGhie, A., & Chapman, T. (1961). Disorders of attention and perception in early schizophrenia. *British Journal of Medical Psychology, 34*, 103–116.
Meehl, P.E. (1978). Theoretical risks and tabular asterisks: Sir Karl, Sir Ronald, and the slow progress of soft psychology. *Journal of Consulting and Clinical Psychology, 46*, 806–834.
Michon, J.A. (1978). The making of the present; a tutorial review. In J. Requin (Ed.), *Attention and performance. VII* (pp. 89–111). Hillsdale, N.J: Erlbaum.
Norman, D.A., & Bobrow, P.G. (1976). On the role of active memory processes in perception and cognition. In C.N. Cofer (Ed.), *The structure of human memory*. San Francisco: Freeman.
Oltmanns, T.F., & Neale, J.H. (1978). Abstraction and schizophrenia: Problems in psychological deficit research. In B.A. Maher (Ed.), *Progress in experimental personality research* (Vol. 8, pp. 197–243). New York: Academic.
Pass, H.L., Klorman, R., Salzman, L.F., Klein, R.H., & Koskey, G.B. (1980). The late positive component of the evoked response in acute schizophrenics during a test of sustained attention. *Biological Psychiatry, 15*, 9–20.
Polyakov, V.F. (1969). The experimental investigation of cognitive functioning in schizophrenia. In M. Cole & I. Maltzman (Eds), *Handbook of contemporary social psychology*. New York: Basic Books.
Rosenzweig, N., & Gardner, L. (1966). The role of input relevance in sensory isolation. *American Journal of Psychiatry, 122*, 920–928.
Schwartz Place, E.J., & Gilmore, G.C. (1980). Perceptual organization in schizophrenia. *Journal of Abnormal Psychology, 89*, 407–418.
Shakow, D. (1962). "Segmental sets". *Archives of General Psychiatry, 6*, 1–17.
Spohn, H.E., Lacoursiere, R.B., Thompson, K., & Coyne, L. (1977). Phenothiazine effects on psychological and psychophysiological dysfunctions in chronic schizophrenics. *Archives of General Psychiatry, 34*, 633–644.
Straube, E.R. (1979). On the meaning of electrodermal nonresponding in schizophrenia. *Journal of Nervous and Mental Disease, 167*, 601–611.

Strauss, M.E. (1978). The differential and experimental paradigms in the study of cognition in schizophrenia. *Journal of Psychiatric Research, 14*, 316–326.

Treisman, A.M. (1964). Verbal cues, language, and meaning in selective attention. *American Journal of Psychology, 77*, 206–214.

Underwood, G. (Ed.). (1978). *Strategies of information processing*. London: Academic.

Vaughn, C.E., & Leff, J.P. (1976). The influence of family and social factors on the course of psychiatric illness: A comparison of schizophrenic and depressed neurotic patients. *British Journal of Psychiatry, 129*, 125–137.

Wells, D.S., & Leventhal, D. (1984). Perceptual grouping in schizophrenia: replication of Place and Gilmore. *Journal of Abnormal Psychology, 93*, 231–234.

Wing, J.K. (1975). Impairments in schizophrenia; a rational basis for social treatment. In R.D. Wirt, G. Winokur, & M. Roff (Eds.), *Life history research in psychopathology*, (Vol. 4). Minneapolis: University of Minnesota Press.

Wykes, T. (1985). Cognitive impairment in a psychiatric population: Relationship to chronic disability and some implications for rehabilitation. Unpublished M.Phil thesis, University of London.

Zahn, T.P., & Carpenter, W.T. (1978). Effects of short term outcome and clinical improvement on reaction time in acute schizophrenia. *Journal of Psychiatric Research, 14*, 59–68.

Zuckerman, M. (1969). Variables affecting deprivation results. In J.P. Zubek (Ed.), *Sensory deprivation: Fifteen years of research* (pp. 47–84). New York: Appleton-Century-Crofts.

Similarities Between Information-Processing Abnormalities of Actively Symptomatic Schizophrenic Patients and High-Risk Children

K.H. Nuechterlein, and K.M. Zaucha

Research aimed at identifying abnormalities in the processing of information by schizophrenic patients has been an important direction in the search for the mechanisms that may underlie schizophrenic symptomatology. The early systematic descriptions of schizophrenia by Eugen Bleuler gave prominence to the hypothesis that most schizophrenic symptomatology could be traced to a "disconnecting of associative threads" that form the relationships between ideas (Bleuler, 1911/1950, p. 21). Recent investigators have refined the proposition that primary malfunctions in elementary cognitive processes contribute substantially to formal thought disorder (e.g., Maher, 1972, 1983). Hemsley (1977) and Frith (1979), among others, have also suggested ties between a primary cognitive deficit and the secondary formation of delusions and hallucinations, symptoms which are central for the *Diagnostic and Statistical Manual of Mental Disorders*, 3rd edition (DSM-III; 1980) and its revised edition (DSM-III-R; 1987) diagnoses of schizophrenic disorder.

Emil Kraepelin, who described and categorized the manifestations of schizophrenia with classical clarity, suggested that the inadequate control over continuity of thought in schizophrenia was associated with disordered attentional processes: "This behavior is without doubt nearly related to the disorder of attention which we very frequently find conspicuously developed in our patients. It is quite common for them to lose both inclination and ability on their own initiative to keep their attention fixed for any length of time" (Kraepelin, 1913/1919, pp. 5–6). Kraepelin made an early attempt to delineate the type of information processing that malfunctions in schizophrenic disorder by differentiating between *Auffassung* or the registration of information and *Aufmerksamkeit* or active, sustained, directed attention. Kraepelin believed that the ability to register information was generally preserved in schizophrenia, while the ability to sustain or direct attention was almost always deficient (Holzman, Levy, & Proctor, 1978).

From these early attempts to understand the nature of cognition and attention in schizophrenia, the basic concept that deficits in elementary cognitive processes may be causing central systems of the disorder has been debated. The debate has produced three clear needs for research. First, research should incorporate clearly delineated information-processing models and tasks to describe carefully and objectively the specific type or level of cognitive processing that is suspected of being deficient. Such models are provided by the revitalized interest in cognitive psychology and cognitive neuropsychology. Secondly, research needs to incorporate a heuristic model of schizophrenia that addresses how cognitive deficits are hypothesized to be related to the disorder. This chapter will briefly review such a model. Thirdly, because conclusions drawn solely from studies of actively psychotic schizophrenic patients may be reflecting secondary factors such as hospitalization, medication, etc., experimental paradigms that avoid these confounding factors also need to be employed (Mednick & McNeil, 1968). In addition, in order to determine whether cognitive abnormalities on sensitive laboratory measures transcend the acute psychotic state, studies focusing on nonpsychotic states are critical. Studying individuals at heightened risk of developing schizophrenic disorder (Garmezy, 1974; Mednick & McNeil, 1968) and studying individuals in remitted states after schizophrenic episodes (Asarnow & MacCrimmon, 1978; Wohlberg & Kornetsky, 1973) are two prominent ways of identifying abnormalities that are present beyond the period of acute psychotic symptoms. The study of individuals at heightened risk for schizophrenia but who have never experienced a psychotic episode also eliminates prior treatment factors as confounding variables.

The present chapter will focus on the similarities in the findings from studies of individuals at increased risk for schizophrenic disorders and studies of actively psychotic schizophrenic patients. We will concentrate on findings from the continuous performance test, the span of apprehension task, and short-term recall tasks as examples of prominent information-processing deficits in schizophrenia.

Current Conceptions of Processing Capacity and Processing Load

The growing body of research into normal human perception, cognition, and attention has produced models that have refined our conceptions of the processes involved. Information-processing models in this complex field receive continuing revision. For the present discussion, a brief review of processing-capacity models of attention and of levels of processing load will set the stage for description of deficits in schizophrenia. The reader is encouraged to consult Nuechterlein and Dawson (1984b), Knight (1984), Gjerde (1983), and Kietzman, Spring, and Zubin (1980) for more complete reviews of information-processing models related to schizophrenia.

One type of information-processing model posits that incoming sensory information moves through a fixed sequence of processing stages. Early "bottleneck" theories of selective attention attempted to locate the stage at which people select stimuli for further processing from among the many inputs that are registered by the senses. More recent models have emphasized greater flexibility in the control of processing by conceptualizing attention as a limited resource or processing capacity that can be allocated to various stages and levels to facilitate processing.

Kahneman (1973) proposed one of the first information-processing models based on attention as processing capacity. In this model, attention is not specific to a given stage of information processing but is a limited pool of processing resources or cognitive effort. An individual has flexibility in allocating processing capacity to one task or dividing it among several tasks depending on the allocation policy. The allocation policy is influenced by both voluntary factors (such as following instructions) and involuntary factors (such as attending to novel stimuli). Also, the general level of processing capacity may vary from moment to moment because it is partially determined by the general arousal level of the individual.

The type of task and the level of task difficulty are important considerations in determining the demands placed on processing capacity. Greater demands on processing capacity are made by higher-level mental operations occurring near the response end as compared to processes in early stages of processing (Kahneman, 1973). Beatty (1982b) provided a scaling of various types and levels of tasks according to their processing demands. He used pupillary response measurements, as suggested by Kahneman, to provide a physiological index of processing load. According to Beatty (1982b), tasks employing a small amount of information that is clearly presented (e.g., recalling one or two digits, matching two letters, easy perceptual discriminations) have lower processing load than tasks employing a larger amount of information which is difficult to discern or which requires complex language and reasoning operations (e.g., recalling seven digits, difficult word matching, grammatical reasoning).

A distinction has also been made between cognitive processes that make demands on limited processing capacity (attention-demanding, controlled, or effortful processes) and processes that make no demands on processing capacity (automatic processes) (Hasher & Zacks, 1979; Posner & Snyder, 1975; Schneider, Dumais, & Shiffrin, 1984; Shiffrin & Schneider, 1977). Although attention-demanding and automatic processes were initially viewed as qualitatively different from each other, it is possible that they are best conceptualized as representing processes at opposite poles of a dimension of processing-resource demand.

The changing conception of attention leads to notions of attentional abnormalities in flexible allocation models that differ from those based on sequential stage models. Instead of a particular stage or process being dysfunctional, processing capacity models emphasize deficits in overall processing capacity, abnormal allocation policies, or deficient regulation of the level of activation and arousal (Gjerde, 1983: Nuechterlein & Dawson, 1984b). These deficits appear under conditions that create sufficient demands on the processing capacity of the individual. Thus, if deficits in information processing in schizophrenic patients result from limited availability or allocation of overall processing capacity, then performance deficits should appear only under conditions that place sufficient demands on processing capacity. As will be seen below in the discussions of the three different tasks, similarities in performance by schizophrenic patients and high-risk populations appear only under high levels of processing load.

A Tentative Vulnerability/Stress Model of Schizophrenic Episodes

These basic concepts of information processing and attentional functioning improve our ability to describe cognitive processes that may be deficient in schizophrenia and suggest interrelationships of such deficits with abnormalities in other domains. Furthermore, the appearance of certain cognitive deficits throughout the course of the disorder (premorbid, psychotic, and postpsychotic) and in individuals at increased risk for schizophrenia suggests that these deficits are possible indicators of vulnerability to schizophrenic disorder, rather than only part of the acute symptomatology.

Vulnerability indicators or markers have received a great deal of attention recently and have been defined in various ways (Asarnow & Asarnow, 1982; Nuechterlein & Dawson, 1984a; Zubin & Spring, 1977). Our ongoing research on the early course of schizophrenic disorders has resulted in a conceptual separation of variables that are "stable vulnerability indicators" from those that are "mediating vulnerability factors" (Nuechterlein & Dawson, 1984a). Stable vulnerability indicators refer to characteristics of schizophrenic patients that are stably deviant from normal levels, even during remissions of psychotic symptoms, and that are independent of symptomatic changes. Mediating vulnerability factors refer to characteristics that are also deviant from normal levels of symptomatology during both psychotic and asymptomatic states, but that covary with level of symptomatology. We hypothesize that some mediating vulnerability factors may be contributors in the causal chains leading to psychotic symptomatology and would, therefore, be expected to show an increased deviation from normal levels preceding or simultaneous with psychotic episodes (Nuechterlein & Dawson, 1984a).

The University of California, Los Angeles (UCLA) Mental Health Clinical Research Center for the Study of Schizophrenia has developed a working model for the development of schizophrenic psychotic episodes, and this is summarized in Fig. 1. [For more complete presentations of the model, see Nuechterlein and Dawson (1984a), Liberman (1986), and Nuechterlein (1987).] The primary components of this model fall into the five major categories of (a) enduring personal vulnerability characteristics; (b) environmental potentiators and stressors; (c) personal and environmental protective factors; (d) transient intermediate states; and (e) outcome behaviors. The present discussion is primarily concerned with enduring vulnerability characteristics.

This developing heuristic model suggests that enduring vulnerability characteristics, already present in an individual, interact with stressful stimuli in the individual's environment to produce transient intermediate states of processing

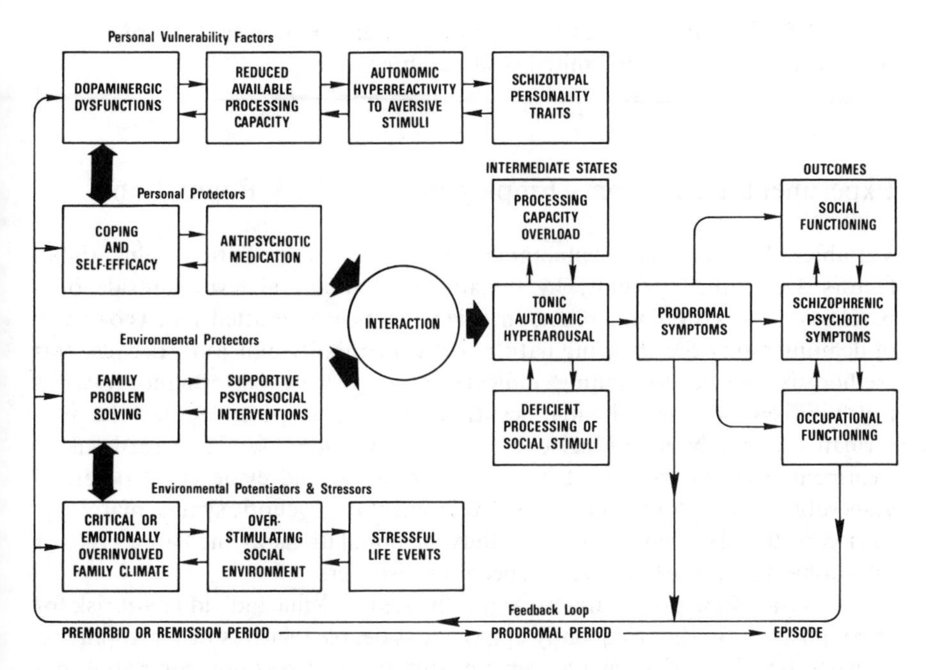

Fig. 1. A heuristic conceptual framework for possible factors in the development of schizophrenic episodes. (From Nuechterlein 1987)

capacity overload, tonic autonomic hyperarousal, and impaired processing of social stimuli before psychotic symptoms develop (Nuechterlein, 1987; Nuechterlein & Dawson, 1984a). The intermediate state of processing capacity overload and the resulting social behaviors are hypothesized to disrupt the immediate family and the broader environmental situation of the individual, resulting in an increase in the level and frequency of environmental stressors and, in turn, more extreme processing capacity overload. This feedback cycle is hypothesized to continue until the transient intermediate states reach the individual's threshold point for the development of schizophrenic psychotic symptoms. Protective factors within the individual and in the environment serve to buffer the vulnerable individual from the environmental potentiators and stressors and to interrupt the feedback cycle.

Laboratory measures of information processing have consistently demonstrated three cognitive processes, among others, to be deviant in schizophrenic populations: sensory storage and read out (as measured by the forced-choice, partial-report span of apprehension), signal detection during sustained focused attention (as measured by the continuous performance test), and short-term recall memory (as measured by digit-span and word-span recall tasks). The convergence of findings across schizophrenic patients and high-risk individuals makes deficits on these tasks potential enduring vulnerability indicators for schizophrenia. Findings from other tasks also lend substantial support to the notion of deficient processes in these three areas. However, for brevity, the present discussion will be limited to these three tasks.

Experimental Paradigms Employing High-Risk Populations

Variables that are stable vulnerability indicators or mediating vulnerability factors are defined partially by remaining at abnormal levels outside of a psychotic state. Examining schizophrenic patients in a remitted state is one way of demonstrating the enduring nature of a vulnerability indicator. Because this method is limited to finding indications of deviant performance after a psychotic episode has already occurred, it remains possible that the performance might be a residual effect of the psychotic episode or methods of treatment. For this reason, it is most desirable to find evidence of potential vulnerability indicators prior to the development of psychotic symptomatology. This consideration has led to the study of populations at increased risk for schizophrenia and schizophrenia spectrum disorders.

Three sampling procedures are typically used to define individuals at risk for schizophrenia. Studies frequently employ first-degree relatives of schizophrenic patients. Children of a schizophrenic parent are used because, compared to a general population risk of 1% or less, such offspring have an approximately 10%–15% risk of developing schizophrenia (Gottesman, 1978). Other first-degree relatives of a schizophrenic index case also have rates that are substantially above the population base rate: 8%–10% for siblings and about 4%–6% for parents (Gottesman, 1978). Although the absolute rates are lower when narrow criteria for schizophrenic disorder (e.g., DSM-III) are applied, the differentially higher rates for first-degree relatives of schizophrenic patients as compared to relatives of nonpsychiatric control subjects remains. Using DSM-III criteria, Kendler, Gruenberg, and Tsuang (1985) found a 3.6% morbidity risk for schizophrenia and a 7.2% risk for all nonaffective psychotic disorders among first-degree relatives of schizophrenic patients, compared to 0.1% and 0.3%, respectively, among first-degree relatives of nonpsychiatric control subjects.

A second strategy has been to select individuals from the population at large who demonstrate personality characteristics that are possibly related to increased risk for schizophrenic disorder (Chapman, Edell, & Chapman, 1980; Nuechterlein, 1985; Steronko & Woods, 1978). The third and least common strategy has been to select subjects based on the presence of biochemical characteristics that have been observed among schizophrenic patients (Buchsbaum, Murphy, Coursey, Lake, & Ziegler, 1978).

With increasing frequency, studies are using laboratory tasks of cognitive performance in an attempt to isolate potential vulnerability indicators in high-risk samples. The following sections will summarize findings from the first two high-risk sampling strategies for the tasks mentioned above.

Forced-Choice Span of Apprehension

The forced-choice span of apprehension, first developed by Estes and Taylor (1964), is generally considered a measure of the amount of information simultaneously processed from briefly presented visual stimuli (Asarnow & MacCrimmon, 1981). During a basic forced-choice span of apprehension task (Asarnow & MacCrimmon, 1978), subjects sit in front of a rear-projection screen or, more recently, a computer monitor on which arrays of letters are presented. Arrays are typically constructed using a 4 × 4 matrix. Subjects are told that one of two target letters, such as T or F, will be very briefly (e.g., 50–70 ms) presented in each trial and that they are to report which is presented. Target stimuli are embedded in arrays containing different numbers of irrelevant letters to vary the level of task difficulty. The target and irrelevant letters are randomly assigned to the 16 possible positions of the matrix. The principal score from this task is the proportion of trials on which the target stimulus is correctly detected.

The forced-choice span of apprehension requires rapid internal scanning of arrays of varying sizes and investigates sensory storage and read-out stages of visual information processing. The task measures the quality and efficiency of the initial sensory memory stage in multistore models of memory, which typically lasts about 250 ms (Atkinson & Shiffrin, 1968). Because subjects need only process targets, and not irrelevant letters, to a recognition level for reporting, the task can estimate the efficiency of visual search in sensory memory (Estes & Taylor, 1964).

Actively Psychotic Schizophrenic Patients

Initial studies of the forced-choice span of apprehension task revealed that symptomatic schizophrenic patients are impaired at identifying target letters in large arrays but not small arrays, as compared to nonpsychotic psychiatric patients and normal subjects (Neale, McIntyre, Fox, & Cromwell, 1969; Neale, 1971). Subsequent studies by Asarnow and MacCrimmon (1978, 1981) supported and extended these findings. Both acutely symptomatic and partially recovered schizophrenic patients performed more poorly than normal control subjects on the forced-choice span of apprehension task (Asarnow & MacCrimmon, 1978). Furthermore, manic-depressive patients in relative remission did not show deficits at most array sizes on this task, suggesting that the task may reveal cognitive deficits that are particularly relevant to schizophrenia (Asarnow & MacCrimmon, 1981). A longitudinal study that examined patients 1 week and 12 weeks after hospitalization also showed that impaired performance on the span of apprehension remains relatively stable among schizophrenic patients even after reductions in thought disorder and general symptomatology (Asarnow & MacCrimmon, 1982). Finally, a recent study has found that span of apprehension performance is uncorrelated with cross-sectional severity of positive symptoms (hallucinations and delusions), but is significantly related to negative symptoms such as blunted affect and motor retardation in recent-onset schizophrenic patients (Nuechterlein, Edell, Norris, & Dawson, 1986).

These studies indicate the presence of a deficit in the amount of information that schizophrenic patients can process from brief stimulus presentations both during and following the presence of an acute schizophrenic episode. The deficit does not seem to be secondary to concurrent positive symptoms of schizophrenia, but may be linked to negative symptoms. The significance of this deficit as a potential vulnerability marker for schizophrenia becomes clearer from a brief review of studies of populations at risk for schizophrenia.

High-Risk Studies

Span of apprehension studies using subjects at risk for schizophrenia have also demonstrated performance deficits on the task. A subgroup of foster children born to schizophrenic mothers demonstrated a level and pattern of impaired performance on the forced-choice span of apprehension task that is very similar to that of acutely disturbed schizophrenic patients (Asarnow, Steffy, MacCrimmon, & Cleghorn, 1977, 1978). As compared to foster children of nonpsychiatric biological parents or nonfoster normal comparison children, the foster children born to schizophrenic mothers identified fewer target letters when targets were presented in large arrays with multiple irrelevant letters.

Harvey, Weintraub, and Neale (1985) did not find this deficit in forced-choice span of apprehension performance among their sample of children born to a schizophrenic parent. Among the possible reasons for these discrepant results are the greater demand for detection of peripherally presented (nonfoveal) stimuli in the Asarnow et al. (1977) study and the possibility that the foster children in the study of Asarnow et al. (1977) had mothers with more severe forms of schizophrenia than those included in the Harvey et al. (1985) study (Asarnow, Steffy, & Waldman, 1985; Neale & Harvey, 1985). Additional research is needed to clarify this matter.

Poorer performance on the forced-choice span of apprehension task has been successfully used to identify a group of young adults without a history of psychiatric disorder but who report a higher level of schizotypal experiences than other subjects drawn from the same temporary employment agencies (Asarnow, Nuechterlein, & Marder, 1983). Although not selected for genetic relationship to a schizophrenic patient, these young adults who report schizotypal experiences are also hypothesized to be at increased risk for psychosis.

In summary, although one study failed to find the span of apprehension deficit among a sample of children of schizophrenic parents, the appearance of a performance deficit on the span of apprehension task prior to the appearance of severe symptoms in another sample at genetic risk and also in subjects reporting a greater number of schizotypal experiences suggests that the task is sensitive to cognitive processes central to schizophrenia. The impairment of early visual search processes when several irrelevant stimuli are present is relatively enduring in some schizophrenic patients, as it is found both during and following a severe psychotic episode. This deficit does not appear in span of apprehension conditions employing single letters, suggesting that a relatively high level of processing load is required to elicit this early visual processing abnormality.

Continuous Performance Test

The inability to sustain focused attention in tasks that have high processing demands is a second potential vulnerability indicator for schizophrenia. Several versions of a visual vigilance task, the continuous performance test (CPT), have provided a consistent pattern of deficient performance in actively symptomatic and remitted schizophrenic patients and in children of schizophrenic parents.

Several versions of the CPT have been derived from the original work by Rosvold, Mirsky, Sarason, Bransome, and Beck (1956). The subject views a series of briefly presented stimuli (typically letters or numbers) that appear in rapid succession at regular intervals over a continuous vigil. The subject is to respond to a predesignated target (e.g., the numeral 0) or target series (e.g., a 7 only when it follows a 3) by pressing a button. The exposure times are typically in the 40–200 ms range, the interstimulus intervals in the 1–1.5 s range, and the total vigilance period from 5–15 min (Kornetsky, 1972; Kornetsky & Orzack, 1978; Nuechterlein, 1983; Rosvold et al., 1956; Sykes, Douglas, & Morgenstern, 1973; Wohlberg & Kornetsky, 1973). The target stimulus occurs with relatively low frequency, ranging from 10% to 25% of presented stimuli.

Performance on the CPT has traditionally been evaluated by examining errors of omission (missed targets) and errors of commission (responses to nontargets). When signal detection theory indices are used instead of traditional raw error scores, two underlying processes of task performance can be examined. The first, d′, characterizes a subject's performance in terms of sensitivity to accurately discriminate targets (signal) from nontargets (noise) (Davies & Parasuraman, 1982; Green & Swets, 1966; McNicol, 1972). The second, the response criterion, indexes the amount of perceptual evidence that a person demands before responding that a given stimulus is a signal or, in other terms, how cautious the person is in saying that a stimulus is a target. This dimension of response criterion is independent of the first dimension, sensitivity (Nuechterlein, 1985).

Tasks such as the CPT that require sustained vigilance typically produce a decrease in sensitivity over time for normal subjects only under sufficient task demands. Combining perceptually degraded (blurred) stimuli and high rates of presentation places high demands on processing capacity by requiring rapid, sustained processing and integration of ambiguous features of each stimulus (Nuechterlein, Parasuraman, & Jiang, 1983). Requiring memory for successive stimuli in a rapidly paced vigilance task also places high demands on processing capacity and produces decreases in sensitivity over time (Parasuraman, 1979). Beatty (1982a) provided psychophysiological evidence of the demands placed on processing capacity during vigilance tasks, using a pupillary dilation index that has been widely used as a measure of processing resource allocation. Beatty discovered that subjects who show sensitivity decrements over time have decreases in phasic pupillary dilations that correlate highly with changes in sensitivity. In other words, decrements in sustained attention are related to changes in the intensity of attention that is evoked by or allocated to vigilance task stimuli.

Actively Psychotic Schizophrenic Patients

Studies using the forced-choice span of apprehension have revealed impaired performance in schizophrenia only under conditions of relatively high processing load. High levels of momentary processing load are also necessary to elicit impaired performance on the CPT among high-risk populations, as will be reviewed below. However, impaired performance on the CPT is found under conditions of lower processing load among chronic schizophrenic patients. Significantly lower target hit rates are obtained by chronic, drug-free schizophrenic patients, as compared to chronic alcoholic or normal control subjects (Orzack & Kornetsky, 1966), on a version of the CPT with a single, clearly focused target letter that fails to elicit deficits among children of schizophrenic parents. This pattern suggests that the active schizophrenic period may be characterized by a more severe impairment in vigilance than is present preceding the episode. Recognition of single, highly familiar targets (such as a letter or digit) requires little processing capacity (Posner, 1978; Shiffrin & Schneider, 1977); thus, information-processing dysfunction during an episode of active symptomatology may involve processes that are normally relatively automatic in addition to those that require high levels of processing capacity.

Decreased target detection rates have also been demonstrated among remitted schizophrenic patients, but only in versions of the CPT with a relatively high processing load (Asarnow & MacCrimmon, 1978; Wohlberg & Kornetsky, 1973). These studies employed CPT versions with either short-term memory loads or stimuli that moved from one screen location to another from trial to trial. In addition, auditory distraction was added to some conditions, which would further increase the demand on processing resources relative to the version with a single, clearly focused target letter employed by Orzack and Kornetsky (1966).

A recent attempt to find relationships between performance on high processing load, degraded stimulus, and short-term memory versions of the CPT and major symptom dimensions in recent-onset schizophrenic patients revealed that deficits in discriminating target from nontarget stimuli during these CPT versions were correlated with negative symptoms (e.g., blunted affect, motor retardation) but not positive symptoms during an inpatient period (Nuechterlein et al., 1986). Furthermore, the outpatient level of CPT target discrimination was related to the inpatient level of negative symptoms even though there was no concurrent outpatient relationship between CPT performance and negative symptoms. This pattern suggests that a target discrimination deficit on high processing load versions of the CPT may serve as a vulnerability factor for development of schizophrenic negative symptoms.

High-Risk Studies

The processing load of the task is also important in detecting deficits in CPT performance for populations at increased risk for schizophrenia. Studies of children and adolescents that have used clearly focused numerals or letters without a short-term memory burden have failed to find significant differences in performance between children of schizophrenic parents and normal comparison groups (Asarnow et al., 1977; Cornblatt & Erlenmeyer-Kimling, 1984; Grunebaum, Cohler, Kauffman, & Gallant, 1978; Nuechterlein, 1983).

Versions of the CPT that involve higher processing loads have been more successful in uncovering performance deficits in various samples of populations at risk for schizophrenia. Erlenmeyer-Kimling and Cornblatt (1978) asked 7- to 12-year-old children to respond each time two identical slides of playing cards appeared in sequence. This CPT version places increased load on memory by requiring sustained processing of two dimensions (suit and number) with no single, absolute target stimulus. Children of schizophrenic patients showed impaired performance by identifying fewer targets, making more false alarm responses, and showing lower sensitivity than children of parents without psychiatric disorder (Erlenmeyer-Kimling & Cornblatt, 1978; Rutschmann, Cornblatt, & Erlenmeyer-Kimling, 1977). In a second sample of 7- to 12-year-old children, a version of the CPT in which the target was two identical double digits appearing in succession also revealed lower sensitivity and fewer target detections in children of schizophrenic parents than in children of normal parents (Cornblatt & Erlenmeyer-Kimling, 1984). These results were extended in research with 9- to 16-year-old children that employed the playing card CPT as well as versions with perceptually degraded digits or reversed response requirements with a single-digit target (Nuechterlein, 1983). Nuechterlein (1983) found that children of schizophrenic mothers had significantly lower scores than stratified normal comparison children on a common sensitivity factor on which five CPT versions loaded. Furthermore, the degraded stimulus CPT was the most effective version for identifying a disproportionately large group of high-risk children with low sensitivity (d′). Children of mothers with nonschizophrenic psychiatric disorders have not shown significant CPT deficits (Nuechterlein, 1983; Rutschmann, Cornblatt, & Erlenmeyer-Kimling, 1986).

Poor signal/noise discrimination (low sensitivity) on a high processing load CPT also characterizes persons believed to be at risk for schizophrenia by virtue of schizotypal characteristics. Nuechterlein, Edell, and West (in preparation) selected three groups of college students, one with the 2-7-8 Minnesota Multiphasic Personality Inventory (MMPI) profile type, which is associated with schizotypal features and later schizophrenic diagnoses; a second group with no scale elevations; and a third group with other scale elevations. The 2-7-8 subjects showed lower sensitivity on a degraded stimulus CPT. Also, Nuechterlein, Asarnow, and Marder (in preparation) found that young adults without a personal psychiatric history who demonstrated lower sensitivity on a degraded stimulus version of the CPT had significantly higher scores on several measures of schizotypal characteristics.

A consistent pattern of impaired performance on vigilance tasks that have relatively high processing load requirements is found among children of schizophrenic parents and individuals who demonstrate schizotypal characteristics in their responses to personality questionnaries. Vigilance tasks with low processing loads reveal deficits in chronic, symptomatic schizophrenic patients but not high-risk groups. These findings suggest that low signal/noise discrimination on CPT versions with high momentary processing loads may be an indicator of vulnerability to schizophrenia.

Rehearsal During Free Recall Tasks

Findings of differential processing deficit in short-term memory tasks are of particular interest since the cognitive processes are more directly under the conscious control of the subject. Four basic conclusions can be drawn from research on memory in schizophrenia:

1. Schizophrenic patients appear capable of using mnemonic organizational strategies to encode information, but they fail to do so spontaneously (Koh, Kayton, & Schwartz, 1974; Lutz & Marsh, 1981; Traupmann, 1980).
2. Deficient recall of many types of verbal material is found within various schizophrenic groups across a variety of research paradigms, including free recall (Depue & Fowles, 1974; Koh, Kayton, & Berry, 1973; Larsen, McGhie, & Chapman, 1964; Russell & Beekhuis, 1976; Spence & Lair, 1964).
3. Because recognition memory tasks do not appear to require use of specific mnemonic strategies during encoding (Kintsch, 1970), they usually do not show performance deficits in schizophrenia (Bauman, 1971; Bauman & Murray, 1968; Koh, Grinker, Marusary, & Foreman, 1981; Koh, Kayton, & Berry, 1973; Koh & Peterson, 1978; Nachmani & Cohen, 1969; Russell; Bannatyne, & Smith, 1975),
4. The schizophrenic recall deficit is significantly lessened when incidental learning paradigms are used to insure effective organization of information at encoding (Koh et al., 1981; Koh, Kayton, & Peterson, 1976; Koh, Marusary, & Rosen, 1980; Larsen & Fromholt, 1976).

These findings consistently suggest that poorer short-term recall performance by schizophrenic patients results, at least in part, from a failure to generate or maintain effective mnemonic strategies. The short-term memory store, as conceptualized by Atkinson and Shiffrin (1968), is an active, limited capacity, processing component where conscious mental processes occur. Information is held in this store for a brief period of time that may be increased by allocating attention to the material. Maintaining an item in the short-term store through rehearsal permits transfer of the item into a more enduring, stable, and relatively unlimited memory structure, the long-term store (Atkinson & Shiffrin, 1968). Effective mnemonic strategies serve two basic purposes. One function is to maximize the limited capacity of the short-term memory store by associating bits of information through chunking or grouping during the encoding stage of processing. A second purpose is to allocate attention to material to maintain it in the short-term store for a longer period of time, allowing transfer to the long-term store. The mnemonic strategies generated by schizophrenic patients apparently fail to serve these two functions.

Distraction Effects

Neutral and distraction conditions during serial recall tasks have been used to examine the level of information processing that is impaired in schizophrenia. In this type of task, strings of numbers or words are presented, on some trials with several irrelevant items being read between relevant items. Accuracy of recall of individual positions may be tested, or recall of the entire list in appropriate order may be required. If the percentage of correct recall is plotted by serial position, a U-shaped recall curve is found for normal subjects, indicating better recall of items that are presented at the beginning and end of lists (Craik, 1970; Glanzer & Cunitz, 1966). Recall of items from initial positions in a list is viewed as output from the long-term store. Enhanced recall of initial items in a list, which is termed a "primacy effect," reflects more rehearsal and deeper strategic processing of these items as compared to items in the middle of the list. The enhanced recall of items at the end of the serial position curve, which is termed a "recency effect," represents recall of items from the short-term store because they can be recalled immediately and therefore do not require as much rehearsal as early list positions.

Recall of primacy items presented under distraction conditions is impaired in schizophrenic patients compared to normal control subjects (Oltmanns, 1978). This deficit in recall performance seems to be specific to items requiring active rehearsal, because no significant difference in recall of recency items occurs between groups. Oltmanns noted that schizophrenic performance under distraction conditions was quite similar to the performance of normal subjects in an earlier study who were constrained from practicing or organizing items for recall (Hamilton & Hockey, 1974). The findings suggest the presence of a deficit in the control and direction of attention to meet the increased task demands caused by distraction.

Frame and Oltmanns (1982) examined the effects of distraction on the serial position curve for recall across clinical states within schizophrenic patients. Again, impaired recall of primacy items was found both during an episode and at relative recovery. The impairment seems to be somewhat specific to schizophrenia because a comparison group of depressed patients recalled primacy items better than the schizophrenia group. This finding indicates an enduring deficit in schizophrenia involving active, organizational processes such as rehearsal. Recall of recency items by schizophrenic patients remained intact across clinical states.

The similarity of serial recall performance under distraction by children of schizophrenic parents is striking. Harvey, Winters, Weintraub, and Neale (1981) tested children of schizophrenic, bipolar, and unipolar patients as well as children of normal parents on a digit span task, using neutral and distraction conditions. Analysis of the serial position curve demonstrated that, under distraction conditions, poorer recall performance for primacy as compared to recency positions differentiated children of schizophrenics from the other groups. Harvey et al. (1981) interpreted these findings as indicating that distraction may interfere with the rehearsal of items during presentation in children at risk for schizophrenia. The presence of this form of distractibility during and following a schizophrenic psychotic episode and in children of schizophrenic parents suggests that a deficit in active, controlled information processing is a possible vulnerability factor for schizophrenia.

Rehearsal

Although the studies of distractibility in schizophrenia have been interpreted as indicating a disruption in rehearsal processes, direct assessment of schizophrenic rehearsal deficits in such tasks has not been undertaken until recently. We have recently completed a study that supports the hypothesis that schizophrenic patients in a relatively remitted clinical state are deficient in spontaneously generating and maintaining optimal mnemonic strategies and that this deficiency extends beyond simple rehearsal (Zaucha, Nuechterlein, and Asarnow, in preparation). The study examined the rehearsal and recall of word lists among schizophrenic patients and a normal control group. Subjects rehearsed lists of 20 nouns for immediate free recall under a silent baseline condition, an overt baseline condition, and then under three induced rehearsal conditions.

The baseline conditions permitted examination of recall and self-generated rehearsal strategies in a relatively unconstrained situation. Two of the three induced rehearsal conditions constrained subjects to rehearse list items in ways that would allocate different amounts of rehearsal to early list items, while the third acted as a modified baseline condition in that subjects could rehearse as they desired provided their rehearsal filled the presentation interval and contained only repetitions of items from the present list. One of the constrained rehearsal conditions required the subject to repeat the presented word three times immediately after presentation (one-item rehearsal), which equates rehearsal for all serial positions. The other constrained rehearsal condition (three-item rehearsal) required the subjects, after each word, to repeat once the last three words that had been presented. For the first serial position, this strategy involved repeating the first word three times and, for the second serial position, repeating the first word twice and the second word once. Thus, three-item rehearsal forced disproportionate rehearsal of the word in the first serial position. We hypothesized that the two induced rehearsal conditions, by creating equivalent rehearsal of primacy items across groups, would equate recall of primacy items for the control and schizophrenia groups. We hypothesized that the groups would show no primacy effect in the one-item rehearsal condition and a prominent primacy effect in the three-item rehearsal condition.

When rehearsal of primacy items was made equivalent to rehearsal of items in other serial positions (one-item rehearsal), the schizophrenic patients showed a large, significant drop in recall of primacy items from their counterbalanced baseline recall of primacy items, resulting in the disappearance of any primacy effect. However, the normal control subjects surprisingly decreased their primacy recall only to a small and statistically nonsignificant degree relative to the counterbalanced baseline level. Thus, even when overt rehearsal was equated for all serial positions and should have eliminated the primacy effect that can be attributed to simple rehearsal, normal subjects continued to show significantly more primacy effect than schizophrenic patients. Normal subjects apparently employ mnemonic strategies that go beyond rehearsal when the required rehearsal strategy is simple and not optimal.

When rehearsal of primacy items was increased by induction of the three-item rehearsal strategy, the recall of primacy items between the two groups was equated as predicted. The increased rehearsal of primacy items, compared to the one-item rehearsal condition, boosted the recall of these items for schizophrenic patients as expected. At the same time, compared to the relatively unstructured, counterbalanced baseline condition, this complex rehearsal condition produced a significant drop in the recall of primary items for the control group but not for the schizophrenia group. It appeared that, for recall of primacy items, the relatively complex three-item rehearsal procedure was an improvement over the one-item rehearsal procedure and equivalent to naturally used mnemonic strategies for schizophrenic patients, but was inferior to the naturally used mnemonic strategies of normal subjects.

In summary, we (Zaucha, Nuechterlein, and Asarnow, in preparation) have found that inducing similar types of rehearsal can have differential effects on schizophrenic patients and control subjects, depending on the complexity of the rehearsal strategy. If an induced rehearsal strategy is easy but inefficient for rehearsal of material, schizophrenic patients appear deficient in spontaneously generating additional mnemonic strategies for more effective recall. On the other hand, if an induced rehearsal procedure is too demanding, it may interfere with the ability of normal subjects to employ additional natural mnemonic strategies. In this situation, the normal subjects can show suppressed recall of primacy items relative to an unstructured rehearsal condition and be made equivalent in primacy recall to schizophrenic patients. Thus, schizophrenic patients appear to be deficient in spontaneous generation of optimal mnemonic strategies that extend beyond rehearsal, whereas normal subjects apparently employ such strategies naturally unless other task demands produce interference.

At present, no data exist on the effects of induced rehearsal strategies on serial recall in high-risk populations. However, preliminary findings from a sample of adults who had been autistic as children suggest that these rehearsal tasks may be sensitive to differences in cognitive functioning across these diagnostic groups. Thus, the use of overt rehearsal and induced rehearsal strategies appears to be a promising way to examine further the deficit in recall of primacy items that has been found among children of schizophrenic patients in previous research (Harvey et al., 1981).

Conclusions

Similar cognitive deficits have been found in schizophrenic patients and in populations at risk for schizophrenia on large letter arrays in the forced-choice span of apprehension task, during high processing load versions of the CPT, and in the early serial positions within recall tasks. The deficits in initial sensory storage and read out in the span of apprehension task, of signal detection during sustained attention in the CPT, and of controlled, effortful processing during recall meet the requirements for vulnerability indicators as they appear to be consistently present during actively symptomatic as well as remitted periods within many schizophrenic patients. Furthermore, their presence in populations at risk for developing schizophrenia suggests that these information-processing deficiencies may be present in the premorbid period and are good candidates for predictors of increased probability of schizophrenia and related disorders. The specificity of these deficits to risk for schizophrenia needs additional investigation, but preliminary evidence suggests that the lowered sensitivity in the high processing load CPT versions and the suppressed primacy effect in recall tasks are not present at significantly increased frequency among children of parents with nonschizophrenic psychiatric disorders as compared to normal control groups. These cognitive processing abnormalities appear to have the common feature of involving conditions of high momentary processing demands.

The tentative vulnerability/stress model of schizophrenia that we have presented suggests that these enduring cognitive deficits can interact with stressful events in a person's external environment, resulting in periods of processing capacity overload. This transient state is hypothesized to be one of the precursors to schizophrenic symptomatology. Research on populations at risk for schizophrenia and schizophrenia spectrum disorders permits an important test of this and similar heuristic models because the potential vulnerability factors can be examined before the general disruption associated with the acute illness. Thus, as compared to cross-sectional studies of actively symptomatic schizophrenic patients, these studies can separate more easily the vulnerability factors and precipitating stressors for schizophrenic episodes from the immediate consequences of acute symptomatology. Continuing research encompassing both schizophrenic patients in varying clinical states and populations at risk for schizophrenia is needed to refine our basic understanding of the vulnerability factors that contribute to schizophrenia.

Acknowledgment. Preparation of this chapter was supported by National Institute of Mental Health grants MH14584, MH37705, and MH30911.

References

Asarnow, R.F., & Asarnow, J.R. (1982). Attention-information processing dysfunction and vulnerability to schizophrenia: Implications for preventive intervention. In M.J. Goldstein (Ed.), *Preventive intervention in schizophrenia: Are we ready?* (DHHS Publication No. ADM 82-1111). Washington, DC: US Government Printing Office.

Asarnow, R.F., & MacCrimmon, D.J. (1978). Residual performance deficit in clinically remitted schizophrenics: A marker of schizophrenia? *Journal of Abnormal Psychology, 87*, 597–608.

Asarnow, R.F., & MacCrimmon, D.J. (1981). Span of apprehension deficits during the post-psychotic stages of schizophrenia: A replication and extension. *Archives of General Psychiatry, 38*, 1006–1011.

Asarnow, R.F., & MacCrimmon, D.J. (1982). Attention/information processing, neuropsychological functioning, and thought disorder during the acute and partial recovery phases of schizophrenia: A longitudinal study. *Psychiatry Research, 7*, 309–319.

Asarnow, R.F., Steffy, R.A., MacCrimmon, D.J., & Cleghorn, J.M. (1977). An attentional assessment of foster children at risk for schizophrenia. *Journal of Abnormal Psychology, 86*, 267–275.

Asarnow, R.F., Steffy, R.A., MacCrimmon, D.J., & Cleghorn, J.M. (1978). An attentional assessment of foster children at risk for schizophrenia. In L.C. Wynne, R.L. Cromwell, & S. Matthysse (Eds.), *The nature of schizophrenia: New approaches to research and treatment.* New York: Wiley.

Asarnow, R.F., Nuechterlein, K.H., & Marder, S.R. (1983). Span of apprehension performance, neuropsychological functioning, and indices of psychosis proneness. *Journal of Nervous and Mental Disease, 171*, 662–669.

Asarnow, R.F., Steffy, R., & Waldman, I. (1985). Comment on Harvey, Weintraub, and Neale: Span of apprehesion deficits in children vulnerable to psychopathology. *Journal of Abnormal Psychology, 94*, 414–417.

Atkinson, R.C., & Shiffrin, R.M. (1968). Human memory: A proposed system and its control processes. In K.W. Spence & J.T. Spence (Eds.), *Advances in the psychology of learning and motivation: Research and theory* (Vol. 2). New York: Academic.

Bauman, E. (1971). Schizophrenic short-term memory: The role of organization at input. *Journal of Consulting and Clinical Psychology, 36*, 14–19.

Bauman, E., & Murray, D.J. (1968). Recognition versus recall in schizophrenia. *Canadian Journal of Psychology, 22*, 18–25.

Beatty, J. (1982a). Phasic not tonic pupillary responses vary with auditory vigilance performance. *Psychophysiology, 19*, 167–172.

Beatty, J. (1982b). Task-evoked pupillary responses, processing load, and the structure of processing resources. *Psychological Bulletin, 91*, 276–292.

Bleuler, E. (1950). *Dementia praecox or the group of schizophrenias* (J. Zinkin, Trans.). New York: International Universities Press. (Original work published 1911).

Buchsbaum, M.S., Murphy, D.L., Coursey, R.D., Lake, C.R., & Ziegler, M.G. (1978). Platelet monoamine oxidase, plasma dopamine-beta-hydroxylase, and attention in a "biochemical high risk" sample. *Journal of Psychiatric Research, 14*, 215–224.

Chapman, L.J., Edell, W.S., & Chapman, J.P. (1980). Physical anhedonia, perceptual aberration, and psychosis proneness. *Schizophrenia Bulletin, 6*, 639–653.

Cornblatt, B., & Erlenmeyer-Kimling, L. (1984). Early attentional predictors of adolescent behavioral disturbances in children at risk for schizophrenia. In N.F. Watt, E.J. Anthony, L.C. Wynne, & J.E. Rolf (Eds.), *Children at risk for schizophrenia: A longitudinal perspective*. New York: Cambridge University Press.

Craik, F.I. (1970). The fate of primary memory items in free recall. *Journal of Verbal Learning and Verbal Behavior, 9*, 143–148.

Davies, D.R., & Parasuraman, R. (1982). *The psychology of vigilance*. London: Academic.

Depue, R.A., & Fowles, D.C. (1974). Conceptual ability, response interference, and arousal in withdrawn and active schizophrenics. *Journal of Consulting and Clinical Psychology, 42*, 509–518.

Diagnostic and statistical manual of mental disorders, 3rd. ed. (DSM-III). (1980). Washington, DC: American Psychiatric Association.

Diagnostic and statistical manual of mental disorders, 3rd. ed. rev. (DMS-IIIR). (1987) Washington, DC: American Psychiatric Association.

Erlenmeyer-Kimling, L., & Cornblatt, B. (1978). Attentional measures in a study of children at high risk for schizophrenia. In L.C. Wynne, R. Cromwell, & S. Matthysse (Eds.). *The nature of schizophrenia: New approaches to research and treatment*. New York: Wiley.

Estes, W.K., & Taylor, H.A. (1964). A detection method and pobabilistic models for assessing information processing from brief visual displays. *Proceedings of the National Academy of Sciences of the United States of America, 52*, 446–454.

Frame, C.L., & Oltmanns, T.F. (1982). Serial recall by schizophrenic and affective patients during and after psychotic episodes. *Journal of Abnormal Psychology, 91*, 311–318.

Frith, C.D. (1979). Consciousness, information processing and schizophrenia. *British Journal of Psychiatry, 134*, 225–235.

Garmezy, N. (1974). Children at risk: The search for the antecedents of schizophrenia. Part II. Ongoing research programs, issues, and intervention. *Schizophrenia Bulletin, 1*, (9), 55–125.

Gjerde, P.F. (1983). Attentional capacity dysfunction and arousal in schizophrenia. *Psychological Bulletin, 93*, 57–72.

Glanzer, M., & Cunitz, A.R. (1966). Two storage mechanisms in free recall. *Journal of Verbal Learning and Verbal Behavior, 5*, 351–360.

Gottesman, I.I. (1978). Schizophrenia and genetics: Where are we? Are you sure? In L.C. Wynne, Cromwell, R.L., & Matthysse, S. (Eds.), *The nature of schizophrenia: New approaches to research and treatment*. New York: Wiley.

Green, D.M., & Swets, J.A. (1966). *Signal detection theory and psychophysics*. New York: Wiley.

Grunebaum, H., Cohler, B.J., Kauffman, C., & Gallant, D. (1978). Children of depressed and schizophrenic mothers. *Child Psychiatry and Human Development, 8*, 219–228.

Hamilton, P., & Hockey, R. (1974). Active selection of items to be remembered: The role of timing. *Cognitive Psychology, 6*, 61–83.

Harvey, P., Winters, K., Weintraub, S., & Neale, J.M. (1981). Distractibility in children vulnerable to psychopathology. *Journal of Abnormal Psychology, 90*, 298–304.

Harvey, P.D., Weintraub, S., & Neale, J.M. (1985). Span of apprehension deficits in children vulnerable to psychopathology: A failure to replicate. *Journal of Abnormal Psychology, 94*, 410–413.

Hasher, L., & Zacks, R.T. (1979). Automatic and effortful processes in memory. *Journal of Experimental Psychology: General, 108*, 356–388.

Hemsley, D.R. (1977). What have cognitive deficits to do with schizophrenic symptoms? *British Journal of Psychiatry, 130*, 167–173.

Holzman, P.S., Levy, D.L., & Proctor, L.R. (1978). The several qualities attention in schizophrenia. *Journal of Psychiatric Research, 14*, 99–110.

Kahneman, D. (1973). *Attention and effort*. Englewood Cliffs, NJ: Prentice-Hall.

Kendler, K.S., Gruenberg, A.M., & Tsuang, M.T. (1985). Psychiatric illness in first-degree relatives of schizophrenic and surgical control patients. *Archives of General Psychiatry, 42*, 770–779.

Kietzman, M.L., Spring, B., & Zubin, J. (1980). Perception, cognition, and attention. In H.I.

Kaplan, A.M. Freedman, & B.J. Sadock (Eds.), *Comprehensive textbook of psychiatry* (3rd ed.). Baltimore: Williams and Wilkins.

Kintsch, W. (1970). Models for free recall and recognition. In D.A. Norman (Ed.), *Models of human memory*. New York: Academic.

Knight, R.A. (1984). Converging models of cognitive deficit in schizophrenia. In W.D. Spaulding & J.K. Cole (Eds.), *1983 Nebraska Symposium on motivation: Vol. 31. Theories of schizophrenia and psychosis*. Lincoln: University of Nebraska Press.

Koh, S.D., & Peterson, R.A. (1978). Encoding orientation and the remembering of schizophrenic young adults. *Journal of Abnormal Psychology, 87*, 303–313.

Koh, S.D., Kayton, L., & Berry, R. (1973). Mnemonic organization in young nonpsychotic schizophrenics. *Journal of Abnormal Psychology, 81*, 299–310.

Koh, S.D., Kayton, L., & Schwartz, C. (1974). The structure of word storage in the permanent memory of non-psychotic schizophrenics. *Journal of Consulting and Clinical Psychology, 42*, 879–887.

Koh, S.D., Kayton, L., & Peterson, R.A. (1976). Affective encoding and subsequent remembering in schizophrenic young adults. *Journal of Abnormal Psychology, 85*, 156–166.

Koh, S.D., Marusary, T.Z., & Rosen, A.J. (1980). Remembering of sentences by schizophrenic young adults. *Journal of Abnormal Psychology, 89*, 291–294.

Koh, S.D., Grinker, R.R., Marusary, T.Z., & Foreman, P.L. (1981). Affective memory and schizophrenic anhedonia. *Schizophrenia Bulletin, 7*, 292–307.

Kornetsky, C. (1972). The use of a simple test of attention as a measure of drug effects in schizophrenic patients. *Psychopharmacologia, 24*, 99–106.

Kornetsky, C., & Orzack, M.H. (1978). Physiologic and behavioral correlates of attention dysfunction in schizophrenic patients. In L.C. Wynne, R.L. Cromwell, & S. Matthysse (Eds.), *The nature of schizophrenia: New approaches to research and treatment*. New York: Wiley.

Kraepelin, E. (1919). *Dementia praecox and paraphrenia*. (R.M. Barclay, Trans.). Edinburgh: Livingston. (Original work published 1913).

Larsen, S.F., & Fromholt, P. (1976). Mnemonic organization and free recall in schizophrenia. *Journal of Abnormal Psychology, 85*, 61–65.

Larsen, S.F., McGhie, A., & Chapman, J. (1964). Perception of speech in schizophrenia. *British Journal of Psychiatry, 110*, 375–380.

Liberman, R.P. (1986). Coping and competence as protective factors in the vulnerability-stress model of schizophrenia. In M.J. Goldstein, I. Hand, & K. Hahlweg (Eds.), *Treatment of schizophrenia: Family assessment and intervention*. Berlin, Heidelberg, New York: Springer.

Lutz, J., & Marsh, T.K. (1981). The effects of a dual level word list on schizophrenic free recall. *Schizophrenia Bulletin, 7*, 509–717.

Maher, B.A. (1972). The language of schizophrenia: A review and interpretation. *British Journal of Psychiatry, 120*, 4–17.

Maher, B.A. (1983). A tentative theory of schizophrenic utterance. *Progress in Experimental Personality Research, 12*, 1–52.

McNicol, D. (1972). *A primer of signal detection theory*. London: Allen and Unwin.

Mednick, S.A., & McNeil, T.F. (1968). Current methodology in research on the etiology of schizophrenia: Serious difficulties which suggest the use of the high-risk group method. *Psychological Bulletin, 70*, 681–693.

Nachmani, G., & Cohen, B.D., (1969). Recall and recognition free learning in schizophrenia. *Journal of Abnormal Psychology, 74*, 511–516.

Neale, J.M. (1971). Perceptual span in schizophrenia. *Journal of Abnormal Psychology, 77*, 196–204.

Neale, J.M., & Harvey, P.D. (1985). Span of apprehension deficits in vulnerable children: Further comments. *Journal of Abnormal Psychology, 94*, 418–419.

Neale, J.M., McIntyre, C.W., Fox, R., & Cromwell, R.L. (1969). Span of apprehension in acute schizophrenics. *Journal of Abnormal Psychology, 74*, 593–596.

Nuechterlein, K.H. (1983). Signal detection in vigilance tasks and behavioral attributes among offspring of schizophrenic mothers and among hyperactive children. *Journal of Abnormal Psychology, 92*, 4–28.

Nuechterlein, K.H. (1985). Converging evidence for vigilance deficit as a vulnerability indicator for schizophrenic disorders. In M. Alpert (Ed.), *Controversies in schizophrenia: Changes and constancies*. New York: Guildford.

Nuechterlein, K.H. (1987). Vulnerability models for schizophrenia: State of the art. In H. Hafner, W.F. Gattaz, & W. Janzarik (Eds.), *Search for the causes of schizophrenia*. Berlin, Heidelberg, New York: Springer.

Nuechterlein, K.H., & Dawson, M.E. (1984a). A heuristic vulnerability/stress model of schizophrenic episodes. *Schizophrenia Bulletin, 10*, 300–312.

Nuechterlein, K.H., & Dawson, M.E. (1984b). Information processing and attentional functioning in the developmental course of schizophrenic disorders. *Schizophrenia Bulletin, 10*, 160–203.

Nuechterlein, K.H., Parasuraman, R., & Jiang, Q. (1983). Visual sustained attention: Image degradation produces rapid sensitivity decrement over time. *Science, 220*, 327–329.

Nuechterlein, K.H., Edell, W.S., Norris, M., & Dawson, M.E. (1986). Attentional vulnerability indicators, thought disorder, and negative symptoms. *Schizophrenia Bulletin, 12*, 408–426.

Oltmanns, T.F. (1978). Selective attention in schizophrenic and manic psychosis: The effect of distraction on information processing. *Journal of Abnormal Psychology, 87*, 212–225.

Orzack, M.H., & Kornetsky, C. (1966). Attention dysfunction in chronic schizophrenia. *Archives of General Psychiatry, 14*, 323–326.

Parasuraman, R. (1979). Memory load and event rate control sensitivity decrements in sustained attention. *Science, 205*, 924–927.

Posner, M.I. (1978). *Chronometric explorations of mind.* Hillsdale, NJ: Erlbaum.

Posner, M.I., & Snyder, C.R.R. (1975). Attention and cognitive control. In R.L. Solso (Ed.), *Information processing and cognition: The Loyola Symposium*. Hillsdale, NJ: Erlbaum.

Rosvold, H.E., Mirsky, A., Sarason, I., Bransome, E.D. Jr., & Beck, L.H. (1956). A continuous performance test of brain damage. *Journal of Consulting Psychology, 20*, 343–350.

Russell, P.N., & Beekhuis, M.E. (1976). Organization in memory: A comparison of psychotics and normals. *Journal of Abnormal Psychology, 85*, 527–534.

Russell, P.N., Bannatyne, P.A., & Smith, J.F. (1975). Associative strength as a mode of organization in recall and recognition: A comparison of schizophrenics and normals. *Journal of Abnormal Psychology, 84*, 122–128.

Rutschmann, J., Cornblatt, B., & Erlenmeyer-Kimling, L. (1977). Sustained attention in children at risk for schizophrenia: Report on a continuous performance test. *Archives of General Psychiatry, 34*, 571–575.

Rutschmann, J., Cornblatt, B., & Erlenmeyer-Kimling, L. (1986). Sustained attention in children at risk for schizophrenia: Findings with two visual continuous performance tests in a new sample. *Journal of Abnormal Child Psychology, 14*, 365–385.

Schneider, W., Dumais, S.T., & Shiffrin, R.M. (1984). Automatic and control processing and attention. In R. Parasuraman & D.R. Davies (Eds.), *Varieties of attention* (pp. 1–27). Orlando, FL: Academic.

Shiffrin, R.M. & Schneider, W. (1977). Controlled and automatic human information processing. II. Perceptual learning, automatic attending, and a general theory. *Psychological Review, 84*, 127–190.

Spence, J.T., & Lair, C.V. (1964). Associative interference in the verbal learning performance of schizophrenics and normals. *Journal of Abnormal and Social Psychology, 68*, 204–209.

Steronko, R.J., & Woods, D.J. (1978). Impairment in early stages of visual information processing in nonpsychotic schizotypal individuals. *Journal of Abnormal Psychology, 87*, 481–490.

Sykes, D.H., Douglas, V.I., & Morgenstern, G. (1973). Sustained attention in hyperactive children. *Journal of Child Psychology and Psychiatry, 44*, 267–273.

Traupmann, K.L. (1980). Encoding processes and memory for categorially related words by schizophrenic patients. *Journal of Abnormal Psychology, 89*, 704–716.

Wohlberg, G.W., & Kornetsky, C. (1973). Sustained attention in remitted schizophrenics. *Archives of General Psychiatry, 28*, 533–537.

Zubin, J., & Spring, B. (1977). Vulnerability – A new view of schizophrenia. *Journal of Abnormal Psychology, 86*, 103–126.

Vulnerabilities to Schizophrenia: Information-Processing Markers

B. Spring, M. Lemon, and P. Fergeson

The search for a fundamental anomaly in the way schizophrenics process information has a history that dates back to Bleuler (1911/1950) and Kraepelin (1913/1919). Inpatients reliably exhibit many processing deviations. Studies of other populations have been necessary, however, to determine whether these deviations reflect more than iatrogenic effects of treatment or consequences of the stress accompanying symptom exacerbation. One research strategy has been to separate disturbances that are episode markers (i.e., deviations that emerge with psychotic exacerbation and that normalize when psychosis remits) from more enduring characteristics that are vulnerability markers (i.e., deviations that precede the episode, persist after symptoms have remitted, and appear in a significant subgroup of patients' relatives). Vulnerability markers are likely to be indicators of the predisposition to schizophrenia, since they occur in individuals who are vulnerable to schizophrenia but not actively symptomatic (Cromwell & Spaulding, 1978; Spring & Zubin, 1978; Zubin & Spring, 1977).

Heterogeneous Vulnerabilities

So far the search for markers has been guided by the hypothesis that there is a single diathesis for schizophrenia. Schizophrenics differ, however, in whether or not they manifest information-processing anomalies (Freedman & Chapman, 1973), and the anomalies they do exhibit are often uncorrelated (Asarnow & MacCrimmon, 1978; Kopfstein & Neale, 1972). Moreover, findings increasingly suggest that schizophrenia is heterogeneous in clinical expression, course, and probably etiology (Buchsbaum & Rieder, 1979; Crow, 1980; Kety, 1980). If so, vulnerabilities to schizophrenia and their laboratory markers may also be heterogeneous. By analogy vulnerability research to date can be likened to a quest for the single source of the Nile – overlooking the possibility that a disorder embracing as many tributaries as schizophrenia may have more than a single source.

Florid, positive, or psychotic symptoms (e.g., hallucinations, delusions, thought disorganization) are emphasized by the *Diagnostic and Statistical Manual of Mental Disorders*, 3rd revised edition (DSM-IIIR; 1987) and many research diagnostic criteria (e.g., Research Diagnostic Criteria, RDC). Other negative or deficit symptoms (e.g., flattened affect) also appear in many schizophrenic patients and are uncorrelated with positive symptoms (Pogue-Geile & Harrow, 1984). The etiology of negative symptoms remains controversial. One proposal (Zubin, 1985) is that they reflect premorbid personality features; another (Wing & Brown, 1970) is that they are after-effects of the schizophrenic illness and its treatment. A third proposal (Crow, 1980) is that positive and negative symptoms result from different pathophysiological processes which result in different psychological manifestations and pharmacologic responses. Crow suggests that a disturbance in dopaminergic neurotransmission (type I) gives rise to neuroleptic-responsive positive symptoms, and that a progressive dementia leading to a loss of viable dopaminergic neurons (type II) results in negative symptoms that are not improved – and sometimes even worsened – by neuroleptics (Johnstone, Crow, Frith, Husband, & Kreel, 1976).

Recent findings suggest that specific processing deviations correlate selectively with either positive or negative symptoms (Cornblatt, Lenzenweger, Dworkin, & Erlenmeyer-Kimling, 1985; Green & Walker, 1985; Nuechterlein, Edell, Norris, & Dawson, 1986). One hypothesis that could accommodate these findings is that the deviations indicate discrete causal processes that give rise to vulnerabilities to different symptoms. As a heuristic device, we propose an elaboration of the original (Spring & Zubin, 1978; Zubin & Spring, 1977) criteria for vulnerability markers to specify whether processing deviations indicate vulnerability to positive or negative symptoms. Table 1 gives three criteria for determining whether a deviation is a positive or negative symptom-linked marker, and two additional criteria for establishing whether the deviation is a vulnerability marker.

Positive symptom-linked markers should:

- Be correlated with the severity of positive symptoms.
- Be improved by the administration of neuroleptics.
- Show episodic state fluctuations, worsening with positive symptom exacerbations and lessening with symptom remission.

Table 1. Criteria for positive and negative symptom-linked vulnerability markers

Positive	Negative
Symptom linkage criteria	
1. Correlation with positive symptoms	1. Correlation with negative symptoms
2. Improvement with neuroleptics	2. No effect or adverse effect of neuroleptics
3. Episodic fluctuation with positive symptom exacerbation and remission	3. No episodic fluctuation with positive symptom exacerbation and remission
Vulnerability criteria	
4. Persistence in remitted patients	4. Persistence in remitted patients
5. Deviation in relatives of patients with marked positive symptoms	5. Deviation in relatives of patients with marked negative symptoms

If the deviation is also a marker of vulnerability to positive symptoms, it should:

- Persist in clinically improved patients.
- Appear in a subgroup of relatives of those patients who are characterized by marked positive symptoms.

Although it seems paradoxical that positive symptom-linked deviations should both lessen with clinical improvement and persist in remitted patients, both findings are expected. Because the processing impairment lessens as positive symptoms subside, the degree of deviation in remitted patients or relatives should be less than that produced by the dual influences of vulnerability and an episode of florid psychosis. Nonetheless, a smaller impairment should persist, and differentiate vulnerable populations from normal controls who are not at risk.[1] A further point is that positive symptom-linked markers may show imperfect diagnostic specificity because some nonschizophrenic patients (and a subgroup of their relatives) are also predisposed to neuroleptic-responsive psychotic symptoms. Even so, positive symptom-linked markers should be more prevalent among active and remitted schizophrenics and their relatives than psychiatric controls, since all schizophrenics meeting current diagnostic criteria are predisposed to psychosis, as contrasted with only a minority of patients with other (e.g., affective) diagnoses.

In contrast, negative symptom-linked markers should:

- Be correlated with the severity of negative symptoms.
- Be unaffected or slightly adversely affected by the administration of neuroleptics.
- To the extent that they are exclusively associated with negative symptoms, performance on this second category of markers should not be affected by exacerbations of florid positive symptoms.

Deviations linked only to negative symptoms fail to meet the criteria for episode markers; if patients' deficit symptoms remain stable, performance should not decline when positive symptoms emerge. To qualify as an indicator of vulnerability to negative symptoms, the deviation should also occur in:

- Remitted patients.
- A subgroup of relatives of patients characterized by marked negative symptoms.

---

[1] Not all positive symptom-linked markers remain deviant in clinically improved patients. If the processing deviation is purely an episode indicator, performance will normalize as psychotic symptoms abate. In contrast, if the deviation is an indicator of positive symptom-linked vulnerability, performance will remain somewhat deviant. Our distinction between episode indicators versus positive symptom-linked vulnerability markers resembles Nuechterlein and Dawson's (1984a) differentiation between symptom indicators versus mediating vulnerability factors. Nuechterlein and Dawson's mediating vulnerability factors are, in our framework, positive symptom-linked vulnerability markers. Their stable vulnerability indicators may, in our terms, be negative symptom-linked vulnerability markers.

If laboratory information-processing measures do, in fact, mark different vulnerabilities, the study of relatives becomes more complex. Relatives of schizophrenics are heterogeneous in the likelihood that they will possess a predisposition to schizophrenia at all, in the kinds of schizophrenic manifestations to which they may be predisposed, and, finally, in their actual risk for developing symptoms. Offspring and first-degree relatives of a schizophrenic person share, on average, 50% of the proband's genes, but only 10% $\pm$4% will become schizophrenic themselves. Most of this latter group of most vulnerable relatives will be excluded from studies of adult relatives of schizophrenics to avoid contaminating the at-risk sample with ill or formerly ill cases. Because negative symptoms are omitted from current diagnostic criteria for schizophrenia, not all schizophrenic patients will be vulnerable to this process, nor show its laboratory markers.

Considering only the patients who do show negative symptom-linked markers, similar deviations can be expected in approximately 50% of their first-degree relatives if the deviations indicate a genetic predisposition, and in a much smaller proportion if the markers are more closely associated with the partial phenotypic expression of symptoms. In light of this picture of diminishing proportions, analyses more powerful than group mean comparisons are warranted to test for deviations predicted in such small minorities of relatives. Comparisons of extreme groups of very poorly performing high risk subjects and controls (Nuechterlein, 1983), correlational analyses comparing the performance of patients and their relatives (Spring, 1985), and studies of relatives of patients preselected for exhibiting a laboratory marker (DeAmicis & Cromwell, 1979) all warrant special attention, as discussed below.

Information Processing Markers of Vulnerability

Four well-studied information-processing markers hold promise as vulnerability markers: distractibility, short-term verbal memory impairments, reaction-time deficits, and vigilance deficits measured by the continuous performance test (CPT). Findings suggest that distractibility and verbal memory deficits meet many criteria for positive symptom-linked vulnerability markers. In contrast, deficits in sustained attention, measured by reaction time and the CPT, appear sensitive to processes generating negative symptoms. Although not discussed here because of space limitations, deviations in smooth pursuit eye movements are another promising negative symptom-linked vulnerability marker (Holzman, Levy, & Proctor, 1978). After evaluating the diagnostic specificity of each marker, we review findings on whether each processing deviation occurs in first-degree relatives of schizophrenics.

Distractibility

Much evidence indicates that schizophrenics have diminished capacity to maintain a figure-ground relationship between relevant and irrelevant impinging stimulation (cf. Payne, Hochberg, & Hawks, 1970; Wishner & Wahl, 1974). Their impairment may reflect difficulties in filtering out distracting physical stimuli, suppressing responses to irrelevant meanings, or allocating processing capacity preferentially to a primary task.

Distractibility assessments can be grouped into two main categories: immediate response tests and delayed response tests. *Immediate response tests* evaluate the degree to which distractors presented simultaneously with target stimuli disrupt responses to targets. Measures include:

- Shadowing tests in which subjects continuously repeat back a string of verbal stimuli presented with and without a distracting message.
- The information overload test (IOT) (Cornblatt & Erlenmeyer-Kimling, 1984), in which intermittent auditory distraction occurs while subjects select a picture that matches a spoken target word.
- Distractor versions of the CPT, in which intermittent auditory or visual distractors occur as subjects search for targets interspersed amid a continuous series of visual stimuli.

Delayed response tests of distractibility assess the degree to which distractors presented in temporal proximity to target stimuli disrupt later recall of these targets. On span tests, for example, subjects hear short strings of target words or digits with and without competing stimuli and then recall the targets in correct order (Oltmanns & Neale, 1975). Because more than one target must be retained in short-term memory for an interval before recall, delayed response measures impose a greater memory load than do immediate response tests of distractibility.

Status as a Positive Symptom-Linked Marker

Distractibility is most pronounced in less chronic patients (Oltmanns, Ohayon, & Neale, 1978) and has been correlated with a positive symptom, formal thought disorder, in relatively acute (Oltmanns et al., 1978) but not more chronic schizophrenics (Manschreck, Maher, Weisstein, Shapiro, Ames, & Dorsey, 1989). Although paranoid schizophrenics present some signs that they allocate greater than normal attention to distractors, distraction does not actually impair their performance (Finkelstein, 1983; Rund, 1982/83; Spring, 1985). As expected of a positive symptom-linked marker, distractibility is somewhat more pronounced in schizophrenics than in affective controls, but it is not entirely specific to schizophrenia. Manic patients especially (Oltmanns, 1978), and sometimes patients with major depression (Cornblatt et al., 1985), also show heightened distractibility in proportion to their florid positive symptoms (Cornblatt et al., 1985; Spring, 1985).

Distractibility meets two criteria for a positive symptom-linked marker with inconsistent evidence for the third criterion. First, the degree of distractibility covaries with the severity of positive and not negative symptoms (Cornblatt et al., 1985; Oltmanns et al., 1978; Spring, 1985). Secondly, lessened distractibility accompanies adequate treatment with neuroleptics (Oltmanns et al., 1978; Pigache & Norris, 1973; Strauss, Lew, Coyle, & Tune, 1985). Although some investigators find that distractibility lessens in clinically improved patients (Pigache & Norris, 1973; Blum, Livingston, & Shader, 1969), others (Asarnow & MacCrimmon, 1978; Frame & Oltmanns, 1982) find little change, rendering the sensitivity of distractibility to changes in clinical state unclear.

Status as a Marker of Vulnerability to Positive Symptoms

To our knowledge, there have been only three studies of distractibility in remitted patients. Two used the CPT, with one (Wohlberg & Kornetsky, 1973) finding that remitted schizophrenics show a specific differential deficit due to distraction, and the other finding a slightly but not significantly greater impairment with distraction than without (Asarnow & MacCrimmon, 1978). The third study (Frame & Oltmanns, 1982) examined clinically improved schizophrenics prior to hospital discharge and found that a tendency toward distractibility (large in magnitude but nonsignificant with this small sample of eight) persisted. Clinically improved schizophrenics, therefore, remain at least somewhat distractible.

Although results have all been in the predicted direction, high-risk children have only inconsistently been found significantly more distractible than controls. Two likely explanations concern problems in devising tests of appropriate difficulty for multiple age groups and the low statistical power of the group mean comparisons used in all studies. Three studies involved immediate response tests of distractibility. Asarnow, Steffy, MacCrimmon, and Cleghorn (1978) failed to find impairments on a competing voices test among a small sample of foster home-reared adolescents whose mothers had been hospitalized for schizophrenia. Differences did approach significance, however, in the most difficult experimental condition. Comparing the IOT performance of children of a schizophrenic parent to normal controls, Cornblatt and Erlenmeyer-Kimling (1984) did find the high-risk children significantly more adversely affected by both noise and voice distractors. On CPT performance with and without distraction, high-risk children from the same sample were more than normally susceptible to distraction in some (Erlenmeyer-Kimling & Cornblatt, 1978; Rutschmann, Cornblatt, & Erlenmeyer-Kimling, 1977), but not all analyses (Cornblatt & Erlenmeyer-Kimling, 1985).

Findings with delayed response tests of distractibility have also been directionally consistent, but not always significant. In one study, preadolescent and adolescent offspring of a schizophrenic parent heard very short distractor span items. Although the high-risk group recalled fewer target digits than controls, the differences were small and nonsignificant (Orvaschel, Mednick, Schulsinger, & Rock, 1979). In a similar study administering longer neutral and distractor span tests to 7–12-year-old children of a schizophrenic parent, Cornblatt and Erlenmeyer-Kimling (1984) failed to find a differential deficit due to distraction.

Since the distractor items produced a very marked performance decline in all the children, they may have been too difficult for this age group. In a third study of children aged 6–16 years (Winters, Stone, Weintraub, & Neale, 1981), both children of schizophrenics and children of unipolar depressed patients performed worse than normal controls on the distractor span tests, with the children of schizophrenics showing a slightly but not significantly greater performance decrement with distraction. Children of a bipolar parent did not differ from controls. Examining this sample's older, 13–18-year-old, children, for whom span tests were matched on discriminating power, Harvey, Winters, Weintraub, and Neale (1981) derived the same results. Children of schizophrenics were unique, however, in that distraction disrupted the primacy effect, the usual advantage for words presented early in a memory list. Distraction apparently prevented the capacity-demanding mental rehearsal needed to recall early list items. In fact, with rehearsal demands greatly increased by lengthening the list to 15, Driscoll (1984) found that only children of schizophrenics showed a significant recall decrement due to distraction.

In what is, to our knowledge, the only study of distractibility in adult first-degree relatives of schizophrenics, Spring (1985) compared the shadowing performance of parents and siblings of schizophrenics, bipolar and unipolar affective patients, and normal controls. These adult relatives showed neither generalized deficits in repeating a verbal message, nor specific deficits due to distractibility. The relatives of schizophrenics did, however, exceed normal controls in intrusions, interjecting phonemes from a distracting message. The number of intrusions was also significantly correlated between schizophrenic patients and their family members, and not for the other diagnostic groups, as would be expected if distractibility is a familially transmitted vulnerability marker for schizophrenia.

Given the limited statistical power of the analyses used in most studies, the findings show sufficient directional consistency to encourage further research on distractibility as a positive symptom-linked vulnerability marker. The overlapping performance distributions of relatives of schizophrenics and psychiatric controls may arise because some relatives of affective patients are also predisposed to florid psychosis.

Short-Term Verbal Memory

Short-term memory is an intermediate process in the information-processing sequence, preceded by the sensory register and followed by the larger capacity long-term memory store (Atkinson & Shiffrin, 1968). Two major categories of short-term memory assessment are tests of *recognition*, which require only encoding and storage, and tests of *recall*, which in addition require active rehearsal and retrieval of test items. In recognition testing, the subject receives a training list of verbal stimuli and must then identify these "old" stimuli from a second test list including both "old " and "new" stimuli. In recall testing, by contrast, no second list follows the training list, and subjects must retrieve the items directly from short-term memory. Two kinds of recall procedures are widely used: *memory span tests* and *free recall tests*. In memory span a limited number of items (usually no more than eight) is presented for subsequent recall in the originally given sequence (serial recall). Whereas later list items can be recalled passively or automatically from sensory storage, earlier items require active rehearsal or recoding in order to be retained. More demanding recall tests present a large number of items (more than ten) to be remembered, but permit subjects to recall them in any order (free recall).

Status as a Positive Symptom-Linked Marker

Recall memory impairments appear reliably in schizophrenic patients, as do recognition impairments when tests of adequate psychometric discriminating power are used (cf. Calev, 1984). The recall impairment of schizophrenics tends to exceed that of depressed patients (Frame & Oltmanns, 1982), but not manics (Oltmanns, 1978).

Like distractibility, verbal memory deficits meet two criteria for positive symptom-linked markers, with insufficient evidence to evaluate the third criterion. First, verbal memory impairment specifically covaries with the severity of positive symptoms and is uncorrelated with negative symptoms (Green & Walker, 1985). Secondly, recall deficits are sensitive to changes in the florid psychotic state. When tested on memory span shortly after hospitalization and retested after clinical improvement, schizophrenics, unlike depressed patients, showed significant improvements in recall (Frame & Oltmanns, 1982). Inconsistent with the criteria for positive symptom-linked markers, neuroleptics have not been found to appreciably benefit the recall of schizophrenic patients (Pearl, 1962). However, since anticholinergic drugs, given to attenuate neuroleptic-induced extrapyramidal side effects, have adverse effects on recall memory (Baker, Cheng, & Amara, 1983; Calev, 1984; Potamianos & Kellet, 1982; Tune, Strauss, Lew, Breitlinger, & Coyle, 1982), it may be that a beneficial neuroleptic effect has been masked.

Status as a Marker of Vulnerability to Positive Symptoms

As expected of a vulnerability marker, recall impairment persists in clinically improved schizophrenic patients (Frame & Oltmanns, 1982). Verbal memory deficits also appear in children of schizophrenics, although, again, differences based on group mean comparisons reach significance only inconsistently.

Testing memory span for six items paced at one per 2 s, neither Harvey et al. (1981) nor Winters et al. (1981) found significant differences between high-risk children and controls, although the high-risk children performed somewhat more poorly. In contrast, with lists paced twice as fast, or with longer lists, high-risk children showed significant deficits in serial recall (Erlenmeyer-Kimling & Cornblatt, 1978; Cornblatt & Erlenmeyer-Kimling, 1984). High-risk children have also shown impairments in recognition, especially when test items are difficult to encode (Cornblatt & Erlenmeyer-Kimling, 1984; Rutschmann, Cornblatt & Erlenmeyer-Kimling, 1980). On the other hand, no differences emerged on a test of intentional learning (Driscoll, 1984), perhaps because subjects could control the pacing of the task and thus compensate for subtle deficits (Nuechterlein & Dawson, 1984b).

Although short-term verbal memory impairments are promising markers of vulnerability to positive symptoms, this inference should not be generalized to visual memory, because nonverbal memory deficits covary with the severity of negative symptoms (Green & Walker, 1985).

Reaction Time

In simple reaction time (RT) tests of attention (e.g., crossover and crossmodal tests) response speed is timed while the subject performs a fingerlift response as rapidly as possible. *Crossover* tasks vary the length and regularity of the preparatory interval (PI) that begins with the ready signal and ends with the imperative signal to respond. Some trials involve a series of PIs that are identical in length, making the timing of the imperative signal predictable. Other trials involve PIs that vary in length, making the imperative signal unpredictable. Normal subjects profit from the regularity of the PIs and respond faster to the regular than the irregular series until the PIs become very long. Schizophrenics, however, lose the advantage of the regular series before PIs reach approximately 7 s. At a PI duration of 7 s or less, their response curves for the regular and irregular series meet or cross over, because reactions to irregular trials become just as fast or even faster than reactions to regular trials.

Early crossover suggests an inability to sustain attention and maintain a set to respond at regular intervals (Huston, Shakow, & Riggs, 1937). After using a slightly different procedure, Bellissimo and Steffy (1972) concluded that crossover could reflect a specific deficit in reacting to redundancy. Usually all of the regular PI trials are presented first with PIs of increasing duration and are followed by the irregular series. Bellissimo and Steffy (1972), however, administered an embedded set version of the task in which short sequences of four regular trials (isotemporal sets) were embedded within the irregular series. Response times grew longer with each subsequent trial of the isotemporal set, demonstrating the redundancy-associated deficit: a progressively greater slowing in response to regularity.

Another simple RT paradigm, the *crossmodal* procedure, assesses the ability to shift attention from one modality to another. Sound and light imperative stimuli are presented in alternation (crossmodally) and in sequences involving the same modality (ipsimodally). Crossmodal retardation, the greater lengthening of RT to crossmodal as compared to ipsimodal sequences, indexes the degree of difficulty in shifting attention.

Status as a Negative Symptom-Linked Marker

Overall response speed is a highly nonspecific measure, slowed in many diagnostic groups (Rosofsky, Levin, & Holzman, 1982; Spring, 1980) and affected by many different processes. Positive symptoms (King, 1954; Spohn, Coyne, Lacoursiere, Mazur, & Haynes, 1985), generalized deficits, tardive dyskinesia, and brain damage (Olbrich, 1972; Spohn et al., 1985) are all accompanied by slowed RT. Nor do neuroleptics produce consistent effects on response speed. Some evidence suggests facilitation (Brooks & Weaver, 1961; Spohn, Larcoursiere, Thompson, & Coyne, 1977), other evidence suggests no influence (Held, Cromwell, Frank, & Fann, 1970), and some evidence even suggests that high-dose neuroleptics may slow RT by inducing abnormal involuntary movements (Spohn et al., 1985).

Crossmodal retardation is also found in several diagnostic groups, perhaps slightly more consistently in schizophrenics. Spring (1980) found that schizophrenics showed greater than normal retardation with shifts from both sound to light and light to sound. For depressed patients, crossmodal retardation exceeded normal only when the shift was from light to sound.

Very early crossover has, among psychiatric patients, shown greater specificity for schizophrenia (Bohannon & Strauss, 1983), although it can appear in organic conditions (Greiffenstein, Milberg, Lewis, & Rosebaum, 1981) or aging (Botwinick, Brinley, & Robbin, 1959; Strauss, Wagman, & Quaid, 1983). Early crossover is most prevalent in chronic process schizophrenics (Bellissimo & Steffy, 1972; Steffy & Galbraith, 1974; Zahn & Rosenthal, 1965): on the embedded set procedure 42%–72% of process patients exhibit strong early crossover.

Unlike other laboratory markers reviewed so far, early crossover meets at least two criteria for a negative symptom-linked marker. First, crossover is unaffected by neuroleptics (Spohn et al., 1977; Wynne & Kornetsky, 1960). Secondly, crossover is not responsive to changes in the florid psychotic state (Zahn & Carpenter, 1978). Although correlations with negative symptoms have not been examined, crossover is most prevalent in the patient subgroups most likely to show brain ventricular enlargement (Andreason, 1982; Johnstone et al., 1976; Weinbergber, Cannon-Spoor, Potkin, & Wyatt, 1980), a sign that may be correlated with negative symptoms.

Status as a Marker of Vulnerability to Negative Symptoms

Early findings by Marcus (1973) suggested that RT slowing might be a vulnerability marker. Children in grades 5–8 who had been born to schizophrenic mothers showed slower than normal RT across all PIs in both the regular and irregular series. Moreover, their RT remained significantly slowed under reward and informational conditions designed to facilitate performance. Relatives of schizophrenics showed significantly slowed RT in one other study. Adult siblings of patients reacted more slowly than normal on a choice RT task (Wood & Cook, 1979). In another study of adults, Van Dyke, Rosenthal, and Rasmussen (1975) examined all four combinations of: (a) rearing by a schizophrenic parent; and (b) being the offspring of a schizophrenic parent. Regardless of whether they were biologically related to a schizophrenic parent, subjects who were reared by a schizophrenic showed slowed RT. Four other studies failed to find significant slowing in relatives of schizophrenics. In one (Asarnow et al., 1978), results were in the direction of slower RT in children of schizophrenics, but in three other studies of both children and adults, the mean RTs of relatives and controls were virtually identical (DeAmicis & Cromwell, 1979; Phipps-Yonas, 1984; Spring, 1980).

Like mean RT, crossmodal retardation has not proved to be a promising vulnerability marker. Neither child (Phipps-Yonas, 1984) nor adult (Spring, 1980) relatives of schizophrenics have shown greater than normal crossmodal retardation.

Although early crossover is an enduring phenomenon in outpatients (Bohannon & Strauss, 1983), crossover has failed to emerge in two studies of children of schizophrenics (Asarnow et al., 1978; Marcus, 1973) and one study of adult offspring (Van Dyke et al., 1975). Crossover did, however, significantly differentiate adult relatives of schizophrenics from normal controls in one study (DeAmicis & Cromwell, 1979). The DeAmicis and Cromwell study was unique in two respects. First, the investigators used the embedded set paradigm. This technique may differ importantly from the traditional crossover RT procedure, since it also revealed early crossover in another sample identified as high risk on the basis of personality features (Simons, MacMillan, & Ireland, 1982). Secondly, DeAmicis and Cromwell accepted only process patients who demonstrated early crossover and tested their relatives, maximizing the likelihood that relatives, if predisposed to schizophrenia, would possess the kind of vulnerability marked by early crossover. If crossover is a negative symptom-linked vulnerability marker, such powerful methodologies may be necessary to detect significant differences between high-risk populations and controls. Only relatives of the subgroup of patients predisposed to negative symptoms would be expected to exhibit negative symptom-linked markers themselves, creating an effect easily lost in the variance for the entire group of relatives of schizophrenics.

Continuous Performance Test

Like crossover RT and shadowing without distraction, the CPT tests sustained attention. More specifically, it tests vigilance for visual targets. Several adaptations of the task exist: a conventional version using a single clearly focused target (Rosvold, Mirsky, Sarason, Bransome, & Beck, 1956) and modified versions to increase the task's difficulty. Difficulty has been increased in three ways: by adding distraction, by adding a memory load, or by stimulus degradation. The memory load CPT uses a designated target sequence rather than a single target. The sequence may involve two identical stimuli (e.g., two playing cards identical in number and suit) or a sequence of different stimuli (e.g., A–X or 3–7). The degraded stimulus CPT burdens the early information processing stages of encoding and recognition by presenting stimuli out of focus, partially masked, and at high tachistoscopic speeds (Nuechterlein, Parasuraman, & Jiang, 1983).

Status as a Negative Symptom-Linked Marker

As on other measures of sustained attention (e.g., shadowing without distraction, crossover RT), schizophrenics perform less well than psychiatric controls on the CPT (Orzack & Kornetsky, 1966; Walker, 1981). Only a subgroup (40%–50%) of actively symptomatic schizophrenic patients show marked CPT impairments (Orzack & Kornetsky, 1966, 1971; Walker, 1981) and these tend to have a family history of schizophrenia (Orzack & Kornetsky, 1966; Walker & Shaye, 1982).

CPT performance deficits covary with negative symptoms and are uncorrelated with delusions and hallucinations (Nuechterlein et al., 1986). Also consistent with citeria for a negative symptom-linked marker, CPT performance is apparently unaffected by changes in the acute psychotic state. Asarnow and MacCrimmon (1978) found no significant differences in the number of targets missed by actively psychotic and clinically remitted schizophrenics. Some joint influence of a positive symptom-linked process is suggested, however, by the fact that neuroleptic medications improve schizophrenics' performance on the CPT (Orzack, Kornetsky, & Freeman, 1967; Spohn et al., 1977) and by a correlation (albeit inconsistent) between CPT performance and formal thought disorder (Nuechterlein et al., 1986). The latter result highlights the need to examine associations between information-processing deviations and specific positive and negative symptoms, since some controversy still surrounds the assignment of particular symptoms to each dimension (Sommers, 1985).

Status as a Marker of Vulnerability to Negative Symptoms

Deficits do persist in relatively asymptomatic schizophrenics on demanding versions of the CPT (Asarnow & MacCrimmon, 1978; Wohlberg & Kornetsky, 1973). CPT impairments also emerge consistently in the offspring of schizophrenics, even though differences are not always significant with mean comparison procedures. The conventional CPT usually fails to discriminate high-risk children from controls (Asarnow et al., 1978; Grunebaum, Cohler,

Kauffman, & Gallant, 1978; Nuechterlein, 1983) unless the children are very young (cf. Grunebaum, Weiss, Gallant, & Cohler, 1974). The more demanding memory load CPT has detected impairments in older children at risk even with group mean comparison procedures (Cornblatt & Erlenmeyer-Kimling, 1985; Erlenmeyer-Kimling & Cornblatt, 1978; Rutschmann et al., 1977). The degraded stimulus CPT is also a discriminating procedure with extreme group comparisons, in which it isolates a disproportionately large subgroup of very poor performers among children of schizophrenics (Nuechterlein, 1983).

Conclusions

In light of evidence suggesting the possibility of more than a single diathesis for schizophrenia, we propose new criteria for determining whether an information-processing deviation marks vulnerability to the positive or negative symptoms of schizophrenia. We hypothesize that positive symptom-linked markers should, by definition, correlate with positive symptoms, be improved by the administration of neuroleptics, and show episodic changes with the exacerbation and remission of positive symptoms. Negative symptom-linked markers, in contrast, should correlate with negative symptoms, be unaffected or slightly adversely affected by neuroleptics, and be unaffected by episodes of florid psychotic symptoms. If they mark the predisposition to schizophrenia, markers should also remain deviant in clinically improved schizophrenics and appear in a significant subgroup of relatives of schizophrenics. A review of the literature on information-processing deviations suggests that distractibility and verbal memory deficits meet many criteria for positive symptom-linked vulnerability markers, whereas deficits in sustained attention, measured by RT crossover and the CPT, may be more sensitive to vulnerability to negative symptoms.

Different methodological challenges are posed by the study of positive and negative symptom-linked vulnerability markers. Positive symptom-linked markers present the problem of imperfect diagnostic specificity, perhaps because some proportion of psychiatric (e.g., affective) controls and their relatives are also predisposed to neuroleptic-responsive positive symptoms. Negative symptom-linked markers present a different problem – nonubiquitousness – because the DSM-IIIR criteria for schizophrenia emphasize florid psychotic symptoms, and overlook deficit symptoms. As a result, only a subgroup of schizophrenics exhibits negative symptoms and only some of their relatives can be expected to demonstrate the markers for this predisposition. According to the most liberal estimate, 50% of all relatives of schizophrenics are predicted to demonstrate an information-processing deviation, and this estimate shrinks considerably for negative symptom-linked markers. As a result, performance distributions for the entire group of relatives of schizophrenics often contain sufficient within-group variability to render mean differences between high-risk subjects and controls nonsignificant. We have reviewed several conceptually meaningful data-analytic strategies that are more powerful than the group mean comparison approach and suggest that the development of these methodologies constitutes a pressing need in contemporary vulnerability research.

Acknowledgment. This study was supported in part by a grant from the Graduate School of Arts and Sciences, Texas Tech. University.

References

Andreasen, N.C. (1982). Negative and positive symptoms in schizophrenia. *American Journal of Psychiatry, 140*, 1507–1509.

Asarnow, R.F., & MacCrimmon, D.J. (1978). Residual performance deficit in clinically remitted schizophrenics: A marker of schizophrenia? *Journal of Abnormal Psychology, 87*(6), 597–608.

Asarnow, R.F., Steffy, R.A., MacCrimmon, D.J., & Cleghorn, J.M. (1978), An attentional assessment of foster children at risk for schizophrenia. In L.C. Wynne, R.L. Cromwell & S. Matthysse (Eds.), *The nature of schizophrenia: New approaches to research and treatment* (pp. 339–358). New York: Wiley.

Atkinson, R.C., & Shiffrin, R.M. (1968). Human memory: A proposed system and its control processes. In K.W. Spence & J.T. Spence (Eds.), *Advances in the psychology of learning and motivation: Research and theory (Vol. 2)*. New York: Academic

Baker, L.A., Cheng, L.Y., & Amara, I.B. (1983). The withdrawal of benztropine mesylate in chronic schizophrenic patients. *British Journal of Psychiatry, 143*, 584–590.

Bellissimo, A., & Steffy, R.A. (1972). Redundancy-associated deficit in schizophrenic reaction time performance. *Journal of Abnormal Psychology, 84*, 210–220.

Bleuler, E. (1950). *Dementia praecox or the group of schizophrenias* (J. Zinkin, Trans.). New York: International Universities Press. (Original work published 1911).

Blum, R., Livingston, P., & Shader, R. (1969). Changes in cognition, attention, and language in acute schizophrenia. *Diseases of the Nervous System, 1*, 31–36.

Bohannon, W.E., & Strauss, M.E. (1983). Reaction-time in psychiatric outpatients. *Psychiatry Research, 9*, 17–22.

Botwinick, J.S., Brinley, J.F., & Robbin, J.S. (1959). Maintaining set in relation to motivation and age. *American Journal of Psychology, 72*, 585–588.

Brooks, G.W., & Weaver, L. (1961). Some relations between psychiatric and psychomotor behavior changes associated with tranquilizing medications. *Comprehensive Psychiatry, 2*, 203–210.

Buchsbaum, M.C., & Rieder, R.O. (1979). Biologic heterogeneity and psychiatric research. *Archives of General Psychiatry, 36*, 1163–1169.

Calev, A. (1984). Recall and recognition in mildly disturbed schizophrenics: The use of matched tasks. *Psychological Medicine, 14*, 425–429.

Cornblatt, B., & Erlenmeyer-Kimling, L. (1984). Early attentional predictors of adolescent behavioral disturbances in children at risk for schizophrenia. In N.F. Watt, E.J. Anthony, L.C. Wynne, & J.E. Rolf (Eds.), *Children at risk for schizophrenia: A longitudinal perspective*. New York: Cambridge University Press.

Cornblatt, B., & Erlenmeyer-Kimling, L. (1985). Global attentional deviance as a marker of risk for schizophrenia: Specificity and predictive validity. *Journal of Psychology, 94*(4), 470–486.

Cornblatt, B., Lenzenweger, M.F., Dworkin, R.H., & Erlenmeyer-Kimling, L. (1985). Positive and negative symptoms, attention and information processing. *Schizophrenia Bulletin, 11*(3), 397–407.

Cromwell, R.L., & Spaulding, W. (1978). How schizophrenics handle information. In W.E. Fann, I. Karacan, A.D. Pokorny, & R.L. Williams (Eds.), *Phenomenology and treatment of schizophrenia* (pp. 127–162). New York: Spectrum.

Crow, T.J. (1980). Molecular pathology of schizophrenia: More than one disease process? *British Medical Journal, 280*, 66–68.

DeAmicis, L.A., & Cromwell, R.L. (1979). Reaction time crossover in process schizophrenia patients, their relatives, and control subjects. *Journal of Nervous and Mental Disease, 167*(10), 593–600.

Diagnostic and Statistical Manual of Mental Disorders, 3rd ed. rev. (DSM-IIIR) (1987). Washington, DC: American Psychiatric Association

Driscoll, R.M. (1984). Intentional and incidental learning in children vulnerable to psychopathology. In N.F. Watt, E.J. Anthony, L.C. Wynne, & J.E. Rolf (Eds.), *Children at risk for schizophrenia: A longitudinal perspective*. New York: Cambridge University Press.

Erlenmeyer-Kimling, L., & Cornblatt, B. (1978). Attentional measures in a study of children at high risk for schizophrenia. In L.C. Wynne, R. Cromwell, & S. Matthysse (Eds.), *Nature of schizophrenia: New approaches to research and treatment* (pp. 359–365). New York: Wiley.

Finkelstein, R.J. (1983). Distractibility among paranoid and non-paranoid schizophrenics subtests matched for discriminating power. *British Journal of Clinical Psychology, 22*, 237–244.

Frame, C.L. & Oltmanns, T.F. (1982). Serial recall by schizophrenic and affective patients during and after psychotic episodes. *Journal of Abnormal Psychology, 91*(5), 311–318.

Freedman, B., & Chapman, L.J. (1973). Early subjective experience in schizophrenic episodes. *Journal of Abnormal Psychology, 82*, 46–54.

Green, M. & Walker, E. (1985). Neuropsychological performance and positive and negative symptoms in schizophrenia. *Journal of Abnormal Psychology, 94*(4), 460–469.

Greiffenstein, M., Milberg, W., Lewis, R., & Rosenbaum, G. (1981). Temporal lobe epilepsy and schizophrenia: Comparison of reaction time deficits. *Journal of Abnormal Psychology, 90*, 105–112.

Grunebaum, H., Weiss, J.L., Gallant, D., & Cohler, B.J. (1974). Attention in young children of psychotic mothers. *American Journal of Psychiatry, 131*, 887–891.

Grunebaum, H., Cohler, B.J., Kauffman, C., Gallant, D. (1978). Children of depressed and schizophrenic mothers. *Child Psychiatry and Human Development, 8*, 219–228.

Harvey, P. Winters, K., Weintraub, S., & Neale, J.M. (1981). Distractibility in children vulnerable to psychopathology. *Journal of Abnormal Psychology, 90*, 298–304.

Held, J.M., Cromwell, R.L., Frank, E.T., & Fann, W.E. (1970). Effect of phenothiazines on reaction time in schizophrenics. *Journal of Psychiatric Research, 7*, 209–213.

Holzman, P.S., Levy, D.L., & Proctor, L.R. (1978). The several qualities of attention in schizophrenia. In L.C. Wynne, R.L. Cromwell, & S. Matthysse (Eds.), *The nature of schizophrenia; New approaches to research and treatment* (pp. 295–306), New York: Wiley.

Huston, P.E., Shakow, D., & Riggs, L.A. (1937). Studies of motor function in schizophrenia. II. Reaction time. *Journal of General Psychology, 16*, 39–82.

Johnstone, E.C., Crow, T.J., Frith, C.D., Husband, J., & Kreel, L. (1976). Cerebral ventricular size and cognitive impairment in chronic schizophrenia. *Lancet, II*, 924–926.

Kety, S.S. (1980). The syndrome of schizophrenia: Unresolved questions and opportunities for research. *British Journal of Psychiatry, 136*, 421–436.

King, H.E. (1954). *Psychomotor aspects of mental disease*. Cambridge, MA: Harvard University Press.

Kopfstein, J.H., & Neale, J.M. (1972). A multivariate study of attention dysfunction in schizophrenia. *Journal of Abnormal Psychology, 80*, 294–298.

Kraepelin, E. (1913/1919). *Dementia praecox and paraphrenia*. (R.M. Barclay, Trans.). Edinburgh: Livingston.

Manschreck, T.C., Maher, B.A., Weisstein, C.C., Shapiro, A., Ames, D., & Dorsey, S. (1989). The effect of distraction on focal attention in thought disordered and non-thought disordered schizophrenic patients. *Journal of Abnormal Psychology* (in press).

Marcus, L.M. (1973). Studies of attention in children vulnerable to psychopathology (Doctoral dissertation, University of Minnesota, 1972). *Dissertation Abstracts International, 33*, 5023-B. (University Microfilms No. 7310, 606).

Nuechterlein, K.H. (1983). Signal detection in vigilance tasks and behavioral attributes among offspring of schizophrenic mothers and among hyperactive children. *Journal of Abnormal Psychology*, *92*(1), 4–28.
Nuechterlein, K.H., & Dawson, M.E. (1984a). A heuristic vulnerability/stress model of schizophrenic episodes. *Schizophrenia Bulletin*, *10*, 300–312.
Nuechterlein, K.H., & Dawson, M.E. (1984b). Information processing and attentional functioning in the developmental course of schizophrenic disorders. *Schizophrenia Bulletin*, *10*(2), 160–202.
Nuechterlein, K.H., Parasuraman, R., & Jiang, Q. (1983). Visual sustained attention: Image degradation produces rapid sensitivity decrement over time. *Science*, *220*, 327–329.
Nuechterlein, K.H., Edell, W.S., Norris, M., & Dawson, M.E. (1986). Attentional vulnerability indicators, thought disorder, and negative symptoms in schizophrenia. *Schizophrenia Bulletin*, *12*, 408–426.
Olbrich, R. (1972). Reaction-time in brain-damaged and normal subjects to variable preparatory intervals. *Journal of Nervous and Mental Disease*, *155*, 356–362.
Oltmanns, T.F. (1978). Selective attention in schizophrenia and manic psychoses: The effect of distraction on information processing. *Journal of Abnormal Psychology*, *87*(2), 212–225.
Oltmanns, T.F., & Neale, J.M. (1975). Schizophrenic performance when distractors are present: Attentional deficit or differential task difficulty. *Journal of Abnormal Psychology*, *84*(3), 205–209.
Oltmanns, T.F. Ohayon, J., & Neale, J.M. (1978). The effect of antipsychotic medication and diagnostic critera on distractibility in schizophrenia. *Journal of Psychiatric Research*, *14*, 81–91.
Orvaschel, H., Mednick, S., Schulsinger, F., & Rock, D. (1979). The children of psychiatrically disturbed parents. *Archives of General Psychiatry*, *36*, 691–695.
Orzack, M.H., & Kornetsky, C. (1966). Attention dysfunction in chronic schizophrenia. *Archives General Psychiatry*, *14*, 323–326.
Orzack, M.H., & Kornetsky, C. (1971). Environmental and familial predictors of attention behavior in chronic schizophrenia. *Journal of Psychiatric Research*, *9*, 21–29.
Orzack, M.H., Kornetsky, C., & Freeman, H. (1967). The effects of daily administration of carphenazine on attention in the schizophrenic patient. *Psychopharmacologia*, *11*, 31–38.
Payne, R.W., Hochberg, A.C., & Hawks, D.V. (1970). Dichotic stimulation as a method of assessing disorder of attention in over-inclusive schizophrenic patients. *Journal of Abnormal Psychology*, *76*, 185–193.
Pearl, D. (1962). Phenothiazine effects in chronic schizophrenia. *Journal of Clinical Psychology*, *18*, 86–89.
Phipps-Yonas, S. (1984). Visual and auditory reaction time in children vulnerable to psychopathology. In N.F. Watt, E.J. Anthony, L.C. Wynne, & J.E. Rolf, (Eds.), *Children at risk for schizophrenia: A longitudinal perspective*. New York: Cambridge University Press.
Pigache, R.M., & Norris, H. (1973). Selective attention as an index of the antipsychotic action of chlorpromazine in schizophrenia. *Bulletin of the British Psychonomic Psychology Society*, *23*, 160.
Pogue-Geile, M.F., & Harrow, M. (1984). Negative and positive symptoms in schizophrenia and depression: A follow-up. *Schizophrenia Bulletin*, *10*, 371–387.
Potamianos, G., & Kellet, J.M. (1982). Anticholinergic drugs and memory: The effects of benzhexol on memory in a group of geriatric patients. *British Journal of Psychiatry*, *140*, 470–472.
Rosofsky, I., Levin, S., & Holzman, P.S. (1982). Psychomotility in the functional psychoses. *Journal of Abnormal Psychology*, *91*, 71–74.
Rosvold, H.E., Mirsky, A., Sarason, I., Bransome, E.D., & Beck, L.H. (1956). A continuous test of brain damage. *Journal of Consulting Psychology*, *20*, 343–350.
Rund, B.R. (1982/1983). The effects of distraction on focal attention in paranoid and non-paranoid schizophrenic patients compared to normals and non-psychotic psychiatric patients. *Journal of Psychiatric Research*, *17*(3), 241–250.

Rutschmann, J., Cornblatt, B., & Erlenmeyer-Kimling, L. (1977). Sustained attention in children at risk for schizophrenia. *Archives of General Psychiatry, 34*, 571–575.

Rutschmann, J., Cornblatt, B., & Erlenmeyer-Kimling, L. (1980). Auditory recognition memory in adolescents at risk for schizophrenia: Report on a verbal continuous recognition task. *Psychiatry Research, 3*, 151–161.

Simons, R.F., MacMillan, F.W., & Ireland, F.B. (1982). Reaction-time crossover in preselected schizotypic subjects. *Journal of Abnormal Psychology, 91*, 414–419.

Sommers, A.A. (1985). "Negative symptoms": Conceptual and methodological problems. *Schizophrenia Bulletin, 11*(3), 364–379.

Spohn, H.E., Lacoursiere, R., Thompson, K., & Coyne, L. (1977). Phenothiazine effects on psychological and psychophysiological dysfunction in chronic schizophrenics. *Archives of General Psychiatry, 34*, 633–644.

Spohn, H.E., Coyne, L., Lacoursiere, R., Mazur, D., & Haynes, K. (1985). Relation of neuroleptic dose and tardive dyskinesia to attention, information-processing and psychophysiology in medicated schizophrenics. *Archives of General Psychiatry, 42*, 849–859.

Spring, B. (1980). Shift of attention in schizophrenics, siblings of schizophrenics, and depressed patients. *Journal of Nervous and Mental Disease, 168* (3), 133–139.

Spring, B. (1985). Distractibility as a marker of vulnerability to schizophrenia. *Psychopharmacology Bulletin, 21* (3), 509–512.

Spring, B., & Zubin, J. (1978). Attention and information processing as indicators of vulnerability to schizophrenic episodes. *Journal of Psychiatric Research, 14*, 289–302.

Steffy, R.A., & Galbraith, K.A. (1974). A comparison of segmental set and inhibitory deficit explanations of the crossover pattern in process schizophrenic reaction time. *Journal of Abnormal Psychology, 83*, 227–233.

Strauss, M.E., Wagman, A.M.I., & Quaid, K.A. (1983). Preparatory interval influences on reaction-time of elderly adults. *Journal of Gerontology, 38*, 55–57.

Strauss, M.E., Lew, M.F., Coyle, J.T., & Tune, L.E. (1985). Psychopharmacologic and clinical correlates of attention in chronic schizophrenia. *American Journal of Psychiatry, 142*, 497–499.

Tune, L.E., Strauss, M.E., Lew, M.F., Breitlinger, E., & Coyle, J.T. (1982). Serum levels of anticholinergic drugs and impaired recent memory in chronic schizophrenic patients. *American Journal of Psychiatry, 139*, 1460–1462.

Van Dyke, J.L., Rosenthal D., & Rasmussen, P.V. (1975). Schizophrenia: Effects of inheritance and rearing on reaction time. *Canadian Journal of Science Review, 7* (3), 224–236.

Walker, E. (1981). Attentional and neuromotor functions of schizophrenics, schizoaffectives, and patients with other affective disorders. *Archives of General Psychiatry, 38*, 1355–1358.

Walker, E., & Shaye, J. (1982). Familial schizophrenia: A predictor of neuromotor and attentional abnormalities in schizophrenia. *Archives of General Psychiatry, 39*, 1153–1156.

Weinberger, D.R., Cannon-Spoor, E., Potkin, S.G., & Wyatt, R.J. (1980). Poor premorbid adjustment and CT span abnormalities in chronic schizophrenia. *American Journal of Psychiatry, 137*, 1410–1430.

Wing, J.K., Brown, G.W. (1970). *Institutionalism and schizophrenia.* New York: Cambridge University Press.

Winters, K.C., Stone, A.A., Weintraub, S., & Neale, J.M. (1981). Cognitive and attentional deficits in children vulnerable to psychopathology. *Journal of Abnormal Child Psychology, 9* (4), 435–453.

Wishner, J., & Wahl, B. (1974). Dichotic listening in schizophrenia. *Journal of Consulting and Clinical Psychology, 4*, 538–546.

Wohlberg, G.W., & Kornetsky, C. (1973). Sustained attention in remitted schizophrenics. *Archives of General Psychiatry, 28*, 533–537.

Wood, R.L., & Cook, M. (1979). Attentional deficit in the siblings of schizophrenics. *Psychological Medicine, 9*, 465–467.

Wynne, R.D., & Kornetsky, C., (1960). The effects of chlorpromazine and secobarbital on the reaction times of chronic schizophrenics. *Psychopharmacologia, 1*, 294–302.
Zahn, T.P., & Carpenter, W.T. (1978). Effects of short-term outcome and clinical improvement on reaction time in acute schizophrenia. *Journal of Psychiatric Research, 14*, 59–68.
Zahn, T.P. & Rosenthal, D. (1965). Preparatory set in acute schizophrenia. *Journal of Nervous and Mental Disease, 141*, 352–358.
Zubin, J. (1985) Negative symptoms: Are they indigenous to schizophrenia? *Schizophrenia Bulletin, 11* (3), 461–470.
Zubin, J., & Spring, B. (1977). Vulnerability: A new view of schizophrenia. *Journal of Abnormal Psychology, 86*, 103–126.

Part III

Psychophysiology and Vulnerability

Current Issues in the Application of P300 to Research in Schizophrenia

C.C. Duncan

The Core Symptom in Schizophrenia: Disturbed Attention

Perhaps the earliest formal description of the deficit in attention in schizophrenic symptomatology was provided by Kraepelin: "It is quite common for them to lose both inclination and ability on their own initiative to keep their attention fixed for any length of time. It is often difficult enough to make them attend at all" (Kraepelin, 1919/1971, p. 6). Matthysse (1978) noted more recently that deficits in attention and information processing are still more consistent than neurochemical findings in schizophrenia. Such results have led many theorists to view impaired attention as the fundamental or core cognitive deficit in the disorder and have led to the suggestion that study of the neurobiological mechanisms of attention may provide keys to understanding schizophrenia (Mirsky & Duncan, 1986).

The premise of this paper is that the P300 component of the event-related brain potential (ERP) is a unique tool for studying this most fundamental deficit in schizophrenia. To understand fully the strategy of P300 as an investigative tool in schizophrenia research, it is helpful to review some ideas and rationales about that body of work. I will begin by describing briefly the P300 technique and will then review recent data on factors that affect the P300 in schizophrenic patients. In subsequent sections, I will discuss three major substantive issues pertaining to the application of P300 to research on schizophrenia: prediction, state versus trait issues, and specificity. The chapter concludes with a brief review of the status of P300 as a trait marker of schizophrenia and some suggestions for applications of P300 to schizophrenia research.

The P300 as a Measure of Attention

In recent years, psychophysiological researchers have sought to apply ERPs to the study of attention and information processing as these processes are defined by cognitive psychology. The aim of the field of "cognitive psychophysiology" is to identify ERP components as indices of specific aspects or stages of information processing (Donchin, 1982).

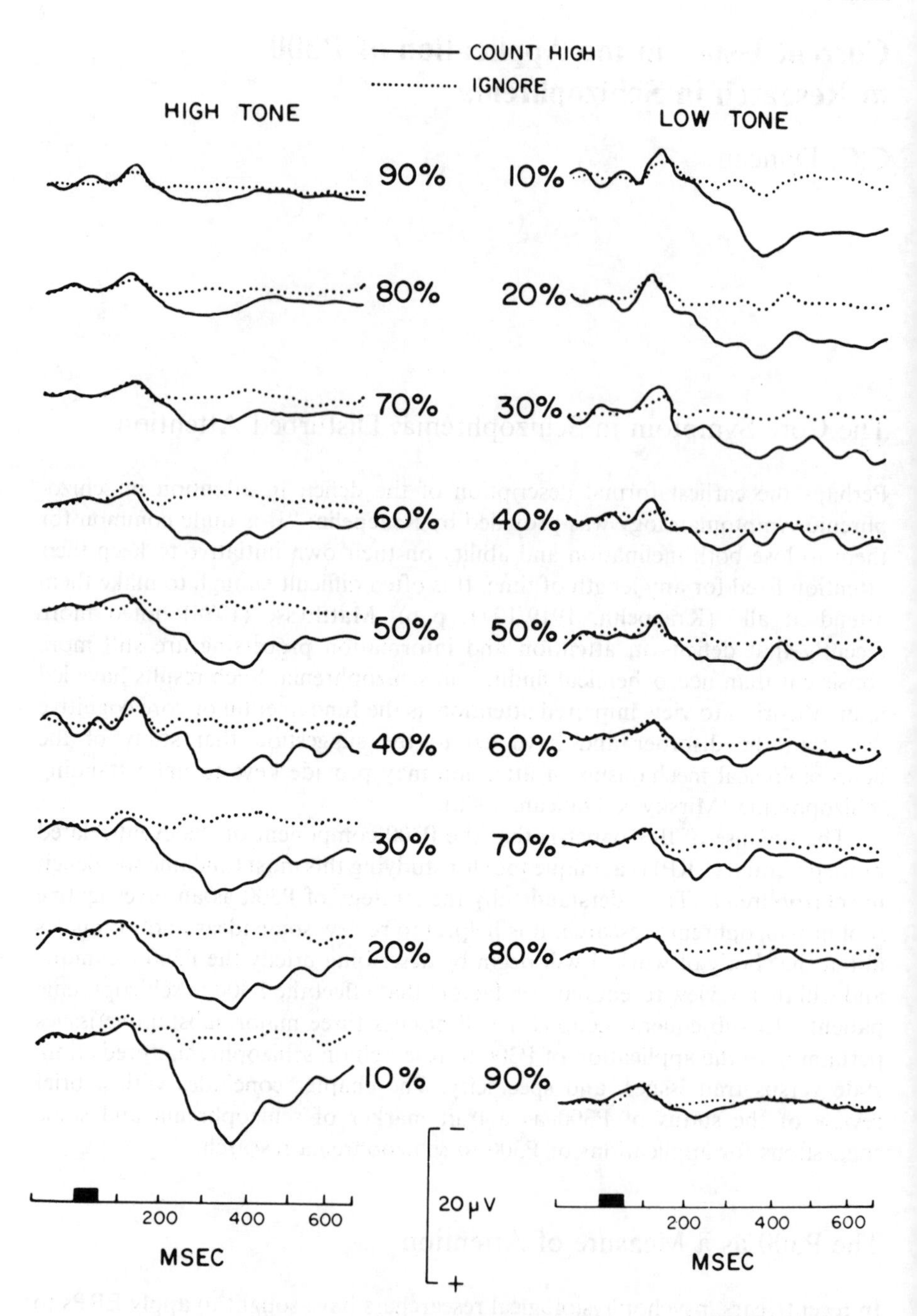

Fig. 1. ERPs elicited by stimuli at nine levels of probability, recorded from the midline parietal scalp area and averaged over ten subjects. High- and low-frequency tones were presented in random order at complementary probabilities. Data are superimposed for two task conditions in which subjects either counted the high tones (*solid lines*) or

A widely studied ERP component, the P300, is a manifestation of cognitive activity invoked by task-relevant stimuli. The discovery of the P300 component was a direct result of the study of attentional deficit in schizophrenia: response time had been shown to increase when the modality of a stimulus differs from that of the immediately preceding stimulus in the sequence; the effect of this "cross-modality shift" was found to be exaggerated in schizophrenic patients (Sutton, Hakerem, Zubin, & Portnoy, 1961). The newly developing ERP technique was applied to an investigation of the cause of this increase in response latency. Sutton, Braren, Zubin, and John (1965) observed a previously unreported phenomenon in the ERP elicited by a shift in modality – a late positive wave that varied in amplitude as an inverse function of stimulus probability. This wave was not related to the modality of the stimulus nor to its physical attributes, but to the informational characteristics of the stimulus. This was the research context that gave rise to the P300 component.

The most commonly applied experimental procedure for eliciting the P300 component is the "oddball paradigm," in which a random sequence of two distinctive stimuli is presented to the subject. In early studies, no task was assigned; however, in recent studies, the subject has generally been required to discriminate between the stimuli and to make a differential response to each. The response may involve a motor reaction or an updating of a covert count of the stimuli. The stimulus that occurs with the lower probability (i.e., the "oddball") elicits a P300 that is larger than the P300 to the higher probability stimulus. The two categories of stimuli may differ in terms of physical qualities (such as tone frequency) or in terms of complex rules (such as words belonging to different semantic categories).

The amplitude of P300 has been shown to be highly responsive to manipulations of stimulus probability, as Sutton et al. first reported in 1965. Using the oddball task, we varied parametrically the relative probabilities of high and low tones presented in a random series (Duncan-Johnson & Donchin, 1977). The subject either counted the high tones ("Count high") or performed a distraction task to which the tones were irrelevant ("Ignore"). It is apparent from the data shown in Fig. 1 that when the stimuli were "task relevant," the amplitude of P300 depended on their a priori probability. That is, the rarer the stimulus, the

ignored the tones and performed a word puzzle (*dotted lines*). Stimulus occurrence is indicated by a *black rectangle* on the *time scale*. Positivity of the scalp electrode with respect to the reference electrodes is plotted as a downward deflection. It is apparent that when the stimuli were task relevant, the amplitude of P300 was inversely related to probability. Note, however, that when the tones were irrelevant to the subject's task, no P300 was elicited even by low-probability tones. (Copyright 1977, The Society for Psychophysiological Research; reproduced with permission of the publisher from Duncan-Johnson & Donchin, 1977) larger the P300 it elicited. In contrast, when the subject was not paying attention to the tones, no P300 was elicited. It is apparent, then, that P300 amplitude varies monotonically with the probability of a task-relevant stimulus. Thus, P300 appears to be a sensitive index of expectancy and attention deployment. These characteristics suggest that the process manifested by P300 is associated with the updating of the subject's template of the environment (Duncan-Johnson & Donchin, 1977).

The P300 component varies in peak latency from less than 300 to nearly 1000 ms post stimulus, depending on the complexity of the stimuli and the task. P300 latency has been shown to be proportional to the time required to classify and evaluate a stimulus, independent of response-production factors (Duncan-Johnson, 1981; Duncan-Johnson & Kopell, 1981; Kutas, McCarthy, & Donchin 1977; McCarthy & Donchin, 1981).

The P300 technique appears to hold promise for the study of the attention or information-processing deficit in schizophrenia, since it can help to clarify the timing and order of neural events involved in information-processing activities (Duncan-Johnson & Donchin, 1982; Hillyard & Kutas, 1983). Moreover, the functional significance of the P300 is sufficiently well established to make it a viable candidate for the study of impaired attention in schizophrenia.

The P300 in Schizophrenia

Because the P300 is derived from cerebral electrical activity, it offers the potential to study dynamic brain function. Thus, the P300 component has been an attractive tool for investigating putative neurobiological mechanisms underlying the attention deficit in schizophrenia.

In 1972 Roth and Cannon reported a finding that has since been replicated many times, namely, that the P300 component of the ERP is reduced in schizophrenic patients (Fig. 2). They used an auditory oddball task in which subjects were instructed to ignore the stimuli as much as possible. Whereas the normal subjects tended to show relatively large P300s to the lower probability stimuli, the P300s recorded from the schizophrenic patients were small or absent. This observation by Roth and Cannon provided evidence which suggested that the physiological process underlying attention is disturbed in schizophrenia.

Despite differences in paradigms, stimulus modalities, instructional sets, diagnostic criteria, medication status, matching of patient and control groups, and data analysis techniques, there has been remarkable consistency in the finding of reduced amplitude of P300 in schizophrenic patients as compared with normal controls (for reviews, see Holzman, 1987; Mirsky & Duncan, 1986; Pritchard, 1986). If we assume that the amplitude of P300 is an index of orienting or allocating attention to task-relevant stimuli, then the results suggest that these functions may be disturbed in schizophrenic patients.

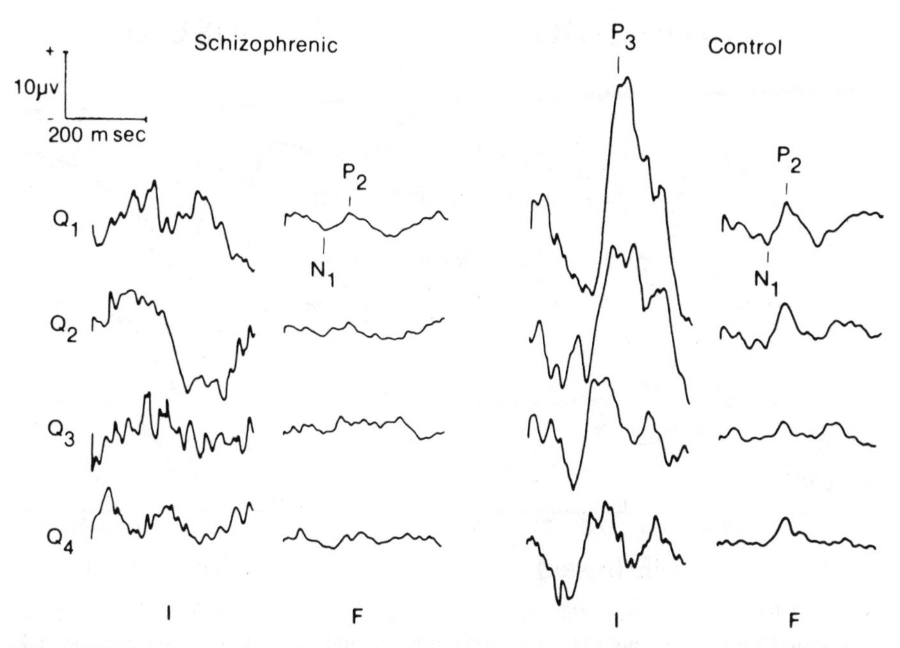

Fig. 2. ERPs recorded from the vertex and elicited by infrequent (*I*, $p=.07$) and frequent (*F*, $p=.93$) tones in a passive (no-task) paradigm. That data for one schizophrenic patient and one normal control are shown. Positivity of the scalp electrode with respect to the reference electrodes is plotted as an upward deflection in this figure. *Q1–Q4* refer to the quartile of trials comprising the averages. It is evident that the infrequent tones elicited a large-amplitude P300 in the control subject but not in the schizophrenic patient. (Copyright 1972, American Medical Association; reproduced with permission from Roth & Cannon, 1972)

We have recently attempted to extend and broaden the finding of attenuated P300 by evaluating the relative effects of modality and probability on P300 in schizophrenic patients and normal controls (Duncan, Perlstein, & Morihisa, 1987). We used the oddball paradigm with a choice reaction time task. In separate series, the probabilities of the stimuli were varied. Subjects were 14 patients who met Research Diagnostic Criteria (Spitzer, Endicott, & Robins, 1977) for schizophrenia and ten matched normal controls. Figure 3 shows the data elicited by the auditory and visual stimuli at three levels of probability. Grand-mean waveforms computed from the data acquired from the two groups of subjects are superimposed.

The ERPs of the two groups differed in both the latency and amplitude of the P300 component. P300 was of longer latency in the schizophrenic patients (378 ms) than in the normal controls (353 ms) ($p<.05$). As in previous studies, the P300 was smaller for the schizophrenic patients than the controls; this difference was larger for low-probability stimuli in the auditory modality. These findings are represented in quantitative form in Fig. 4, which depicts this

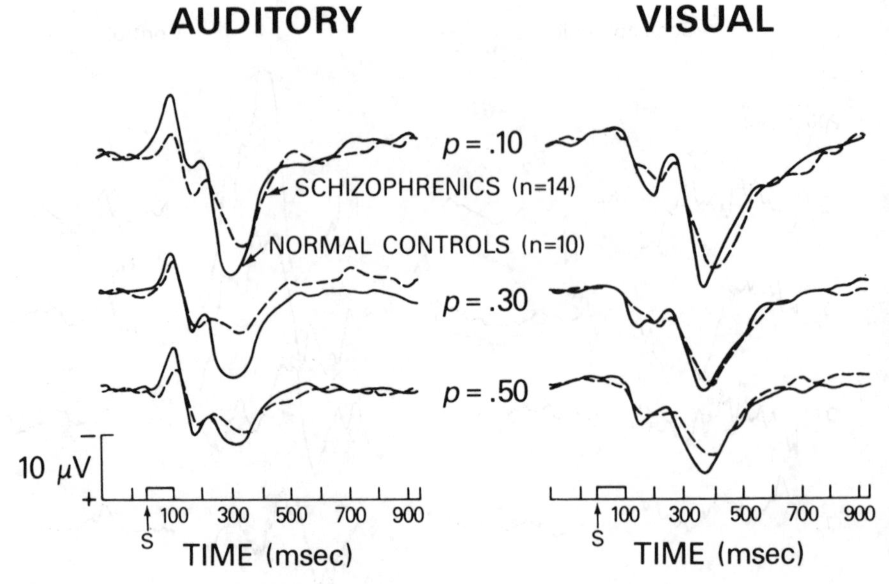

Fig. 3. ERPs recorded from the vertex and averaged over subjects, elicited by auditory and visual stimuli presented at three levels of probability in a choice reaction time task. The data collected from the normal control (*solid lines*; $n = 10$) and schizophrenic (*dashed lines*; $n = 14$) subjects are superimposed. Stimulus onset is indicated by an *arrow* on the *time scale*. It is apparent that the P300 was smaller and later for the schizophrenic patients than the controls, a difference that was maximal for low-probability stimuli in the auditory modality. Note also that the auditory N100 component was attenuated in the schizophrenic patients, a finding that replicates previously reported results (e.g., Roth, Pfefferbaum, Kelly, Berger, & Kopell, 1981). (From Duncan, Perlstein, & Morihisa, 1987)

significant group × modality × probability interaction on P300 amplitude ($p < .025$, Greenhouse-Geisser correction).

Given that the amplitude of P300 elicited by auditory stimuli differentiates normal controls from schizophrenic patients with high reliability, the question remains as to how to interpret this difference. Because only ERPs elicited by stimuli associated with accurate responses comprised the averages, low-amplitude P300 in schizophrenic patients is clearly more than an inevitable concomitant of poor performance. Shagass (1986) interprets the P300 attenuation as a reflection of a deficit of the underlying neurophysiological mechanisms probed by the task. Moreover, our data suggest that schizophrenic patients have a deficit in auditory rather than visual information processing (Duncan et al., 1987). This finding is reminiscent of the relative prevalence of auditory as compared with visual hallucinations in schizophrenic symptomatology.

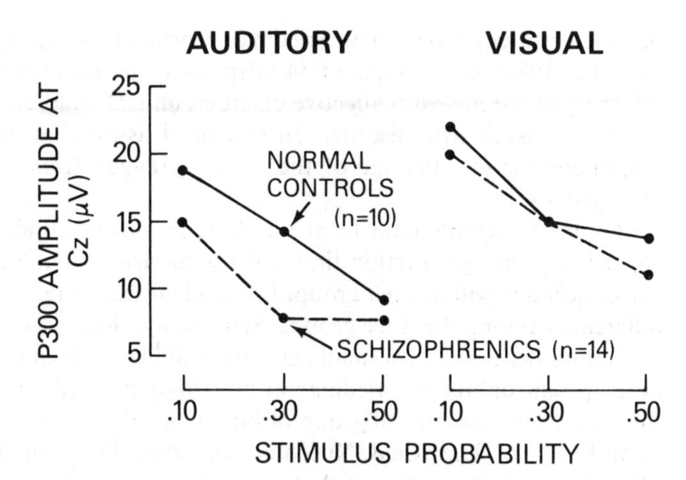

Fig. 4. Mean P300 amplitude at the vertex for the control (*solid lines*; $n = 10$) and schizophrenic (*dashed lines*; $n = 14$) subjects as a function of stimulus modality and probability. Note the significant interaction of group × modality × probability on P300. (From Duncan, Perlstein, & Morihisa, 1987)

Prediction of Schizophrenia with P300: High-Risk Research

It is useful to discuss the concept of traits in an analysis of symptoms and deficits in schizophrenia. As Baron (1986) noted, vulnerability traits refer to biological characteristics that are correlated with the genetic susceptibility to the disorder. A trait is considered to be stable over time, regardless of clinical state; whereas a state variable is evident only during episodes of the disorder. It is critical to be able to differentiate those attributes of schizophrenia that are primarily trait related from those that are primarily state related, since this information can be useful in understanding the pathophysiology of the disorder.

One of the research strategies to evaluate whether P300 is a vulnerability marker of schizophrenia selects individuals who are known to be at high statistical risk for schizophrenia and studies them prospectively, before onset of the disorder. The question is whether reduced P300 predicts future psychopathology.

If one parent is schizophrenic, there is a 10%–15% chance that the offspring of that parent will develop schizophrenia. This is in contrast to a risk estimate of only 1% for the children of normal parents (Gottesman & Shields, 1982). A primary purpose of this approach is to discover markers by comparing the premorbid data on the 10%–15% who eventually develop the disorder with the 85%–90% of high-risk children who do not.

Because reduced P300 amplitude is the most robust ERP abnormality in adult schizophrenics, an amplitude reduction in children at genetic risk would suggest that the P300 reduction is a vulnerability trait of schizophrenia. This high-risk strategy was used by Friedman, Cornblatt, Vaughan, and Erlenmeyer-Kimling (1986) who compared 34 offspring of parents with schizophrenia, 26 offspring of parents with affective disorder, and 74 children of parents with no history of psychiatric disorder. In this third assessment of the subjects in a longitudinal study, the age of the subjects ranged from 11 to 19 years and averaged 14–15.

Figure 5 presents data from the three groups of children. The data were elicited in go/no-go reaction time tasks with visual stimuli and were averaged across subjects within each group. It is evident from Fig. 5 that there were few differences among the three groups. Specifically, there was no evidence of P300 reduction. Because only a small percentage of high-risk children are expected to develop schizophrenia, Friedman et al. (1986) checked on the possibility that there may have been a subgroup of high-risk subjects with disproportionately small P300s (cf. Dawson & Nuechterlein, 1984). They found no clear evidence of a deviant subgroup that could be considered to comprise the most vulnerable children.[1]

There are methodological differences between the cross-sectional and high-risk studies that could account for their failure to find a reduction in P300. One difference is that the sample used by Friedman et al. (1986) was restricted to intact families and, presumably, therefore to parents with less severe schizophrenic disorders. A second issue in interpreting high-risk data is that only a small percentage of the offspring of schizophrenics are expected to develop the disorder. Because of the limited number of high-risk subjects in the Friedman et al. sample, the odds of detecting a subgroup of deviant subjects (i.e., comprising perhaps three to five children) were low. A third issue to consider when interpreting the lack of differences between the high-risk and control children was the use of a task that was not sufficiently demanding. Pritchard (1986) suggested that the processing load for clinically well subjects needs to be greater than that for patients before differences between family members of patients can be detected (cf. Nuechterlein & Dawson, 1984). Fourthly, Friedman et al. (1986) used visual stimuli to elicit ERPs: as shown in Fig. 3 above, we recently found that adult schizophrenic patients differed from normal controls only when their P300s were elicited by infrequent stimuli in the auditory modality (Duncan et al., 1987).

Despite the fact that the findings in this study were disappointing, the strategy is an excellent one; and it may be that further research using other

---

[1] When the children were seen for the first time in the laboratory (round 1), a battery of behavioral tasks was administrated that assessed attentional functioning. These subjects were later characterized as deviant or nondeviant on the basis of their performance (Cornblatt & Erlenmeyer-Kimling, 1985). Friedman et al (1986) reported that the P300s at round 3 (an average of 7 years later) of the high-risk children classified as attentionally deviant at round 1 did not differ from the P300s of the nondeviant children in the same sample. A correlational analysis of attentional performance and P300 amplitude might have been fruitful, and the power of the analysis would have been greater if the behavioral and ERP measures had been obtained at the same assessment.

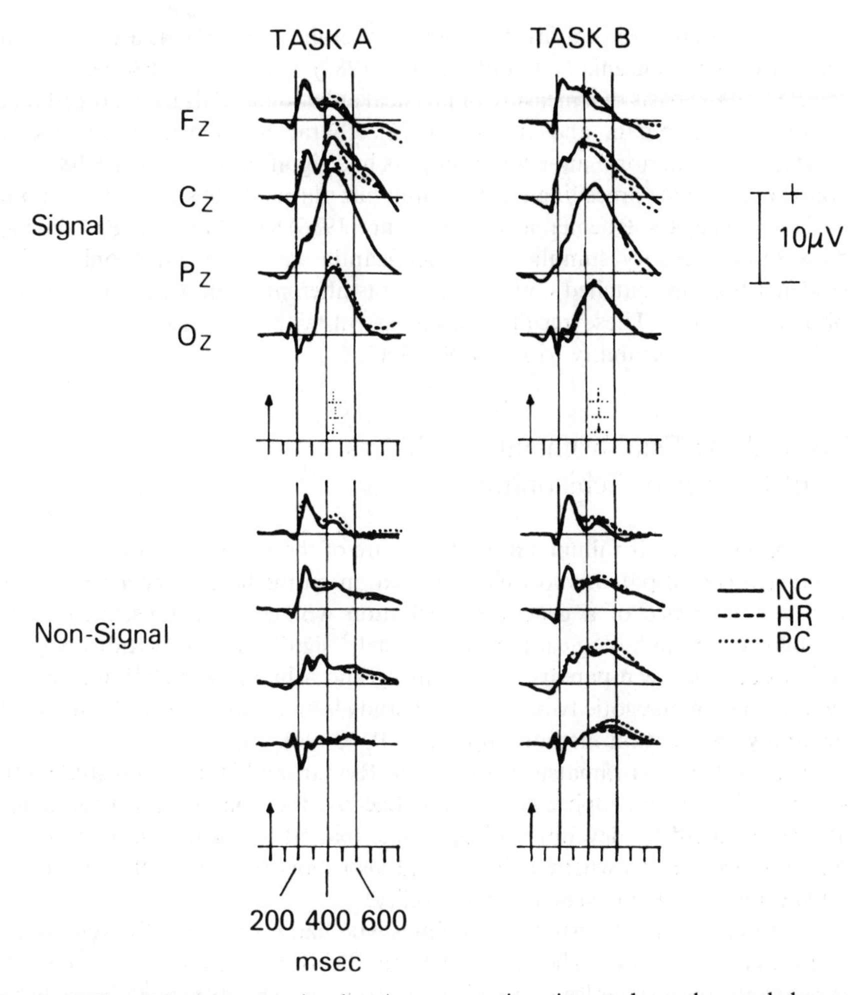

Fig. 5. ERPs elicited in two visual go/no-go reaction time tasks and recorded over midline frontal (F_z), central (C_z), parietal (P_z), and occipital (O_z) scalp areas. In both tasks, the signal stimulus occurred with a probability of .25. Subjects responded to signals with a finger lift. The data were averaged over subjects and are superimposed. *Solid lines*, normal control group; *dashed lines*, high-risk group; *dotted lines*, psychiatric control group. Stimulus onset is indicated by an *arrow* on the *time scale*. Positivity of the scalp electrodes is plotted as an upward deflection in this figure. It is evident that the differences among the three groups were minimal. (From Friedman, Cornblatt, Vaughan, & Erlenmeyer-Kimling, 1986)

paradigms would be fruitful. It is also conceivable that other ERP differences in a high-risk population presage the P300 differences. It is, of course, also possible that reduced P300 is an episode or state marker rather than a vulnerability or trait marker of schizophrenia and thus would not be apparent in high-risk children.

A study that does support the potential usefulness of P300 as a vulnerability marker of schizophrenia is that of Simons (1982), who studied P300 in subjects selected on the basis of a measure of physical anhedonia. This trait, according to Chapman, Chapman, and Raulin (1976), characterizes persons at risk for schizophrenia. Simons' anhedonic subjects had significantly smaller P300s than controls to signals preceding erotic stimuli but normal P300s to neutral stimuli. Josiassen, Shagass, Roemer, and Straumanis (1985) found that the P300 elicited by a somatosensory stimulus was significantly smaller in anhedonic college students than in matched controls and not different from a group of schizophrenic patients. These results are consistent with the view of P300 as an indicator of vulnerability to schizophrenia.

Toward the Establishment of P300 as a Trait Marker of Schizophrenia

A second strategy for illuminating the nature of the P300 marker evaluates the adult relatives of patients to yield information on the hereditary nature of this variable. Evidence of a genetic contribution would be demonstrated by resemblance among biological relatives, namely, significant correlations between siblings and between parents and offspring and a higher correlation in monozygotic than in dizygotic twins. The next study is an example of the family study or family aggregation method applied to P300 research.

Saitoh, Niwa, Hiramatsu, Kameyama, Rymar, and Itoh (1984) studied the siblings of adult schizophrenic patients. Because the siblings of schizophrenics are more likely to develop schizophrenia than the general population, the question arises as to whether they would also show reduced P300s. That is, is P300 a marker of this genetic vulnerability?

Saitoh et al. (1984) tested only siblings who had no history of psychiatric or neurologic disorders.[2] The task involved dichotic listening, in which four consonant-vowel syllables of a male voice were presented through headphones to one ear, and the same syllables of a female voice were presented to the other ear. Subjects attended to one ear at a time and counted one of the syllables in the attended ear ("targets"). They observed reduced P300s to targets in the siblings, similar to the reduction seen in the patients. Figure 6 shows data points corresponding roughly to P300s for a sample of 20 normal controls, 20 siblings of schizophrenic patients, and groups of ten unmedicated and 12 medicated patients who met the *Diagnostic and Statistical Manual of Mental Disorders*, 3rd edition (DSM-III; 1980) criteria for schizophrenia. Twelve of the siblings were related to their sample of schizophrenic patients.

They reported that mean P300 in the siblings was significantly smaller than in the normals and not different from that in the patients. They concluded that a

[2] By studying only well relatives of schizophrenic patients, Saitoh et al. may have reduced the chances of finding an attenuated P300 in the siblings.

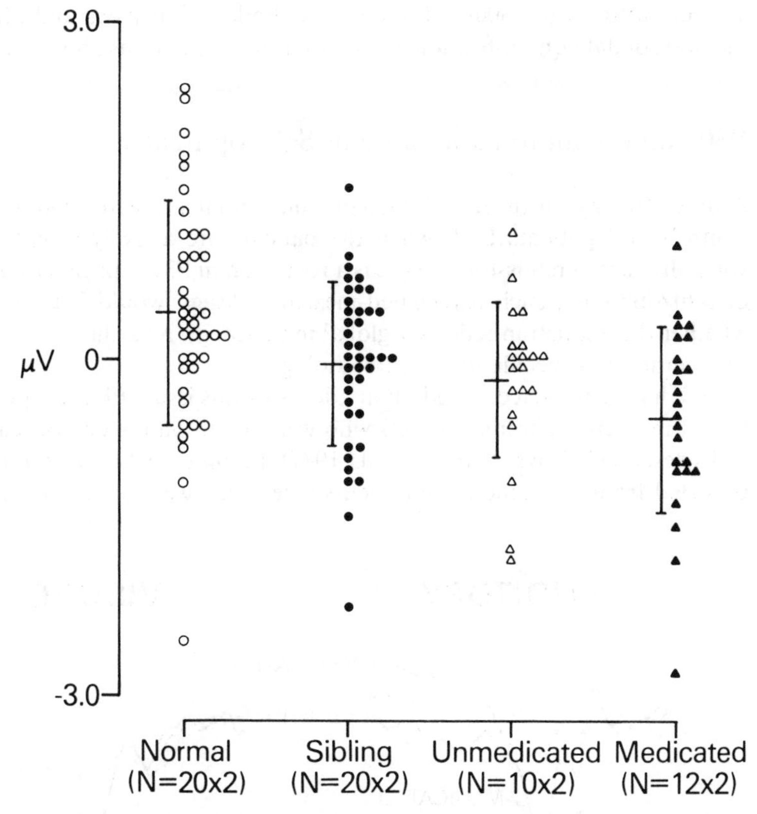

Fig. 6. Mean amplitude at the vertex of an estimate of the P300 component (mean amplitude in the latency region 50– 330 ms after the P200 peak). The ERPs were elicited by auditory target stimuli, which occurred with a probability of .125. Two values for each subject in the four groups are shown, one for each of two target stimuli. Whereas the main effect of group on P300 was significant in the comparison between siblings and normal controls as well as between siblings and medicated schizophrenics, the siblings and unmedicated schizophrenics did not differ. It should be noted, however, that the different analyses of variance were not independent and did not use a repeated-measures design. Moreover, the mean difference between the siblings and normal controls appears to have resulted from a small group of normals with large P300s. (From Saitoh, Niwa, Hiramatsu, Kameyama, Rymar, & Itoh, 1984)

disturbance in attention, as reflected by P300, is a specific deficit in schizophrenia that is genetically determined. The discrepancy between these findings and those of Friedman et al. (1986) may be due to the differences in the difficulty levels between the two tasks (Pritchard, 1986).

However, it is important to note the amount of overlap in P300 among the four groups. In fact, the mean difference between the siblings and the normal controls appears to have been due largely to a small subgroup of the normal subjects with large P300s. Moreover, methodological flaws and idiosyncratic methods of data quantification and analysis raise questions about their findings.

P300 and Symptomatic State in Schizophrenia

A third strategy for the use of P300 in schizophrenia research compares normal controls and patients both when the patients are actively symptomatic and when they are in remission. Whereas a reduction in P300 appears to be a marker of schizophrenia, such a repeated-measures design would help to determine whether this reduction reflects a global impairment, regardless of clinical state, or whether it is specific to symptomatology.

We have conducted a study that addresses this issue. Figure 7 presents data from three schizophrenic patients who were tested on the choice reaction time tasks described above (Duncan et al., 1987). In this case, however, the data were collected from the same three patients when they were on and off neuroleptic

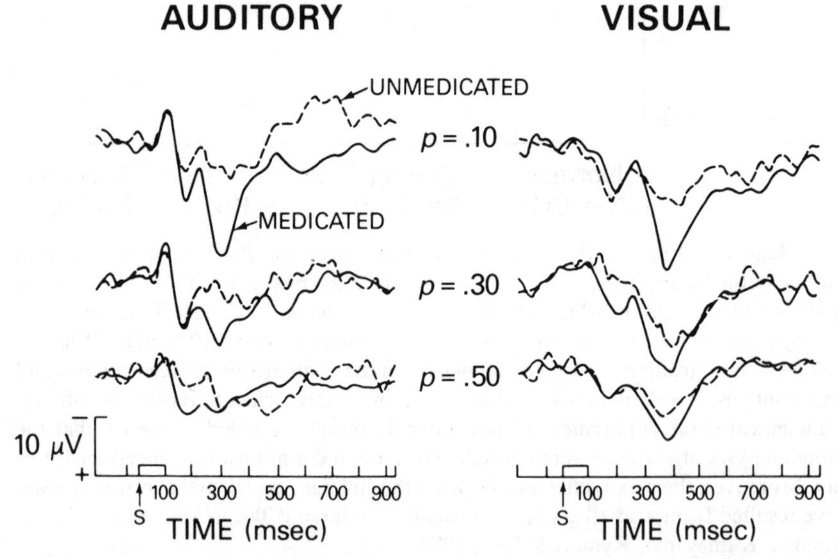

Fig. 7. ERPs recorded from the vertex and averaged over three schizophrenic patients who were tested twice, first when they were free of psychotropic medication (*dashed lines*), and an average of 5 months later when they were stabilized on neuroleptic medication (*solid lines*). The ERPs were elicited by auditory and visual stimuli presented at three levels of probability in a choice reaction time task. Stimulus onset is indicated by an *arrow* on the *time scale*. Note that whereas there was no change in N100, P300 amplitude increased substantially following the administration of neuroleptics. Although the effect of medication appears to be significant, it is the clinical response to medication that correlates with enhanced P300s. (From Duncan, Perlstein, & Morihisa, 1987)

medication. It is evident that mean P300 amplitude increased substantially following the administration of medication. This increase in P300 appears to have been of equal magnitude in the two modalities.[3] Moreover, the enhancement of P300 was related directly to the degree of clinical response to the medication, as assessed by the Brief Psychiatric Rating Scale (Overall & Gorham, 1962): one patient who showed no improvement on neuroleptic medication also showed no change in P300. In contrast, the patient with the greatest clinical response exhibited the greatest increase in P300. Whereas several studies have shown that the medication status of schizophrenic patients is not related to P300 amplitude[4] (e.g., Baribeau-Braun, Picton, & Gosselin, 1983; Pass, Klorman, Salzman, Klein, & Kaskey, 1980; Roth, Pfefferbaum, Kelly, Berger, & Kopell, 1981), others have reported that treatment with neuroleptics is associated with increased P300s (e.g., Josiassen, Shagass, Straumanis, & Roemer, 1984; Roth, Horvath, Pfefferbaum, Tinklenberg, Mezzich, & Kopell, 1979). Moreover, there have been previous reports that P300 amplitude in schizophrenics is inversely correlated with the degree of psychopathology (Josiassen, Shagass, Roemer, & Straumanis, 1981; Roth et al., 1979; Roth, Horvath, Pfefferbaum, & Kopell, 1980), although other studies have reported that the two measures are not correlated (Brecher & Begleiter 1983; Roth et al., 1981).

Figure 8 shows data from the same reaction time tasks for a group of five normal controls who were also tested twice to assess the stability of the P300 over time. The interval between subsequent tests matched that of the inter-test interval of the schizophrenic patients. The overlap of the waveforms indicates that, in normal subjects, P300s are very stable.

Our preliminary data indicate that, when evaluated on a within-subject basis, P300 amplitude in schizophrenic patients is inversely correlated with symptom severity, a relation that in this instance appears to be mediated by the patient's responsiveness to neuroleptic medication. If this finding should hold up, it suggests that the P300 attenuation associated with schizophrenia may be a state rather than a trait marker of the disorder. A related question concerns the specific symptom (or group of symptoms) to which P300 is related. We are continuing to collect data on additional patients in an attempt to replicate this finding and to assess whether there are characteristics of the ERP that predict responsiveness to medication.

Specificity of P300 Changes to Schizophrenia

Few studies using the P300 metric have included nonschizophrenic psychotic patients as controls, so the issue of the specificity of the P300 attenuation in

---

[3] Data from additional patients has confirmed that this correlation is highly significant for P300s elicited by *visual* stimuli. In contrast, auditory P300 does not appear to vary as a function of clinical state.

[4] Including the between-groups analysis of the Duncan et al. (1987) study.

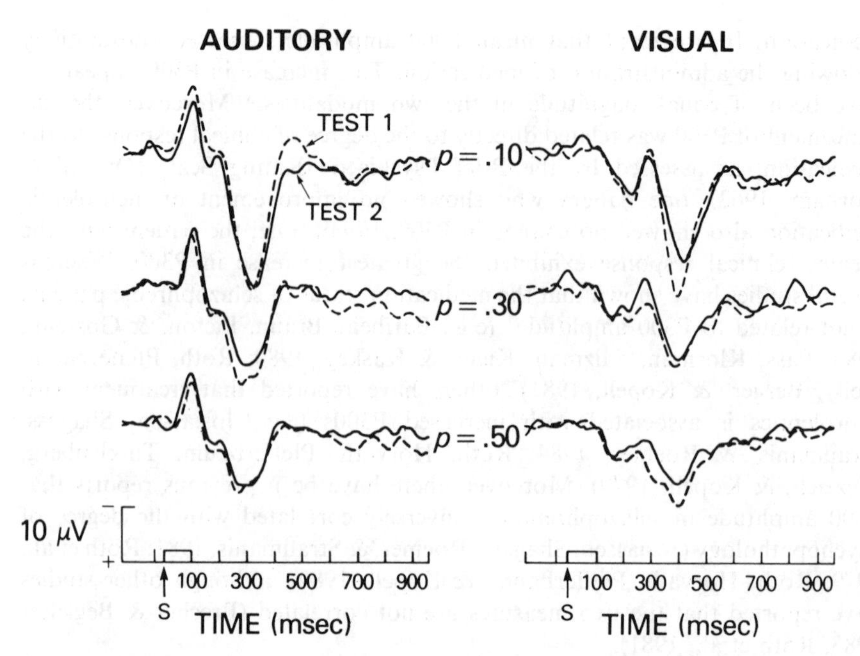

Fig. 8. ERPs recorded from the vertex and elicited by auditory and visual stimuli presented at three levels of probability in a choice reaction time task. The waveforms are averaged over five normal control subjects who were tested twice (*dashed lines*, test 1; *solid lines*, test 2). The mean interval between tests was 5 months, the same as the interval between the two tests of the patients shown in Fig. 7. Stimulus onset is indicated by an *arrow* on the *time scale*. The overlap of the waveforms indicates that ERPs in normal subjects are very stable over time.

schizophrenia has not been addressed adequately. Specificity is perhaps suggested by studies that have reported differences between patients with affective disorders and schizophrenia, with the former exhibiting P300s similar to those of normal subjects (Levit, Sutton, & Zubin, 1973; Pfefferbaum, Wenegrat, Ford, Roth, & Kopell, 1984, Roth et al., 1981; Shagass, 1979; Steinhauer & Zubin, 1982). However, it is noteworthy that P300 attenuation has been observed in other clinical disorders, such as dementia (Goodin, Squires, & Starr, 1978; Josiassen, Shagass, Mancall, & Roemer, 1984), absence epilepsy (Duncan, 1988), and anorexia nervosa (Duncan, Kaye, Perlstein, Jimerson, & Mirsky, 1985). Thus, it is possible that the attenuation of P300 is a nonspecific concomitant of impaired attention. The magnitude of the correlation of behavioral and P300 measures of attention in schizophrenia remains to be investigated. The extent to which reduction in P300 amplitude represents general organismic impairment regardless of clinical diagnosis or represents processes that are specific to a clinical state or diagnosis remains to be determined (Duncan in Roth, Duncan, Pfefferbaum, & Timsit-Berthier, 1986).

Summary and Recommendations

The data on P300 as a vulnerability marker are incomplete, for want of repeated-measures designs and systematic family studies. P300 amplitude may be genetically influenced, as evidenced from higher correlations in monozygotic twins than in unrelated persons (Polich & Burns, 1987; Surwillo, 1980); however, data on dizygotic twins and other family members are needed to evaluate the extent of genetic control. Family data on ill versus well relatives of schizophrenic patients are not yet available.[5]

We have observed intrasubject variability in P300 as a function of clinical state. This variability is at odds with the state independence criterion for a trait variable. Although these data were obtained on only a few patients, they temper our enthusiasm about the potential usefulness of P300 as a vulnerability trait of schizophrenia.

Even if P300 reduction were found not to meet the criteria for a vulnerability trait marker of schizophrenia, the P300 technique would still be useful in understanding the symptoms of schizophrenia. For example, research using P300 could help to identify specific stages or aspects of information processing that are responsible for impaired attention (e.g., Duncan-Johnson, Roth, & Kopell, 1984). The dynamic, noninvasive nature of P300 also makes it especially attractive as a means of studying the biological bases of schizophrenia. For example, study of the effects on P300 of centrally acting drugs that affect brain areas implicated in schizophrenia could lead to a P300 marker for neurochemical imbalances or structural abnormalities (e.g., Duncan & Kaye, 1987). The temporal resolution of P300 could support inferences about brain events on time scales not possible in studies using tissue assays or radioactivity (Duncan in Roth et al., 1986).

The examples I have cited illustrate the potential usefulness of the P300 method in schizophrenia research. Ideally, the full power of this method would be attained by studying diverse types of patients with valid and current diagnoses, using paradigms that tap different aspects of information processing, studying the effects of the experimental variables on P300 as well as other ERP components, identifying homogeneous clinical and biological subtypes of schizophrenia, and correlating ERPs with behavioral responses and measures of brain structure and function. Despite the difficulties inherent in such an approach to schizophrenia research, the potential reward is substantial.

Acknowledgment. The author wishes to thank Allan F. Mirsky for his helpful comments on the manuscript.

---

[5] If P300 amplitude were found to distinguish ill from well relatives of schizophrenic probands in a large number of families, P300 would meet one of the criteria for a vulnerability trait.

References

Baribeau-Braun, J., Picton, T.W., & Gosselin, J.-Y. (1983). Schizophrenia: a neurophysiological evaluation of abnormal information processing. *Science*, *219*, 874–876.

Baron, M. (1986). Genetics of schizophrenia. II. Vulnerability traits and gene markers. *Biological Psychiatry*, *21*, 1189–1211.

Brecher, M., & Begleiter, H. (1983). Event-related brain potentials to high-incentive stimuli in unmedicated schizophrenic patients. *Biological Psychiatry*, *18*, 661–674.

Chapman, L.J., Chapman, J.P., & Raulin, M.L. (1976). Scales for physical and social anhedonia. *Journal of Abnormal Psychology*, *85*, 374–382.

Cornblatt, B.A., & Erlenmeyer-Kimling L. (1985). Global attentional deviance as a marker of risk for schizophrenia: specificity and predictive validity. *Journal of Abnormal Psychology*, *94*, 470–486.

Dawson, M.E., & Nuechterlein, K.H. (1984). Psychophysiological dysfunctions in the developmental course of schizophrenia disorders. *Schizophrenia Bulletin*, *10*, 204–232.

Diagnostic and Statistical Manual of Mental Disorders (1987) (DSM-IIIR) Third edition revised. Washington: American Psychiatric Association.

Donchin, E. (Ed.) (1982). *Cognitive psychophysiology: event-related potentials and the study of cognition*. Hillsdale, NJ: Erlbaum.

Duncan, C.C. (1988). Application of event-related brain potentials to the analysis of interictal attention in absence epilepsy. In M.S. Myslobodsky, & A.F. Mirsky (Eds.), *Elements of petit mal epilepsy* (pp. 341–364). New York: Peter Lang.

Duncan, C.C., & Kaye, W.H. (1987). Effects of clonidine on event-related potential measures of information processing. In R. Johnson, Jr., J.W. Rohrbaugh, & R. Parasuraman (Eds.), *Current trends in event-related potential research* (EEG supplement 40) (pp. 527–531). Amsterdam: Elsevier Science.

Duncan, C.C., Kaye, W.H., Perlstein, W.M., Jimerson, D.C., & Mirsky, A.F. (1985). Cognitive processing in eating disorders: an ERP analysis. *Psychophysiology*, *22*, 588.

Duncan, C.C., Perlstein, W.M., & Morihisa, J.M. (1987). The P300 metric in schizophrenia: effects of probability and modality. In R. Johnson, Jr., J.W. Rohrbaugh, & R. Parasuraman (Eds.), *Current trends in event-related potential research* (EEG supplement 40) (pp. 670–674). Amsterdam: Elsevier Science.

Duncan-Johnson, C.C. (1981). P300 latency: a new metric of information processing. *Psychophysiology*, *18*, 207–215.

Duncan-Johnson, C.C. & Donchin, E. (1977). On quantifying surprise: the variation of event-related potentials with subjective probability. *Psychophysiology*, *14*, 456–467.

Duncan-Johnson, C.C., & Donchin, E. (1982). The P300 component of the event-related brain potential as an index of information processing. *Biological Psychology*, *14*, 1–52.

Duncan-Johnson, C.C. & Kopell, B.S. (1981). The Stroop effect: brain potentials localize the source of interference. *Science*, *214*, 938–940.

Duncan-Johnson, C.C., Roth, W.T., & Kopell, B.S. (1984). Effects of stimulus sequence on P300 and reaction time in schizophrenics: a preliminary report. In R. Karrer, J. Cohen, & P. Tueting (Eds.), *Brain and information: event-related potentials* (pp. 570–577). New York: The New York Academy of Sciences.

Friedman, D., Cornblatt, B., Vaughan, H., Jr., & Erlenmeyer-Kimling, L. (1986). Event-related potentials in children at risk for schizophrenia during two versions of the continuous performance test. *Psychiatry Research*, *18*, 161–177.

Goodin, D.S., Squires, K.C., & Starr, A. (1978). Long latency event-related components of the auditory evoked potential in dementia. *Brain*, *101*, 635–648.

Gottesman, I.I., & Shields, J. (1982). *Schizophrenia: The epigenetic puzzle*. Cambridge: Cambridge University Press.

Hillyard, S.A., & Kutas, M. (1983). Electrophysiology of cognitive processing. *Annual Review of Psychology*, *34*, 33–61.

Holzman, P.S. (1987). Recent studies of psychophysiology in schizophrenia. *Schizophrenia Bulletin, 13*, 49–75.

Josiassen, R.C., Shagass, C., Mancall, E.L., & Roemer, R.A. (1984). Auditory and visual evoked potentials in Huntington's disease. *Electroencephalography and Clinical Neurophysiology, 57*, 113–118.

Josiassen, R.C., Shagass, C., Roemer, R.A., & Straumanis, J.J. (1981). The attention—related somatosensory evoked potential late positive wave in psychiatric patients. *Psychiatry Research, 5*, 147–155.

Josiassen, R.C., Shagass, C., Roemer, R.A., & Straumanis, J.J. (1985). Attention-related effects on somatosensory evoked potentials in college students at high risk for psychopathology. *Journal of Abnormal Psychology, 94*, 507–518.

Josiassen, R.C., Shagass, C., Straumanis, J.J., & Roemer, R.A. (1984). Psychiatric drugs and the somatosensory P400 wave. *Psychiatry Research, 11*, 151–162.

Kraepelin, E. (1971). *Dementia praecox and paraphrenia*, (R.M. Barclay, Trans.). Huntington, NY: Krieger. (Originally published, 1919).

Kutas, M., McCarty, G., & Donchin, E. (1977). Augmenting mental chronometry: the P300 as a measure of stimulus evaluation time. *Science, 197*, 792–795.

Levit, R.A., Sutton, S., & Zubin, J. (1973). Evoked potential correlates of information processing in psychiatric patients. *Psychological Medicine, 3*, 487–494.

Matthysse, S. (1978). Missing links. In J.M Tanner (Ed.), *Psychiatric research: the widening perspective* (pp. 148–150). New York: International Universities Press.

McCarthy, G., & Donchin, E. (1981). A metric for thought: a comparison of P300 latency and reaction time. *Science, 211*, 77–80.

Mirsky, A.F., & Duncan, C.C. (1986). Etiology and expression of schizophrenia: neurobiological and psychosocial factors. *Annual Review of Psychology, 37*, 291–319.

Nuechterlein, K.H., & Dawson, M.E. (1984). Information processing and attentional functioning in the developmental course of schizophrenic disorders. *Schizophrenia Bulletin, 10*, 160–203.

Overall, J.E., & Gorham, D.R. (1962). The brief psychiatric rating scale. *Psychological Reports, 10*, 799–812.

Pass, H.L., Klorman, R., Salzman, L.F., Klein, R.H., & Kaskey, G.B. (1980). The late positive component of the evoked response in acute schizophrenics during a test of sustained attention. *Biological Psychiatry, 15*, 9–20.

Pfefferbaum, A., Wenegrat, B.G., Ford, J.M., Roth, W.T., & Kopell, B.S. (1984). Clinical application of the P3 component of event-related potentials: II. Dementia, depression and schizophrenia. *Electroencephalography and Clinical Neurophysiology, 59*, 104–24.

Polich, J., & Burns, T. (1987). P300 from identical twins. *Neuropsychologia, 25*, 299–304.

Pritchard, W.S. (1986). Cognitive event-related potential correlates of schizophrenia. *Psychological Bulletin, 100*, 43–66.

Roth, W.T., & Cannon, E.H. (1972). Some features of the auditory evoked response in schizophrenics. *Archives of General Psychiatry, 27*, 466–471.

Roth, W.T., Horvath, T.B., Pfefferbaum, A., Tinklenberg, J.R., Mezzich, J., & Kopell, B.S. (1979). Late event-related potentials and schizophrenia. In H. Begleiter (Ed.), *Evoked brain potentials and behavior* (pp. 499–515). New York: Plenum.

Roth, W.T., Horvath, T.B., Pfefferbaum, A., & Kopell, B.S. (1980). Event-related potentials in schizophrenics. *Electroencephalography and Clinical Neurophysiology, 48*, 127–139.

Roth, W.T., Pfefferbaum, A., Kelly, A.F., Berger, P.A., & Kopell, B.S. (1981). Auditory event-related potentials in schizophrenia and depression. *Psychiatry Research, 4*, 199–212.

Roth, W.T., Duncan, C.C., Pfefferbaum, A., & Timsit-Berthier, M. (1986). Applications of cognitive ERPs in psychiatric patients. In W.C. McCallum, R. Zappoli, & F. Denoth (Eds.), *Cerebral psychophysiology: studies in event-related potentials (EEG Supplement 38)*, (pp. 419–438). Amsterdam: Elsevier.

Saitoh, O., Niwa, S.-I., Hiramatsu, K.-I., Kameyama, T., Rymar, K., & Itoh, K. (1984). Abnormalities in late positive components of event-related potentials may reflect a genetic predisposition to schizophrenia. *Biological Psychiatry, 19*, 293–303.

Shagass C. (1979). Sensory evoked potentials in psychosis. In H. Begleiter (Ed.), *Evoked brain potentials and behavior*. New York: Plenum.

Shagass, C. (1986). Commentary on *Current evoked potential research and information processing in schizophrenics*, by J. Baribeau. *Integrative Psychiatry*, *4*, 109–121.

Simons, R.F. (1982). Physical anhedonia and future psychopathology: an electrocortial continuity? *Psychophysiology*, *19*, 433–441.

Spitzer, R.L., Endicott, J., & Robins, E. (1977). *Research diagnostic criteria (RDC) for a selected group of functional disorders* (3rd ed.). New York: Biometrics Research, New York State Psychiatric Institute.

Steinhauer, S., & Zubin, J. (1982). Vulnerability to schizophrenia: information processing in the pupil and event-related potential. In E, Usdin & I. Hanin (Eds.), *Biological markers in psychiatry and neurology* (pp. 371–385). Oxford: Pergamon.

Surwillo, W.W. (1980). Cortical evoked potentials in monozygotic twins and unrelated subjects: comparisons of exogenous and endogenous components. *Behavior Genetics*, *10*, 201–209.

Sutton, S., Braren, M., Zubin, J., & John, E.R. (1965). Evoked-potential correlates of stimulus uncertainty. *Science*, *150*, 1187–1188.

Sutton, S., Hakerem, G., Zubin, J., & Portnoy, M. (1961). The effect of shift of sensory modality on serial reaction-time: a comparison of schizophrenics and normals. *American Journal of Psychology*, *74*, 224–232.

Functional Role of the Different Autonomic Nervous System Activity Patterns Found in Schizophrenia – A New Model

E.R. Straube, and A. Öhman

Correlates of the Heterogeneous Autonomic Nervous System Response in Schizophrenia

Orienting Response and Psychopathology

Autonomic nervous system (ANS) reactivity is as elusive as almost any other characteristic in providing a uniform pattern for describing schizophrenia. Thus, trying to use this type of information to reduce the heterogeneous clinical phenomenon called schizophrenia to a limited number of basic psychobiological factors is not likely to be successful.

However, seen from a different perspective, data suggest that ANS heterogeneity reflects – as do other biological measures – the psychobiological basis of the heterogeneous clinical phenomena. We will describe a model which may serve as a conceptual tool to organize the heterogeneous data in order to elucidate the functional role of ANS activity in different phases of the developmental course of the illness. The model, therefore, should predict differences in vulnerability and developmental course of schizophrenia by means of the different ANS activity patterns found in schizophrenia.

Before we describe such a model, a short review of the empirical background is presented, focused on ANS responses to a certain set of relatively well-defined stimuli, the orienting stimuli. Most studies define orienting stimuli as a series of 10–15 medium intensity tones (75–85 dB) of short duration (1–2 s). The subject is instructed to ignore the tones and to relax. This, therefore, is considered a nondemanding experimental condition.

The usual ANS variable measured here is the skin conductance (SC) response (SCR), primarily reflecting activity in the sympathetically innervated palmar sweat glands. The specific response is called the skin conductance orienting response (SCOR).

The results of the large number of studies reporting SCOR activity in schizophrenics provide an excellent example of the heterogeneous psychobiological response pattern often found in this disorder. Öhman (1981) examined the literature in a comprehensive review article including more than 30 studies. In all these investigations, SCOR activity differed within the schizophrenic group and among studies. A few patients may show the expected type of response, that is, habituating SCOR activity as the orienting stimulus is repeated. Some patients fail to habituate within the number of stimuli used (nonhabituators), whereas other patients (in most studies the largest subgroup) typically do not respond at all to the stimuli used. This latter group is labelled SC nonresponders, and its relative size varies between 0% and 66% in different studies (see Öhman, 1981 and Fig. 1). Figure 1 gives the results of an orienting response (OR) experiment with unmedicated schizophrenic patients (no medication for at least 4 weeks). Electrodermal responses as well as pulse amplitude reductions due to ten orienting stimuli (85-dB, 1000-Hz tones) were measured (Straube and Heimann, 1985).

Even when very similar studies using identical procedures for data reduction and analysis are considered (see the multicenter study of Bernstein et al., 1982), the frequency of SCOR in different subgroups may still show marked differences. Such differences in spite of similar methodologies seem to imply that differences in sample selection play an important role in the SCOR differences reported.

This assumption is supported by the findings of Gruzelier (1976), Straube (1979), and Bernstein et al. (1982), which showed that (SCOR) nonresponders (as defined above) differed significantly from responders (three or more SCORs elicited) in their psychopathological pattern. Gruzelier (1976) found that responders had a more "active" symptom pattern than nonresponders. The responders scored significantly higher than nonresponders in scales measuring anxiety, manic state, and psychotic belligerence, and in attention-demanding and assaultive behavior in the nurses' rating using the Wittenborn Psychiatric Rating Scale. Straube (1979) and Bernstein et al. (1982) both employed the Brief Psychiatric Rating Scale (BPRS) of Overall and Gorham (1962). Straube (1979) investigated a newly admitted acute sample and Bernstein et al. (1981), a chronic sample. Both studies agreed that responders displayed more "active" behaviour since they had significantly higher excitement ratings, whereas the symptom of emotional withdrawal was significantly more frequent in nonresponders. In both studies the incidence of conceptual disorganization was also significantly higher in nonresponders than in responders. Other measures were also significantly different between the two groups in the study of Straube (1979): nonresponders showed more signs of depressive mood, somatic concern, motor retardation, and fewer mannerisms and less posturing than responders; these differences were not found in the chronic sample of Bernstein et al. (1981).

Nonresponding, therefore, appears more prominent in samples with predominantly negative symptoms, but, as we have seen, not all types of negative symptoms are always displayed by nonresponders. Responders, on the other hand, seem to be more prevalent in samples with predominantly positive symptoms.

Indirect evidence for this assumption comes from studies which intentionally limited sampling to one section of the schizophrenic population, i.e., to patients with dominant positive symptoms (Bartfai, Levander, Edman,

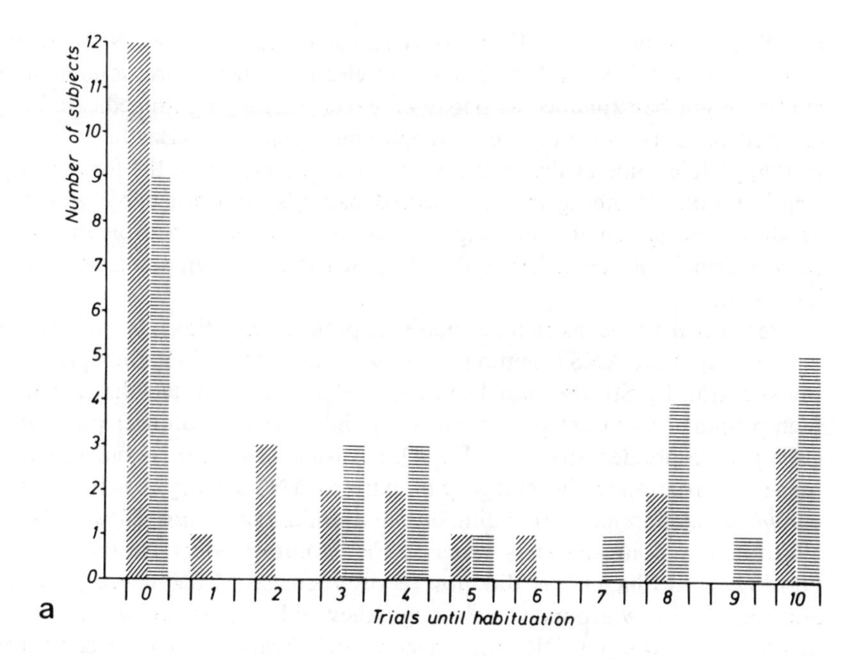

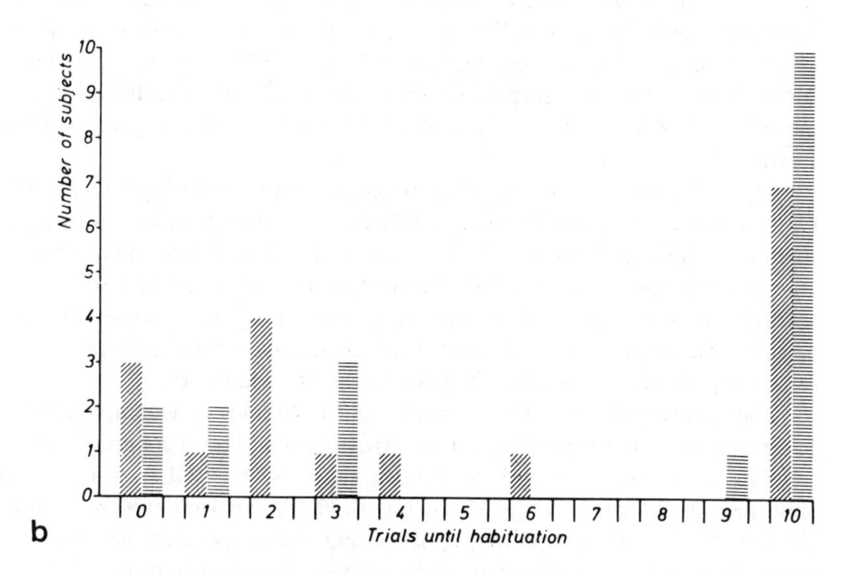

Fig. 1a, b. Distribution of two components of the orienting response until habituation; skin conductance orienting response (*diagonally shaded columns*) and finger pulse volume orienting response (*horizontally shaded columns*) to ten orienting stimuli, 85-dB, 1000-Hz tones. **a** Response distribution of unmedicated schizophrenics, $n=27$. **b** Response distribution of healthy controls, $n=18$

Schalling, & Sedvall, 1983; Frith, Stevens, Johnstone, & Crow, 1979). Bartfai et al. (1983) maintained that the absence of electrodermal nonresponders in their study "might be explained as partly an effect of studying unmedicated hyperaroused patients with positive schizophrenic symptoms" (Bartfai et al., 1983, p. 186). While some evidence exists for the latter assertion, the former suggesting less nonresponding in unmedicated patients does not agree with results produced by systematic investigation of the effects of neuroleptics on the electrodermal OR (Gruzelier et al., 1981; Gruzelier & Hammond, 1978; Venables, 1975).

Peripheral vasoconstriction (pulse amplitude reduction), a cardiovascular component of the ANS orienting response, is also reduced in schizophrenia. An investigation by Straube and Heimann (1985) demonstrated that a relatively high proportion of electrodermal *non*responders were also finger pulse volume (FPV) *non*responders (64%, see Fig. 1). Bernstein et al. (1981) observed an even higher covariation in this category of extreme ANS activity reduction: in their *chronic* schizophrenics, depending on the stimulus conditions, 64%–85% of the electrodermal nonresponders were also FPV nonresponders. However, Öhman, Nordby, & d'Elia (1989) did not report increased FPV nonresponding in electrodermal *non*responders, although they did find attenuated response in another cardiovascular OR component, namely heart rate (HR) deceleration. It has been shown in several studies that other physiological variables are also reduced in SC *non*responder groups (see, for example, the review by Straube, 1980). However, in the SCOR *responders* in the study of Straube and Heimann (1985) the correlation between SC responding and FPV responding was low and insignificant. This is not surprising when we consider that the different components of the ANS are also poorly correlated in healthy subjects (see, for example, Fowles, 1980).

From this perspective, the relatively consistent relationship between SC and cardiovascular components of the OR in the *non*responding category is an interesting finding. However, because the correlation is low in the responding category (Bernstein et al., 1981; Straube & Heimann, 1985) and since most investigations of the OR in schizophrenics are based solely on the SC component, further considerations of the functional role of the ANS deviation in schizophrenics will essentially refer to the SC component.

The absence of an SCOR in many schizophrenics is accompanied by low levels of activity in other SC measures. Most studies show a covariation between number of SCORs to reach habituation, SC level (SCL), and number of spontaneous fluctuations (SFs) during the OR experiment (for review, see Öhman, 1981). In other words, schizophrenic nonresponders generally have a lower SCL with fewer SFs than schizophrenic slow habituators.

Although SCOR differences are related to different patterns of symptomatology within schizophrenia, no SCOR pattern is specific to schizophrenia, i.e., the same response patterns can be found in all groups including normal control groups. However, one exception may be nonresponding, which seems to be more prevalent in psychopathological states and less frequent in normal populations (approximately 7% in normals; see, for example, Straube, 1979). It has, for instance, been shown that the incidence of electrodermal nonresponding is enhanced in depressives (Giedke, Heimann, & Straube, 1982) and chronic alcoholics (Cohen, Sommer, & Hermanutz, 1981; Sommer, 1982).

Considering the fact that at least some of the negative symptoms can be considered nonspecific (see, for example, Carpenter, Heinrichs, & Alphs, 1985), the nonspecificity of nonresponding seems plausible. Many negative symptoms, like anhedonia, withdrawal, generalized retardation, and energy loss, are also transient or enduring signs of depressives, alcoholics, and individuals with other psychiatric disorders.

Carpenter et al. (1985) assumed that diminution in emotional expression, curiosity, and interpersonal involvement, for example, could constitute a "defensive maneuver to dampen external stimuli" (p. 442). Thus, it can be interpreted as a nonspecific coping strategy. Consistent with this interpretation, Rubens and Lapidus (1978) reported that SCOR nonrespnders displayed higher stimulus barrier functions than responders on the Bellak scale.

To summarize the findings reported in this section, the data suggest that attenuated SCOR activity among schizophrenics may be related to reduced orienting activity in cardiovascular measures and to a specific psychopathological state of potential significance for coping processes.

OR and Information Processing

If schizophrenics are allocated to subgroups of nonresponders and responders depending on whether they fail to exhibit or exhibit SCORs, different patterns of information processing seem to emerge. The two-flash threshold is higher in schizophrenic SCOR nonresponders than in schizophrenic SCOR responders (Gruzelier & Venables, 1974). Patterson and Venables (1980) found that the discrimination of signal from noise on a signal detection task (d′ criterion) was poorer in nonresponders *and* responders as compared to a group of schizophrenics with fast habituation of the SCOR. Fast habituators habituated in one or two trials, and their performance did not differ from normals. In the study by Straube (1979) the nonresponders made more errors, predominantly *errors of omission*, on a dichotic shadowing task regardless of distraction conditions. Consequently, a disturbance of selective attention, i.e., higher distractibility, does not appear to be the basis of the poorer performance in the nonresponders. The errors due to distraction from the irrelevant channel were not higher in the responders than in the nonresponders. Alm, Lindström, Öst, and Öhman (1984) found no differences between nonresponders and responders in a short-term memory distraction test.

A possible interpretation of these findings is that the nonresponders have a higher perceptual threshold or – according to the interpretation of Dawson and Nuechterlein (1984) – allocate less processing capacity to external events.

Cornblatt, Lenzenweger, Dworkin, and Erlenmeyer-Kimling (1985), using an information overload task, report reduced processing capacity in negative-symptom schizophrenics. Nonresponders tend to display a pattern of negative symptoms, as was discussed in the previous section. Nonresponding and reduced processing capacity may therefore be related. The nature of information-processing characteristics of the responders is less clear. The four studies done so far compare SCOR nonresponder patients with patients who have three or more SCORs. It may be possible to reveal the exact nature of the processing deficit in a more extreme subgroup, i.e., schizophrenics who fail to habituate. Dawson and Nuechterlein (1984) speculate that the responders allocate processing capacity indiscriminantly and should, therefore, be more easily distracted in a selective attention task. This speculation is indirectly supported by findings reported by Walker and coworkers (Green & Walker, 1986; Walker & Harvey, 1986). They found positive-symptom schizophrenics to be more susceptible to distraction in a digit span, short-term memory task than were negative-symptom schizophrenics. With regard to the small number of studies done so far, Dawson and Nuechterlein (1984) conclude that "the relationship between SCORs and information processing in schizophrenia is in need of further investigation and appears to be a particularly promising area for further research" (p. 213).

ANS Response to Demand and Stress

Actively Symptomatic Patients

So far, we have discussed ANS responses to nondemanding, innocuous orienting stimuli. We now turn to ANS responses of schizophrenics to a category of stimuli to which healthy subjects elicit an effortful, increased ANS response. Under such experimental conditions, we will see again that different ANS response patterns can be provoked within actively symptomatic schizophrenics and in subjects with a genetic risk for schizophrenia.

The area of ANS response to demand and stress is the most interesting, but, for methodological reasons, the most difficult to evaluate. Nevertheless, a relatively uniform pattern of ANS activation to various types of demanding or stressing stimuli emerges *within* the different subgroups.

Again, reduced electrodermal reactivity, in addition to increased reactivity, was observed in earlier studies of schizophrenics (Peterson & Jung, 1907; for other psychophysiological variables, see Hoskins, 1946, and Lang & Buss, 1965). A review of earlier Russian studies revealed that some schizophrenic patients never showed a response to painful stimulation (Lynn, 1963). These studies are especially interesting because they were all conducted *before* the introduction of neuroleptics.

A perusal of recent studies gives the impression that deficient ANS reactivity is found predominantly in chronic schizophrenics. Unfortunately, no systematic comparisons between acute and chronic schizophrenics are available and, in some studies, the patients were on neuroleptics. Öhman, Nordby, and D'Elia (1986) examined the ANS response of chronic schizophrenics during a reaction time task. The schizophrenics displayed smaller and less discriminating SC, FPV, and HR responses to signal and nonsignal tones than did controls. Rist and Cohen (1979) observed lower cardiac reactivity in response to emotional stimuli: significantly *smaller* HR changes in response to *negative* emotional words were observed in chronic schizophrenics than in normals and psychiatric controls, particularly when these words had social significance. Moreover, this selectively lower reactivity correlated with a BPRS factor indicative of lower affective involvement with events in the environment (emotional withdrawal, depression, drive reduction, affective blunting). Since the patients received neuroleptics, it is possible that the findings may have been influenced by the medication. The latter interpretation, however, is refuted by the extensive study of Gray (1975) who investigated drug-free chronic patients. Gray reported relatively *smaller* tonic ANS activity (SCL and tonic HR) changes from baseline to *high* intensity stimulation and demand as compared to the ANS activity change under low-intensity stimulation. (Low-intensity stimuli were 70-dB tones, and high-intensity stimuli were 110-dB tones. Demand and no demand conditions were reaction time task and no reaction time task; see Fig. 2.) The normal control group did not show this pattern of reduced ANS activity under high-intensity stimulation and demand. To investigate the possible effect of long-term institutionalization, a group of long-term prisoners were tested as an additional control group; no differences were found between this group and the normal control group (Gray, 1975). Therefore, it appears that the paradoxical decrease in SCL and the attenuated HR change under more demanding stimulation are correlates of schizophrenia and possibly of the chronic subtype with predominantly negative symptoms.

Davis, Buchsbaum, van Kammen, and Bunney (1979) established that the N100 component of the evoked potential to painful stimuli in unmedicated chronic schizophrenics is correspondingly lower. The amplitudes of evoked potentials increased after administration of naloxone, an endorphin antagonist.

High-Risk Subjects

Because acute schizophrenics are less able to participate in complex tasks, limited information is available on this population. The study of populations at increased risk of developing a schizophrenic disorder, because of genetic loading, may provide important insights concerning the role of ANS deviations as vulnerability indicators.

In contrast to the findings in actively symptomatic schizophrenics, *no* reduced reactivity has been observed in high-risk populations. In this respect,

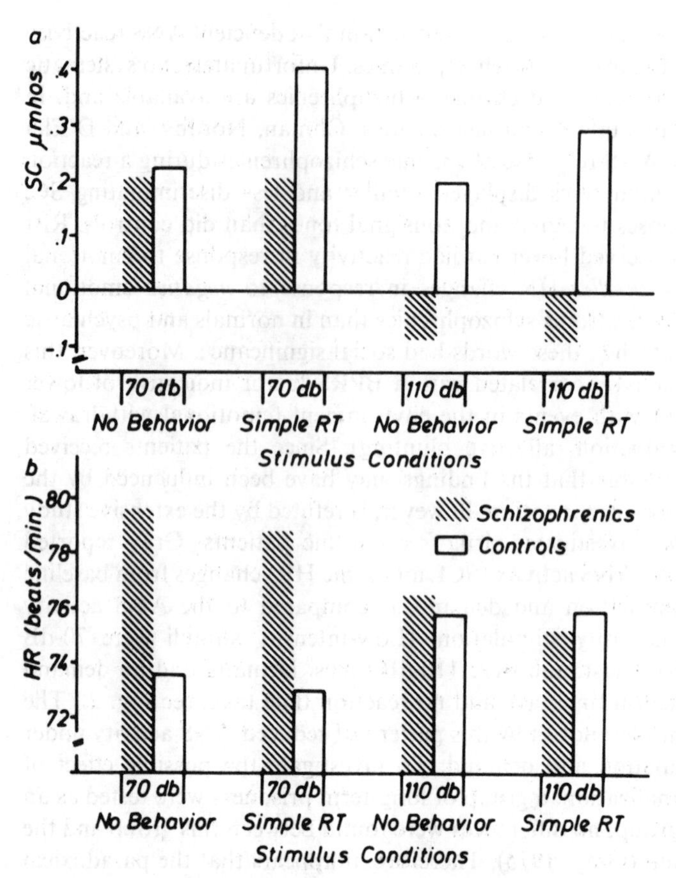

Fig. 2a Skin conductance (SC) anticipatory response changes as a function of stimulus conditions. **b** Heart rate (HR) tonic level changes as a function of stimulus conditions. *RT*, reaction time task. *Shaded columns,* schizophrenics; *unshaded columns,* controls (After Gray, 1975)

the findings clearly differ from the test results in actively symptomatic (chronic) patients.

To date, offspring of schizophrenics have been examined in eight larger high-risk projects. Reports on ANS reactivity of children of schizophrenics and corresponding control populations are now available from five of these projects. The authors of three of these studies report no alteration of ANS reactivity. Elevated ANS reactivity was observed in two studies. The three studies that reported no alteration in ANS (electrodermal) reactivity are the New York (Fein, Tursky, & Erlenmeyer-Kimling, 1974), the St. Louis (Janes & Stern, 1976; Janes, Hesselbrock, & Stern, 1978), and the Israeli (Kugelmass, Marcus, & Schmuell, 1985) high-risk projects.

The oldest and largest high-risk study with respect to the number of cases (207 high-risk subjects) was started in 1962 by Mednick and Schulsinger

(Mednick & Schulsinger, 1968; Parnas, Schulsinger, & Mednick, this volume). SC changes to orienting stimuli and high-intensity stimuli (96-dB noise) were examined. The high-risk children responded to the orienting and the unpleasant high-intensity stimuli with stronger SC activity (higher amplitude, shorter latency, and higher SCL) than the control group of children of nonschizoprenic mothers.

A psychiatric follow-up of the children was performed in 1972. At this time, most of the subjects in the high-risk group had entered the risk period for schizophrenia, i.e., the age at which schizophrenia could develop. Investigation of whether signs of elevated electrodermal reactivity were related to later development of a schizophrenic disorder showed an association for men at high risk, but not for women (Mednick et al., 1978).

Negative findings from other high-risk studies led Mednick and Schulsinger to reanalyze their material. They suspected that sampling differences (particularly in comparison to the New York high-risk project by Erlenmeyer-Kimling, 1975) were responsible for the discrepancies. As Fig. 3 shows, it could, in fact, be established that evidence of enhanced SC reactivity was found most frequently in high-risk children who came from *nonintact homes* (e.g., mother or father frequently absent, children reared in institutional settings). The SC amplitudes of high-risk children from an *intact* home were only marginally higher than those of children from the low-risk group, that is, children without a schizophrenic parent. In the latter group, intactness of the home only played an insignificant role with respect to electrodermal activity (Mednick, 1978). Higher SC activity here means higher amplitude, shorter response latency, and higher conductance level. The differential SC amplitude responses of the low-and high-risk children are depicted in Fig. 3.

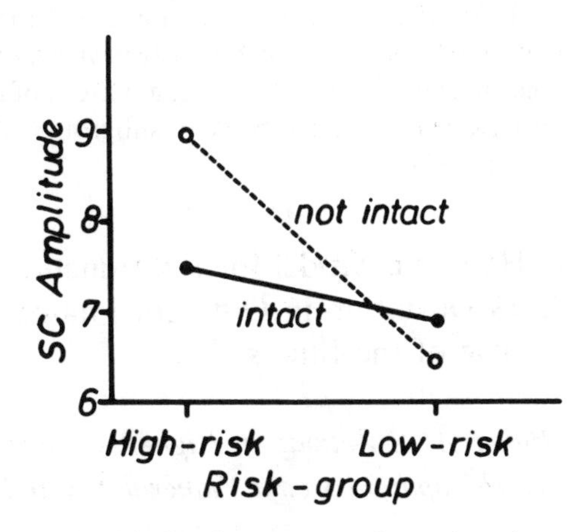

Fig. 3. Skin conductance amplitudes (over all trials, i.e., innocuous and aversive stimulus conditions) of high-risk and low-risk groups by intactness of family (*solid line*, intact; *dotted line*, not intact). (After Mednick, 1978)

This finding may reflect the interaction between unfavorable environmental conditions and ANS arousability due to genetic disposition. In other words, electrodermal arousability was elevated in children at high risk *only* under unfavorable psychosocial environmental conditions.

Salzman and Klein (1978) of the University of Rochester high-risk project used a method similar to that of Mednick and Schulsinger. They reported higher SCL during presentation of the orienting tones, but no significant deviation in other measures (SC amplitude, etc.). The SCR to high-intensity tones, however, was again clearly stronger in the high-risk subjects than in the controls. This study, however, did not analyze interaction between ANS activity and "noxious" psychosocial conditions.

Adopted children represent a population that is at increased risk only because of genetic reasons. That is to say, although they have inherited genes from a schizophrenic biological parent, they have been reared in "normal" homes. Studying foster-reared offspring of schizophrenics is, therefore, methodologically superior to the other high-risk designs, since the possible effect of living with a latent or manifest psychotic parent does not influence the developmental course of the offspring.

Van Dyke, Rosenthal, and Rasmussen (1974) compared foster-reared children born to schizophrenic parents with a control group of foster-reared children of nonschizophrenic biological parents. They used nearly the same measures and stimulation methods employed by Mednick and Schulsinger since the study was done in Mednick and Schulsinger's laboratory in Denmark. This increases the comparability of the results. Their findings again showed higher electrodermal activity to innocuous and aversive stimuli in the index group than in the control group (adopted children with *non*schizophrenic biological parents). However, as with the Salzman and Klein (1978) study, the differences were not as clearcut as in the results of the Mednick and Schulsinger study.

In summary, it may be assumed that the ANS response, i.e., SCR, in high-risk populations is not necessarily deviant. However, in the presence of unfavorable environmental conditions, a pattern of *higher* SC activity to innocuous and aversive stimuli may emerge in subgroups of potentially more vulnerable high-risk subjects.

A Heuristic Model for the Functional Meaning of ANS Deviation in Different Phases of the Developmental Course of the Illness

Higher ANS Activity in High-Risk Individuals and Preschizophrenics as a Vulnerability Indicator

ANS deviations are not reported in all high-risk studies. The results of the Mednick and Schulsinger project suggest that unfavorable life conditions provoke a rise in SC activity to innocuous and aversive stimuli in children at genetic risk. Slight disturbances of information processing, however, are present in these high-risk subjects (see Parnas & Schulsinger, 1986; or review by Nuechterlein & Dawson, 1984; and Nuechterlein & Zaucha, this volume).

How can this discrepancy be explained? Applying a vulnerability-stress model (e.g., Zubin & Spring, 1977) to the reported findings, it can be hypothesized that a liability to cognitive disturbance is the underlying (genetically transmitted) deficit, the diathesis. Since the majority of high-risk children will never develop schizophrenia, other factors must have a modulating effect. It can be assumed that two factors are responsible: the amount of genetic loading and the amount of stress (e.g., adverse life events or enduring adverse life conditions encountered in the environment of the high-risk individual).

This assumption is supported by a recent analysis of Burman, Mednick, Machon, Parnas, and Schulsinger (1987). The authors revealed that the family relationships of high-risk offspring who later developed schizophrenia were significantly less satisfactory than the family relationships of high-risk offspring who were later diagnosed as having only a schizotypal personality disorder or no severe mental illness. Burman et al. (1987) conclude that the "findings of this study are intriguing in that they provide additional support for the diathesis-stress model by suggesting that people at high genetic risk for schizophrenia decompensate in part because of the environmental stress associated with unsatisfactory family relationships" (p. 366).

The role of stress in the development of schizophrenia is of interest in connection with the interpretation of the ANS findings: first of all, according to the models of Kahneman (1973) and Öhman (1979), the ANS plays a functional role in information processing in normal subjects as a component in the allocation of processing resources. Secondly, stress leads to a rise of ANS activity in normal subjects and also in high-risk subjects, as we have seen. Because the information processing of subjects at genetic risk for schizophrenia is already characterized by a slight lability, an enduring change in ANS activity due to enduring stress (adverse events) aggravates the disturbance of information processing in these individuals. According to Mandler (1984), emotional events have a disruptive effect on information processing in normals. When information-processing mechanisms are intact, this disruptive effect is only transitory. This is not, however, the case when cognitive processes are already slightly deviant.

Indirect evidence for this suggestion comes from investigations with actively symptomatic patients. Several authors have found that the performance in cognitive tasks declines in schizophrenics when the stimulus material has a positive or negative emotional meaning (Chapman, 1961; Dunn, 1954; Turbiner, 1961; Webb, 1952). Brodsky (1963), for example, compared the performance of acute schizophrenics, chronic schizophrenics, and psychiatric and normal controls in a card-sorting test. Some cards contained emotional scenes, others objects and nonemotional scenes. Both schizophrenic groups performed poorly when the content of the cards was emotional (scenes of people expressing emotions). The control groups did not perform differently according to the emotional or neutral content of the cards. Feffer (1961) presented schizophrenics and a normal control group with verbal material consisting of target words and background words. The content of the target and the background was systematically varied. Feffer found that response errors through intrusion were higher in a subgroup of schizophrenics when the target word had an affective meaning and the background was neutral. The errors were significantly lower in this group when the target had a neutral meaning and the background consisted of emotional stimuli. The performance of the normals was not influenced by stimulus content. Feffer concluded that schizophrenics try to avoid emotional material, since the errors appeared only with emotional targets where intrusions from the neutral background occurred. This was, however, only true for the subgroup of schizophrenic patients who failed in a proverb interpretation pretest, i.e., had a certain type of cognitive disturbance. The role of emotions in vulnerability and developmental course is further elucidated by the finding that high expressed emotion in a key relative is related to early relapse (Leff & Vaughn, 1984).

The hypothesized change from subclinical cognitive deviation to pathological cognitive deviation mediated by stressful events is illustrated in Fig 4. Similar reasonings have been put forward by Nuechterlein and Dawson (1984).

Some of the high-risk individuals, however, will not develop psychopathological states, even under stressful life conditions, since the magnitude of the genetically determined diathesis is lower or stress effects are less enduring in these individuals.

The best index variable for testing the model, according to the reported findings, seems to be the electrodermal activity during experimental innocuous and aversive stimulation, i.e., SCR and SCL to orienting stimuli (SCOR) and to mildly aversive stimuli.

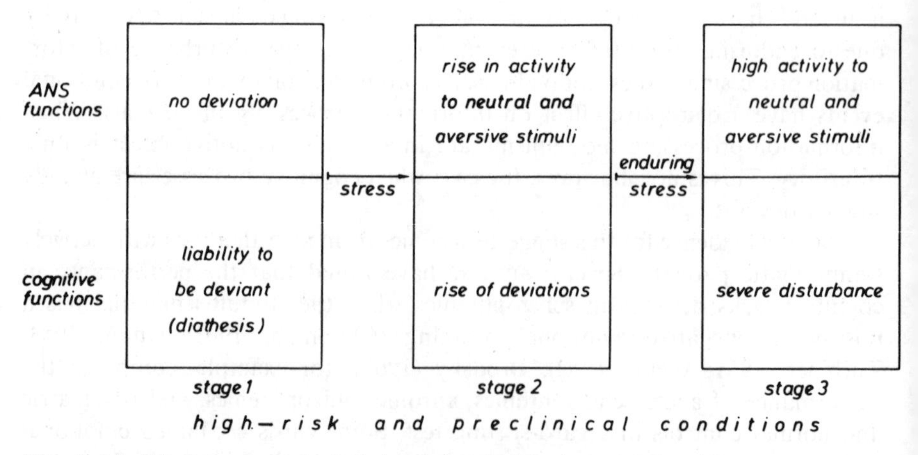

Fig. 4. Model of the hypothetical developmental course of SC activity and cognitive disturbance from high-risk to preclinical phases of the illness.

Two important facts, however, seem to contradict the model: a considerable proportion of actively symptomatic schizophrenics are nonresponders to the innocuous orienting stimuli or, what seems to be even more devastating to the model, display paradoxically *reduced* electrodermal and/or cardiovascular responses to aversive, stressful stimuli.

For further development of the model, therefore, we have to consider that schizophrenia is a heterogeneous illness, i.e., heterogeneous with respect to vulnerability, symptomatology, coping ability, and outcome.

Heterogeneity of the Developmental Course and Symptoms as Reflected by Differences in ANS Activity

According to the results of the long-term outcome study of Tsuang and Dempsey (1979), 54% of schizophrenics have a "poor" long-term outcome and 46% have a "fair" to "good" outcome. "Long-term outcome" in this context refers to the development of the illness over an average of 33 years after admission. These figures confirm similar results reported by Bleuler (1972), as well as the results of Ciompi and Müller (1976). They were further corroborated by Huber, Gross, and Schüttler (1979).

From the model developed thus far, it can be predicted that acute schizophrenics, i.e., patients in the early clinical phase, who display high SC activity to innocuous (orienting) stimuli have a poorer outcome than schizophrenics with early habituation. The available data seem to support this hypothesis. However, data are available only for relatively short follow-up periods (4 weeks to 2 years).

Frith, Stevens, Johnstone, and Crow (1979) studied the 9-week prognosis under placebo and under neuroleptic medication. The prognosis for acute schizophrenics, regardless of whether they were on placebo or neuroleptic medication, was poorer in the group with late habituation of the SCOR. Straube, Schied, Rein, and Breyer-Pfaff (1987) applied a Stepwise Discriminant Analysis to the ANS data for newly admitted, drug-free patients. SCOR, together with three other measures, was again selected as the best predictor of the 4-week outcome of neuroleptic therapy when change in formal thought disorder was the outcome criterion. Schizophrenics with late SCOR habituation had the worst outcome. When change of the total BPRS score was the criterion, the group with late habituation of the FPVOR had the worst outcome. The two outcome groups differed significantly with respect to this variable. In the study of Zahn, Carpenter, and McGlashan (1981b), late habituation of the SCOR, together with two other variables, was again selected by Discriminant Analysis. Here the criterion was change in symptomatology over a 3-month period. In the study of Straube, Wagner, Foerster, Schied, Gaertner, and Heimann (in preparation), Discriminant Analysis selected the (admission test) SCL during orienting and other innocuous stimuli out of ten ANS factors (Principal Component Analysis) as the best predictor of the 9-month outcome. The schizophrenics with relapse (worsening of symptoms as the criterion) had significantly higher SCLs than the group with no relapse. As in the studies of Frith et al. (1979) and Zahn et al. (1981b), this was independent of the drug status of the patients, i.e., the results were the same in the groups on and off medication.

In summary, it can be said that the results seem to be fairly consistent. The schizophrenic group with poor short- or medium-term outcome shows higher SC activity during the presentation of *innocuous stimuli*. Higher SC activity, in most of the five recent studies mentioned, means late habituation of SCOR which was usually connected with higher SCLs. In one study (Straube et al., 1987), cardiovascular OR (FPVOR) was additionally selected as a predictor for one of the four outcome criteria applied. These data, therefore, confirm the model: higher SC activity under innocuous stimulation indicates a high risk for breakdown or, in extension of the model, poor short- and medium-term outcome, which means early relapse in the case of medium-term outcome [(9-month period in the Straube et al. study (in preparation)].

The mentioned contradiction to the model, however, stems from the fact that a subgroup of schizophrenics are (SCOR) nonresponders. It is logical, therefore, to assume that schizophrenics with early habituation *and* schizophrenic nonresponders have a good outcome. The data clearly support the first assumption. With respect to nonresponding, the possible role is less clear. Since nonresponding is linked to negative symptoms, the assumption of good outcome in nonresponders seems to contradict clinical experience and is, in fact, less clearly supported by the studies mentioned above: in the studies of Frith et al. (1979), Zahn et al. (1981a,b), and Straube et al. (in preparation), nonresponders were underrepresented. This could be due to the fact that the majority of these patients were acute first-breakdown patients with predominantly positive symptoms. Frith et al. (1979) intentionally excluded negative-symptom schizophrenic patients from their sample (see first section of this paper). Straube et al. (1987) restricted their sample to good premorbid patients, but did not exclude negative-symptom schizophrenics. They therefore found a considerable number of nonresponders in the sample. In fact, at admission testing, more nonresponders were found in the group which was to improve than in the group which was to have a poorer outcome. The good-outcome group, however, is better characterized as an early habituating group, since this group displayed an average of two responses (cardiovascular OR) to habituation. (The poor-outcome group displayed about five responses to the orienting stimuli at admission testing.)

A result of Schneider (1982) may shed some light on the question of whether negative-symptom nonresponders have a good or a poor prognosis. Schneider examined, in contrast to the other studies, a chronic sample with predominantly negative symptoms. He found that patients who displayed less benefit from a 6-month neuroleptic treatment had less pretreatment electrodermal activity and lower SCLs.

The relationship between SC nonresponding and outcome was recently examined more directly by Öhman's group (Öhman, Öhlund, Alm, Öst, Wieselgren, & Lindström, submitted for publication). They followed a mixed group of schizophrenics – some of them acute and in a first episode and some chronic patients – over a 2-year period. They found that SCOR nonresponding was associated with poor *social* outcome, measured in terms of social contact and ability to support oneself by applying the outcome scale of Strauss and Carpenter (1972). However, the discrepancy between these findings and those previously reviewed may be more apparent than real because of the different outcome criteria used. There is, indeed, no such thing as a unidimensional construct of, say, "poor" outcome in schizophrenia (e.g., Bland, 1982). Outcome is multidimensional and is composed of only moderately intercorrelated measures (Strauss & Carpenter, 1974). The studies by Frith et al. (1979), Zahn et al. (1981b), and Straube et al. (1987, and in preparation) all relied on symptomatic outcome, whether directly assessed (Frith et al., 1979; Zahn et al., 1981b) or assessed through relapse (Straube et al., 1987, and in preparation). According to the vulnerability-stress model (e.g., Zubin & Spring, 1977) aggravation of schizophrenic symptoms occurs in vulnerable individuals as a consequence of excessive stress and strain in daily life. Examples of such stresses may be arguments with friends or conflicts at work. Thus, for vulnerable individuals stress may be a consequence of relatively good social adjustment in terms of social contacts or job performance. However, the poor-outcome nonresponders studied by Öhman et al. (submitted for publication) avoided this type of stress and strain by isolating themselves socially, that is to say, they saw no friends and they did not support themselves on the open job market. By avoiding the potential stress and strain of social life, nonresponders may evade occasional symptom aggravations, but at a considerable social cost. Conversely, responding schizophrenics may have a social life, but at the cost of being exposed to stress and thus risking a worsening of their symptoms. In sum, therefore, nonresponding and extreme responding may both be related to poor outcome, but to different types of poor outcome. Indeed, if the heterogeneous nature of outcome in schizophrenia is accepted (e.g., Strauss & Carpenter, 1974), a natural research priority would be to try to delineate predictors of different types of outcome. According to the present discussion, such differential predictions may follow from the different types of ANS reaction patterns discussed in this paper.

The second apparent contradiction to the model concerns the mentioned findings of *reduced* ANS response to more demanding, stressful stimuli in laboratory testing. These results, usually found in chronic samples, are in sharp contrast to the findings with high-risk subjects, who show no reduction but – under some conditions – *higher* SC activity to aversive stimulation, as discussed in the previous sections. A shift in ANS responsivity, therefore, appears to occur from the early phases of schizophrenia to the later chronic stages. In this context, it is interesting to note that Zahn et al. (1981b) found *reduced* ANS responses to more *demanding and stressful* stimulation in the group with poor outcome. As was already reported, the same poor prognosis patients had a higher ANS activity to *non*demanding orienting stimuli. The demanding task was a reaction time task, and the stressful task was mental arithmetic. Zahn et al. (1981b) report that the number of SCRs to the ready signal and to the imperative stimulus was significantly reduced and that HR deceleration was significantly less pronounced in the poor-outcome group than in the group with good outcome. The response pattern of the good-outcome group was more similar to that of the normal control group, but good- and poor-outcome patients did not differ with respect to severity of psychopathology when initially tested at admission to the research ward of the National Institute of Mental Health (NIMH). Roughly the same pattern appeared when the subjects were tested under more stressful task conditions (reduced SCR frequency), i.e., when the subjects were doing the mental arithmetic task. (Here, the group which was to improve during the 3-month period had an intermediate position with respect to ANS responsivity between the normal control group and the group with poor prognosis, which again displayed reduced ANS activity.) Straube et al. (1987) found a similar pattern of ANS reduction (reduced SCR frequency) under more demanding task conditions (dichotic shadowing task) in the group which was to show less improvement than in the group which was to improve. The shadowing performance did not, however, differ significantly between the outcome groups. In the other outcome studies mentioned above, the subjects were not tested under more demanding task conditions.

More studies, therefore, are needed before a well-founded conclusion can be reached; the results mentioned above, however, support the tentative hypothesis that this paradoxical response pattern can be interpreted as attempts to reduce the effects of demand and stress. A further speculation is that when such attempts are driven to the extreme, they may also result in social withdrawal and SC nonresponding (See Öhman et al., submitted for publication).

Further support for this hypothesis comes from quite a different field: the research group of Venables examined the effect of stimulus intensity on reaction time. In normals, the usual finding is a quickening of reaction time concurrent with an increase of stimulus intensity. In the nonparanoid, chronic schizophrenic patients examined, however, a *slowing* of the reaction time occurred concurrently with an *increase* in stimulus intensity: "... there was a paradoxical increase in reaction time that could be attributed to an increase in Pavlovian transmarginal inhibition" (Venables, 1977, p. 50; see also Venables & Tizard, 1956, 1958). This finding was later replicated by Venables and O'Connors (1959). Unfortunately, no comparison was made between nonparanoid chronic patients and acute schizophrenics with predominantly positive symptoms. A concomitant examination of ANS activity would also have been interesting since, surprisingly, the paradoxical slowing of reaction time with increasing intensity parallels the paradoxical reduction of ANS activity.

It is obvious that the paradoxical reduction of ANS activity should be interpreted as a similar attempt to cope with aversive stimulation. If this is the case, why will these patients have a poor outcome?

The model presented in Fig. 4 postulates that a rise in ANS activity in response to innocuous and aversive stimuli characterizes the preclinical phase. In extension of this it is postulated that a shift in ANS arousal occurs in the further development of the illness: in one group (the group with good prognosis), ANS activity returns to "normal" modulation in accordance with the varying demands in the environment. The subjects with poor prognosis or with an already chronic course show a maladapted pattern of ANS activity, some with high activity to innocuous stimuli, i.e., SCOR hyperresponding, and some with lack of responding to innocuous stimuli, i.e., SCOR nonresponding, and/or paradoxically reduced activity under task demand and stressful stimulation. This model is depicted in Fig. 5. SCOR nonresponding seems to express a pathological coping style which seems to be supported by clinical features found in the nonresponder group, as was already discussed above. The functional meaning of reduced ANS activity under high-intensity stimulation might have the same protective origin. Both patterns might also be – at least in some patients – just the expression of a maladapted nervous system which is incapable of modulating the recruitment of processing resources according to varying external demands. The combination of high ANS activity in response to the nondemanding orienting stimuli with reduced ANS responsivity to demand and aversive stimulation in the studies of Zahn et al. (1981b) and Straube et al. (1987) may be another type of expression of maladaptation. Because the terms "high" and "low activity" have to be understood as relative differences in relation to the responses of the good-prognosis group and the normals, the same response pattern could theoretically be predicted by the assumption of an unmodulated physiological output system which displays a continuous activity in the medium range. Medium activity, unmodulated by external events, would, therefore, be too high for nondemanding situations and too low for demanding situations. Indeed, Öhman et al. (1986) reported a group of chronic schizophrenics to be above normals in SCORs to task-irrelevant visual stimuli, but below normals in ANS responses to task-relevant stimuli. Thus, their paradigm was able to pick up both features of the deviant schizophrenic ANS response profile in the same experimental session.

We need, however, many more experiments in order to uncover the exact functional significance of the different ANS patterns in schizophrenia, i.e., whether they signify coping, defective pathological coping, or a maladapted cognitive-physiological response system. Only follow-up periods of up to 2 years have been tested until now. The different ANS pattern might have a different meaning in relation to longer periods of prediction as compared to short- and medium-term outcome. At present we can only state that deviation from normal ANS variability in any direction – without understanding the exact nature of this deviation – signifies poor short- and medium-term outcome in

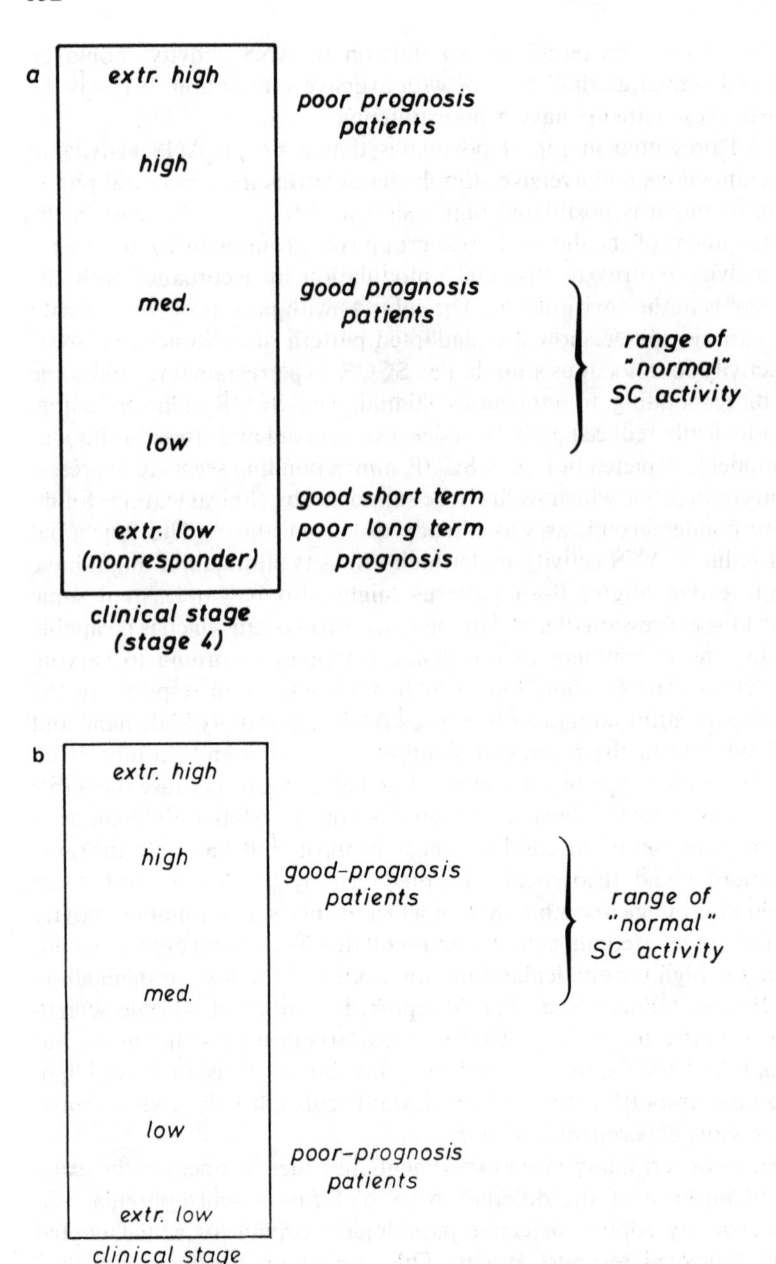

Fig. 5a, b. Model to explain the heterogeneous SC activity of actively symptomatic schizophrenics as a predictor of the heterogeneous outcome of the illness, and comparison with the "normal" SC response range (i.e., in a healthy control group) to different types of stimuli. **a** SC activity to nondemanding, i.e., orienting stimuli. **b** SC activity to demanding or aversive stimuli schizophrenia, which is, however, not a trivial statement since in all outcome studies the poor-outcome and good-outcome patients did not differ from each other with respect to the severity of their illness at admission testing but with respect to their ANS pattern (see, for example, Frith et al., 1979; Öhman et al., submitted for publication; Straube et al., 1987, and in preparation; Zahn et al., 1981b).

For further investigations of the subject, in order to increase the comparability of the findings we propose to examine SCR, SC fluctuations, and SCL to orienting stimuli, to high-intensity noise, and to different degrees of demand.

Although the existence of the different ANS patterns in different subgroups of schizophrenia is supported by cross-sectional data, the model is, however, highly speculative as far as the longitudinal development of ANS activity is concerned. No study exists which has tested the developmental course of ANS activity from preclinical to symptomatic stages of the illness. The same is true for later, long-term development of ANS activity after appearance and change of schizophrenic symptomatology.

We know, however, that a change in ANS activity during short-term treatment occurs (Alm, Öst, & Öhman, 1987; Straube, 1983; Zahn et al., 1981b). Zahn et al. (1981b) demonstrated that change in symptomatology was accompanied by a change in ANS activity. ANS activity has, therefore, to be considered as a state-dependent variable, which is in accordance with our conceptualization of the different ANS patterns, i.e., that they indicate different stages of the developmental course of the illness.

Summary and Conclusion

A conceptual model is proposed to explain heterogeneous ANS activity patterns found in schizophrenia. Characteristic ANS deviations occur in the various stages of the developmental course and predict the heterogeneous development. Electrodermal activity (SCR, SCL) is proposed as the criterion to test the model.

In preclinical stages (the high-risk phases) ANS activity, i.e., SC activity, is usually not deviant. When, however, unfavorable life conditions are present, a rise in SC activity is observed. This is explained within the framework of a diathesis stress model and as a forerunner of clinical breakdown.

Further development of the illness leads to a splitting of the ANS response pattern. Good-prognosis patients modulate ANS activity according to the different degrees of demand and do not differ from normals. Poor-prognosis patients show hyperresponding to nondemanding stimuli (as do high-risk children) and paradoxical reduction to demand. This can be interpreted as a defective capability of the CNS to modulate the physiological output or as an attempt to protect the organism, an interpretation which can be put forward for the poor-prognosis nonresponders as well. Support for both positions can be found in the experimental literature. Because the functional meaning of ANS activity patterns has been tested only for relatively short-term follow-up periods (up to 2 years), it is possible that different subgroups with different long-term development are concealed behind the same ANS pattern.

The model should, therefore, serve as a conceptual framework to allow a more precise testing of hypotheses in order to develop better, i.e., more precise, models of the functional meaning of the different ANS patterns found in schizophrenia.

References

Alm, T., Lindström, L.H., Öst, L.G., & Öhman, A. (1984). Electrodermal non-responding in schizophrenia: Relationships to attentional, clinical, biochemical, computed tomographical and genetic factors. *International Journal of Psychophysiology*, *1*, 195–208.

Alm, T., Öst, L.G., & Öhman, A. (1987). The stability of electrodermal orienting responses in schizophrenic patients. Abstracts of papers presented at the Twenty-Seventh Annual Meeting of the Society for Psychophysiological Research. *Psychophysiology*, *24*, 576.

Bartfai, A., Levander, S., Edman, G., Schalling, D., & Sedvall, G. (1983). Skin conductance responses in unmedicated recently admitted schizophrenic patients. *Psychophysiology*, *20*, 180–187.

Bernstein, A.S., Taylor, K.W., Starkey, P., Juni, S., Lubowsky, J., & Paley, H. (1981). Bilateral skin conductance, finger pulse volume and EEG orienting response to tones of differing intensities in chronic schizophrenics and controls. *Journal of Nervous and Mental Disease*, *169*, 513–528.

Bernstein, A.S., Frith, C.D., Gruzelier, J.H., Patterson, T., Straube, E., Venables, P.H., & Zahn, T.P. (1982). An analysis of the skin conductance orienting response in samples of American, British and German schizophrenics. *Biological Psychology*, *14*, 155–211.

Bland, R.C. (1982). Predicting the outcome in schizophrenia. *Canadian Journal of Psychiatry*, *27*, 52–62.

Bleuler, M. (1972). *Die schizophrenen Geistesstörungen im Lichte langjähriger Kranken- und Familiengeschichten*. Stuttgart: Thieme.

Brodsky, M. (1963). Interpersonal stimuli as interference in a sorting task. *Journal of Personality*, *31*, 517–533.

Burman, B., Mednick, S.A., Machon, R.A., Parnas, J., & Schulsinger, F. (1987). Children at high risk for schizophrenia: Parent and offspring perceptions of family relationships. *Journal of Abnormal Psychology*, *96*, 364–366.

Carpenter, W.T., Heinrichs, D.W., & Alphs, L.D. (1985). Treatment of negative symptoms. *Schizophrenia Bulletin*, *11*, 440–452.

Chapman, L.J. (1961). Emotional factors in schizophrenic deficit. *Psychological Reports*, *9*, 564.

Ciompi, L., & Müller, C. (1976). *Lebensweg und Alter der Schizophrenen. Eine katamnestische Langzeitstudie bis ins Senium*. Berlin, Heidelberg, New York: Springer.

Cohen, R., Sommer, W., Hermanutz, M. (1981). Auditory event-related potentials in chronic schizophrenics. *Advances in Biological Psychiatry*, *6*, 180–185. Basel: Karger.

Cornblatt, B.A., Lenzenweger, M.F., Dworkin, R.H., & Erlenmeyer-Kimling, L. (1985). Positive and negative schizophrenic symptoms, attention, and information processing. *Schizophrenia Bulletin*, *11*, 397–408.

Davis, G.C., Buchsbaum, M.S., van Kammen, D.P., & Bunney, W.E. (1979). Analgesia to pain stimuli in schizophrenics and its reversal by naltrexone. *Psychiatry Research*, *1*, 61–69.

Dawson, M.E., & Nuechterlein, K.H. (1984). Psychophysiological dysfunction in the developmental course of schizophrenic disorders. *Schizophrenia Bulletin*, *10*, 204–232.

Dunn, W.L. (1954). Visual discrimination of schizophrenic subjects as a function of stimulus meaning. *Journal of Personality*, *23*, 48–64.

Erlenmeyer-Kimling, L. (1975). A prospective study of children at risk for schizophrenia: Methodological considerations and some preliminary findings. In R.D. Wirt, G. Winokur, & M. Roff (Eds.), *Life history research on psychopathology* (Vol. 4). Minneapolis: University of Minnesota Press.

Feffer, M.H. (1961). The influence of affective factors on conceptualization in schizophrenia. *Journal of Abnormal Psychology*, *63*, 588–596.

Fein, G., Tursky, B., & Erlenmeyer-Kimling, L. (1974). *Stimulus sensitivity and reactivity in children at high risk for schizophrenia.* Presented at the Annual Meeting of The Society for Psychophysiological Research, Salt Lake City, UT. October 18–21.

Fowles, D.C. (1980). The three-arousal model: Implications of Gray's two-factor learning theory for heart rate, electrodermal activity and psychopathology. *Psychophysiology*, *17*, 87–104.

Frith, C.D., Stevens, M., Johnstone, E.C., & Crow, T.J., (1979). Skin conductance responsivity during acute episodes of schizophrenia as a predictor of symptomatic improvement. *Psychological Medicine*, *9*, 101–106.

Giedke, H., Heimann, H., & Straube, E. (1982). *Vergleichende Ergebnisse psychophysiologischer Untersuchungen bei Schizophrenien und Depressionen.* Stuttgart: Schattauer.

Gray, A.L. (1975). Autonomic correlates of chronic schizophrenia: A reaction time paradigm. *Journal of Abnormal Psychology*, *84*, 189–196.

Green, M.F., & Walker, E. (1986). Attentional performance in positive- and negative-symptoms schizophrenia. *Journal of Nervous and Mental Disease*, *174*, 203–213.

Gruzelier, J.H. (1976). Clinical attributes of schizophrenic skin conductance responders and non-responders. *Psychological Medicine*, *6*, 245–249.

Gruzelier, J.H., & Hammond, N. (1978). The effect of chlorpromazine upon psychophysiological, endocrine and information processing measures in schizophrenia. *Journal of Psychiatric Research*, *14*, 167–182.

Gruzelier, J.H., & Venables, P.H. (1974). Two-flash threshold, sensitivity, and beta in normal subjects and schizophrenics. *Quarterly Journal of Experimental Psychology*, *26*, 594–604.

Gruzelier, J.H., Connolly, J., Eves, J., Hirsch, S., Zaki, S., Weller, M., & Yorkston, N. (1981). Effect of propranolol and phenothiazines on electrodermal orienting and habituation in schizophrenia. *Psychological Medicine*, *11*, 93–108.

Hoskins, R.G. (1946). *The biology of schizophrenia.* New York: Norton.

Huber, G., Gross, G., & Schüttler, R. (1979). *Schizophrenie. Eine verlaufs- und sozialpsychiatrische Langzeitstudie.* Berlin, Heidelberg, New York: Springer.

Janes, C.L., & Stern J.A. (1976). Electrodermal response configuration as a function of rated psychopathology in children. *Journal of Nervous and Mental Disease*, *162*, 184–194.

Janes, C.L., Hesselbrock, V., & Stern, J.A. (1978). Parental psychopathology, age, and race as related to electrodermal activity of children. *Psychophysiology*, *15*, 24–34.

Kahneman, D. (1973). Attention and effort. In J.J. Jenkins (Ed.), *Arousal and attention.* Englewood Cliffs, NJ: Prentice-Hall.

Kugelmass, S., Marcus, J., & Schmuell, J. (1985). Psychophysiological reactivity in high-risk children. *Schizophrenia Bulletin*, *11*, 66–73.

Lang, P.J., & Buss, A.H. (1965). Psychological deficit in schizophrenia. II. Interference and activation. *Journal of Abnormal Psychology*, *70*, 77–108.

Leff, J., & Vaughn, C. (1984). *Expressed emotion in families: Its significance for mental illness.* New York: Guilford.

Lynn, R. (1963). Russian theory and research on schizophrenia. *Psychological Bulletin*, *60*, 486–498.

Mandler, G. (1984). *Mind and body. Psychology of emotion and stress.* New York: Norton.

Mednick, S.A. (1978). Berkson's fallacy and high-risk research. In L.C. Wynne, R.L. Cromwell, & S. Matthysse (Eds.), *The nature of schizophrenia: New approaches to research and treatment.* New York: Wiley.

Mednick, S.A., & Schulsinger, F. (1968). Some premorbid characteristics related to breakdown in children with schizophrenic mothers. In D. Rosenthal & S.S. Kety (Eds.), *The transmission of schizophrenia.* Oxford: Pergamon.

Mednick, S.A., Schulsinger, F., Teasdale, T.W., Schulsinger, H., Venables, P., & Rock, D. (1978). Schizophrenia in high-risk children: Sex differences in predisposing factors. In G. Serban (Ed.), *Cognitive defects in the development of mental illness*. New York: Brunner/Mazel.

Nuechterlein, K.H., & Dawson, M.L. (1984). Information processing and attentional functioning in the developmental course of schizophrenic disorders. *Schizophrenia Bulletin*, *10*, 160–203.

Öhlund, L., Alm, T., Lindström, L., Wiesegren, I.M., Öst, L.G., & Öhman, A. (1987). Electrodermal nonresponding in schizophrenics: Relationship to social outcome. Abstracts of papers presented at the Twenty-Seventh Annual Meeting of the Society for Psychophysiological Research. *Psychophysiology*, *24*, 603.

Öhman, A. (1979). The orienting response, attention, and learning: An information-processing perspective. In H.D. Kimel, E.H. van Olst, & J.F. Orlebecke (Eds.), *The orienting reflex in humans*. Hillsdale, N.J: Erlbaum.

Öhman, A. (1981). Electrodermal activity and vulnerability to schizophrenia. A review. *Biological Psychology*, *12*, 87–145.

Öhman, A., Nordby, H., & D'Elia, G. (1986). Orienting and schizophrenia: Stimulus significance, attention, and distraction in a signaled reaction time task. *Journal of Abnormal Psychology*, *95*, 326–334.

Öhman, A., Nordby, H., & D'Elia, G. (1989). Orienting in schizophrenia. Habituation to auditory stimuli of constant and varying intensity. *Psychology*, 26 (in press).

Overall, J., & Gorham, D. (1962). The Brief Psychiatric Rating Scale. *Psychological Reports*, *10*, 799–812.

Parnas, J., & Schulsinger, H. (1986). Continuity of formal thought disorder from childhood to adulthood in a high-risk sample. *Acta Psychiatrica Scandinavica*, *74*, 246–251.

Patterson, T., & Venables, P.H. (1980). Auditory vigilance: Normals compared to chronic schizophrenic subgroups defined by skin conductance variables. *Psychiatry Research*, *2*, 107–112.

Peterson, F., & Jung, C.G. (1907). Psycho-physical investigations with the galvanometer and pneumograph in normal and insane individuals. *Brain*, *30*, 153–218.

Raine, A., & Venables, P.H. (1984). Electrodermal nonresponding, antisocial behavior, and schizoid tendencies in adolescents. *Psychophysiology*, *21*, 424–433.

Rist, F., & Cohen, R. (1979). Paradoxical response reduction and flattening of affect in schizophrenia. Abstracts of papers presented 18th Meeting Society for Psychophysiological Research. *Psychophysiology*, *16*, 201.

Rubens, R.L., & Lapidus, L.N. (1978). Schizophrenic patterns of arousal and stimulus barrier functioning. *Journal of Abnormal Psychology*, *87*, 199–211.

Salzman, L.F., & Klein, R.H. (1978). Habituation and conditioning of electrodermal response in high risk children. *Schizophrenia Bulletin*, *4*, 210–222.

Schneider, S.J. (1982). Electrodermal activity and therapeutic response to neuroleptic treatment in chronic schizophrenic in-patients. *Psychological Medicine*, *12*, 607–613.

Simons, R.F., Losito, B.D., Rose, S.C., & MacMillan, F.W. (1983). Electrodermal nonresponding among college undergraduates: Temporal stability, situational specificity, and relationship to heart rate change. *Psychophysiology*, *20*, 498–505.

Sommer, W. (1982). Event-related potentials in electrodermal responders and nonresponders. Dissertation, University of Konstanz.

Straube, E. (1979). On the meaning of electrodermal nonresponding in schizophrenia. *Journal of Nervous and Mental Disease*, *167*, 601–611.

Straube, E. (1980). Reduced reactivity and psychopathology – Examples from research on schizophrenia. In M. Koukkou, D. Lehman, & J. Angst (Eds.), *Functional states of the brain: Their determinants*. Amsterdam: Elsevier.

Straube, E.R. (1983). High and low arousability in schizophrenia. In C. Perris, D. Kemali, & M. Koukkou-Lehmann (Eds.), *Advances in biological psychiatry: Vol. 13. Neurophysiological correlates of normal cognition and psychopathology*. Basel: Karger.

Straube, E., & Heimann, H. (1985). Kompensatorische Mechanismen – spezifisch oder unspezifisch? In G. Huber (Ed.), *Basisstadien endogener Psychosen und das Borderline-Problem*. Stuttgart: Schattauer.

Straube, E.R., Schied, H.-W., Rein, W., & Breyer-Pfaff, U. (1987). Autonomic nervous system differences as predictors of short-term outcome in schizophrenics. *Pharmacopsychiatry, 20*, 105–110.

Strauss, J.S., & Carpenter, W.T. (1972). The prediction of outcome in schizophrenia. I. Characteristics of outcome. *Archives of General Psychiatry, 27*, 739–746,

Strauss, J.S., & Carpenter, W.T. (1974). The prediction of outcome in schizophrenia. II. Relationship between predictor and outcome variables. *Archives of General Psychiatry, 31*, 37–42.

Tsuang, M.T., & Dempsey, M. (1979). Long-term outcome of major psychoses. II. Schizoaffective disorder compared with schizophrenia, affective disorders, and a surgical control group. *Archives of General Psychiatry, 36*, 1302–1304.

Turbiner, M. (1961). Choice discrimination in schizophrenia and normal subjects for positive, negative and neutral affective stimuli. *Journal of Consulting Psychology, 25*(1), 92.

Van Dyke, J.L., Rosenthal, D., & Rasmussen, P.V. (1974). Electrodermal functioning in adopted-away offspring of schizophrenics. *Journal of Psychiatry Research, 10*, 199–215.

Venables, P.H. (1975). Psychophysiological studies of schizophrenic pathology. In: Venables, J.H. & Christie, M.J. (Eds.). *Research in psychophysiology*. London: Wiley.

Venables, P.H. (1977). Input dysfunction in schizophrenia. In B.A. Maher (Ed.), *Contributions to the psychopathology of schizophrenia*. New York: Academic.

Venables, P.H., & O'Conners, N. (1959). Reaction times to auditory and visual stimulation in schizophrenic and normal subjects. *Quarterly Journal of Experimental Psychology, 11*, 175–179.

Venables, P.H., & Tizard, J. (1956). Paradoxical effects in the reaction time of schizophrenics. *Journal of Abnormal and Clinical Psychology, 33*, 220–224.

Venables, P.H., & Tizard, J. (1958). The effect of auditory stimulus intensity on the reaction time of schizophrenics. *Journal of Mental Science, 104*, 1160–1164.

Walker, E., & Harvey, P. (1986). Positive and negative symptom in schizophrenia: Attention performance correlates. *Psychophysiology, 19*, 294–302.

Webb, W.W. (1952). Conceptual ability of schizophrenics as a function of threat or failure. *American Psychologist, 7*, 335.

Zahn, T.P., Carpenter, W.T., & McGlashan, T.H. (1981a). Autonomic nervous system comparison with normal controls. *Archives of General Psychiatry, 38*, 251–258.

Zahn, T.P. Carpenter, W.T., & McGlashan, T.H. (1981b). Autonomic nervous system activity in acute schizophrenia. II. Relationships to short term prognosis and clinical state. *Archives of General Psychiatry, 38*, 260–266.

Zubin, J., & Spring, B. (1977). Vulnerability: A new view of schizophrenia. *Journal of Abnormal Psychology, 86*, 103–126.

Part IV

Intervention Programs: Cognitive, Social, and Emotional Disturbances in Schizophrenics

Cognitive Treatment in Schizophrenia

H.D. Brenner, S. Kraemer, M. Hermanutz, and B. Hodel

Introduction

We are presently witnessing an increasing interest in integrative concepts of schizophrenia (e.g., Brenner, 1987; Ciompi, 1985; Strauss & Carpenter, 1981; Zubin & Spring, 1977). Despite considerable differences in their initial assumptions, viewpoints, and emphasis, we can detect a trend towards a vulnerability-stress model in which earlier considerations in this direction are integrated in a new form. Impairments in information processing, i.e., elementary cognitive disorders, are regarded as indicators or traits of vulnerability to schizophrenia, and these impairments are held responsible for a reduction in the capacity to cope with stress (e.g., Nuechterlein & Dawson, 1984; Zubin, 1986).

Thus, it is not surprising that there has been an increased realization of the clinical significance of cognitive disorders for the treatment and rehabilitation of schizophrenia, and possibly even for its prevention. In none of the current concepts of the vulnerability-stress model, however, are these disorders in information processing taken into account in a sufficiently differentiated form. No real insight has therefore been gained into the mediating processes between preexisting or residual cognitive deficiencies and manifest psychotic behavior. For this reason, the relevant therapeutic recommendations remain general and vague: avoiding stimulation, reducing the quantity of information, clear and unambiguous information, structuring, simplifying, and clarifying contact with the patient and the general treatment milieu – unspecific measures which at best make information processing easier, but do not directly affect the cognitive disorders themselves (cf. Ciompi, 1986; Liberman, 1982). This is an unsatisfactory state of affairs, deserving greater attention both in practice and in research.

The neglect of cognitive processes in the therapy of schizophrenia is very difficult to understand, even if the vulnerability-stress model is not referred to. After all, that cognitive disturbances are pivotal to as well as characteristic of schizophrenia and form the basis of the clinically observable symptoms is a view which in its essence is as old as schizophrenia research itself and has a long clinical tradition. The Anglo-American literature of the past decades in particular displays a continuous interest in experimental psychological and psychopathological research into a "core psychological deficit" of schizophrenia (cf. Hemsley, this volume; Nuechterlein & Zaucha, this volume; and surveys by Lang & Buss, 1965, and Nuechterlein & Dawson, 1984).

However, our understanding of the experimental psychological approach has undergone considerable changes since the first studies were carried out. At the beginning, relevant work involved widely diverging definitions and operationalizations of theoretical constructs, and the methods of measurement that were used often turned out to be inadequate or inappropriate for covering and testing the constructs which had been postulated. Since the last decade, however, when researchers started to adopt models and methods used in cognitive psychology to study information processing in healthy subjects, relevance and results of experimental psychological schizophrenia research have improved considerably. The question as to the existence of cognitive and psychophysiological deficits is no longer approached in an isolated manner, but with regard to the sequence of cognitive processes proceeding from the reception of information to its transformation into observable behavior. Indicators of abnormalities in the processing of information have been found on every level (cf. George & Neufeld, 1985).

Cognitive Disorders in Schizophrenia

The following disorders are currently cited in the literature as being basic cognitive deficiencies of schizophrenics: disturbances in the selection between relevant and irrelevant stimuli, in the maintenance or flexible allocation of focused and sustained attention, and in the availability of stored information for comparison processes to recognize and identify stimuli, an impaired capacity for abstraction, unusual concept formation, inadequate concept modulation, errors in syllogistic and analogical inference, and disturbances in the choice of responses arising from mutual interference of competing reactions. Correlates to psychophysiological peculiarities are sometimes postulated (e.g., Öhman, 1981; Straube, 1983).

In doing so, numerous authors start out from a basic deficit in the early stages of information processing (e.g., Broga & Neufeld, 1981). In these perceptual disorder models, deficits, for example, in selective attentional functions, are assumed to be the cause of inadequate concept formation and impaired response selection. Yet, according to conceptual disorder models, deficits at later stages of processing reactively lead to perceptive disorders via a poor overall organization of the individual (e.g., Dingemans, Space, & Cromwell, 1983). In the course of information processing, however, perception and conceptualization are likely to be connected in a process of circular interaction in which each complements and controls the other (cf. Magaro, 1980). As a consequence, it is the directing, evaluating, and integrating operations that must be impaired, rather than isolated subprocesses.

In cognitive psychology, it is undisputed that such disorders of information processing can affect not only higher mental functions such as judgement, but also emotions and overt behavior. For instance, lack of availability of information stored in the long-term memory can lead to an inadequate coordination of thought, imagination, and perception, an inadequacy which might become so extreme that the individual concerned experiences thoughts as foreign, perhaps even as being produced externally. Description of such relationships, however, has largely remained on a very general level (cf. also George & Neufeld, 1985).

Considering the cognitive disturbances of schizophrenics within the framework of various recent formulations of the vulnerability-stress concept of schizophrenia (e.g., Ciompi, 1986; Falloon, McGill, & Boyd, 1984; Hahlweg, 1986; Zubin, 1986) compels us to abandon a purely linear etiological understanding in the sense of a core psychological deficit in favor of a systemic approach. Although there is no consensus with regard to a differentiated conceptualization of vulnerability, authors more or less generally concur that it comprises a broad spectrum of structural components ranging from deviations from biological norms to deficits in social competence. Aside from psychophysiological peculiarities, cognitive disturbances in the sense of deficits in information processing are also mostly considered to be structural vulnerability characteristics (cf. Nuechterlein & Dawson, 1984) and, as already mentioned, regarded as a cause or at least a preliminary stage of an increased susceptibility to stress (cf. Ciompi, 1986; Spring, 1981; Zubin, 1986).

In our opinion, this approach neglects the systemic aspect of the vulnerability-stress concept. Basically, deficits in information processing are likely to reduce the potential for adapting to or compensating for both autonomous biological changes and changes in the demands of the environment. From a systemic point of view, these deficits are thus not so much structural vulnerability characteristcs or a transphenomenal basis of schizophrenic symptoms (Huber, 1983; Süllwold, 1983) as moderating variables within a positive feedback between those biological and psychosocial factors which – according to Ciompi (1984) – can lead to acutely productive psychotic forms of behavior in the manner of a "run-away" via vicious circles: therefore, cognitive disorders can exert a pervasive influence extending to overt behavior (cf. Brenner, 1987; Spaulding, 1986).

Based on this systemic viewpoint, relationships between the features described are best understood within a hierarchically organized model which we have presented in detail elsewhere (Brenner, 1987). In this model (Fig. 1), overt behavior – whether it be so-called microsocial forms of behavior in immediate social interaction or macrosocial behavior in the sense of fulfilling the demands of social roles – is based fundamentally on integrative performances of specific processes on the more elementary functional levels of attention, perception, concept formation, attribution, etc. Schizophrenia is characterized by dysfunctions or deficits on all of these functional levels (cf. George & Neufeld, 1985).

Some of these disturbing influences can be self-sufficient, others have to accumulate or interrelate, either among themselves or with environmental or organismic variables. On account of the hierarchical organization of behavior, deficiencies on elementary levels lead to disturbances on complex levels. For

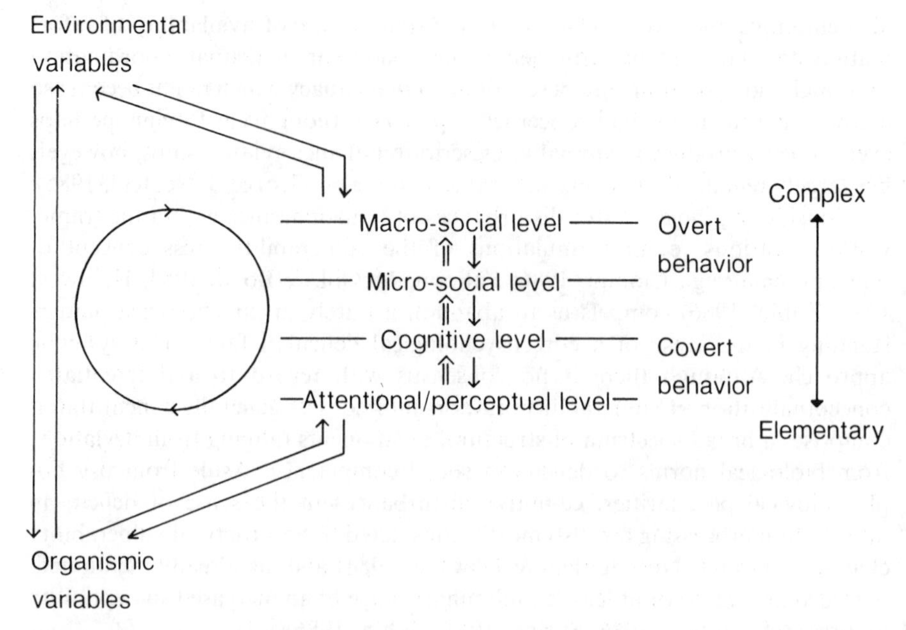

Fig. 1. Schematic representation of the hierarchical development and organization of deficient behavior in schizophrenics

example, an individual having difficulties with the control, intensity, and processing of information will display reduced tolerance to interpersonal strains, especially if the latter are ambiguous or ambivalent. Because of attentional and perceptual disorders, the subject experiences these strains in a more complex manner than would be the case if his/her information processing were undisturbed. Discrepancies arising between perception and interpretation prevent the necessary integration, which further intensifies the cognitive deficiencies. An additional increase in the level of arousal can indirectly provoke an even greater deterioration, e.g., if the patient's environment reacts to the emergence of such disorders with irritation or rejection. If these interactions between impaired attentional functions, situational interpretation, emotion, and arousal enter into a vicious circle, they can ultimately lead to a total breakdown of systematic information processing.

This approach allows us to understand not only why therapy programs exclusively focusing on overt behavior remain partly ineffective and frequently achieve merely short-lived improvements, but also why it is not so uncommon for such therapies to lead to an exacerbation of attentional, perceptual, and cognitive deficiencies (cf. Hemsley, 1977; Schooler & Spohn, 1982). It also becomes directly apparent that neuroleptic medication, by normalizing psychophysiological overarousal, can partly or completely normalize certain very elementary cognitive dysfunctions such as simple attentional processes or the preattentional processing of visual stimuli, whereas it cannot influence higher dysfunctions such as disturbances in the capacity for abstraction, concept formation, or concept modulation, i.e., disorders in the flexible adaption of schemata of information organization to changing situational demands (e.g., Braff & Saccuzzo, 1982; Strauss, Lew, Coyle, & Tuna, 1985; Zahn, Carpenter, & McGlaskin, 1981).

Therapeutic Approaches

These considerations make it apparent that attentional, perceptual, and cognitive disorders displayed by schizophrenics are relevant not only with regard to the pathogenesis of symptoms or symptom clusters, but also with regard to any form of behavior-oriented therapeutic intervention.

Cognitive therapy in the sense of purposive reduction of these disorders or of mediation of adequate functioning allows for specific psychopathological features of schizophrenia and would thus in many cases seem to be a precondition for successful therapeutic intervention on other behavioral levels. This is valid irrespective of accepting the vulnerability-stress model of schizophrenia. The fact that specific deficits of schizophrenics, particularly on the more elementary functional levels, have been ascertained to be vulnerability linked only serves to increase their importance in this respect. Logically enough, schizophrenia research of the last decade – above all in the area concerned with behavioral therapy – increasingly demanded that the basic cognitive disorders of schizophrenic patients be taken into specific account (e.g., Florin, 1976/77; Hemsley, 1977; Lauterbach, Pelzer, & Awiszus, 1979; Liberman, 1982). However, the literature about this kind of cognitive therepy for schizophrenic patients is on the whole rather scarce. More particularly, there are hardly any systematic therapeutic approaches which concern themselves with specific attentional, perceptual, and (in the narrower sense of the word) cognitive dysfunctions of schizophrenics and which are integrated into a multimodal treatment plan.

Magaro (1980) and Spaulding, Storms, Goodrich, and Sullivan (1986) have recently surveyed the results of several studies about training aimed at isolated deficits. In the majority of these studies, the training involved attentional exercises, either in connection with the capacity for abstraction (Wagner, 1968) or with auditory and visual recognition skills (cf. Wishner & Wahl, 1974). As all these exercises took place in a laboratory situation, it remains questionable whether the improvements achieved may be generalized. Such quasiexperimental proceedings also raise the problem of a differential therapeutic efficacy for subdivisions of schizophrenia (Magaro, 1980). Paranoid patients possibly learn to compensate for their perceptive deficits rather than to mitigate them. Through such compensation, which presumably is restricted to isolated perceptive deficits, the capacity for integration or concept formation would remain neglected. For nonparanoid schizophrenics, whose disturbances lie more in the area of conceptualization than perception, isolated laboratory exercises in attention would be to no advantage (Brenner, Stramke, & Brauchli, 1982a).

Wallace (1978) demonstrated the importance of taking perceptive disorders in schizophrenics into account by utilizing therapy programs that were primarily concerned with other levels of behavior. They elaborated a model for the development of social skills, allowing for perceptual disorders and problem-solving deficits. By means of video, social situations were analyzed with regard to their most significant parameters so that the patients could answer given causal questions. Follow-up studies (Wallace, 1982; Wallace & Boone, 1984) confirmed the effectiveness of this method. Purely conceptual problem solving based on the model of D'Zurilla and Goldfried (1971), however, proved to be of little use to schizophrenics (Wallace, Nelson, Liberman, Aitchison, Lukoff, Elder, & Ferris, 1980).

Meichenbaum and Cameron (1973, 1974) described the first systematic therapeutic approaches which primarily aimed at normalizing attentional and conceptual functions. For instance, while completing tasks that call for attentional performances, the patients give themselves first spoken and then silent instructions to focus attention, to maintain purposive attention, and to avoid distraction. Further self-instruction involves self-reinforcement and self-reassurance in the case of frustrating failures. The findings of these investigations imply that their methods yield good overall treatment results, provided the therapeutic interventions are based on a careful inquiry into the specific attentional and perceptual disorders of each individual case.

Liberman (1982) developed a series of practical recommendations for allowing for cognitive deficits in the training of social skills. They include, for example: keep the therapeutic setting surveyable and free from disturbing stimuli; prepare diagrams with clear and simple visual indications for cognitive strategies; use both mild censorship for inappropriate response behavior and praise for appropriate behavior, introduce task analyses and classifying questions in small and simple steps, reduce the unfamiliarity of new material (elements, scenes) by repeating it several times, etc. Ciompi (1985) has recently attempted to relate the therapeutic milieu to the disorders in information processing found in schizophrenics. For him, it is of the utmost importance that information includes affective as well as cognitive contents. Like Liberman, he proposes numerous measures such as reducing complexity, alleviating tension, upholding the continuity of care, etc. in order to protect the schizophrenic patient from emotional tension which could affect information processing.

According to our own experiences with early case studies (Brenner, Seeger, & Stramke, 1980), actual therapy even within the area of individual and closely defined cognitive disorders has to allow for both the numerous other simultaneously existing cognitive deficits and the social dimensions of the disorder, and this from the very beginning. As a result of these experiences and on the basis of our fundamental objections to "cold cognition," it is our conviction that cognitive therapy for schizophrenia should not be restricted to the training

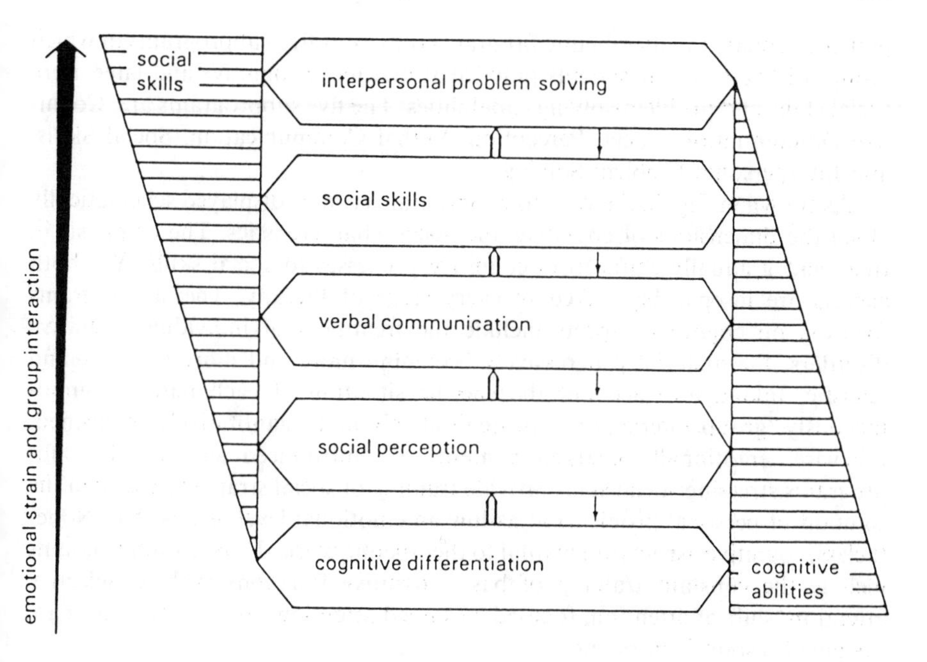

Fig. 2. Schematic representation of the treatment program

of disturbed cognitive functions in isolation (Fig. 2). On the contrary, cognitive therapy has to aim at breaking up two vicious circles: on the one hand, the connections between impaired attentional/perceptual and conceptual processes and their integrating organizations and, on the other hand, the positive feedback between cognitive dysfunctions and psychosocial stressors found to be relevant for triggering off a schizophrenic episode (cf. Brenner, 1986, 1987; Spaulding, Cannell, & Hargrove, in preparation).

Integrated Treatment of Cognitive, Communicative, and Social Skills

Treatment Program

With the objective of considering the social dimension of the deficiencies also, we resolved the problem of integrating cognitive and social therapeutic components by a prolonged step-by-step process of testing, rearranging, and retesting. Our efforts over several years resulted in a systematic treatment program for the integrated treatment of cognitive, communicative, and social disorders afflicting schizophrenic patients. Various publications on this subject reflect changes in our theoretical attitudes as well as scientific and practical experience gained in different therapeutic settings with different populations of patients. Today, the therapeutic program consists of five subprograms in which groups of five to seven patients practice at first more cognitive and later more social skills and problem-solving capabilities. The five subprograms are: Cognitive Differentiation, Social Perception, Verbal Communication, Social Skills, and Interpersonal Problem Solving.

As shown in Fig. 2, the various subprograms can be displayed schematically along the dimensions of cognitive and social characteristics. The emphasis in treatment gradually shifts from cognitive processes to social skills. Yet both aspects are inseparably linked in every stage of therapy. The subprograms focusing on cognitive aspects include the treatment of individual cognitive disorders, the material progressively becoming more and more complex and realistic, taking into account the specific situation of each patient. Simultaneously, group interactions are qualitatively and quantitatively intensified. Likewise, emotionally charged contents are introduced slowly. The subprograms stressing social skills provide training of social strategies useful in the solution of personal problems at as low an emotional level as possible. Nonetheless, cognitive aspects are pivotal to therapeutic work. Thus, all subprograms include the constant training of basic cognitive functions such as selective attention, shift of attention, focused sustained attention over a long time span, sustained responsiveness, etc.

Subprogram 1: Cognitive Differentiation

Specifically, the first subprogram is concerned with functions such as concept formation, abstraction abilities, concept modulation, recall and recognition, and both the formation and the use of associatively linked concept hierarchies. Here, a deficit exists when a class or concept is formed according to inessential features, which leads to unusual and overgeneralized combinations, or when fixation onto concrete thought occurs. Correspondingly, training in cognitive differentiation starts with exercises in concept formation, using small cards on which several systematically varying characteristics are given. The second step involves exercises with verbal concept systems (synonyms, antonyms, definitions, concepts with different meanings according to context, hierarchies of concepts, etc.), and, finally, a third step practices systematic strategies to find given concepts.

Subprogram 2: Social Perception

The second subprogram primarily aims at the processes of stimulus discrimination and interpretation, making use of previous experience in the perception and evaluation of social interactions. Relevant deficits affect size constancy, depth perception, figure-ground discrimination, contrast perception, and assessing probability by context, familiarity, etc. This subprogram is described in greater detail below.

Subprogram 3: Verbal Communication

The third subprogram is based on the numerous findings about impaired communication in the families of schizophrenics, which are caused by ambiguous or contradictory information, talking at cross-purposes, disqualifying other people's opinions, etc. Above all, these impairments arise whenever the conversational situation becomes emotionally charged. The objective consists in enabling group members to pay attention to the contributions of others, to understand other thoughts while disregarding one's own, to establish connections between one's own thoughts and those of others, as well as in training the associative-semantic processes involved in the production of speech. Training begins with the literal repetition of given sentences, followed by repeating the meaning of spontaneous phrases. In the next step, patients practice producing so-called basic questions (who, where, what, why, how) and the corresponding answers, passing on to free questioning and answering. In the concluding step, the group goes on to free communication, which – as in the preceding exercises – is repeatedly examined with regard to the above-mentioned difficulties in communication.

Subprogram 4: Social Skills

The fourth subprogram can best be characterized by indicating its fundamental differences to the familiar behavior modification techniques of role performance and self-assertiveness training, such as detailed cognitive prestructuring and preparation; at first only informative, and then motivational reinforcement; interventions directly influencing internal processes of self-direction, such as self-perception and self-evaluation, etc. This and the following subprogram do not essentially differ from the exercises the literature discribes for training social skills and problem-solving skills (Liberman et al., 1987).

Subprogram 5: Problem-Solving Skills

The training of problem-solving skills in fact attempts to convey more effective possibilities for coping with potential stressors, the individual therapeutic steps being closely linked with the cognitive analysis of problem-solving strategies.

Example

The subprogram Social Perception will now be presented in more detail, as it fuses cognitive, communicative, and social therapeutic elements in a particularly expressive manner. Like all the other subprograms, it is structured in such a way as to increase the demands made on the group from the moment its members enter into therapy, i.e., by passing on from simple and surveyable tasks to more complex and difficult tasks. The therapeutic material consists of a pool of slides illustrating scenes which have been evaluated by naive subjects in a previous experiment with regard to the intensity of the feelings and emotions straining the people involved as well as to the lack of ambiguity of each given situation. At the beginning of the subprogram, the patients are shown very simple and well-structured slides of individuals expressing only little emotion; in the course of the subprogram, slides showing emotionally more stressful and complex social interactions are introduced, which means that the amount of information the patient has to process increases progressively. For each slide, the therapeutic procedure is divided into three main steps: at first, only details are described and summarized again and again by the therapist or by patients suffering from merely slight dysfunctions. Then, individual interpretations are selected for discussion by the group, continuously referring to details for argumentation until a joint statement can be made by the group as a whole.

This exercise is meant to foster subjective perception and experience while simultaneously relating them to the group's opinion. Conscious cognitive restructuring of the perceptual field and the explicit treatment of initially present cognitive dissonances are absolutely essential for this process.

Finally, each member of the group is asked to state the theme of the slide in question briefly and succinctly. This step allows the therapist to recheck how adequately the content of the picture has been cognitively grasped and processed. With more complex pictures, which permit differing interpretations, the group collects several meaningful interpretations, attempting to make each member accept as many of these as possible before the slide's theme is stated. The factors speaking for and against each interpretation must be carefully discussed and compared.

For the process of understanding, it has also proved helpful to ask the group what kind of additional information would be necessary to specify a particular interpretation. Again, a group consensus for each possible interpretation should be attained. The therapist acts exclusively in a directive and supporting manner with respect to the theme in question. Use is made of methods derived from learning theory, such as self-reinforcement and self-control, as well as informative reinforcement. The therapist especially encourages direct interaction between patients. Furthermore, special attention is paid to a positive alteration of the self-concept. At present, similar exercises are being carried out with auditory therapeutic material. However, they are still at an experimental stage and have yet to be fully evaluated.

Evaluation Studies

General Efficacy

Since its conception, an overall evaluation of the treatment program described here has been carried out in several controlled experimental studies. In all the designs used, group comparisons were made between experimental and control groups. Psychological tests for cognitive performance and standardized rating and self-rating scales indicating psychopathological status and self-perception served to assess the treatment's success. (Brenner, Stramke, Hodel, & Rui, 1982b; Brenner, Hodel, Kube, & Roder, 1987a; Brenner, Böker, & Hodel, 1987b; Roder, Studer, & Brenner, 1987; Stramke, Hodel, & Brauchli, 1983). Until now, the complete treatment program has been employed with moderately and severely chronic schizophrenic patients. Since the various studies were carried out using approximately the same experimental design and produced comparable results, our main study (study 1) – which will now be briefly presented – can serve as an example for the overall evaluations of the treatment program. After this, investigations isolating and evaluating the mainly cognitive therapeutic components and concerning the possibility of implementing the treatment program in the setting of a large psychiatric hospital with a rural catchment area will be discussed.

Study 1 (Brenner et al., 1987, a, b)
The main study was carried out as a controlled group design using pre- and post-measurements. Six groups were formed: two experimental, two placebo-attention, and two "blank" control groups. The main hypothesis included the following supposition: after treatment, the experimental groups should surpass the control groups with regard to improvements in cognitive disorders and symptomatology. Furthermore, this superiority should still be detectable in a follow-up examination, in our case 18 months after the patients had left the hospital.

The main criteria for including a patient in study 1 were that at least two psychiatrists – one of whom was not taking part in the research project – had independently diagnosed the disease as chronic schizophrenia in accordance with the International Classification of Diseases (ICD) 295 (except 295.5 and 295.7) and that no clinical indications of alcoholism or organic cerebral damage were found. Additional criteria were: at least 1 year's duration of hospitalization, age between 20 and 50 years, IQ not below 85. All the patients fulfilling the inclusion criteria were allocated to one of the six groups according to the order in which they were admitted to the hospital. Forty-three patients participated in the study; their average age was 33 years, their average IQ 98, and the average duration of the illness was 6 years. One patient could not be located for the follow-up examination. There were no significant differences between the groups with regard to age, intelligence, and duration of the illness. All patients joined the conventional rehabilitation program. In addition to that, the patients of the experimental groups participated in daily treatment sessions (five per week) of 60–75 min, and the patients of the placebo-attention groups participated in unspecific group activities (e.g., discussions, games, etc.).

The following standardized psychological tests were used as dependent variables for pre- and post-measurements:

- Benton Test A (Benton-A) (to assess the ability to recognize figures; Benton, 1981)

- Attention Encumbrance Test (d2) (to assess attentional performance; Brickenkamp, 1978)
- Brief Psychiatric Rating Scale (BPRS) (to assess the psychopathological condition; Overall & Gorham, 1962)
- Frankfurt Complaints Questionnaire (FCQ) (for the self-assessment of various, mainly cognitive, subjectively experienced basic disorders, e.g., loss of automatism or disturbances of perception; Süllwold, 1977)
- Minnesota Multiphase Personality Inventory (MMPI) (schizophrenia scales, Sc, only)

Benton-A, d2, and subscores of the FCQ, MMPI (Sc), and BPRS were used for the analysis of cognitive abilities. MMPI and BPRS characterized the psychopathological state. For the follow-up examination, five tests were employed as dependent variables, i.e., BPRS, Benton-A, d2, FCQ, and, additionally, the Scale of Psychosocial Adjustment (PSA)[1] monitoring performance in the areas of self-care, working abilities, role performing, stress tolerance, and finally the readmission rates.

Because of general therapeutic considerations, patients of all three groups could not be kept hospitalized for up to $2\frac{1}{2}$ months, the time needed to complete the treatment program. Therefore, the following procedures were used: the physician in charge of a particular patient decided when he/she should be discharged according to the usual criteria. However, by means of weekly tests drawn up for the five subprograms, patients of the experimental groups were monitored to assess whether or not they had reached a "plateau of performance," i.e., whether or not they had reached the "maximum benefit point."

Table 1 shows the result of an analysis of covariance with the three factors "group membership," the pretreatment measures as covariables, and the pre-post differences as the dependent variables: the results of the F tests showed significant differences in three out of five measures (FCQ, d2, BPRS). An additional analysis of means showed that the experimenal groups were superior to the other groups in exactly the same three post-measurements (FCQ, d2, BPRS). The pre-post scores within the individual groups were also analyzed using the Wilcoxon test. The test showed that the experimental groups were characterized by significant improvements covering all six dependent variable measures, in comparison to two significant positive changes respectively for the placebo-attention groups and the "blank" control groups.

Table 2 shows the results of another analysis of covariance of the follow-up data. Again considering different pretest levels, all measures (FCQ, d2, BPRS, PSA) were discriminatory at the follow-up. Additional analyses of the means showed superior improvements of the experimental groups in all measures (see Brenner et al., 1982b). Once more, there were significantly better results for the experimental groups compared to the control groups in the five follow-up

[1] Available from the authors.

Table 1. Study 1: effects of group membership (experimental vs, control groups) on immediate treatment results, with the control variable "pre-treatment measurement" kept constant by an analysis of-covariance ($n=43$)

	Experimental group ($n=14$)				Placebo-attention group ($n=15$)				"Blank" control group ($n=14$)				After treatment	
	$\bar{X}$		SD		$\bar{X}$		SD		$\bar{X}$		SD			
Control measures	Pre	Post	Pre	Post	Pre	Post	Pre	Post	Pre	Post	Pre	Post	Effect (F value)	p
Benton-A	81.92	91.00	15.30	10.13	74.53	86.07	4.99	12.47	79.86	89.86	12.59	13.73	0.56	NS
MMPI (Sc)	66.07	56.64	11.54	13.82	66.8	61.6	11.11	13.39	64.74	65.36	20.44	13.61	1.493	NS
FCQ	25.79	5.29	11.78	5.34	22.27	13.6	11.94	10.34	25.57	13.57	11.57	8.78	6.037	≤ 0.01
Test d2	92.14	105.21	11.41	12.60	88.93	92.8	10.97	17.34	85.36	91.57	10.19	13.77	2.399	≤ 0.01
BPRS	50.86	32.14	11.04	5.44	46.33	42.53	8.06	9.42	53.61	38	12.18	10.13	6.788	≤ 0.01

Table 2. Study 1: effects of group membership on the follow-up data after about 18 months, with control variable "pre-treatment measurement" kept constant by an analysis of covariance ($n=43$)

Control measures	Experimental group ($n=14$)		Placebo-attention group ($n=14$)		"Blank" control group ($n=14$)		Follow-up after about 18 months Effect	
	$\bar{X}$	SD	$\bar{X}$	SD	$\bar{X}$	SD	(F value)	p
FCQ	11.29	9.26	19.77	12.78	18.57	9.26	5.37	0.05
Test d2	108.36	11.74	92.21	10.76	87.71	16.87	9.10	0.01
BPRS	33.14	14.38	44.5	14.29	42.86	14.26	6.58	0.05
PSA	5.57	1.74	4.36	2.13	4.43	1.45	5.99	0.05

control measurements. The difference in readmission rate was tested by the Mann-Whitney U test, a nonparametric test. The significance level was found to be 5% (z value = -2.6). Within the experimental groups, Spearman rank correlations were used to investigate whether there were significant correlations between the attainment of the maximum benefit point with regard to the specific treatment program and the long-term treatment effects. Significant correlations were found in four of the five follow-up variables (FCQ, d2, BPRS, PSA, readmission rate).

With regard to these results, some points are of particular interest. The usual claim of cognitive treatments that models and results from experimental psychology would be directly applicable to the treatment of specific cognitive deficits in schizophrenics could not be upheld, at least not in its strict sense. However, experiences with the treatment program necessitated both rendering the therapeutic material more concrete and fashioning realistic problems. In addition to that, group dynamic processes became increasingly important in the course of the treatment. Finally, the usual claim is further weakened in view of the complex nature of the constructs which need to be used to explain cognitive deficits.

These critical remarks must be considered in relation to the clear-cut findings which were obtained. The results show that cognitive treatment makes it possible to improve cognitive impairments as well as concomitant effects on instrumental and social handicaps. In this respect, however, the results might have been confounded by social therapeutic components and by the effects of developing group processes. Thus, this study alone does not enable us to make any definitive statement about the contribution of normalizing cognitive functions to observable improvements in overt behavior.

Further directive questions have been brought up following a more detailed analysis of the data obtained from another evaluation study concerning the overall efficacy of the treatment program. This study had the same controlled pre-post design, although there was a control group and no placebo-attention-group (experimental group $n=10$, control group $n=8$). Patient sample, assessment parameters, and therapeutic effect were comparable with those of study 1 (cf. Brenner et al., 1987). Nearly the same control measures were used: Benton-A, d2, FCQ, BPRS, PSA, and additionally SASKA (Riegel, 1967) – a verbal intelligence test with subscores for synonyms, antonyms, classification, and selection – and Konzentrations-Veslaufs-Test (KVT; Abel, 1961) – a concentration test considering time and mistakes.

One question presented here was the spectrum of improvements. This problem was approached with the help of the multidimensional scaling model (MDS) analysis. The corresponding MDS diagram displays a clear horizontal structure over all pre- and post-data (Fig. 3). The structure is supported by the following stress values: stress $\hat{d} = 0.077$, which is a theoretical stress value, and stress $1 = 0.1635$, which is an empirical stress value. Thus, stress $\hat{d}$ lies below stress 1, and stress 1 is below the 0.2 limit, rendering the result of the MDS analysis significant.

As can also be seen in Fig. 3, the behavioral and drive tests are situated in the upper half, the more cognitively determined measures in the lower half. Within the behavioral level, the drive tests (points 16 and 18) form their own hierarchy, while a second hierarchy is constituted by the behavioral rating and self-rating assessments (points 3, 4, 9, 10, 11). In the lower cluster, points 12, 14, and 15 are

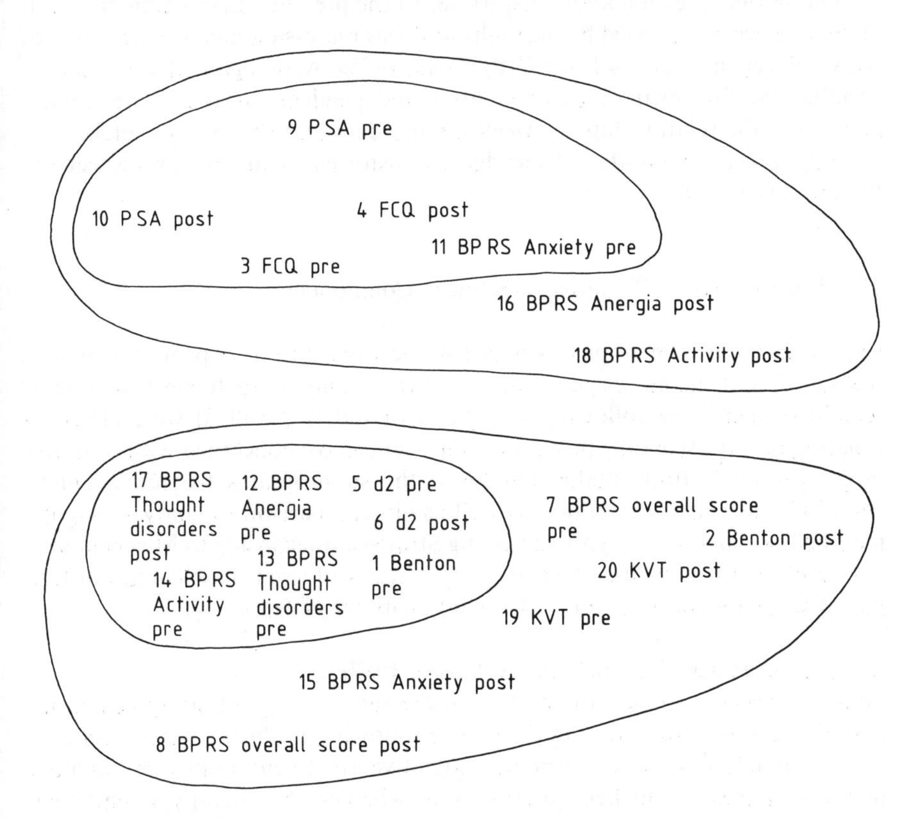

Fig. 3. Hierarchic cluster analysis of the dependent variable data

not cognitive, despite which a predominance of cognitive measures may be ascertained. The two inner hierarchies, however, are not separable to the same extent as on the behavioral level. The inner stage could be described as the measures of thought disorder, the outer stage as the measures of concentration.

As the MDS analysis depicts similarities in content of data graphically, as distance or closeness, respectively, two interpretations of the MDS diagram are permissible. The diagram shows cognitive and behavior-oriented functions from the start. The post-data, which depict the effects of the treatment program, are generally situated in the diagram close to the pre-data, often even immediately next to them. Consequently, the treatment program has, on the one hand, a general effect on the cognitive and on the behavior-oriented functions. On the other hand, the effect of the treatment program is likely to be greater on the cognitive functions, as the cognitive cluster is, on average, closer together than the behavior-oriented one. This interpretation has additionally been investigated by means of multiple linear regression analysis (Hodel, 1985). The results show that the treatment effects are rather of a cognitive nature. The positive alterations in overt behavior should be accordingly supported by improvements in basic cognitive performances.

The second question about distortions of the pre-data due to different levels of intelligence was tackled by the multiple linear regression model. The values of the Wechsler Intelligence Test (WIP) (Dahl, 1975a) were regarded as dependent variables, all further pre-measurements as independent variables. The findings imply that the relationships between the pre-data and the level of intelligence are negligible, the pre-data being hardly distorted at all in this respect (cf. Brenner et al., 1987).

The Effectiveness of Cognitive Treatment Components

Even after the treatment program as a whole seemed to have proven its worth, the question of the more specific effects of the cognitive treatment components remained open. The following two studies (studies 2 and 3) were aimed at isolating and verifying the program components most concerned with cognitive target variables. Both studies employed the subprograms Cognitive Differentiation and Social Perception as well as – in comparison to study 1 – slightly modified Social Skills/Cognitive Coping Strategies (according to Meichenbaum & Cameron, 1973, 1974). The first study consists of single case studies of four patients, the second of a controlled study with 30 patients.

Study 2 (Kraemer, Sulz, Schmid, & Lässle, 1987)
Study 2 concerns single case studies, in the sense of a pilot study generating hypotheses rather than testing them. The following problems were raised: the fundamental question was whether cognitive treatment improves cognitive target variables; a further question was whether the therapy components Cognitive Differentiation and Social Perception (cognitive training) could be

distinguished from the more complex Cognitive Strategies (problem solving) in their effects on different variables.

Basically, it was expected that the forms of treatment used would generally lead to an improvement in cognitive performance (direct objective). Furthermore, the patients were expected to profit more from cognitive training and less from problem solving in the short term, since the complexity involved in problem solving might have an unsettling effect on them.

The investigational design was an extended A/B design with a short determination of the basic phase (A: 7 days) and two alternating twice-repeated treatment phases (B1 and B2 as training component 1 with Cognitive Differentiation and Social Perception, in both cases 2 weeks of treatment with ten sessions each; C1 and C2 as training component 2 with Cognitive Coping Strategies, 2 weeks with ten treatment sessions each).

The four patients formed a relatively homogeneous group in inpatient rehabilitation, homogeneous with regard to several factors related to the illness (ICD 295.1: $n=2$; ICD 295.3: $n=2$): their ages ranged from 23 to 26 years, the illness had lasted for 2–3 years, and they had previously been in inpatient psychiatric treatment once or twice. All were being administered oral and individually dosed neuroleptic medication. Regarding social status and intelligence, one patient displayed a clear deviation: he was highy intelligent (IQ 130) and came from an academic family, while the other three were of average intelligence (IQ approximately 100) and came from lower-middle or lower class families.

The methods of assessment used included various tests, as well as rating and self-rating questionnaires containing cognitive and social variables concerned with subjective condition (activation) and with psychopathology. The cognitive variables involved were:

- From Repeated Psychological Measurement (RPM) (Fahrenberg, Kuhn, Kulick, & Myrtek, 1977) (covering specific cognitive abilities such as the speed of Gestalt formation and concentration):
  Word Recognition
  Crossing Out Numbers
  Remembering Syllables

- FCQ (Süllwold, 1977)

- From Assessment Sheet for Therapeutic Personnel (*Einschätzungsbogen für das Personal*; EBP) (Schmid, 1984):
  Concentration
  Perseverance
  Attention

Word Recognition and EBP were used daily, the other variables at the beginning of the determination of the baseline and every 2 weeks during the treatment phases (regarding the social and subjective variables, see Kraemer et al., 1987).

The four patients participated in almost all of the 40 therapy sessions, which had been declared as a course and involved daily sessions (i.e., every working day). They expressed interest, were cooperative, and regularly completed the relevant forms, even at weekends. The therapists were surprised at this obviously good motivation, as the material appeared dry and the sessions were mainly additional to the standard therapeutic program (ergotherapy, various group sessions).

Figure 4 shows the graphic representation of one cognitive test, the RPM subtest Word Recognition. The curves of all four patients display a visible decline, which corresponds to an improvement in performance. However, this decline is clearly more pronounced in patients A and B. (Testing for trend monotony yielded a highly significant result for all four patients: $p \leq 0.001$).

The remaining results of the trend tests for the other cognitive variables shows that in the course of the treatment, patients A and B improved both on the psychological test level (with the exception of short-term memory) and the level of staff-rating (EBP), but not in the self-rating of different basic disorders (FCQ) of an essentially cognitive nature. Patients C and D displayed less consistent improvement with regard to the cognitive variables involved, and even some deterioration in the staff-ratings. Through additional tests of significance, however, this study shows significant improvements in three out of the four patients in several cognitive target variables (seven, six, or five respectively, from a total of nine, all with a high significance level: $p \leq 0.01$); these improvements emerged in Word Recognition (time, mistakes, and general index), Crossing Out Numbers from the RPM and Concentration, Perseverance, and Attention from the EBP.

The outcome of a special single-case method (time series analysis – ARIMA[2] model) showed that the patients profited more from the pure training than from complex problem solving: three of the four patients displayed significant differences between baseline and the first treatment phase, and these patients also showed further clear – if less pronounced – differences in the treatment phase. Thus, this study as a whole confirms the basic expectation that cognitive methods of treatment lead to significant improvements in cognitive performance.

Study 3 (Kraemer et al., 1987)
Study 3 was carried out as a control group study, aimed at comparing cognitive treatment components with an unspecific so-called placebo-attention therapy. Unlike the placebo-attention group, patients undergoing treatment were expected to improve in various target variables.

The sample ($n = 30$) consisted of severely chronic patients of relatively high age (average: 46 years) with a low IQ (average: 93) and long-term hospitaliz-

[2] Autoregressive method using moving averages as a basis of calculation.

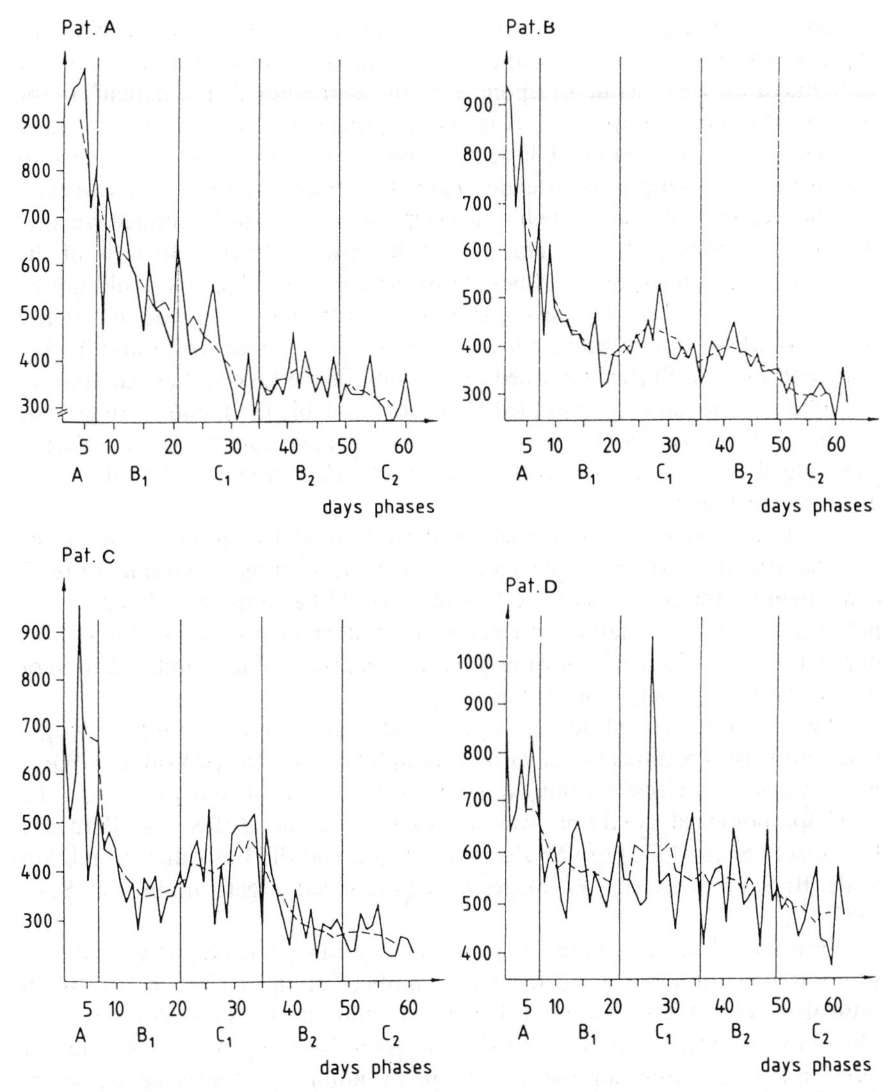

Fig. 4. Study 2: Results of the time series analysis (ARIMA model, error-adjusted time) for the variable Word Recognition (RPM). *Solid lines*, original data; *dotted lines*, seventh step of means

ation (average: 14 years). All patients involved in the study fulfilled the criteria of the *Diagnostic and Statistical Manual of Mental Disorders*, 3rd edition (DSM-III; 1980) for schizophrenia (chronic paranoid psychosis: $n=15$; residual syndromes: $n=15$). The psychopathological status was examined using the PSE (Wing, Cooper, & Sartorius, 1982). Group allocation of the patients was randomized. Before the treatment began, the experimental group and the placebo-attention group varied only with regard to age: the patients in the experimental group were significantly older than those in the control group. The contents of the treatment corresponded to those in Study 2. The patients in the placebo-attention group were assigned to practicing handicrafts and other manual tasks. The treatment lasted 12 weeks, with five weekly sessions: in addition to that, all groups attended relaxation training three times a week.

The treatment was evaluated in two steps: first, it had to be verified whether or not the contents of the therapy were directly conveyable. In view of the pronounced chronicity of the illness in the sample, this objective could not be taken for granted. For this reason, tasks derived from the therapeutic material were formulated for several areas: Ability for Abstraction (AT) and Verbal Differentiation (DT) (distinguished by solution of the task and explanation of the solution), Social Perception (SP), Problem Solving (PS), and strategies for Coping with Stress (CS); the correctness, or rather the quality of each solution was judged on points. These tasks were given to all patients both before and after the treatment.

The treatment groups improved significantly in all training tasks, while the placebo-attention groups displayed no change (verified by a two-tailed *t* test): consequently, the contents of the treatment could be conveyed. However, the patients only rarely attained the maximal number of points. In this patient population the tasks would obviously have to be practiced for a longer period of time (objective: principle of overlearning).

It was only the second step that applied external criteria in a pre-post design. Once more, the cognitive target variables employed were the two subtests Word Recognition and Crossing out Numbers from the RPM and the FCQ. The psychopathological condition was assessed using the BPRS, the Paranoid Depression Scale (PDS) of von Zerssen (1973a), and the Individual Condition Scale (BFS; von Zerssen, 1973b) (regarding the social target variables, cf. Sulz, 1987).

Even though the experimental groups improved significantly in the subtests Word Recognition and Crossing Out Numbers of the RPM, in the BPRS subscales anergia and Thought Disorders, and in the subscales Paranoid Thoughts and Depression of the PDS and BFS these improvements were not significant in a group comparison. More pronounced improvements, which remained significant compared to the control groups, emerged in five out of eight factors of the FCQ: the treatment obviously reduced such nonspecific basic disorders as loss of automatized skills, disturbances in movement and thought, intimated delusional moods, persisting listlessness, etc. (Table 3). Thus, the results of this study, too, confirm the expectations that had been formulated: the methods of cognitive treatment employed obviously appear to be effective in improving performance more in the area of specific cognitive than of psychopathological variables.

It is interesting to note that the effects in both studies seem to be independent of age, sex, intelligence, and above all of psychopathology or subgroup diagnosis. Unfortunately, it is not possible to make any definitive statement about

Table 3. Study 3: effect of the external criteria of the therapeutic success by a t test (double verification) ($n=30$)

Variable external criteria	Experimental group ($n=17$) Pre $\bar{X}$	SD	Post $\bar{X}$	SD	p	Placebo-attention group ($n=13$) Pre $\bar{X}$	SD	Post $\bar{X}$	SD	p	Group differences Pre D	Change D
Language	9.5	7.3	7.5	7.0	NS	10.5	7.2	11.7	7.9	NS	NS	NS
Perception	3.2	4.0	2.4	3.1	NS	5.3	5.2	5.3	5.7	NS	NS	NS
Loss of automatism	5.1	2.7	3.1	2.8	$<.01$	5.2	3.6	5.1	4.0	NS	NS	$p<.05$
FCQ:												
Motoric	4.1	3.6	1.6	1.9	$<.01$	4.6	4.4	5.2	5.4	NS	NS	$p<.01$
Cognition	3.4	2.2	1.8	2.1	$<.05$	3.7	3.1	4.0	2.9	NS	NS	$p<.05$
Perception disorders	1.1	1.2	1.1	1.3	NS	1.5	1.3	1.0	1.0	NS	NS	NS
Chimera tendency	4.1	2.9	1.6	1.6	$<.01$	4.5	3.4	4.2	3.3	NS	NS	$p<.05$
Constant dislike	2.2	1.9	0.8	1.0	$<.01$	2.6	2.2	2.8	2.4	NS	NS	$p<.05$

D, difference.

the intriguing question as to the stability of the therapeutic results achieved, since both studies only had a short-term design. However, a longer-lasting treatment is likely to be indispensable – at least for severely chronic patients – in order to ensure the stability of the therapeutic effects. This ought to be taken into account in planning treatment. (cf. Sulz, 1987). As far as practical clinical work is concerned, our experience suggests that daily sessions are advantageous but not necessary. Daily sessions are particularly recommendable for the first therapeutic sections, i.e., Cognitive Differentiation and Social Perception. In the case of the more complex components of the therapy, such as Cognitive Coping Strategies, the sessions may be separated by longer intervals. Furthermore, fulfilling a particular criterion (e.g., a given number of points in solving specific tasks or tests) could lead to further treatment sessions being punctuated by longer periods of time.

Program Implementation in a Large Psychiatric Hospital

Varying external factors (characteristics of the patient population, conditions of hospitalization, number and training of the personnel involved in therapy, etc.) demand corresponding modifications of therapeutic programs, especially if they transcend standard forms of care, as in the current cognitive treatment of schizophrenic patients. The following study (study 4) discusses the practicability of the treatment program under the conditions of an admission ward of a large psychiatric hospital with a rural catchment area (see also Hermanutz & Gestrich, 1987).

Study 4 (Hermanutz & Gestrich, 1987)
Study 4 was implemented as a control group study, trying to verify the effects of the modified cognitive treatment program on performance in attention and

perception, on psychopathological symptoms, and on social behavior. Thirty-two schizophrenic patients participated in the treatment program after being selected by the resident physicians according to ICD criteria after the acute symptoms had remitted. The average age was 28 years, the average length of total inpatient treatment amounted to 17 months. Thirty-two patients, who paralleled the test group as far as age and education were concerned, were evaluated and used as a control group. All patients were administered neuroleptic medication.

The comparably large fluctuation of patients in an admission ward made it necessary for the therapy components to be modified so as to prevent them from becoming contingent on one another in degree of difficulty. It had to be possible for a patient to join the treatment program at any time. Moreover, the treatment was meant to start immediately after the acute symptoms had begun to remit. In order to achieve the required minimal attention in spite of remaining symptoms, simple exercises were used to improve focused attention. Finally, the time spent on each subprogram was restricted to approximately 10 min so that different exercises could be carried out simultaneously to include as wide a spectrum of dysfunctions as possible and to maintain the patients' motivation during the 30-min sessions.

To improve the impaired focusing of attention on those aspects of the tasks that are relevant as far as behavior is concerned, we used simple reaction and concentration exercises in which the patients – as in reaction time experiments – have to react quickly to simple stimuli at either regular or irregular intervals. The relevance of these exercises is explained to the patients by means of examples from everyday life, e.g., switching on household appliances, working at the conveyor belt, counting the strokes of a clock, etc. The first exercises consist in counting forward and backward in turn around the circle, or in naming weekdays or letters of the alphabet, etc. A memory component is added when a sequence of railway stations or the individual steps of given and partially automatized procedures such as making a telephone call or starting a car have to be recited in turn. In these simple exercises, the patients can easily prepare themselves for the moment when they must focus their attention, since they know when their turn is coming. In the following exercises, however, they cannot predict when they have to be prepared to react, and thus constant readiness is required. One such exercise, which trains the ability to react to a changing situation, consists in having the patients randomly throw a ball back and forth while simultaneously reciting the name or birthdate of the other patients. This exercise corresponds more closely to the exigencies placed on one's attention span in everyday life, where a more spontaneous focusing of one's attention is required, as for example, in conversation. Many patients complain of a lack of concentration when reading or watching television. This specific weakness is combated with written exercises; for example, the patients complete an ascending number series or a picture or they look for errors in drawings. If the patients are able to be attentive for a short time, it is possible for them to take in information. Thus, further exercises aim at improving the ability to remember. The patients are expected to remember names, routes, dates, or foreign words. Mnemonics are constructed and relayed together. The various memory contents are checked several times by questioning, and the corresponding retaining strategies are regularly repeated.

After these preparatory exercises, the subprograms Cognitive Differentiation, Social Perception, and Verbal Communication of the treatment program were applied.

The effects of the treatment were measured with various instruments. Clinical symptoms and behavior before the start of the program were documented by the resident physicians and the nursing staff using the BPRS, the Global Assessment Scale (GAS; Endicott, Spitzer, Fleiss, & Cohen, 1976), and the Nurses' Observation Scale for Inpatient Evaluation (NOSIE; Honigfeld, Gills, & Klett, 1976). In order to determine cognitive ability, the d2 test as well as the picture arrangement and picture completion tests from the Wechsler Adult Intelligence Scale (WAIS; Dahl, 1975b) were employed. These tests were repeated after the patients had attended between 20 and 30 treatment sessions. During these 6–10 weeks, the control group took part in occupational therapy and leisure time activities offered by the ward.

The results of covariance analyses show that the experimental group benefitted from the cognitive therapy in two ways: not only were they rated much better on the GAS with regard to their social, occupational, and family skills, but they were also judged significantly less tense and paranoid than the patients in the control group on the corresponding BPRS scales (GAS: f value $= 5.07$, $p \leq 0.05$; BPRS subscale Tension: f value $= 4.99$, $p \leq 0.05$; BPRS subscale Hostility: f value $= 4.49$, $p \leq 0.05$). However, no significant differences between the experimental and control groups could be found on d2, NOSIE, and WAIS. These advantages on GAS and BPRS of the experimental group as opposed to the control group are of importance since they cannot be attributed to the differing severity of symptoms between the two groups at the time of the first assessment.

An additional investigation of the connection between changes in different variables (product-moment correlations) led to more differentiated results. Only in the experimental group does the increased performance in distinguishing between essential and inessential details in the picture completion test display a significant correlation with the improvement of clinical symptoms: the greater the improvement that takes place in the pre-post scores of this test, the greater the reduction in thought impairments and tension ($r = 0.36$). There is no such correlation to be found in the control group ($r = 0.01$). The relationship between improved GAS ratings and thought disorder on the one hand, and the duration of hospitalization on the other hand proved significant in the experimental group ($r = -0.34$), whereas this was not the case in the control group ($r = -0.03$), i.e., the longer a patient stays in hospital, the less he/she profits from cognitive treatment. Since the experimental group had been in hospital for an average of 7.5 months longer than the control group, the psychopathological improvements we ascertained are all the more remarkable.

The results of this study demonstrate that improvements in the psychopathological condition of schizophrenic patients above and beyond those usually achieved with neuroleptic medication and occupational therapy can be attained through additional cognitive treatment. Indications of physical activation as well as uncooperative behavior in connection with hostility towards others could be distinctly reduced after treatment for 6–10 weeks. These improvements were coupled with reduced impairments in the areas of social, family, and occupational skills. However, in this study, the experimental group did not surpass the control group in the simple concentration exercises of the d2 test and in picture arrangement and picture completion tests at the post-measuring. Between pre- and post-measuring, the performances improved to the same extent in both groups in all three test procedures, which suggests declining psychopathological symptoms in the course of general therapy rather than a specific effect of cognitive treatment. The lack of direct proof for the effects of the cognitive treatment program on just those abilities which ought to benefit most from such a program is without doubt astonishing: namely, attention and concentration as examined by the d2 test, and the organization of perception as measured by the WAIS subtests. Yet, this is possibly a consequence of the patient sample, brought about by the integration of the treatment program into an admission ward. Contrary to study 1, the patients participating in this study did so shortly after being hospitalized on account of an acute psychotic episode. They simultaneously underwent acute treatment with neuroleptic medication, which led to dramatic improvements in some members of the control group as well. Over and above these unspecific changes, the effects of the treatment program cannot be proven statistically.

The connection between the duration of hospitalization and symptom improvements as well as the increased average test performances of the experimental group at the post-measuring date could indicate that the effects of the therapy would be more pronounced if the therapy were carried out with greater intensity and increased frequency, involving patients with a shorter history of hospitalization.

Discussion

The efficacy of a therapeutic intervention is usually judged by its effects. In the studies verifying general efficacy, significant changes served to prove the effectiveness of the therapy, particularly in the case of moderately chronic schizophrenic patients, provided the treatment lasts for 2–3 months. Follow-up data covering – at least summarily – the most important improvements that were aimed at by assessing the level of psychosocial functioning and the readmission rate 18 months after completion of the therapy provide further evidence for the general validity of the results achieved. Still, proof of significant change does not tell us anything about the substance of the therapeutic effects in a narrower sense.

From a methodological point of view, however, these studies are not free of shortcomings. On the one hand, one negative aspect would be that in study 1 randomization was impossible in view of the fact that all groups had to be treated on the same ward. On the other hand, this meant that interward variation was kept relatively constant. Another shortcoming concerns the fact that probably not all methods of measurement used were sufficiently specific. When research was started, more specific methods were not available. These circumstances led to using methods of measurement and ratings which were already in use and appeared to lend themselves to assessing the kind of change which was anticipated in the hypotheses. Finally, the superiority of the experimental groups at follow-up may allow us to presume the reliability of the treatment results, but a further-reaching interpretation of these data should only be made with caution. Not only time, but also other factors can lead to a learning decay. Social support, chances of integration after discharge from the hospital, compliance, etc. are merely some of the factors affecting the stability of the treatment results. Corresponding controls for the follow-up period are lacking.

According to Spaulding (1986) and Brenner (1986, 1987), the cognitive disorders of schizophrenics have a pervasive character. If the present treatment program correspondingly claims to proceed in a systemic instead of an isolated manner, the individual therapeutic measures would have to be indirectly effective on all levels. The control methods applied are only partially adequate in this respect. Even though an additional MDS analysis revealed the control methods to be divided into cognitive and behavioral spectra, there emerged a tendency towards cognitive optimization without an equivalent increase in social skills. The significant improvements in performance lie mainly in the cognitive area. This could imply that the treatment program primarily optimizes cognitive processes. That general IQ value displayed hardly any relationship to the dependent variables could confirm the further assumption that the treatment program purposively improves schizophrenia-specific cognitive deficits instead of general deficits. Compared to that, the behavioral measures present a mixed showing. Against this background, the interpretation that the normalization of cognitive functions leads indirectly to improvements on the functional level of overt behavior cannot be accepted without reservation. Nevertheless, the significant improvements found with the modified version of the treatment program rather refer to variables of overt behavior. Hermanutz and Gestrich (1987) explain this by the fact that the patients taking part in this study were in an acute episode of the illness at the beginning of the treatment and therefore were being treated with intensive neuroleptic medication. However, the results on which they base the argument for the relationships between different levels of measurement by means of product-moment correlations provide evidence for a connection to elementary cognitive functions. Yet this investigation must be criticized on the grounds that the selection of samples by parallelization was decided on the basis of only a few criteria and that no information is given about fluctuations in the open group, so that there is plenty of room for confounding effects.

Neither can the question as to the pervasive nature of cognitive therapy effects be answered based on the results of studies about the effectiveness of cognitive treatment components, in which the main interest was not aimed at the global effectiveness of the treatment program, but rather at the differential effectiveness on each level. Indeed, the control measures were classified according to cognitive functioning, susceptibility to stress in social interaction, and psychopathological symptoms; and, in addition to that, a partial distinction was made between "internal" and "external" criteria of success, but the relationships between the changes on different functional levels were not examined. The results of these investigations, however, strongly support the finding that the treatment program leads to improvements in cognitive performance, even though objections with respect to the methodology can be made: e.g., in the single-case analysis with regard to the baseline that could be too short for statistical comparisons, which would hamper efficiency testing; or in the group studies with regard to the lack of information about the comparability of the initial levels of both groups in various dependent variables. Furthermore, there is no answer to the question as to whether the pervasive effects of the therapy exert not only an optimizing influence, but sometimes also a disturbing influence in the sense of undesirable interferences.

Although the overall results of the various studies point to the conclusion that the therapeutic effects are based on reducing cognitive deficits, they could essentially also be due to a training in effective compensation strategies. These two levels are likely to be interrelated through a continuous process of circular interaction. Besides the reduction of cognitive disorders aimed at by means of cognitive treatment components, this treatment might achieve a broader and better self-perception of these disorders and of relevant internal and external stressors in the course of therapy. On this basis, coping strategies in the sense of successful attempts at self-stabilization may be developed (cf. Böker & Brenner, 1983). If cognitive dysfunctions in the sense of deficient information processing diminish the potential for coping with autonomous biological changes as well as changing environmental demands, this aspect of the effects of cognitive therapy would gather foremost importance.

Conclusions

The results of the different studies support the demand initially made on the basis of theoretical considerations, namely that the present treatment and rehabilitation programs be complemented by integrated cognitive treatment methods. At the same time, however, they also show that the cognitive treatment of schizophrenia is not yet sufficiently developed and differentiated. If cognitive treatment is to be derived from existing cognitive deficits more stringently than before, we need both exact operationalization and a conditional model of these disorders. Until now, most models and theories of cognition in schizophrenia constitute – as in other areas of schizophrenia research – attempts to explain the fundamental nature of observable or measurable deficits. They do not specify how such deficits can arise, although this would be a precondition for further optimizing cognitive treatment. Dysfunctions even on elementary functional levels can just as well be an expression of compensatory attempts at reorganizing as a primary disorder: e.g., on the attentional/perceptual functional level, the development of a deviant style of attention which reduces the amount of information taken in and thus should help to reduce overarousal; or on the conceptual level, the development of restricted and rigid conceptualization of perceived information in order to avoid ambiguity and the concurrent stress. In these cases of compensatory dysfunctions, direct therapeutic interventions intended to normalize cognitive disorders without simultaneous control of the quantity of information available or of psychophysiological arousal would be detrimental. Thus, a corresponding cognitive treatment would require simultaneous neuroleptic medication (or its modification) and very specific sociotherapeutic or psychotherapeutic interventions.

The fact that in therapy cognitive disorders have to be understood in the context of the patient's current social situation and environment will presumably pose particular problems. Specific disorders are frequently connected to specific factors lying outside the mere consideration of the hierarchic organization of behavior. Thus, it is only in the rarest of cases that effect relationships can be understood exclusively by means of experimental and clinical covering of deficiencies on the different functional levels of behavior. For this reason, one should not count on improvements on a given functional level just continuing to be effective on another level, just as one must not expect such improvements to be generalized to the natural environment without the transfer of cues, instructions, or reinforcements, which is best achieved by including reference persons as social mediators.

A further conclusion suggests itself after reading the literature on the cognitive treatment of schizophrenia: the problems which are still unsolved – e.g., greater specificity concerning existing cognitive dysfunctions, a better understanding of therapeutic effects, differential indications, etc. – demand a still closer connection between experimental psychopathology and hypothesis-directed therapy. Most suitable for this process are single-case studies, in which the multiple assessment of the deficiencies present on a patient's different functional levels of behavior provides the basis for deducing hypotheses about the hierarchic interrelationships between these deficiencies, leading to hypothesis-directed programs of intervention. It would then be possible for the underlying theoretical assumptions to be further verified, modified, or abandoned, depending on the success or failure of the treatment based on these hypotheses. That this is indeed a possible way of proceeding has been demonstrated by Spaulding et al. (1986). In contrast to this, further group studies should above all endeavor to find appropriate control measures and ensure adequate investigational designs (e.g., extended "counter-balance design"), where the different treatment phases take place several times, nevertheless their order is changed reciprocally. Additionally, homogeneity within groups should be considered (Hodel & Brenner, 1986) in order to reveal the connections between improvements in cognitive functions and clinically and socially relevant changes in psychopathological status, behavior, and the level of psychosocial functioning of the patient. Such a research strategy is most likely to lead to the overdue development and optimization of the cognitive treatment of schizophrenia, and at the same time to a clarification of the limits of this form of therapy and of the necessity of its integration into a multimodal treatment concept.

References

Abel, D. (1961). *Konzentrations-Verlaufs-Test*. Göttingen: Hogrefe.

Benton, A.L. (1981). *Der Benton-Test*. Bern: Huber.

Böker, W. & Brenner, H.D. (1983). Selbstheilungsversuche Schizophrener: Psychopathologische Befunde und Folgerungen für Forschung und Therapie. *Nervenarzt*, *54*, 578–589.

Braff, D., & Saccuzzo, D. (1982). Effect of antipsychotic medication on speed of information processing in schizophrenic patients. *American Journal of Psychiatry*, *139*, 1127–1130.

Brenner, H.D. (1986). Zur Bedeutung von Basisstörungen für Behandlung und Rehabilitation schizophrener Menschen. In W. Böker & H.D. Brenner (Eds.), *Bewältigung der Schizophrenie. Multidimensionale Konzepte, psychosoziale Therapien, Angehörigenarbeit und autoprotektive Anstrengungen*. Bern: Huber.

Brenner, H.D. (1987). On the importance of cognitive disorders in treatment and rehabilitation. In: J.S. Strauss, W. Böker, & H.D. Brenner (Eds.), *Psychosocial treatment of schizophrenia*. Toronto: Huber.

Brenner, H.D., Seeger, G., & Stramke, W.G. (1980). Evaluation eines spezifischen Therapieprogramms zum Training kognitiver und kommunikativer Fähigkeiten in der Rehabilitation chronisch schizophrener Patienten in einem naturalistischen Feldexperiment. In M. Hautzinger & W. Schultz (Eds.), *Klinische Psychologie und Psychotherapie* (Vol. 4). Cologne, Tübingen; Gesellschaft für wissenschaftliche Gesprächspsychotherapie e.V.; Deutsche Gesellschaft für Verhaltenstherapie e.V.

Brenner, H.D., Stramke, W.G., & Brauchli, B. (1982a). Integriertes psychologisches Therapieprogramm bei chronisch schizophrenen Patienten. Untersuchungen zur Differentialindikation. In H. Helmchen, M. Linden & U. Rueger (Eds.), *Psychotherapie in der Psychiatrie*. Berlin, Heidelberg, New York, Toronto: Springer.

Brenner, H.D., Stramke, W.G., Hodel, B., & Rui, C. (1982b). Untersuchungen zur Effizienz und Indikation eines psychologischen Therapieprogrammes bei schizophrenen Basisstörungen: Ergebnisse einer 18-monatigen Feldstudie. In F. Reimer (Ed.), *Verhaltenstherapie in der Psychiatrie*. Weinsberg: Weissenhof.

Brenner, H.D., Böker, W., & Hodel, B. (1987b). Cognitive treatment of basic pervasive dysfunction in schizophrenia. In S.C. Schulz & C.A. Tamminga (Eds.), Proceedings of the International Congress on Schizophrenia Research. Belleview-Biltmore, Clearwater, FL, March 28–April 9.

Brenner, H.D., Hodel, B., Kube, G., & Roder, V. (1987a). Kognitive Therapie bei Schizophrenen: Problemanalyse und empirische Ergebnisse. *Nervenarzt*, *58*, 72–83.

Brickenkamp, R. (1978). *Test d2. Aufmerksamkeits-Belastungs-Test*. Göttingen: Hogrefe.

Broga, M.I., & Neufeld, R.W.J. (1981). Evaluation of information sequential aspects of schizophrenic performance: framework and current findings. *Journal of Nervous and Mental Disease*, *169*, 558–568.

Ciompi, L. (1984). Modellvorstellungen zum Zusammenwirken biologischer und psychosozialer Faktoren in der Schizophrenie. *Fortschritte der Neurologie-Psychiatrie*, *52*: 200–206.

Ciompi, L. (1985). Schizophrenie als Störung der Informationsverarbeitung – Eine Hypothese und ihre therapeutischen Konsequenzen. In H. Stierlin, L.C. Wynne, & M. Wirsching (Eds.), *Psychotherapie und Sozialtherapie der Schizophrenie. Ein internationaler Ueberblick*. Berlin, Heidelberg, New York: Springer.

Ciompi, L. (1986). Auf dem Weg zu einem kohärenten multidimensionalen Krankheits- und Therapieverständnis der Schizophrenie: Konvergierende neue Konzepte. In W. Böker, & H.D. Brenner (Eds.), *Bewältigung der Schizophrenie: Multidimensionale Konzepte, psychosoziale und kognitive Therapien, Angehörigenarbeit und autoprotektive Strategien*. Bern: Huber.

Dahl, G. (1975a) Reduzierter Wechsler Intelligenz Test. In R Brickenkamp (Ed.), *Testhandbuch*. Göttingen: Hogrefe.

Dahl, G. (1975b). Der Hamburger Wechsler-Intelligenztest (HAWIE). In R. Brickenkamp (Ed.), *Testhandbuch*. Göttingen: Hogrefe.

Diagnostic and statistical manual of mental disorders, 3rd ed. (DSM-III) (1980). Washington DC: American Psychiatric Association.

Dingemans, P., Space, L.B., & Cromwell, R.L. (1983). Repertory grid, consistency and schizophrenia. In J. Adams-Webber (Ed.), *Personal constructs: Theory and application*. Toronto: Academic.

D'Zurilla, T., & Goldfried, M. (1971). Problem solving and behavior modification. *Journal of Abnormal Psychology*, *78*, 107–126.

Endicott, Y., Spitzer, R.L., Fleiss, Y.L., & Cohen, Y. (1976). Global Assessment Scale. *Archives of General Psychiatry*, *33*, 766–771.

Fahrenberg, J., Kuhn, M., Kulick, B., & Myrtek, M. (1977). Methodenentwicklung für psychologische Zeitreihenstudien. *Diagnostica*, *23*, 15–36.

Falloon, I.R.H., McGill, C.W., & Boyd, J.L. (1984). *Family care of schizophrenia*. New York: Guildford.

Florin, J. (1976/1977). Group social skills training for chronic psychiatric patients. Comment to Williams M.T. et al. *European Journal of Behavioral Analysis and Modification*, *1*, 230–232.

Friedrich, W., & Henning, W. (1980). *Der sozialwissenschaftliche Forschungsprozess*. Berlin: DVW.

George, L., & Neufeld, R.W.J. (1985). Cognition and symptomatology in schizophrenia. *Schizophrenia Bulletin*, *11*(2): 264–285.

Hahlweg, K. (1986). Einfluss der Familieninteraktion auf Entstehung, Verlauf und Therapie schizophrener Störungen. In E. Nordmann & M. Cierpka (Eds.), *Familienforschung in Psychiatrie und Psychotherapie*. Heidelberg, Berlin, New York: Springer.

Hemsley, D.R. (1977). What have cognitive deficits to do with schizophrenic symptoms? *British Journal of Psychiatry*, *130*, 167–173.

Hermanutz, M., & Gestrich, J. (1987). Kognitives Training mit Schizophrenen: Beschreibung des Trainings und Ergebnisse einer kontrollierten Therapiestudie. *Nervenarzt*, *58*, 91–96.

Hodel, B. (1985). *Weiterführende Datenanalyse der Retest Untersuchung zum integrierten psychologischen Therapieprogramm*. Internes Arbeitspapier der Abteilung für theoretische und evaluative Psychiatrie. University of Bern, Psychiatric Hospital.

Hodel, B., & Brenner. H.D. (1986). Kriterien zur Homogenität von Therepiegruppen mit chronisch schizophrenen Patienten. *Zentralblatt für Neurologie und Psychiatre*, *245* (8), 674.

Honigfeld, G., Gills, R.D., & Klett, L.I. (1976). Observation Scale for Inpatient Evaluation. In W. Guy (Ed.), *ECDEU, Assessment manual for psychopharmacology* (rev.ed). Rockville, MA: USGPO.

Huber, G. (1983). Das Konzept substratnaher Basissymptome und seine Bedeutung für Theorie und Therapie schizophrener Erkrankungen. *Nervenarzt*, *54*, 23–32.

Kraemer, S., Sulz, K.H.D., Schmid, R., & Lässle, R. (1987). Cognitive therapy of schizophrenic patients under standard care. *Nervenarzt*, *58*, 84–90.

Lang, P.J., & Buss, A.H. (1965). Psychological deficit in schizophrenia. II. Interference and activation. *Journal of Abnormal Psychology*, *70*, 77–106.

Lauterbach, W., Pelzer, U., & Awiszus, D. (1979). Is social skills training effective in European schizophrenics? *Behavioral Analysis and Modification*, *3*, 21–31.

Liberman, R.P. (1982). Social factors in schizpophrenia. In. L. Grinspoon (Ed.), *Psychiatry: 1982 Annual review.* Washington: American Psychiatric Press.

Liberman, R.P., Jacobs, H.E., Boone S.E. et al. (1987). Skills training for the community adoption of schizophrenics. In J.S. Strauss W. Böker, & H.D. Brenner (Eds.), *Psychosocial treatment of schizophrenia.* Toronto: Huber.

Magaro, P.A. (1980). *Cognition in schizophrenia and paranoia. The integration of cognitive processes.* Hillsdale, N Y: Erlbaum.

Meichenbaum, D., & Cameron, R. (1973). Training schizophrenics to talk to themselves. A means of developing attentional controls. *Behavior Therapy, 4,* 515–534.

Meichenbaum, D., & Cameron, R. (1974). The clinical potential modifying what clients say to themselves. In M. Mahoney, & C.T. Thoresen (Eds.), *Self-control: Power to the person.* Monterey, CA: Brooks-Cole.

Nuechterlein, K.H., & Dawson, M.E. (1984). Information-processing and attentional functioning in the developmental course of schizophrenic disorders. *Schizophrenia Bulletin, 10,* 160–203.

Öhman, A. (1981). Electrodermal activity and vulnerability to schizophrenia: A review. *Biological Psychology, 12,* 87–145.

Overall, J.E., & Gorham, P.R. (1962). The brief psychiatric rating scale. *Psychological Reports, 10,* 799–812.

Riegel. K.F. (1967). *Der sprachliche Leistungstest SASKA.* Göttingen: Hogrefe.

Roder, V., Studer, K., & Brenner, H.D. (1987). Erfahrungen mit einem integrierten psychologischen Therapieprogramm zum Training kommunikativer und kognitiver Fähigkeiten in der Rehabilitation schwer chronisch schizophrener Patienten. *Schweizer Archiv für Neurologie and Psychiatrie, 138* (1), 31–34.

Schmid, R. (1984). *Psychotherapeutische Zusatzbehandlung zur Verbesserung kognitiver Basisstörungen schizophrener Patienten.* Unpublished thesis. Ludwigs-Maximilians-University, Munich. Institute of Clinical Psychology.

Schooler, C., & Spohn, H.E. (1982). Social dysfunction and treatment failure in schizophrenia. *Schizophrenia Bulletin, 8,* 85–98.

Spaulding, W. (1986). Assessment of adult-onset pervasive behavior disorders. In A. Cummero, K. Calhoun, H. Adams (Eds.), *Handbook of behavioral assessment* (2nd ed.). New York: Wiley.

Spaulding, W., Storms, L., Goodrich, V., & Sullivan M. (1986). Applications of experimental psychopathology in psychiatry rehabilitation. *Schizophrenia Bulletin, 4,* 560–577.

Spring, B., (1981). Stress and schizophrenia: Some defitional issues. *Schizophrenia Bulletin. 7,* 24–33.

Stramke, W.G., Hodel, B., & Brauchli, B. (1983). Untersuchungen zur Wirksamkeit Psychologischer Therapieprogramme in der Rehabilitation chronisch schizophrener Patienten. In H.D. Brenner, E.R. Rey, & W.G. Stramke (Eds.), *Empirische Schizophrenieforschung* (pp. 216–234). Bern: Huber.

Straube, E. (1983). Kann die psychologisch-physiologische Grundlagenforschung einen Beitrag zur Therapie und Prognosenforschung liefern? In H.D. Brenner, E.R. Rey, W.G. Stramke (Eds.), *Empirische Schizophrenieforschung.* Bern: Huber.

Strauss, J.S., & Carpenter, W.T. Jr. (1981). *Schizophrenia.* New York: Plenum.

Strauss, M., Lew, M., Coyle J., & Tuna, L. (1985). Psychopharmacological and clinical correlates of attention in chronic schizophrenia. *American Journal of Psychiatry, 142,* 497–499.

Süllwold, L. (1977). *Symptome schizophrener Erkrankungen: Uncharakteristische Basisstörungen.* Berlin, Heidelberg, New York: Springer.

Süllwold, L. (1983). *Schizophrenie.* Stuttgart: Kohlhammer.

Süllwold, L. (1986). Basis-Störungen; Instabilität von Hirnfunktionen. In W. Böker & H.D. Brenner (Eds.), *Bewältigung der Schizophrenie: Multidimensionale Konzepte, Psychosoziale und kognitive Therapien, Angehörigenarbeit und autoprotektive Anstrengungen.* Bern: Huber.

Sulz, S.K.D. (1987). *Psychotherapie in der klinischen Psychiatrie.* Stuttgart: Thieme.

Von Zerssen D. (1973a) Selbstbeurteilungsskala zur Abschätzung des "subjektiven Befundes" in psychopathlogischen Querschnitt- und Längsschnittuntersuchungen. *Archiv für Psychiatrie und Nervenkrankheiten, 217,* 299–314.

Von Zerssen, D. (1973b). Beschwerdenskalen bei Depressionen. *Therapiewoche*, *46*, 4426–4440.

Wagner, B.R. (1968). The training of attending and abstracting responses in chronic schizophrenics. *Journal of Experimental Research in Personality*, *3*, 77–78.

Wallace, C.J. (1978). The assessment of interpersonal problem-solving skills with chronic schizophrenics. Paper presented at the Annual Meeting of the American Psychological Association, New York.

Wallace, C.J. (1982). The social skills training project of the mental health clinical research center for the study of schizophrenia. In J.P. Curran & P.M. Monti, (Eds.) *Social skills training: A practical handbook for assessment and treatment*. New York: Guilford.

Wallace, C.J., & Boone, St. E. (1984). Cognitive factors in the social skills of schizophrenic patients: Implications for treatment. In W.D. Spaulding & J.K. Cole (Eds.), *Theories of schizophrenia and psychosis. Nebraska Symposium on Motivation 1983*. London: University of Nebraska Press.

Wallace, C.J., Nelson, C., Liberman, R., Aitchison, R., Lukoff, D., Elder J.P., & Ferris, C. (1980). A review and critique of social skills training with schizophrenic patients. *Schizophrenia Bulletin*, *6*, 43–63.

Wing, J.K., Cooper, J.E., & Sartorius, N. (1982). *Die Erfassung und Klassifikation psychiatrischer Symptome. Beschreibung und Glossar des PSE (Present State Examination)*. Weinheim, Basel: Beltz.

Wishner, J., & Wahl, O. (1974). Dichotic listening in schizophrenia. *Clinical Psychology*, *42*, 538–546.

Zahn, T., Carpenter, W., & McGlaskin, T. (1981). Autonomic nervous system activity in acute schizophrenia. II. Relationships to short-term prognosis and clinical state. *Archives of General Psychiatry*, *38*, 260–266.

Zubin, J. (1986). Mögliche Implikationen der Vulnerabilitätshypothese für das psychosoziale Management der Schizophrenie. In W. Böker & H.D. Brenner (Eds.) *Bewältigung der Schizophrenie: Multidimensionale Konzepte, psychosoziale und kognitive Therapien, Angehörigenarbeit und autoperspektive Anstrengungen*. Bern: Huber.

Zubin, J., & Spring, B.J. (1977). Vulnerability – A new view of schizophrenia. *Journal of Abnormal Psychology*, *86*, 102–126.

Training Skills in the Psychiatrically Disabled: Learning Coping and Competence*

R.P. Liberman, K.T. Mueser, C.J. Wallace, H.E. Jacobs, T. Eckman, and H.K. Massel

Given the widening consensus that most major mental disorders are chronic in course, a rehabilitation model that emphasizes the building of skills and prosthetic and supportive environments has supplanted curative and acute treatment models for schizophrenia and other disabling illnesses (Anthony, 1980; Liberman, 1985; Liberman & Evans, 1985). The effectiveness of neuroleptic medications in controlling the positive symptoms of psychosis has enabled many patients to live in the community; however, deinstitutionalization has been accompanied by poor quality of community life (Lehman, Ward, & Linn, 1982) and a "revolving door" pattern of frequent, albeit relatively brief rehospitalizations for individuals suffering from chronic and recurrent forms of affective and schizophrenic disorders (Goldman, Gatozzi, & Taube, 1981; Talbott, 1978). The inadequacy of traditional methods of treating schizophrenia is underscored by the unacceptably high readmission rates of approximately 40% in 1 year and 75% in 5 years following hospital discharge (Kohen & Paul, 1976). Data emerging from longitudinal studies of patients with affective disorders also suggest that chronicity and prolonged social disability mark a significant proportion of individuals suffering from major depressive episodes, including about 22% who suffer from "double depression."

One of the most compelling arguments for a skills training, rehabilitation model of chronic psychiatric disorders comes from the failure of antipsychotic drugs to remediate the negative symptoms of mental disorder (Schooler, 1986); the serious side effects of neuroleptics, which often evoke noncompliance (Kane, 1985, Van Putten, 1974); and the fact that medications, by themselves, cannot teach patients the coping skills they require for survival and maintenance in the community (Liberman & Foy, 1983; Paul, 1969).

The well-documented deficits in social and living skills of chronic mental patients (see Anthony & Liberman, 1986; Wallace, 1986), together with the unsatisfactoriness of current drug and psychosocial treatments for this population provide a strong rationale for developing new interventions. Social skills training – directed at problems in the areas of instrumental roles, family relationships, vocation, and friendships and peer support – has become an innovative avenue for psychosocial intervention with severely disabled psychiatric

---

* This article appeared in *Schizophrenia Bulletin*, *12*, 1986. Reprinted by permission of authors and publishers.

patients. In this article, the authors chart developments in social skills training, beginning with a conceptual model that describes the influences bearing on an individual's social skills from intrapersonal as well as interpersonal sources.

Conceptual Model of Social Skills and Competence

One of the obstacles to the advancement of any new scientific field, whether applied or basic, is the lack of a coherent conceptual framework that enables investigators to (a) find guidance and direction for their research and development activities; and (b) understand the reasons for findings that mesh or appear inconsistent. While the development of social skills training as a major element of psychiatric rehabilitation grew out of the pragmatic "trial and error" traditions of behaviorism and human resource development, it now appears timely to organize and galvanize skills training approaches with an overarching theoretical model. One such model, designed by rehabilitation researchers at the University of California, Los Angeles (UCLA) Clinical Research Center for Schizophrenia and Psychiatric Rehabilitation, is articulated in Fig. 1.

The model has four major components – social schemata, social skills, coping efforts, and social competence. Basic psychobiological and social cognitive processes constitute an individual's *social schemata*, providing the "raw material" for learning social skills. *Social skills* are the cognitive, verbal, and nonverbal behaviors that must be used interpersonally to achieve needs for community survival and a reasonable quality of life. Social skills include accurate perception of incoming social messages, social problem-solving capacity, and "sending" skills. *Coping* efforts are the individual's attempt to put into practice the social skills that exist within his/her repertoire. The impact of the person's social skills on the relevant interpersonal field or environment, favorable or unfavorable, defines that person's *social competence*.

A social schema is a modifiable information structure that is a prototype in memory of a frequently experienced situation (Glaser, 1984; Rumelhart, 1981). The individual uses this prototype to interpret instances of related knowledge and to integrate new information. A schema is, in essence, an individual's theory or model that "enables him/her to make assumptions about events that generally occur in a particular situation" (Glaser, 1984, p. 100).

When applied to a particular social situation, a schema is the individual's assumptions about the qualities that define a competent performance in that general class of situations, the skills required for that performance, and the responses that can be expected of the environment. The more extensive the individual's experience in that general class of situations, the more finely differentiated his/her schema will be, and the more likely he/she will perform competently.

To develop social schemata, certain basic psychobiological functions are necessary, including perception, attention, memory, affect, and concept formation. A deficiency in one of these will severely limit the range and distinctiveness

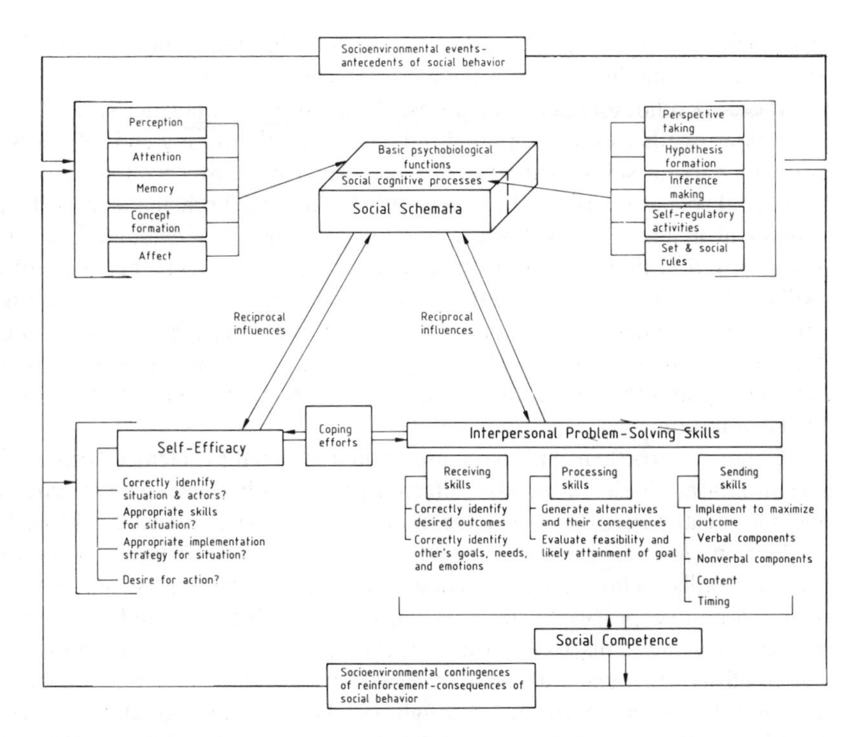

Fig. 1. Conceptual model for constituent variables related to social skills and social competence. Social schemata influence social coping and social skills and are organized from basic psychobiological processes and social cognitions. The effectiveness of an individual's social skills in attaining desirable instrumental and affiliative goals determines social competence.

of the individual's schemata and any subsequent coping efforts. In addition, developing social schemata requires several higher-order cognitive processes, including the ability to take the perspective of others' intentions, and regulate one's own behavior. A deficiency in one of these will result in impoverished social schemata, lower skill level, and impaired social coping.

Thus, social schemata that are poorly developed because of inexperience, a deficiency in the psychobiological functions, or a deficiency in higher order cognitive processes may result in social incompetence. Inexperience may lead to incorrect assumptions about the nature of a competent performance, the required skills, or the type and extent of the environmental responses. The individual's social behaviors may be hasty and poorly fashioned; on the other hand, he/she may be inactive because of an overestimate of the required skills or an underestimate of his/her abilities. Deficiencies in the higher-order cognitive skills may lead to invalid hypotheses about others' behaviors. Misinterpretations may result, and behaviors may be performed that are inappropriate to the individual's and others' actual goals and intentions. Deficiencies in the basic psychobiological functions may lead to either an inattentiveness to the relevant stimuli or an inability to store them for later processing.

Basic psychobiological functions, behavioral competencies, and social cognition together exert reciprocal influences on self-efficacy and interpersonal problem-solving skills. Self-efficacy is governed both by social schemata and successful social outcomes (Bandura, 1977). The social schemata carried by an individual at any time will affect the person's ability to evaluate correctly a social situation that is about to be entered, to determine whether the requisite skills to be effective in the situation are in one's repertoire, to know whether a means to implement the skills is at hand, and to evaluate motivation or desire for using the skills in action. These cognitive and motivational factors represent self-efficacy and they determine the likelihood and persistence of coping efforts in the situation.

Coping efforts then lead to the use of interpersonal problem-solving skills in the situation. These skills, also affected by the individual's social schemata, include social perception (*receiving* skills), generation of alternatives and their evaluation (*processing* skills), and verbal and nonverbal behavioral responses (*sending* skills). Thus, social schemata (basic psychobiological functions plus social cognitive processes) interact with both self-efficacy and interpersonal problem-solving skills to determine the success or failure of the individual's actual efforts in social transactions. The more success the person experiences with more of his/her needs met through social contacts, the greater the person's social competence. Competence is defined by the outcomes of social interactions and the degree to which a person is able to cope and use interpersonal skills to obtain instrumental and affiliative needs.

In Fig. 1, the role of the social environment is shown as a frame or border around the intrapersonal elements of social competence. Life events and social stimuli trigger the operation of an individual's social schemata, leading to self-evaluation of efficacy and coping with the event or social situation. The contingencies of reinforcement and social "rules" and expectancies, at the other end of the process, determine whether the individual has used schemata, coping, and skills appropriately and effectively. Successful social outcome, or competence, in turn, has an impact on social schemata, self-efficacy, and social skills. The feedback loops in Fig. 1 illustrate the bidirectional manner in which these processes influence one another.

Implication of Conceptual Model

The theoretical processes in Fig. 1 are heuristic for both researchers and clinicians. For researchers, they suggest hypotheses to test; for example, will patients suffering from schizophrenia who have deficits in attention, memory, concept formation, and affect exhibit less self-efficacy, coping, and interpersonal problem-solving skills? Can direct training of basic psychobiological functions improve social skills and social competence? Can self-efficacy and coping be shown to increase or decrease depending on the outcomes of social transactions?

For clinicians, several modifications of customary therapy processes are suggested for patients with deficits in basic psychobiological functions. For example, in psychotic patients with anhedonia and amotivational states, it is desirable to build into the therapy or skills training procedure extrinsic sources of motivation or incentives. The use of tokens, food, or monetary reinforcement is helpful in the social teaching of such patients (Paul & Lentz, 1977). In patients lacking perceptual and attentional abilities, offering "prostheses" such as boldly written posters and handouts, use of videotape models, and repetitions of instructions and feedback improve engagement in social skills training (Liberman, Nuechterlein, & Wallace, 1982).

The conceptual framework serves to identify three major focal points for the design and testing of social skills training methods. The first option is to train the basic psychobiological and cognitive functions that form the person's social schemata. For example, attention span and higher-order abstraction have been improved in preliminary studies carried out in experimental psychopathology laboratories (Brenner, 1986; Spaulding, Storms, Goodrich, and Sullivan, 1986). A second approach is to train the *receiving*, *processing*, and *sending* skills of individuals using behavior rehearsal, coaching, reinforcement methods, modeling, and homework. The third strategy that derives from the model is to reprogram the individual's natural environment such that skills – however well developed – can be assured of support and favorable response by others. This strategy is often used in combination with the first two approaches.

Direct Training of Social Cognitive Skills

For regressed, thought-disordered, and highly distractible schizophrenic patients, directive training of basic cognitive processes is a prerequisite to broader induction of social skills. A significant minority of schizophrenic patients have such severe cognitive, memory, and attentional impairments that they cannot productively participate in group-based training of social skills that requires sustained attention, ability to follow general instructions, and voluntary involvement in role playing. Furthermore, conventional social skills training methods assume that patients can generalize social concepts after minimal exposure to multiple elements of a stimulus class: for example, to learn that self-disclosure is appropriate in a situation where one's conversational partner has self-disclosed and is asking open-ended questions that solicit personal information about oneself. As can be seen in Fig. 1, deficiencies in basic psychobiological functions and social cognitive processes – including concept formation and inference making – markedly interfere with generalization of such social experiences.

The use of behavioral learning procedures to teach distractible and incoherent patients better cognitive skills is promising. One group of behavior analysts trained simple greeting responses in regressed State hospital patients by systematically introducing and fading prompts and reinforcers in a discrete trials format (Kale, Kaye, Wheland, & Hopkins, 1968). Overlearning and repetitious training of exemplars of greetings resulted in generalization of the greeting behavior to persons not involved in the training. Several replications and extensions of this approach, using single-subject experimental designs, confirmed the ability of regressed patients to learn social responses under highly constrained and directive training protocols (Fichter, Wallace, Liberman, & Davis, 1976; Wallace & Davis, 1974; Wallace et al., 1980). Training included frequent and immediate reinforcement for minimal social verbalizations. Both positive (e.g., tokens exchangeable for various edibles or cigarettes) and negative (e.g., escape from the noxious social interaction) reinforcers were used to build conversational skills. These studies suggested that patients could extend their social skills development as a consequence of initial training.

Three groups of workers are currently expanding this work by developing programmatic approaches to training attentional, perceptual, and self-regulatory activities. In each group, the focus is on training patients who have been refractory to various psychosocial and pharmacotherapeutic interventions. A group in Switzerland has designed a five-step program that begins with training of attentional skills and, in the course of 3 months, teaches patients basic conversational skills (Brenner, 1986). Spaulding et al. (1986) in Nebraska have focused their training efforts on simple vocational skills as a means of improving attention span. A group at the Camarillo-UCLA Clinical Research Center have developed an attention-focusing procedure for teaching conversational skills (Liberman, Kuehnel, Phipps, & Cardin, 1985).

Attention Focusing, Training of Conversational Skills

The attention-focusing procedure involves systematic repetitions of training content, a graduated prompting sequence, and consistent and immediate reinforcement – all applied within a discrete trials format. This training procedure readily elicits the patient's attention on the relevant training curriculum while minimizing demands on cognitive and information-processing capacities. The repetitious but brief training sessions reduce the chances of distractibility by careful manipulation of the training components in each learning trial. When this type of intensive training is provided twice daily for 20 min each, repertoires of conversational skills can be established.

The discrete trials format requires a trainer and a training confederate, who could be a higher functioning patient or an aide. The confederate serves as the patient's conversational partner and presents conversational "openers" to the patient. The trainer provides instructions, prompts, and reinforcement. In a typical trial – there may be up to 20 trials in a single training session – the training confederate makes a statement to the patient, such as: "I went shopping last night." If the patient makes an appropriate response (e.g., "What did you

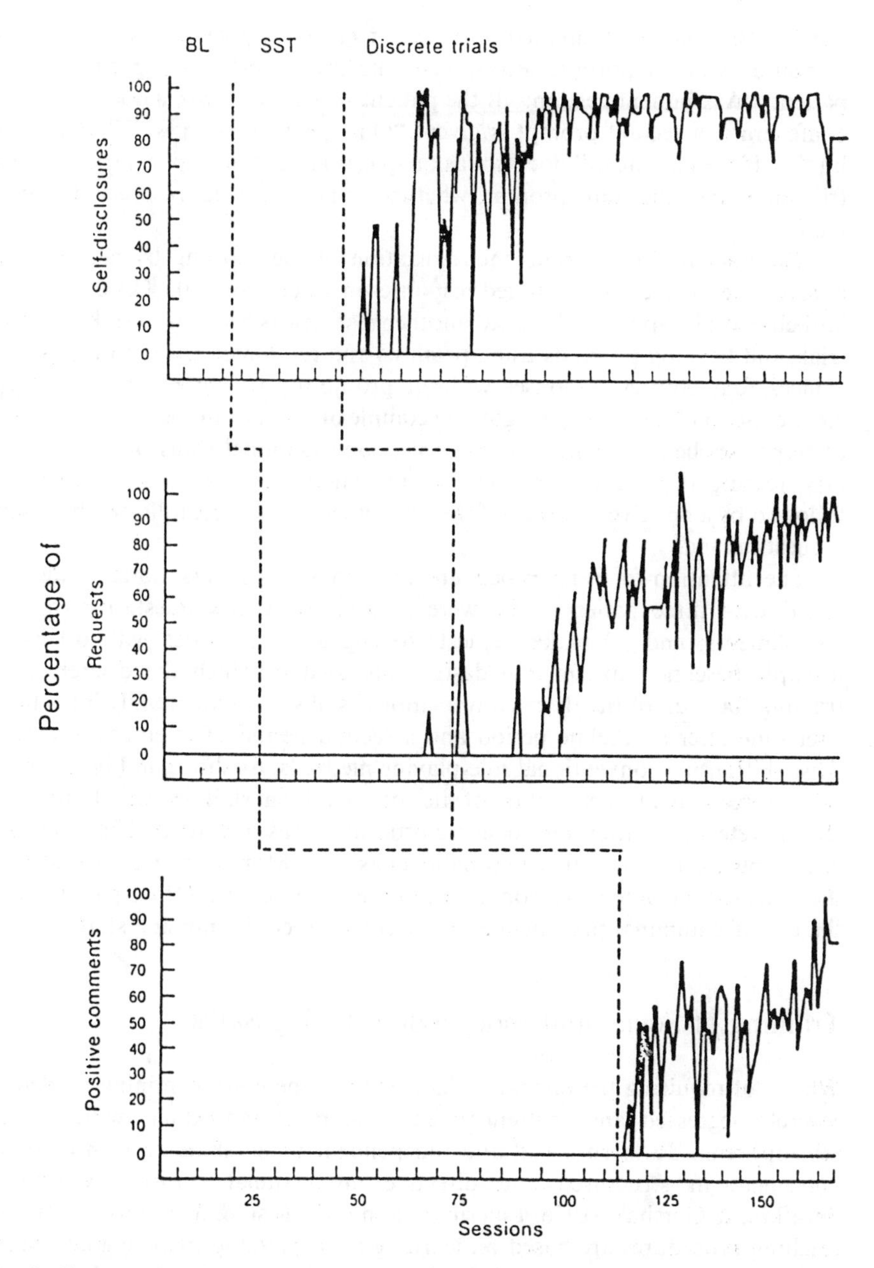

Fig. 2. Conversational skills of a chronic schizophrenic patient as a function of social skills training. A multiple baseline (*BL*) analysis of the conversational skills of a chronic, thought-disordered schizophrenic male as a function of basic social skills training (*SST*) and attention-focusing skills training (*Discrete trials*). Efficacy of training is evaluated by the percentage of correct, unprompted conversational responses made during the training sessions. (Data from Massel, 1985).

buy?"), the trial is terminated and reinforcement is provided. If there is no response or an inappropriate response, the trainer delivers a prompt to the patient: "Ask him a question." If the patient still does not ask a question of the confederate, a second prompt is given: "One good question is 'What did you buy?' " If the patient still does not ask a question, that prompt is repeated. The trial ends after the third prompt, whether or not a correct response has been made.

The patient demonstrates internalization of the learning by making four consecutive, correct, unprompted responses in successive trials. Once a particular behavioral response is learned, another response is brought into the training trials and training proceeds using prompts and reinforcement until the patient evinces four correct responses without prompting in successive trials. Repertoires are built by adding length and complexity to the interactional sequences of responses being taught. For example, conversational skills of a functional type require the use of sequences of responses such as asking a question, followed by a positive comment, followed by self-disclosure, followed by asking a question, etc.

The attention-focusing procedure for teaching conversational skills was tested with three patients who were trained to (a) ask questions; (b) give compliments; and (c) make requests to engage in activities with others. A multiple baseline experimental design was used in which the discrete trials training for each of the three conversational skills was sequentially introduced over time after a baseline period and a second period of attempting to train these skills using conventional role-playing methods. As shown in Fig. 2 for one of the three patients, acquisition of the conversational skills occurred only after the discrete trials, attention-focusing procedure was instituted. These findings were replicated in the other two patients as well. Moreover, generalization of the skills to nonconfederates on the ward was observed in all three patients with the use of a minimal prompt-reinforcement protocol by nursing staff.

Training of Social and Independent Living Skills

While not requiring the intensive, discrete trials method of training needed by severely regressed and inattentive patients, most individuals with chronic schizophrenia do learn social and independent living skills only through involvement in structured and directive instructional sessions (Goldstein, Sprafkin, & Gershaw, 1976; Liberman, King, De Risi, & McCann, 1975). The teaching procedures are based on learning principles and include goal setting, focused instructions modeling, behavior rehearsal, prompting, social reinforcement, shaping successive approximations to desired behaviors, in vivo practice of skills, and homework assignments.

Social skills can be defined as interpersonal behaviors that are: (a) instrumental for maintaining and optimizing independence and community survival; and (b) socioemotional for establishing, maintaining, and deepening supportive personal relationships. While early definitions of social skills were limited strictly to the domain of overt motoric behavior, cognitive and affective behavioral modalities are now included as relevant dimensions of this construct.

Social skills training resembles a classroom teaching environment more than a traditional therapy setting. Sessions require the active participation of the patient(s) and the therapist, they may be conducted with individual patients or in groups, and they may be as brief as 10 min a day or as long as 2 h, depending on the attentional capacities of the patients. Massed practice (i.e., multiple training sessions per week) is preferred to learning less intensively over a longer period. Agendas specifying the behavioral goals are planned with a patient's input and implemented using specific procedures following written guidelines derived from a trainers' manual. Role playing (behavior rehearsal) is the main vehicle for both assessing and teaching social skills, which are targeted for intervention on the basis of their functional relation toward attaining a specific goal important to the patient. Three types of behavior are usually targeted for modification: *response topography* behaviors, such as voice volume, fluency, eye contact; *content* behaviors, such as making a positive statement or requesting additional information; and *cognitive problem-solving* skills (Wallace, Boone, Donahoe, & Foy, 1985).

Basic Model of Social Skills Training

To give a more graphic picture of how social skills training is actually done, the next two sections provide details of the procedures used by trainers/therapists conducting the most commonly used "basic model" and the more recently developed "problem-solving model." The basic model is shown as a clinical decision tree in the flow chart of Fig. 3. The procedures can be described in five steps.

1. The trainer identifies the interpersonal problem of a patient by asking the following questions: *What* emotion, need, or communication is lacking or not being appropriately expressed, and how often does the behavior occur? *With whom* does the patient desire to improve social contact? *When* does the problem occur? *Where* does the problem occur? A wide variety of techniques can be used to assess interpersonal problems, including naturalistic observation, self-report measures, reports of significant others, and role-play performance. As in other behavior therapy interventions, assessment is an ongoing process that occurs before, during, and after social skills training.

2. In specifying the goals of training, the trainer and patient together target new behaviors that either rectify deficits in performance or modulate excessive or overly intense emotional expressiveness. Targeted behaviors are chosen with the patient on the basis of their functional relation to achieving a positive goal that is attainable within the patient's learning capacities. Goals should be articulated as specific behaviors that are high in frequency, to provide more

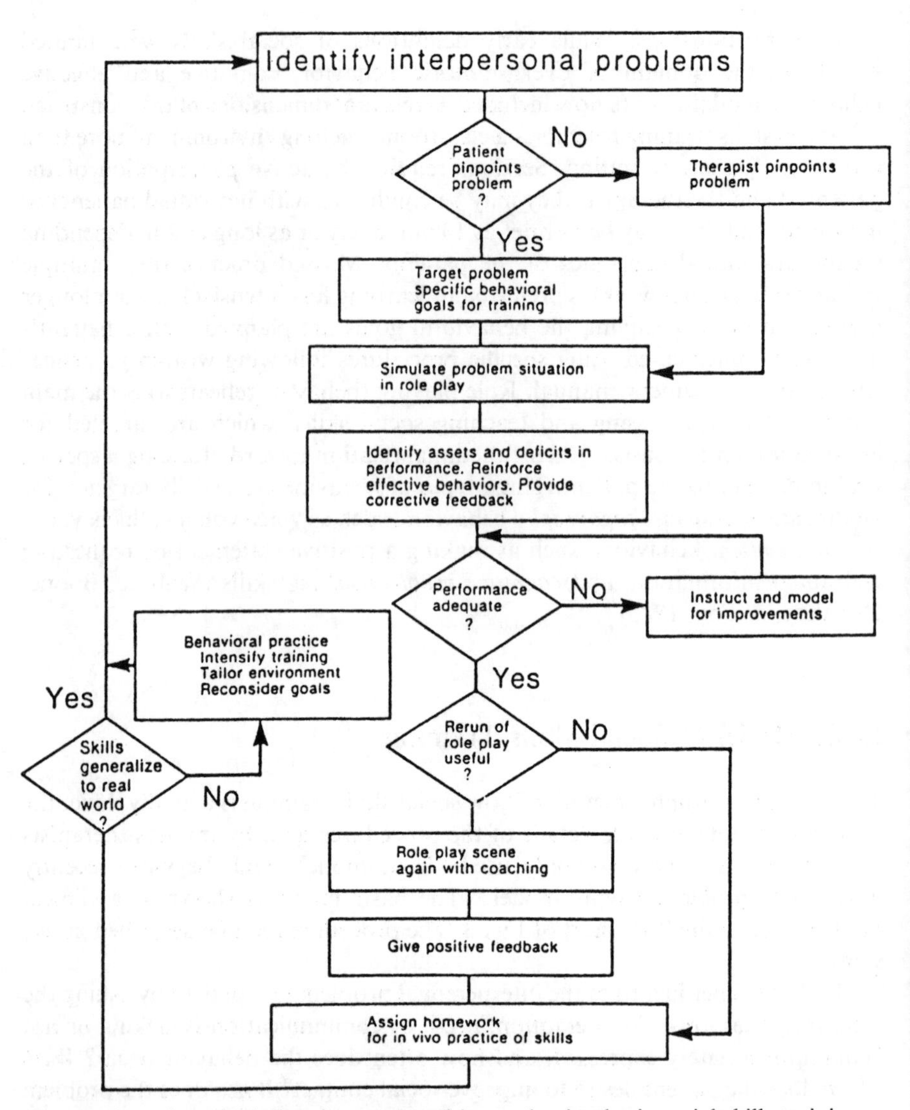

Fig. 3. Flow chart depicting the steps used in conducting basic social skills training.

opportunity for practice and feedback. The relevant domains of goal setting–behaviors and emotions, relationships, and settings–which combine to set the stage for overcoming the problem and moving toward improved social and emotional functioning are outlined in Table 1.

3. The patient is engaged in a role play of the problem situation, using other members of the group to play relevant roles. These scenes are usually events that have occurred in the recent past or are likely to occur in the near future. The first role play of each problem siuation is a "dry run" done "naturally" by the

Table 1. Some characteristics of goal setting in social skills training.

Targeted behaviors
Asking for or giving information
Initiating or terminating conversations
Maintaining conversations
Response topography (eye contact, voice volume, affect).
Targeted emotions
Affection, love
Anger, annoyance, hostility
Assertiveness, dominance
Frustration
Happiness, pleasure, delight
Interest, empathy
Sadness, grief
Interpersonal targets
Employers or employees
Family members
Friends, acquaintances
Hospital or board-and-care staff
Sales persons, agency bureaucrats
Strangers
Settings
Home, board-and-care facility
Hospital, mental health center
Job, school
Public place

patient, who is simply instructed to act as he/she would if he/she were in the actual situation. Following the dry run, which may be videotaped for immediate feedback, the patient's assets, deficits, and excesses in his/her role-play performance are noted. The patient is praised for appropriate behaviors and efforts, and positive feedback is solicited from other group members.

4. In a series of role plays, direct instructions, *modeling* or behavioral demonstration, *shaping* (reinforcing successive approximations), and *coaching* (verbal or nonverbal prompts given by a therapist to elicit specific behaviors in a role play) are used to modify the patient's behaviors toward the goal. Elements of the total "gestalt" are added one by one, such as eye contact, facial expression, vocal tone and loudness, posture, and speech content. After each role play, good elements of the patient's performance are praised by the therapist and group; corrective feedback is given about deficits.

5. The trainer promotes generalization of the newly learned behavior to situations outside the training sessions by giving homework assignments to practice the skills in the natural environment and giving positive feedback for successful transfer of skills. Generalization of skills is improved when training is

not separated from the patient's everyday world, but integrated into it. Whenever possible, therapy should be taken out of the clinician's office and practised in homes, wards, schools, stores, restaurants, and other environments where it is desirable to perform the target behaviors. Transfer of skills can also be facilitated by repeated practice and overlearning, teaching the patient to use self-evaluation and self-reinforcement, fading the structure and frequency of training, and ensuring that the natural environment is indeed socially responsive and reinforcing to the patient's skill performance. Friends, family members, nursing staff personnel, and peers can aid this process by prompting and reinforcing new social behaviors until they are established.

Problem-Solving Training Model

Many chronic psychiatric patients are deficient in basic problem-solving skills (Edelstein, Couture, Cray, Dickens, & Lusebrink, 1980; Wallace, et al., 1980). Recently, training within an information-processing framework has been shown to be effective for those patients capable of learning problem-solving strategies (Foy, Wallace, & Liberman, 1983). In this model patients are taught to improve their perception of incoming stimuli from immediate interpersonal situations, process those stimuli meaningfully to select an appropriate response, and send an effective verbal and nonverbal response back to the other person.

Interpersonal communication is viewed as a three-stage process requiring *receiving, processing*, and *sending* skills (Wallace et al., 1980). Receiving skills refer to the accurate perception, interpretation, and comprehension of relevant situational parameters. Processing skills involve weighing and selecting response options and determining an implementation strategy. Sending skills are the verbal and nonverbal behaviors emitted in the interpersonal situation that are necessary steps toward attaining the specified goal.

As in the basic model, an interpersonal scene is role played and preferably videotaped. After each role play, the therapist asks specific questions to assess the patient's receiving and processing skills, exemplified by the list contained in Table 2. After the patient has shown acceptable receiving and processing skills, his/her sending skills are assessed by reviewing the videotaped role play.

Clinical researchers at the Clinical Research Center for Schizophrenia and Psychiatric Rehabilitation at the Brentwood Psychiatric Division of the West Los Angeles VA Medical Center have developed a comprehensive social skills program for chronic psychiatric patients based on the problem-solving model. This program includes "modules" that are being developed in areas such as medication management, leisure and recreation, self-care and personal hygiene, food preparation, money management, and friendship and dating. Training is done in small groups, meeting in 90-min sessions, one to three times weekly for a period of 2–3 months, depending on the patient's clinical status and premorbid level of adjustment.

Table 2. Receiving and processing skill questions asked in training social problem solving skills

Receiving questions
What did the other person say?
What was the other person feeling?
What were the patient's short-term goals?
What were the patient's long-term goals?
Did the patient obtain his/her goals?
Processing questions
What other alternatives could the patient use in this situation?
If the patient were to do (an alternative), what would the other person feel?
If the patient were to do (an alternative), what would he/she feel?
Would the (alternative) help the patient achieve his/her short-term goals?
Would the (alternative) help the patient achieve his/her long-term goals?

One of the modules, Medication Management, has been empirically evaluated and field tested in 30 facilities nationwide. An example of evaluation data, collected before, after, and at 3 months' follow-up, is shown in Fig. 4. The evaluation of behavioral skills in the four topical areas relevant to reliable use of neuroleptic drugs was carried out through role-play simulation of the criterion situation. Significant improvements in knowledge of medication benefits, self-administration of medication, coping with side effects, and negotiating medication matters with a physician were found. Erosions in knowledge were less than 12% at the 3-month follow-up point. The Medication Management Module is described at length in another publication (Wallace et al., 1985).

Skills Training in Vocational Rehabilitation

Despite the obvious advantages of employment for psychiatric patients, unemployment has been reported to be as high as 70% in the chronically mentally ill in the United States (Goldstrom & Manderscheid, 1982). Unemployment among mental patients reflects their difficulty in both obtaining and maintaining jobs. While approximately 25% of patients return to work within 6 months of hospital discharge, only 15% are still employed by the 1-year follow-up point (Anthony, Cohen, & Vitalo, 1978).

The experience of being chronically unemployed is highly aversive to individuals with psychiatric disorders, common stereotypes and misconceptions to the contrary. In a survey of 500 chronic mental patients residing in Los Angeles board-and-care homes, Lehman et al. (1982) found that lack of work was one of the greatest complaints related to poor quality of life. Even chronically impaired patients supported by Social Security pensions had not

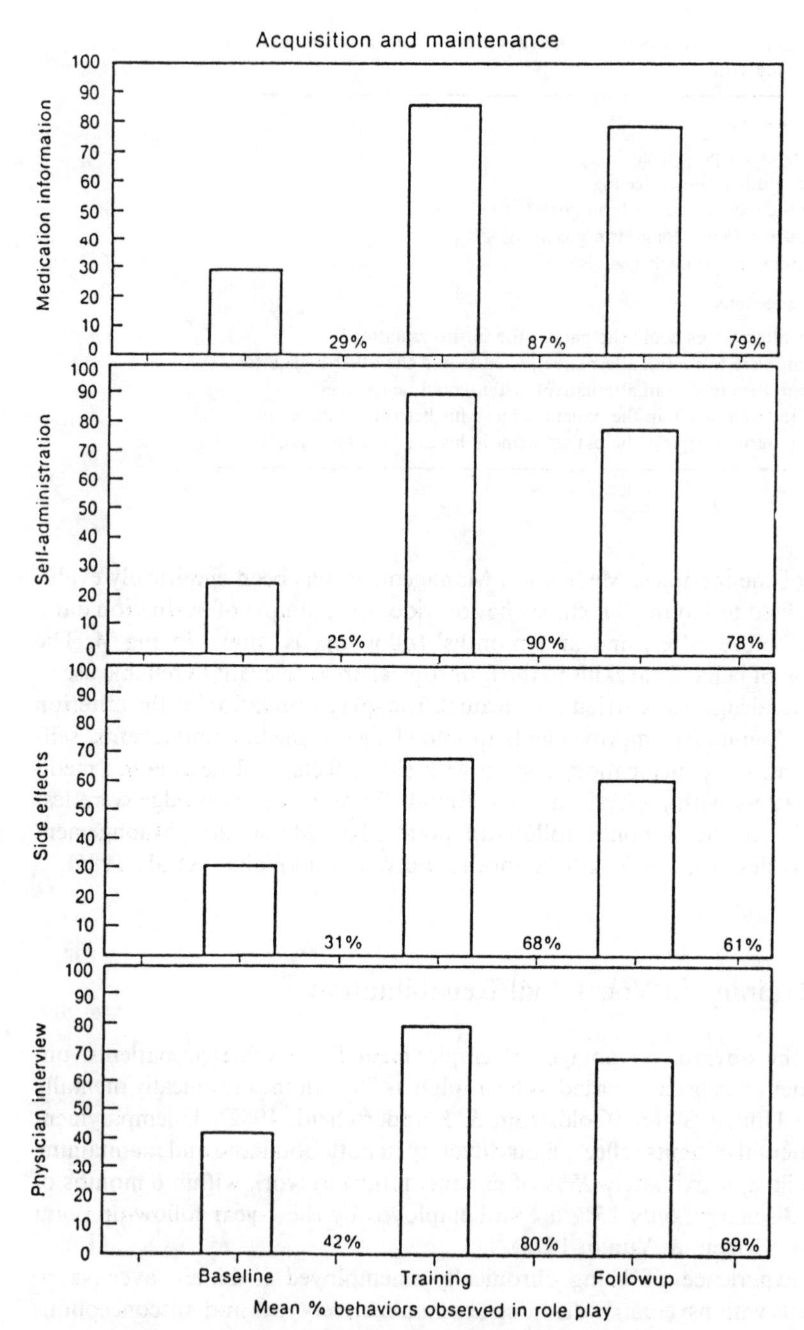

Fig. 4. Evaluation of the medication management module. A group of three chronic schziophrenic patients on maintenance neuroleptic medication were rated for the presence or absence of skills taught in each of four areas. Ratings were made in novel role-played situations that were similar to the situations in which the patients were trained. (Adapted from Wallace et al., 1985).

relinquished their aspirations for a job, and their dissatisfaction with unemployment and leisure time was significantly greater than that of a cross-section of the normal population.

Since many patients who are capable of assuming full-time employment will not have jobs waiting for them when they leave the hospital, job placement is an important element in their rehabilitation and integration back into the community. How patients present themselves at job interviews is a critical determinant of whether they obtain work. Psychiatric patients often have special problems responding to questions about their personal circumstances and recent past. Studies have demonstrated that psychiatric patients can benefit from training in interview skills (Kelly, Laughlin, Claiborne, & Patterson, 1979). Additional skills for obtaining employment include knowing how to solicit job leads and having the motivation and persistence to sustain a long, frustrating job search. One fruitful program for overcoming the obstacles to employment has been the establishment of a Job-Finding Club for recovering psychiatric patients whose symptoms are well enough controlled for them to work full time.

Job-Finding Club. The Job-Finding Club combines several successful techniques in a packaged module first developed by Azrin and colleagues (Azrin & Besalel, 1980; Azrin & Phillip, 1979). Key elements of the module include: (a) the use of an environment conducive to motivating patients in their job search; (b) use of reinforcement strategies; (c) a breakdown of the tasks involved in finding a job; and (d) the training of skills needed to find a job. To adapt this model to the needs of the psychiatrically disabled, it was necessary to increase the structure and motivation inherent in the program, including daily goal-setting activities, monetary rewards, and remedial training in job-seeking skills. The Job-Finding Club for psychiatric patients was designed and evaluated at the Brentwood Division of the West Los Angeles VA Medical Center (Jacobs, Kardashian, Kreinbring, Ponder, & Simpson, 1984). Patients participated in the program full time (6 h per day) while they lived either in the hospital or in the community. While time for participating in the program is unlimited, patients spent an average of 24 days in the Club before locating employment. There are three distinct parts to the Club: training in job-seeking skills, the job search itself, and follow-up and job maintenance.

Training in Job-Seeking Skills. During the 1st week of the program, patients participate in an intensive 6-h per day workshop designed to assess and train basic job-finding skills. The curriculum includes identifying sources of job leads, contacting job leads, writing job résumés, filling out employment applications, participating in job interviews, and using public transport. Instruction is competency based, with trainers using programmed materials, didactic instruction, role plays, and in vivo training exercises. Whenever possible, the program uses materials and situations that the client will face during the job search, such as filling out actual job applications and contacting sources for job leads. The patients' progress is closely monitored and additional instruction is provided as necessary to meet individual needs.

Job Search. After completing the 5-day workshop on skills required for job seeking, patients begin their job search. The program provides areas for telephoning, secretarial support, and identifying current job leads. These leads are gleaned from newspaper advertisements, employment notices, civil service announcements, the yellow pages, and visits to job placement counselors from State employment agencies. A daily, intensive goal-setting session is conducted with each patient to plan his/her job-search activities. During this session counselors and patients identify the most advantageous options for the day's search. They also develop outcome expectations for the daily activities, set a time frame for accomplishing the task, and carry out problem solving of potential obstacles that may be encountered during the day. Patients keep a log of their daily job-seeking activities to account for their time in the program.

Job Maintenance. Club graduates may attend a weekly session that teaches strategies to deal with problems that may threaten job security. Training follows a problem-solving model specifying solutions to an identified issue and then role playing these solutions with feedback before the patient uses the approach in his/her work setting. Problem issues are identified by the participants and may include learning how to get along with co-workers on the job, improving daily living conditions, and managing residual psychiatric symptoms. Graduates may also return to the program if they lose their jobs or wish to upgrade their positions.

Evaluation. The effectiveness of the Club was supported by the outcome of the first 97 patients enrolled in the program. The majority of these patients had hospital admission diagnoses of schizophrenia and a history of psychiatric hospitalization. The average patient had been unemployed for over $1\frac{1}{2}$ years before his/her present hospitalization. The results of the Job-Finding Club during the first 8 months of operation revealed that 66% of all the patients who had entered the Club either had obtained employment or were enrolled in full-time job-training programs. Most jobs were secured in clerical and sales positions (34%); service occupations (25%); technical, managerial, or professional positions (11%); and machine trades (7%).

Six-month follow-up data were collected on the 66 patients who entered jobs or job-training programs from the Job-Finding Club. The percentage of employed people was 75% over the first 6 months after leaving the Club. In comparison, out of the 25 patients who left the Job-Finding Club without successful placement, none of them had found a job 6 months later (Jacobs et al., 1984). Job outcomes have remained stable since the Club's initiation 3 years ago. Out of a total referred patient group of approximately 300, 65% of the participants obtained jobs or entered full-time vocational educational programs. Patients with positive symptoms had greater difficulties finding a job, as did older patients. Previous work history and education did not predict success in finding a job, but did affect the type of employment secured. Thus, the Job-Finding Club is a viable program for training and preparing psychiatric patients in the skills necessary to find employment in the competitive job market.

Generalization of Social Skills Training

The most challenging obstacle to rehabilitation practitioners involved in training skills with chronic mental patients is the difficulty of transferring trained skills into patients' natural living, working, and learning environments. Some patients show no transfer of skills taught them in training sessions, while others evince incomplete generalization or poor maintenance of skills. If skills training is to be a clinically effective method for rehabilitating patients, then it will be necessary to improve the generalization of skills from the clinic or hospital into the patients' natural environment.

Tactics aimed at facilitating generalization from hospital to community have been evaluated in a case study by Liberman, King, and DeRisi (1976). Maintaining consistency in reinforcement contingencies from hospital to community settings, using natural reinforcers, pinpointing functional behaviors as therapeutic goals, overlearning, and training natural caregivers were methods that promoted generalization.

Several specific suggestions for promoting generalization (Stokes & Baer, 1977) have not as yet been fully tested in work with chronic mental patients. The social skills trainer might consider:

- Cueing patient's significant others (families, friends, agency workers, employers) to reinforce the patient's gradually improving skills.
- Training many exemplars of the situations in which the skills need to be used; in particular, diversifying situations during training that prepare patients for a variety of real-life settings.
- Loosening control over the stimuli and responses involved in training; in particular, training different examples concurrently, varying instructions, social reinforcers, and back-up reinforcers.
- Blurring the contingencies and expectations operating during training; in particular, concealing, when possible, the point at which those contingencies stop operating, possibly by delaying reinforcement.
- Using stimuli in the training setting that are likely to be found in generalization settings; in particular, using peers as tutors may aid transfer of skills.
- Reinforcing accurate self-reports of desirable behavior, applying self-recording and self-reinforcement techniques whenever possible.
- When examples of generalization occur, reinforcing at least some of them at least sometimes.

Social skills training techniques, while effective in helping patients acquire interpersonal skills, require the inclusion of procedures that specifically facilitate the generalization of the learned skills into the patient's real-life settings. Generalization does not ordinarily occur spontaneously; it must be planned and programmed. The organization of the real-life settings, orchestrated by the clinician conducting the skills training, to promote support by significant others for the patient's new-found skills, is a key element in the overall training process.

Homework assignments to practice skills in natural environments can be made more successful with the addition of modest efforts at instructing key others to prompt and reinforce the trainee for practicing skills. A study of conversational skills in chronic psychiatric inpatients of a State hospital revealed little or no generalization from the training room to the wards and grounds of the hospital. When systematic homework assignments were provided with back-up reminders and praise from ward staff for completing the practice, generalization was found, even with total strangers (Martinez-Diaz et al., 1983).

Training Recreational and Leisure Skills

For those patients unable to seek sheltered or competitive employment because of persisting and intrusive psychopathology, the skills training approach can still provide benefits. Such patients need to be engaged in activities that might be considered precursors of more demanding social skills and that could "displace" some of their psychopathology. Unless their symptoms and bizarre behaviors are at least partly reduced in frequency and intensity, their self-efficacy and coping efforts will be obliterated and their constructive participation in various forms of skills training will be blocked.

Consider the difficulty an individual would have entering relevant social situations for transacting with others if he had a high rate of talking to himself or showed strange posturing. It is hard enough to overcome social anxiety and long-standing social deficits, but the presence of stigmatizing signs of severe mental disorder will blunt coping efforts and suppress self-efficacy as depicted in Fig. 1. Can individuals be trained to overcome these stigmata of their disorders and thereby to become candidates for social skills training?

Behavioral observations, made objectively with time-sampling rating codes, have repeatedly documented the inverse relation between the frequency of idiosyncratic behaviors (e.g., pacing, repetitive gestures, posturing, and self-verbalizations) and the amount of structured programming present in the living environment. Whether studied in hospitals, mental health centers, or board-and-care homes, patients exhibit significantly more deviant behaviors during unstructured, "free" time (Liberman, De Risi, King, & Wood, 1974; Paul & Lentz, 1977; Rosen, Sussman, Mueser, Lyons, & Davis, 1986).

The corollary of these observations is the displacement of bizarre behaviors by engaging patients in recreational and social activities. A series of controlled studies has been carried out at the Camarillo-UCLA Clinical Research Center that examined the influence of a variety of leisure activities in the reduction of bizarre motoric and verbal behaviors (Wong, Terranova, Bowen, Zarate, Massel, & Liberman, 1987). Unstructured time on the inpatient unit, during which patients had access to recreational materials (e.g., crafts, books, playing cards, and music) but were not prompted to use them, was compared to other times when the patients were prompted and reinforced for participation in these activities. Obsessive-compulsive ruminations, posturings, inappropriate laughter, mumbling to self, and other bizarre behaviors were significantly reduced when patients were engaged in structured recreational activities. The data in Fig. 5 from a case study of a patient with hallucinatory speech illustrate the displacement of dysfunctional behaviors with recreational therapy. Without the structured prompting and reinforcement, the patient's engagement in activities waned and his hallucinatory speech markedly increased. Further analysis of the effective components of recreational therapy showed that instructions and prompting were crucial, but reinforcement was not, aside from the intrinsic

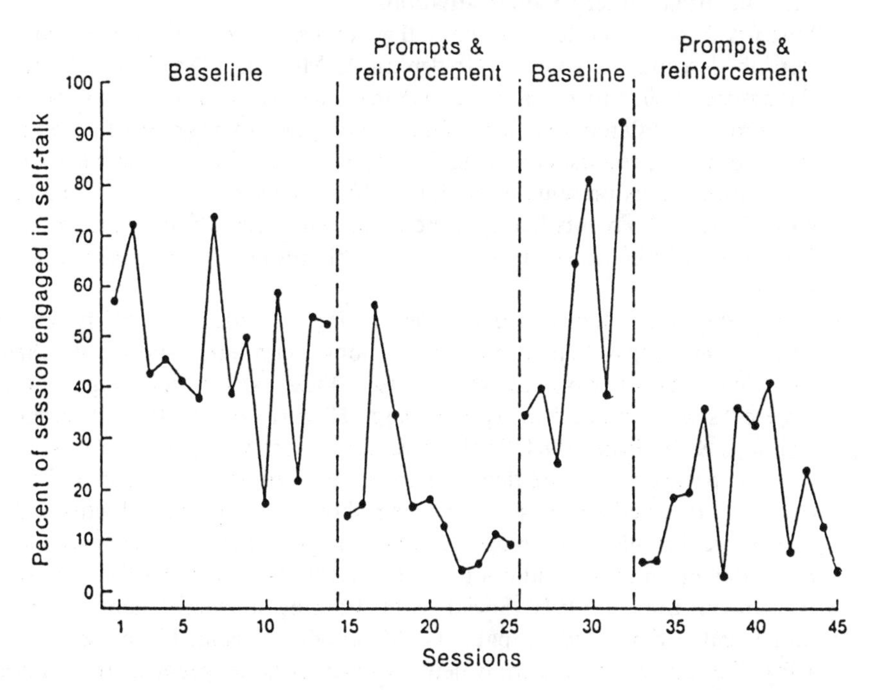

Fig. 5. Displacement of hallucinatory speech behavior with recreational therapy. A chronic schizophrenic male with frequent hallucinations marked by self-vocalizations was exposed to recreational materials and activities with (*independent activity*) and without (*baseline*) supervision by a therapist who provided prompts and reinforcement for task engagement during the supervised periods.

pleasure patients obtained from engaging in the activities. A caveat here is to ensure that the patient's inventory of past and current recreational interests is taken seriously in planning the recreational task.

Conclusion

Over the past 15 years, more than 50 studies have been published on social skills training with psychiatric patients (for reviews, see Brady, 1984 ; Wallace et al., 1980). These studies provided the first evidence that social skills training was a feasible treatment strategy and laid the empirical foundation for recent innovations in training techniques. Many of the early studies suffered from methodological shortcomings, including lack of (a) diagnostic assessment; (b) specifying concomitant psychotropic medications; and (c) widely accepted outcome measures, such as symptomatology or relapse rate. The results of these studies can be summarized by three conclusions:

1. Psychiatric patients can be trained in behaviors that will improve their social skills in specific interpersonal situations.
2. Patients show moderate to substantial generalization of trained behaviors to untrained scenes and items (Goldsmith & McFall, 1975; Kelly, Urey, & Patterson, 1980; Liberman et al., 1984b). The problem of behavioral generalization to different and novel situations appears to be greater for complex behaviors (e.g., requests for behavior change) than simple behavior such as eye contact. This presents a special problem for social skills training with chronic mental patients living in the community, for whom complex social behaviors may be necessary to use accessible resources and generate social support.
3. Comprehensive, intensive social skills training can reduce clinical symptoms and relapse in psychiatric patients. Among neuroleptic-stabilized schizophrenic inpatients or outpatients, intensive social skills training significantly lowered symptoms and delayed relapse (Hogarty et al., 1986; Liberman, Falloon, & Wallace, 1984; Wallace & Liberman, 1985). Similarly, schizophrenic patients who participated in a day hospital program and concurrently received social skills training showed symptom reductions that were more durable over a 6-month follow-up period than patients who were in the day program but did not receive social skills training (Bellack, Turner, Hersen, & Luber, 1984). Social skills training alleviates depression for unmedicated depressed outpatients (McKnight, Nelson, Hayes, & Jarrett, 1984), has clinical effects equivalent to those of antidepressant medication, and is associated with a lower rate of dropout from treatment (Bellack, Hersen, & Himmelhoch, 1983).

Many psychiatric patients manifest learning disabilities that require highly directive behavioral techniques for teaching social skills. Chronic patients often have information-processing and attentional deficits and show hyperarousal or hypoarousal during psychophysiological testing. These patients may experience overstimulation from emotional stressors or even from therapy sessions that are not adequately structured and modulated. Chronic patients often fail to be motivated by customary forms of social and tangible rewards available in traditional therapy. The acquisition of other social skills is impaired in many patients by their lack of conversational skills, an important building block to the attainment of social competence. Patients with schizophrenia often have deficiencies in their social perception and their ability to generate response alternatives for coping with everyday problems such as making an appointment or getting help with annoying drug effects. Patients with verbal dysfluencies, minimal vocal intonation, and poor eye contact may be further impaired in their social learning. The wide variation in cognitive impairment and social deficits among psychiatric patients points to the importance of tailoring social skills training procedures to the needs of individual patients.

The aim of rehabilitation is not to cure disease, but to enhance a deficient individual's functioning, level of adaptation, and quality of life. The necessary design and validation of fully effective technology for skills training in social, family, and vocational domains will require tools from a variety of disciplines – psychopharmacology, social and cognitive psychology, developmental psychology, behavior analysis, psychodynamics, systems theory, and environmental psychology. For example, it has been demonstrated that patients learn social problem-solving skills better when they are taking optimal doses of neuroleptics, when their families are involved in educational activities aimed at improving family emotional climates, when they are exposed to repeated practice with slow and gradual steps, when visual as well as auditory cues and instructions are used, when positive feedback and corrective feedback are liberally provided, when social modeling is provided that uses peers as well as therapists, and when skills training is personalized and overlearned.

Just as neuroleptic drugs require consistent and indefinite use to maintain their therapeutic and prophylactic effects, psychosocial treatments require consistency and long-term application. Remediating psychological and social deficits in patients with schizophrenic disorders involves the same persistent application of the environment as remedying the patient's neurochemical disturbances with medication.

Despite the best efforts at training social, vocational, family, and independent living skills, some patients with major mental disorders require a responsive and compensatory environment to allow them to function with a reasonable quality of life in the community (Stein & Test, 1978). Designing supportive environments to compensate for the residual behavioral and social deficiencies of chronic mental patients can be viewed as akin to the manufacture of prosthetic and orthotic devices for the physically disabled. Just as a paraplegic individual depends on a wheelchair, hydraulic lifts, and sidewalk ramps to exercise independence, mentally disabled individuals require self-help social clubs, transitional employment programs, and sheltered workshops.

References

Anthony, W.A. (1980). A rehabilitation model for rehabilitating the psychiatrically disabled. *Rehabilitation Counseling Bulletin 24*; 6–21.

Anthony, W.A., Cohen, M.R., & Vitalo, R. (1978). The measurement of rehabilitation outcome. *Schizophrenia Bulletin, 4*; 365–383.

Anthony, W.A., & Liberman, R.P. (1986). The practice of psychiatric rehabilitation. *Schizophrenia Bulletin, 12*, 542–559.

Azrin, N.H., & Besalel, V.A. (1980). *Job Club counselors manual: A behavioral approach to vocational counseling*. Baltimore: University Park Press.

Azrin, N.H., & Phillip, R.A. (1979). The Job Club method for the job handicapped: A comparative outcome study. *Rehabilitation Counseling Bulletin, 23*, 144–155.

Bandura, A. (1977). Self-efficacy: Toward a unifying theory of behavioral change. *Psychological Review, 84*, 191–215.

Beard, J.J., Malamud, T.J., & Rossman, E. (1978). Psychiatric rehabilitation and long-term rehospitalization rates. *Schizophrenia Bulletin, 4*, 622–635.

Bellack, A.S., Hersen, M., & Himmelhoch, J.M. (1983). A comparison of social skills training, pharmacotherapy and psychotherapy for depression. *Behaviour Research and Therapy, 21*, 101–107.

Bellack, A.S., Turner, S.M., Hersen, M., & Luber, R.F. (1984). An examination of the efficacy of social skills training for chronic schizophrenic patients. *Hospital and Community Psychiatry, 35*, 1023–1028.

Brady, J.P. (1984). Social skills training for psychiatric patients. *American Journal of Psychiatry, 141*, 491–498.

Brenner, H.D. (1986). Zur Bedeutung von Basisstorungen für Behandlung und Rehabilitation. In W. Böker & H.D. Brenner (Eds.), *Bewältigung der Schizophrenie* (pp. 142–158). Bern: Huber.

Edelstein, B.A., Couture, E., Cray, M., Dickens, P., & Lusebrink, N. (1980). Group training of problem solving with psychiatric patients. In D. Upper & S. M. Ross (Eds.), *Behavioral group therapy: An annual review* (Vol. 2). Champaign, IL: Research Press.

Fichter, M., Wallace, C.J., Liberman, R.P., & Davis, J.R. (1976). Improving social interaction in a chronic psychotic using nagging (discriminated avoidance): Experimental analysis and generalization. *Journal of Applied Behavior Analysis, 9*, 377–386.

Foy, D.W., Wallace, C.J., & Liberman, R.P. (1983). Advances in social skills training for chronic mental patients. In K.D. Craig & R.J. McMahon (Eds.), *Advances in clinical behavior therapy*. New York: Brunner/Mazel.

Glaser, R. (1984). Education and thinking: The role of knowledge. *American Psychologist, 39*, 93–104.

Goldman, H.H., Gatozzi, J., & Taube, R. (1981). The national plan for the chronically mentally ill. *Hospital and Community Psychiatry, 32*, 16–28.

Goldsmith, J.B., & McFall, R.M. (1975). Development and evaluation of an interpersonal skill-training program for psychiatric inpatients. *Journal of Abnormal Psychology, 84*, 51–58.

Goldstein, A.P., Sprafkin, R.P., & Gershaw, M.J. (1976). *Skill training for community living: Applying structured learning therapy*. New York: Pergamon.

Goldstrom, I., & Manderscheid, R. (1982). The chronically mentally ill: A descriptive analysis from the uniform client data instrument. *Community Support Services Journal, 2*: 4–9.

Hogarty, G.E., Anderson, C.M., Reiss, D.J. Kornblith, S.J., Greenwald, D.P., Javna, C.J., & Madania, M.J. (1986). Family psychoeducation, social skills training, and maintenance chemotherapy in the aftercare treatment of schizophrenia. *Archives of General Psychiatry, 43*, 633–642.

Jacobs, H.E., Kardashian, S., Kreinbring, R.K., Ponder, R., & Simpson, A.R. (1984). A skills-oriented model for facilitating employment among psychiatrically disabled persons. *Rehabilitation Counseling Bulletin, 28*, 87–96.

Kale, R.J., Kaye, J.H., Wheland, P.A., & Hopkins, B. (1968). The effects of reinforcement on the modification, maintenance and generalization of social responses of mental patients. *Journal of Applied Behavior Analysis. 1*, 307–314.

Kane, J.M. (1985). Compliance issues in outpatient treatment. *Journal of Clinical Psychopharmacology, 5,* 22S–27S.

Kelly, J.A., Laughlin, C., Claiborne, M., & Patterson, J. (1979). A group procedure for teaching job interviewing skills to formerly hospitalized psychiatric patients. *Behavior Therapy, 10,* 299–310.

Kelly, J.A., Urey, J.R., & Patterson, J.T. (1980). Improving heterosocial conversational skills of male psychiatric patients through a small group training procedure. *Behavior Therapy, 11,* 79–83.

Kohen, W., & Paul, G.L. (1976). Current trends and recommended changes in extended care placement of mental patients. *Schizophrenia Bulletin. 2,* 575–594.

Lehman, A.F., Ward, N.C., & Linn, L.S. (1982). Chronic mental patients: The quality of life issue. *American Journal of Psychiatry, 134,* 1271–1276.

Liberman, R.P. (1985). Psychosocial therapies for schizophrenia. In H.I. Kaplan, & B.J. Sadock, (Eds.), *Comprehensive textbook of psychiatry* (pp. 724–734). Baltimore: Williams and Wilkins.

Liberman, R.P., & Evans, C.C. (1985). Behavioral rehabilitation for chronic mental patients. *Journal of Clinical Psychopharmacology, 5,* 8S–14S.

Liberman, R.P., & Foy, D.W. (1983). Psychiatric rehabilitation for chronic mental patients. *Psychiatric Annals, 13,* 539–545.

Liberman, R.P., DeRisi, W.J., King, L.W., & Wood, D. (1974). Behavioral measurement in a community mental health center. In P. Davidson, F. Clarke, & C. Hamerlynck (Eds.), *Evaluating behavioral programs in community, residential and educational settings* (pp. 103–139). Champaign, IL: Research Press.

Liberman, R.P., King, L.W., DeRisi, W.J., & McCann, M. (1975). *Personal effectiveness: Guiding people to assert themselves and improve their social skills.* Champaign, IL: Research Press.

Liberman, R.P., King, L.W., & DeRisi, W.J. (1976). Behavior analysis and therapy in community mental health. In H. Leitenberg (Ed.), *Handbook of behavior analysis and modification* (pp. 566–603). Englewood Cliffs, NJ: Prentice-Hall.

Liberman, R.P., Nuechterlein, K.H., & Wallace, C.J. (1982). Social skills training and the nature of schizophrenia. In J.P. Curran & P.M. Monti (Eds.), *Social skills training; A practical handbook for assessment and treatment* (pp. 5–56). New York: Guilford.

Liberman, R.P., Falloon, I.R.H., & Wallace, C.J. (1984). Drug-psychosocial interventions in the treatment of schizophrenia. In M. Mirabi (Ed.), *The chronically mentally ill: Research and services* (pp. 175–212). New York: SP Medical and Scientific Books.

Liberman, R.P., Lillie, F.J., Falloon, I.R.H., Harpin, E.J., Hutchinson, W., & Stoute, B.A. (1984b). Social skills training for relapsing schizophrenics: An experimental analysis. *Behavior Modification, 8,* 155–179.

Liberman, R.P., Kuehnel, T.G., Phipps, C.C., & Cardin, V.A. (1985). *Resource book for psychiatric rehabilitation: elements of service for the mentally ill.* Los Angeles: University of California Press.

Martinez-Diaz, J.A., Massel, H.K., Wong, S.E., Wiegand, W., Bowen, L. Edelstein, B.A., Marshall, R.D., & Liberman, R.P. (1983, December). "Training of generalization of conversation skills in chronic schizphrenics." Presented at the World Congress on Behavior Therapy, Washington, DC.

Massel, H.K. (1985). Doctoral dissertation, Georgia State University.

McKnight, D.L., Nelson, R.O., Hayes, S.C., & Jarrett, R.B. (1984). Importance of treating individually assessed response classes in the amelioration of depression. *Behavior Therapy, 15,* 315–335.

Paul, G.L. (1969). The chronic mental patient: Current status, future directions. *Psychological Bulletin, 71,* 81–94.

Paul, G.L., & Lentz, R. (1977). *Psychosocial treatment of chronic mental patients.* Cambridge, MA: Harvard University Press.

Rosen, A.J., Sussman, S., Mueser, K.T., Lyons, J.S., & Davis, J.M. (1986). Behavioral assessment of psychiatric inpatients and normal controls across different environmental contexts. *Journal of Behavioral Assessment, 3,* 25–36,

Rumelhart, D.E. (1981). *Understanding understanding.* La Jolla, CA: University of California, Center for Human Information Processing.

Schooler, N.R. (1986). The efficacy of antipsychotic drugs and family therapies in the maintenance treatment of schizophrenia. *Journal of Clinical Psychopharmacology, 6,* 11S–19S.

Spaulding, W., Storms, L., Goodrich, V., & Sullivan, M. (1986). Applications of experimental psychopathology to psychiatric rehabilitation. *Schizophrenia Bulletin, 12,* 560–577.

Stein, L.I., & Test, M.A. (1978). *Alternatives to mental hospital treatment.* New York: Plenum.

Stokes, T.F., & Baer, D.M. (1977). An implicit technology of generalization. *Journal of Applied Behavior Analysis, 10,* 349–369.

Talbott, J.A. (1978). *The chronic mental patient: Problems, solutions, and recommendations for a public policy.* Washington, DC: The American Psychiatric Association.

Van Putten, T. (1974). Why do schizophrenic patients refuse to take their drugs? *Archives of General Psychiatry, 31,* 67–72.

Wallace, C.J. (1986). Functional assessment. *Schizophrenia Bulletin, 12,* 604–630.

Wallace, C.J., & Davis, J.R. (1974). The effects of information and reinforcement on the conversational behavior of chronic psychiatric patient dyads. *Journal of Consulting and Clinical Psychology, 42,* 656–666.

Wallace, C.J., & Liberman, R.P. (1985). Social skills training for patients with schizophrenia: A controlled clinical trial. *Psychiatry Research. 15,* 239–247.

Wallace, C.J., Nelson, C.J., Liberman, R.P., Aitchinson, R.H., Lukoff, D., Elder, J.P., & Ferris, C. (1980). A review and critique of social skills training with schizophrenic patients. *Schizophrenia Bulletin, 6,* 42–63.

Wallace, C.J., Boone, S.E., Donahoe, C.P., & Foy, D.W. (1985). Psychosocial rehabilitation for the chronic mentally disabled: Social and independent living skills training. In D. Barlow (Ed.), *Behavioral treatment of adult disorders* (pp. 462–501). New York: Guilford.

Wong, S.E., Terranova, M.D., Bowen, L., Zarate, R., Massel, H.K., & Liberman, R.P. (1987). Providing independent recreational activities to reduce stereotypic vocalizations in chronic schizophrenics. *Journal of Applied Behavior Analysis, 20,* 77–81.

Wong, S.E., Massel, H.K., Mosk, M.D., & Liberman, R.P. (1986). Behavioral approaches to the treatment of schizophrenia. In G.D. Burrows, T.R. Norman, & G. Rubinstein (Eds.), *Handbook of studies on schizophrenia* (pp. 239–247). Amsterdam: Elsevier Science.

Family Interventions in the Community Management of Schizophrenia: Methods and Results

I.R.H. Falloon, K. Hahlweg, and N. Tarrier

The treatment of schizophrenia has changed to a great extent over the last 30 years. Owing to the widespread use of neuroleptic medication, the mean length of stay in hospital has shortened considerably, and many patients are now treated in the community. Without question, neuroleptic drug treatment is effective in promoting symptom reduction in acute exacerbations, and it also has a definite prophylactic effect in preventing subsequent exacerbations. The mean relapse rate after 1 year of continuous neuroleptic treatment is 41%, while under placebo conditions 68% of the patients relapse (Hogarty, 1984). However, despite the significant differences between placebo and verum the relapse rates are still high. Furthermore, long-term neuroleptic treatment is frequently accompanied by bothersome and often persistent side effects. These unpleasant effects include a variety of movement disorders, such as slowed, stiff motor behavior, involving facial and gestural expressions, tremor resembling Parkinson's disease, restlessness, apathy, or drowsiness, and may persist irreversibly as in the case of tardive dyskinesia (Falloon, McGill, & Boyd, 1984).

Concerns about these adverse effects of neuroleptic medication have led to a search for alternative long-term medication regimens, in particular low-dose and intermittent treatment. In low-dose therapy, patients receive about 10% of the usual standard dose (Kane et al., 1983), while in intermittent treatment medication is discontinued gradually. If clinical worsening is noted, medication is promptly reinstituted (Carpenter, Stephens, Rey, Hanlon & Heinrichs, 1982).

In general, neuroleptic medication of one form or another seems to be a necessity in the community care of schizophrenics. As suggested from the vulnerability-stress model, the major effect of neuroleptic medication may lie in its remarkable ability to calm patients down by changing the autonomic arousal anomalies found in acute and withdrawn schizophrenic patients (see Straube & Öhman this volume) to normal levels, thus operating on one major vulnerability factor. However, when looking at the relapse rates the protection afforded seems to be only partial because environmental stressors (both ambient stressors and discrete events) play a role in precipitating episodes even when the patient is taking optimal doses of medication (Falloon et al., 1984).

A stressful family environment constitutes such an ambient stressor. Levels of family expressed emotion (EE) have been repeatedly found to predict relapse rates in schizophrenic patients 9 or 12 months after hospital discharge (Brown,

Birley, & Wing, 1972; Jenkins et al., 1986; Leff & Vaughn, 1985; Nuechterlein et al., 1986). These studies have shown that the chance of relapse increases by a factor of approximately four whenever a patient returns to a family environment marked by high levels of criticism and/or emotional overinvolvement. In contrast to the 50%–60% relapse rate for a 9-month period among high-EE families, the base rate of relapse in families rated as low on EE averages 15%.

EE is coded from the individual Camberwell Family Interview (CFI; Vaughn & Leff, 1976) with a relative of a psychiatric patient, and ratings are based on statements made by the relative about the patient. The number of critical comments (statements of irritation, dislike, or resentment about the patient's behavior or personality, usually expressed with corresponding voice tone) in the interview are counted. Degree of emotional overinvolvement (markedly overconcerned, overprotective, or self-sacrificing attitudes/behavior) is rated on a six-point scale for the whole interview. Relatives are classified as high EE if they show evidence of excessive criticism and/or emotional overinvolvement (EOI). Generally, this interview is administered while the patient is hospitalized for an index episode of the disorder, and it is assumed that the EE rating reflects the type of family environment which the patient will encounter after discharge.

Recent studies have shown that the EE measure is not only relevant to schizophrenia, but is also a valuable predictor of relapse in depression (Hooley, Orley, & Teasdale, 1986; Vaughn & Leff, 1976) and in recent-onset mania (Miklowitz, Goldstein, Nuechterlein, Snyder, & Doane, 1987). In view of these findings – and in accordance with the vulnerability-stress model – it seems mandatory to include the family in a comprehensive aftercare treatment program in order to prevent relapse by improving the ability of the family to manage environmental stress.

Besides the compelling evidence from the EE research there are a number of other reasons for involving the family members in the community management of schizophrenia. However, as President Carter's Commission on Mental Health (1978) concluded:

> It is still the rule rather than the exception that most treatment plans for schizophrenics are focused almost entirely on the patient. Either because of treatment philosophy or limited resources, family members are often dealt with only minimally. Clearly, even now, there is enough information to show that there are many reasons to attend to the needs of the families of schizophrenic patients, including providing them with social and community supports to help ease their burden in caring for their impaired family member (Vol. II, p. 20).

Indeed, perhaps the most compelling reason for providing family treatment is that the family support system remains unrivalled in the care of its disabled members, yet the costs of that care, in both monetary and personal burden, are borne almost entirely by the caregiving family. In many cases of schizophrenia, especially in the United States and the United Kingdom, patients who were formerly cared for in the long-stay wards of publicly funded hospitals, with expert nursing and medical supervision, are now cared for by relatives who are not only untrained and ill-informed about the nature of the illness and its optimal management, but are often denied access to this information and criticized by professionals for the harm they have done the patient. The minimal intervention provided for family members and patients should entail dissemination of information about schizophrenia with guidelines on its management. The genetic implications of this condition, albeit relatively minor (with the exception of indentical twins or marriages between two persons with schizophrenia), should be discussed. The omission of such genetic counseling might reasonably be considered malpractice.

Educating families about schizophrenia appears an important first step in providing support. A second component entails the provision of basic social support such as economic aid, housing, and the provision of supportive services for both the patient and his/her family. For the more disabled patients day care and brief periods of residential care to provide family members with relief from arduous caregiving may be a substantial assistance. For most patients the availability of rehabilitation services, both vocational and social, to assist in their return to active community functioning is crucial.

The provision of support to patients and families is an unglamorous, often overlooked family intervention in the management of schizophrenia, but it is arguably one of the most efficient means of reducing family tension and resentment directed towards the index patient. The research on family factors associated with exacerbations of schizophrenia reveals that the levels of support provided to often severely disturbed patients is surprisingly high in more than half the families, and that most appear willing to continue to provide assistance for their disabled relatives (Evans, Bullard, & Solomon, 1960; Leff, 1979). However, a substantial proportion appear unable to cope with recurrent episodes of behavioral disturbance and tend to provide a less optimal milieu that results in more frequent exacerbations and admissions to hospital. These families often show deficits in a more emotional manner. For this group of families, social support alone is insufficient, and family therapy interventions that seek to improve the coping capacity of family members and to reduce family stress are usually indicated.

Methods

Multiple Family Groups

A variant of the supportive model is multiple family group therapy (McFarlane, 1983). Several families (usually three to five) including the patients discuss wide-ranging issues such as practical issues of living, family rules, management of schizophrenia, or expanding social networks. Therapists tend to facilitate problem-solving discussion among families while providing suggestions and professional advice from time to time. Family members and patients are able to share their past experiences and their present difficulties. Psychodynamic interventions are minimized, but the commonality of group themes and reinforcement of a cohesive group milieu are considered useful vehicles to enhance the problem-solving potential of the group format. Advocates of this approach have suggested that working with groups of families is superior to working with one family alone (Lansky, Bley, McVey, & Brotman, 1978; Laqueur, 1972; Norton, Detre, & Jarecke, 1963). These claims of clinical effectiveness have not yet been supported by comparative studies.

Crisis Management

Langsley, Machotka, and Flomenhaft (1968) at the University of Colorado developed a program of family crisis therapy aimed at minimizing admission to hospital. They assumed that the request for hospitalization of one member of the family was often precipitated by a crisis in the family and that removal of an individual from the family at that point in time was likely to complicate the resolution of the crisis by distracting solving of the family problem. Family crisis therapy employs a crisis intervention model with pragmatic problem solving of the current crisis with efforts to aid the recompensation of the patient. The duration of treatment averages 3 weeks with about five office visits, a home visit, and 24-h telephone contact. Treatment is begun at the time of emergency room contact when all members of the family are called together for an emergency family meeting. The sequence of events leading to the crisis is defined and scapegoating of the patient is prevented. Support, advice, and reassurance are provided to alleviate tension, and drugs are given to *any member of the family* where they may assist in symptom relief. A plan is developed to resolve the situation and to restore the functional capacity of each family member. Conflict resolution and symptom relief are usually rapid, but referral to long-term individual or family therapy may be instigated where long-standing conflicts remain. The crisis unit then provides ongoing contact to assist in subsequent crisis episodes.

In a controlled evaluation of family crisis therapy Langsley, Machotka, and Flomenhaft (1971) treated 150 randomly selected families of patients who requested admission to the University of Colorado Medical Center. A matched control group of 150 similar cases where the identified patient had been admitted to hospital for conventional treatment was used for comparison. An 18-month follow-up of 80% of the original sample indicated that not only could hospital admission be avoided in the crisis management phase, but that in many cases the rate of hospitalization could be reduced over a much longer period. In an earlier report, it was suggested that the family approach may greatly reduce the costs associated with hospital care, although no detailed cost was reported (Langsley et al., 1968). Despite avoiding the much vaunted hazards of hospital care, there was no evidence that the social functioning of the family-treated patients was superior to the conventionally treated group. A measure of clinical status did suggest that the family group had less symptomatic impairment at follow-up. However, it is not clear what aftercare was provided for either group of patients after the acute episode; in particular, details of drug therapy and subsequent crisis intervention are lacking. This serious omission limits the conclusions that can be drawn from the long-term follow-up study. At best we can conclude that family crisis therapy is a feasible alternative to hospital admission in the treatment of many psychiatric emergencies.

Changing the Patterns of Family Communication

Conjoint family therapy was a treatment method that developed serendipitously from research studies of communication behavior in the nuclear family group. In order to study the family communication patterns in a relatively simple environment, researchers met with each family as a group in the clinic and attempted to passively observe open-ended family discussions. Jackson and Weakland (1961) noted that it was not uncommon for the families to report substantial benefit from the opportunity to engage in this procedure, and that improvement in the schizophrenic illness of the index patient was evident. Furthermore, the researchers found themselves making more active interventions to facilitate these family discussions. At the same time as these experiments were being conducted at Palo Alto by the anthropologically oriented group under Bateson (Bateson, Jackson, Haley, & Weakland, 1956), Lidz and his researchers at Yale (Lidz, Cornelison, Fleck, & Terry, 1957), and Bowen's group at the National Institute of Mental Health (NIMH) (Bowen, 1961) were conducting very similar studies and were observing similar beneficial effects from their family discussion. The researchers' interest centered primarily on aberrant communication patterns in the families, so that the patients' illness per se was a confounding variable that was given minimal attention and considered somewhat irrelevant.

This research basis offered an important perspective for some of the theories and practice of family therapy for schizophrenia. The systems theory formulation and treatment model was the most influential of these. This approach conceptualized the family as an interactive system in which each component individual functioned within certain prescribed limits and contributed to the combined productivity of the family group. In the case of families where one member had schizophrenia, the illness was considered to be the direct product of ineffective family interaction. The family was considered the unit of pathology – "a *schizophrenic family*" – with the index patient merely the "carrier" of the disorder, the unfortunate "scpegoat" for the family "madness." It was further hypothesized that:

1. In order to understand the index patient's schizophrenia, the communication patterns of the whole family must be clearly understood (Ackermann, 1966; Bell, 1963; Bowen, 1961, Haley, 1959; Laing & Esterson, 1964).

2. Homeostatic mechanisms exist within the dynamic transactions of family members that serve to preserve the status quo and to resist major changes. Change in one family member is always balanced by changes in one or more of the other family members that effectively cancel out the net effect of the change on the family unit. Thus, improvement of the symptoms of schizophrenia of the index patient may be accompanied by increased psychopathology in other family members. Similarly, stress on one family member may result in changes in members other than the recipient of the stressor (Jackson, 1959).

This model of family psychopathology clearly implicated the family in the etiology of schizophrenia, but, apart from pointing to family management as the preferred mode of therapeutic intervention, it offered few specific strategies to foster lasting change. The frustration experienced by the early family therapists in producing sustained changes in the patterns of family transactions appeared to have been captured in the theory of homeostasis and the associated notion that the family is a closed system that effectively isolates itself from the other systems of work, education, social contacts, and the potential benefits offered through social network inputs, including family therapy.

There have been no controlled studies to support the efficacy of the family systems approaches in the treatment of the chronic mental patient. However, clinical reports suggest that family therapy that aims at improving the clarity of family communication may contribute to a reduction in hospitalization and an improved prognosis for schizophrenia (Esterson, Cooper, & Laing, 1965; Friedman et al., 1965; Jackson & Weakland, 1961).

A variant of systemic family therapy was developed by Italian family therapists relying heavily on the prescription of therapeutic paradoxes (Selvini-Palazzoli, Cecchin, Prata, & Boscolo, 1978). It has to be stressed, however, that despite the popularity of this approach its applicability to schizophrenia is still in doubt. As McFarlane (1983) pointed out: "The Milan team has yet to publish even one case description of an adult schizophrenic, let alone controlled evaluations" (p. 227).

Family Treatment Based upon the Vulnerability-Stress Model

The rapid benefits of continued neuroleptic medication and hospital milieu in the treatment of acute episodes of schizophrenia have led to an increased focus on sustaining improvement after the patient returns home. Prevention of relapse has become the aim of recent developments in family treatment. The well-replicated EE finding that high levels of family stress directed towards the index patient result in florid relapse (Leff & Vaughn, 1985) has induced clinicians to develop family therapy methods that seek to minimize the expression of negative attitudes and overinvolved feelings towards the vulnerable family member. In contrast to earlier family interventions, these newer approaches have been empirically evaluated in controlled outcome studies. They include the brief aftercare approach of Goldstein, Rodnick, Evans, May, and Steinberg (1978), Anderson, Reiss, and Hogarty's (1986) psychoeducational method, the supportive method of Leff, Kuipers, Berkowitz, Eberlein-Vries, and Sturgeon (1986), and the behavioral family therapy method of Falloon et al. (1984) and Tarrier, Barrowclough, Vaughn, Bamrah, Porceddu, Watts, & Freeman (1986).

The Brief Focal Family Approach

Goldstein et al. (1978) devised a six-session family treatment model for patients who had been discharged home to their families after brief inpatient treatment of acute episodes of schizophrenia. Patients in the United States were often discharged after only the most disturbing symptoms had remitted and were often still in the restitution phase. It was clear that such patients are at a high risk for subsequent relapse. For this reason, an intervention that assisted the family to understand the nature of the patient's illness and the need for stress reduction in the period immediately after discharge appeared indicated.

The crisis-oriented method involved six weekly (1-h) sessions during which a psychologist met with the patient and family members in a problem-focused group. The major theme of these sessions was dealing with current and anticipated future stressors. Patients and families were encouraged to adopt realistic expectations for full recovery from the illness and to reduce the pressure on the patient to return rapidly to his/her premorbid social status. A gradual return to social functioning was advocated. Although sessions were relatively unstructured, the therapists were provided with four target objectives to achieve in the six sessions.

The first of these aims involved discussion about the nature of schizophrenia, with the therapist educating the patient and the family about the association between stressful events and precipitation of the illness, as well as the serious nature of schizophrenia, its prognosis, and the need for drug treatment and stress management to prevent further episodes. This educational component was not standardized.

Once the family had a grasp of the vulnerability principles, a problem-solving format was employed to identify stressors, to explore strategies for avoiding or coping with stressful situations, and to plan and evaluate attempts to use stress management strategies. Coping with current symptoms of schizophrenia and practical problems of living were commonly identified stressors. Some intrafamilial stressors were dealt with, but attempts to restructure family communication were generally avoided.

A controlled study of the effectiveness of this approach compared the family therapy approach with standard aftercare procedures in a population of predominantly first admission patients who were diagnosed on broadly based criteria for schizophrenia. Patients were all maintained on injections of fluphenazine, either (a) 25 mg every 2 weeks; or (b) 6.25 mg every 2 weeks.

Measures of psychopathology and community tenure were collected before treatment, and after 6 weeks and 6 months.

After the 6-week treatment period only two (4%) of 46 patients who received family treatment were readmitted to hospital, compared to eight (16%) of 50 patients who had standard aftercare. The differences between the high and low dosage of the drugs were not striking, although only one readmission occurred in the cases who received both family therapy and high-dose neuroleptics, while 24% of those in the low-dose neuroleptic and standard aftercare group were readmitted. Patients treated with family therapy had significantly lower psychopathology ratings on the withdrawal, affective disturbance, and thought disorder factors of the Brief Psychiatric Rating Scale (BPRS). These advantages for family therapy were still pronounced 6 months after discharge. The rate of relapse was 0% for the high-dose family therapy group, but 48% for the low-dose, no-therapy group, leaving the other two groups in between. There were significant effects for drug dosage ($p<0.01$) and family therapy ($p<0.05$). A long-term follow-up after 3–6 years of a subgroup of patients has been conducted, showing no differences between the groups (Goldstein & Kopeikin, 1981). To conclude, standard (high-) dose treatment in conjunction with brief family therapy had a significant effect on relapse rates at the 6-month follow-up.

Long-term Family Treatment

In the following, three more extensive family approaches tested in controlled experiments will be discussed and the results will be summarized.

The Psychoeducational Approach

Hogarty and Anderson at the University of Pittsburgh have developed a family model that addresses directly the vulnerability-stress hypothesis (Anderson et al., 1986). They contend that persons with schizophrenia suffer from a "core psychological defect" that interferes with the cognitive processes essential to problem solving and is manifest in excessive physiological arousal under conditions of everyday stress. Additional stressors readily precipitate episodes of schizophrenia. Thus, the goals of their approach are to diminish stimulation while reducing psychophysiological vulnerability through neuroleptic drug therapy. The focus is clearly on prompting social rehabilitation. The family therapy intervention aims to increase the stability of the home environment by reducing the apprehension of family members about schizophrenia and promoting effective stress management. Attention is given to four main areas: (a) increasing family understanding of schizophrenia and strategies for managing symptomatology; (b) reduction of family stress by promoting more effective coping behavior to deal with crises; (c) promotion of extrafamilial social relationships for all family members; (d) resolving long-standing family conflicts.

The family intervention is divided into four temporal phases stretching over a period of 1–2 years. Phase 1 involves contact with the family in twice-weekly meetings while the patient is hospitalized. The patient does not attend these sessions that aim to (a) develop a therapeutic alliance with the family; (b) establish the clinician as the family ombudsman; (c) elicit reactions to the illness; and (d) mobilize family concern and support. This phase is supportive and empathic, with limited discussion about practical coping issues relating to the hospital management and discharge plans. Formulation of the short-term and long-term goals of therapy is carried out mutually between family and therapist. The patient receives parallel relationship-building sessions form a project nurse-therapist on the ward and participates in one conjoint family session before discharge.

Phase 2 consists of a day-long survival skills workshop that includes four or five families. Parents, spouses, and siblings are encouraged to attend, but the index patient is excluded. Goals are the provision of detailed information on the illness and its management as well as assisting families to form a mutually supportive network. Comprehensive discussion of the nature of schizophrenia, theories of etiology, as well as drug and psychosocial interventions is conducted. Specific family management strategies for stress reduction and coping with the illness in the family are outlined. Families are encouraged to attenuate their expectations for full recovery for many months after all the florid symptoms have remitted. The guilt that families may harbor concerning their role in causing schizophrenia or over what they should have done to prevent the illness is discussed openly and realistically. The importance of clear family communication is stressed. At the conclusion of the workshop, families tend to feel substantially less isolated and usually opt to participate in a monthly multiple family group to continue sharing their burdens and offering support to each other.

Phase 3 consists of family sessions every week that are reduced in frequency to biweekly meetings during the first 6 months after the patient returns home. The family management strategies outlined in the survival skills workshop are individualized and applied to the specific concerns and problems of each family. The patient now becomes an active participant in the family sessions and his/her gradual resumption of role fuctioning is a major theme of the sessions. The second major issue dealt with in this phase is the reinforcement of structure within the family to allow increased "psychological space" for the patient and other family members. Concrete methods to deintensify face-to-face contact between the patient and family members are advocated. These include: allowing family members to speak for themselves, to do things separately, to recognize each person's limitations, to encourage "time outs" whereby the patient may retreat to his/her room or take a walk when feeling agitated or overstimulated. The importance of a strong marital alliance between parents is supported. Parents are encouraged to engage in social activites as a couple and to expand their social networks.

A low-key focus on the patient's resumption of activities is maintained. Simple structured tasks are set to encourage a return to the requirements of everyday living. Reinforcement is provided for small successes. The need for exceptional patience is stressed, and attempts to push the anergic patient are dicouraged. As the patient becomes less withdrawn, more ambitious tasks are assigned relating to a return to appropriate work and social functioning. Families are educated in the appropriate use of therapeutic resources such as when and how to seek professional help. Expectations for substantial changes in the patient's social status are kept low and families are supported in their persistent efforts. Neuroleptic drug therapy with intramuscular fluphenazine is continued at optimal doses throughout this phase of management.

Phase 4, the final phase of the family intervention, is attained when the index patient is able to perform expected roles in the community through work or school and when the family is coping effectively with this increased autonomy and role functioning. At this time the family can opt for one of two alternative treatments: (a) maintenance family therapy with contact decreased to once monthly or less; or (b) more intensive family therapy with confrontation of long-standing family conflicts and interpersonal communication deficits. The maintenance therapy seeks to consolidate early gains and to reinforce continued stress management efforts. This phase usually begins 1 year after discharge and continues up to 2 years.

The strength of this intervention appears to lie in its clear conceptualization, concrete objectives, and long-term commitment. The focus is clearly upon the rehabilitation of the index patient and minimizing family stress associated with management of a handicapped family member. Although goal setting and home-work tasks are employed, the teaching of some rather complex behavioral strategies, e.g., time out, is accomplished through family discussions. Little attention is paid to the process of communication or problem solving. Instead the therapist outlines some basic principles. It is not clear how compliant family members are in adhering to such rules in dealing with stressors at home.

A controlled outcome study of the psychoeducational approach including 134 patients has been conducted at the University of Pittsburgh. The family approach ($n=30$) was compared with an equally intensive patient-oriented social skills training program ($n=30$), and a program that combines family and social skills training ($n=29$). All patients received intramuscular neuroleptic drug maintenance, and a control group ($n=45$) receiving drug therapy only was employed (Hogarty et al., 1986).

The Family Members Group

A variant of the stress-education models of family treatment has been developed by the London-based group of Leff, Berkowitz, and Kuipers (Leff et al., 1986). This is most notably an extension of the work on "expressed emotion" in families conducted earlier at the same department. A high level of criticism and/or over-involvement expressed by one or more household members was predictive of a high rate of relapse of schizophrenia. This effect was found to be less prominent where maintenance drug therapy was sustained and when the index patient and the high-EE relatives were physically separated for much of the time (Vaughn & Leff, 1976). A highly pragmatic approach based on these studies was to provide maintenance drug therapy through intramuscular administration and to maximize interpersonal separation. Futhermore, an analysis of the content of most criticism made of the patients revealed considerable confusion about the nature of the illness. This suggested that a further intervention might involve educating the family members about schizophrenia. The need for flexibility in meeting the heterogeneous needs of patients with schizophrenia and their relatives led to the development of several therapeutic modalities to supplement drug therapy; they include: (a) conjoint family interviews; (b) mental health education; (c) a relatives' group; (d) home visits to counsel relatives.

Patients are chosen for the program on the basis of a Present State Examination (PSE) diagnosis of schizophrenia, and a CFI with each household member. Patients who live in contact with one or more relatives are included in the program. The initial session takes place soon after the patient is discharged from hospital. Explicit instructions are given to the patient and the relatives that "it is better that the relative(s) and the patient spend less time together because it is better for the patient" (Berkowitz, Kuipers, Eberlein-Vries, & Leff, 1981, p. 35). This statement is followed by a problem-solving discussion about ways in which such physical separation can be achieved through constructive activities, e.g., by the relative getting a job or the patient attending a day center.

The mental health education modality consists of four short talks about schizophrenia delivered in two sessions. These prepared talks are delivered in a lecture format followed by a question and answer period and written material to take home. They deal with the nature of schizophrenia, but unlike the education provided in the Goldstein and Pittsburgh programs, exclude information about management of the illness. The index patient is excluded from these sessions.

The relatives' group is an open-ended meeting held biweekly to provide support, catharsis, further educational material, and enhancement of personal coping and management strategies for dealing with the patient's symptoms. Relatives who are rated low on the EE index of the CFI are invited to participate as well as those who are rated high on the EE index. The rationale is that the low-EE relatives, who tend to be more effective at coping with the index patient, might participate as models for the less competent and more emotional high-EE relatives. A semistructured, problem-solving discussion format about specific difficulties in the management of the index patients is employed. Relatives are invited to share their experiences with the index patient and their management strategies. High-EE relatives are encouraged to become more empathic listeners and to focus their attention less on their own emotional needs and more on the concerns of others.

Home visits are not a consistent part of the program but are provided on an ad hoc basis for relatives who are unable or refuse to attend the group. Similar supportive problem-solving sessions concerning ways of coping with the index patient are conducted, but in these sessions the patient is invited to attend.

The family members group approach has been evaluated in a controlled experiment. Twenty-four high-EE families were randomly assigned to the family members group or a comparison group in which the patients received standard psychiatric aftercare only (Leff et al., 1986).

Behavioral Family Therapy Approaches

Falloon and Liberman

The behavioral family therapy approach had been developed for treatment of schizophrenia over the past 10–15 years (Falloon & Liberman, 1983). The goal of the method is to provide comprehensive long-term community care for persons suffering from schizophrenia by utilizing the problem-solving potential of their natural support systems (see Falloon et al., 1984). This is achieved through a careful behavioral analysis of the family support system – its strengths as well as its deficits – followed by specific treatment of functional deficits. All family therapy sessions are conducted in the home in order to maximize generalization and to take full advantage of the entire family unit as a powerful agent for effecting social learning and reinforcement. An added advantage of home visits has been to virtually eliminate problems of attendance at family therapy.

The first two sessions are directed towards the education of patients and their families about the nature, course, etiology, and treatment of schizophrenia. The family is asked to share their perceptions and experiences. The index patient is encouraged to lead the discussion about his/her experiences of the illness. Frequently in these sessions, family members come to understand for the first time how frightening, disruptive, and alien symptoms of schizophrenia, such as auditory hallucinations, delusions of external control, thought broadcasting, and persecutory delusions can be to the patient. The effect of these revelations can be dramatic: one often sees immediate softening in previously critical and unsympathetic family attitudes towards the patient.

Theoretical material related to the etiology and treatment of schizophrenia is also presented. It is explained that although the exact causes are unknown, schizophrenia appears to be related to a biochemical defect in the brain that can produce psychotic symptoms at times when the patient is under stress. Individuals who develop symptoms of schizophrenia are probably born with a vulnerability to this and are not responsible nor to blame for it, nor is their family. It is an illness similar, in a sense, to diabetes or hypertension, in that although there is no cure, there are very effective treatments that can reduce and often eliminate symptoms for long periods of time, allowing a gradual return, in many cases, to premorbid levels of functioning. Although families do not *cause* schizophrenia, they can influence its *course*. Since it is a stress-related illness, the amount of tension and stress in the home environment is a critical factor with which to reckon. There are many ways in which families can help maximize the patient's level of functioning, as well as minimize the chances of relapse; therein lies the rationale for a family therapy approach.

An entire session is devoted to discussing issues related to medication. The rationale for using low-dose medication is presented in terms of the need for modification of the combined effects of stress and biochemistry. A cost-benefit analysis is presented with the principal advantages being (a) reduction or elimination of psychotic symptoms; (b) reduction of morbidity due to stressful life events; and (c) prophylaxis against relapse. Disadvantages discussed include bothersome side effects and possible long-term complications such as tardive dyskinesia. Strategies for coping with side effects are discussed, as well as the philosophy of prescribing low-dose neuroleptics (the model daily dosage for patients in this program is 200 mg chlorpromazine or its equivalent).

Following the two educational sessions, the treatment goals for each family shift to enhancing the problem-solving potential of that family unit. Because a minimally sufficient repertoire of interpersonal communication skills is a prerequisite to effective problem solving, several sessions usually focus on improving family communication. Behavioral rehearsal strategies are employed to shape effective expression of positive and negative feelings, reflective listening, making requests for behavioral change in a positive manner, and reciprocity of conversation. These are tailored to the unique communication deficits that each family demonstrates during an extensive battery of pretreatment interactional assessments. The following elements of effective communication are addressed: (a) nonverbal behavior such as voice tone and volume, body language, eye contact, and facial expression; (b) the appropriateness, clarity, and specificity of verbal content; (c) clear expression of positive and negative feelings in the form of "I" statements; (d) reciprocity of conversation. Generalized expression of positive or negative affect is discouraged in favor of praise or criticism for specific behavior. Family members are urged to check out what other people's thoughts and feelings are, rather than speak for them.

This communication skills training is accomplished primarily via behavioral rehearsal and concomitant instruction, modeling, coaching, social reinforcement, and performance feedback. Families are encouraged to practice newly learned communication techniques and are given specific homework assignments to facilitate the daily use of these skills.

When families show competency at basic communication skills, the problem-solving model is introduced as a means of enhancing coping with stressful life events and reducing family tension. Family members are taught a six-step problem-solving method that involves (a) discussing and coming to an agreement on the exact nature of the problem; (b) generating a list of five or more alternative solutions without judging their relative merits as of yet; (c) discussing, in turn, the pros and cons of each proposed alternative; (d) choosing the best solution or combination of solutions; (e) formulating a specific plan of how to implement the solution; and (f) subsequent review of success and praise for people's efforts to implement the solution. Families are encouraged to structure their problem-solving efforts further by taking notes on a worksheet that provides spaces for describing the nature of the problem, listing alternative solutions, choosing the best solution(s), planning implementation, etc. This maximizes group participation and focuses attention on the task. The therapist initially provides much active guidance, but this is gradually withdrawn as the family masters the technique. The problem-solving method seeks to diffuse the burden of coping with a problem to all members of the family system and to draw on the strengths and resources of the entire family. Moreover, its structured nature tends to reduce the level of family tension and negative affect dramatically when discussing even emotionally charged issues.

Few families have an adequate repertoire of coping skills for dealing with the many behavioral disturbances often associated with schizophrenia. Such specific problems as medication compliance, reduction of side effects, dealing with persistent delusions or hallucinations, or when to seek professional intervention are commonly raised by families. Behavioral management strategies that are taught to families include contingency contracting, shaping, time out, limit setting, and identification of warning signals of impending relapse. These specific strategies may be employed in the resolution of numerous family problems not directly related to the index patient, e.g., marital discord.

The behavioral family therapy approach involves a continuous assessment of specific treatment effects and an ongoing behavioral analysis to pinpoint persistent deficits. The major focus is on the enhancement of problem resolution outside of sessions, unassisted by the therapist. The sessions serve as training workshops to develop improved family problem-solving strategies. The content of the treatment sessions is less important than the specific problem-solving behavior learned. Creative solutions arrived at by the family are applauded, and, wherever feasible, the therapist fades out of the sessions to allow the family to function independently. Once the family has demonstrated competent problem solving, the therapist reduces the frequency of sessions and eventually withdraws completely, although he/she will remain available for consultation and further coaching upon request.

Weekly sessions are held during the first 3 months, followed by biweekly sessions for another 3-month period. Thereafter, monthly sessions are conducted for an indefinite period according to the families' needs.

A controlled study of the behavioral family therapy approach has been conducted (Falloon et al., 1982, 1986). This approach was compared with individual supportive psychotherapy of equal intensity over a 9-month period. Thirty-six patients randomly assigned to both conditions (18 each) all received optimal neuroleptic drug therapy, crisis management, and rehabilitation counseling in addition to the specific treatment approaches.

Tarrier and Barrowclough

In a nearly completed study Tarrier, Barrowclough, and their colleagues in Salford, United Kingdom (Tarrier, Barrowclough, Vaughn, et al., 1988) have evaluated a 9-month behavioral intervention, a short educational intervention, and a routine treatment by a National Health Service (NHS) Psychiatric

Service. All patients who were admitted to acute psychiatric wards within hospitals in the Salford Health District were screened, and those who received a diagnosis of schizophrenia using the PSE and were living with a relative were recruited into the study. Relatives were assessed on a number of measures including the CFI. Patients who had a high-EE relative ($n = 51$) were randomly allocated to either "enactive" behavioral intervention, "symbolic" behavioral intervention, education, or routine treatment. Patients with a low-EE relative ($n = 19$) were randomly allocated to education or routine treatment. The rationale behind the intervention was that living with a high-EE relative produced a high level of ambient stress, which resulted in increased relapse risk. If the factors that caused the relative to have a high level of EE, such as behavior of the patient that provoked criticism or hostility or behavior of the relative that was rated as EOI, could be identified and changed then the EE status and associated levels of stress would be reduced. This, then, would also result in a reduction of relapse risk.

Two interventions, "enactive" and "symbolic," which were identical in content, were designed to evaluate the level of intervention required to produce this change. Varying the levels of behavioral intervention has previously been proposed as a better method of evaluation than the use of a placebo intervention (Barrowclough & Tarrier, 1984). The nature of the intervention was strongly influenced by the behavioral writings of Goldiamond (Goldiamond, 1974) who propounded the use of functional analysis to assess clinical problems and a constructional approach to produce change. The behavioral interventions consisted of three phases:

1. Education program (identical to the intervention received by the education alone group): this consisted of two sessions, 1 week apart. The knowledge held by the relative was initially assessed using the Knowledge about Schizophrenia Interview (KASI) (Barrowclough et al., 1987). Then information about schizophrenia was given with special emphasis on the individual patient's symptoms and beliefs already held by the relative (see Tarrier & Barrowclough, 1986). The second session consisted of a feedback and questions session followed by reassessment with the KASI.
2. Stress management: four biweekly sessions during which the relatives were taught how to monitor stress and their responses to it. Stress was defined as anything that provoked a reaction, whether it concerned the patient or not. More adaptive and positive methods to cope with stress were taught where appropriate, and relatives were instructed to practice and implement these.
3. Goal planning: seven sessions followed, initially biweekly and then monthly, during which relatives and patients participated in suggesting problem areas for change. Problems and areas that required change were translated into needs. From the generated list of both the relatives' and patients' needs goals were formulated. Goals were achieved by a gradual process of meeting stepwise objectives using available resources, including strengths within the family. For example, if a relative was overprotective, then the need of the

patient would be to be more independent and that of the relative to develop more interests and activities away from the patient; goals would then be produced to meet these needs.

Results

In the following, the results of the Hogarty et al., Leff et al., Falloon et al., and Tarrier et al. studies will be summarized. In these studies schizophrenic patients [according to the *Diagnostic and Statistical Manual of Mental Disorders*, 3rd edition (DSM-III) or PSE criteria] were randomly assigned after hospital discharge to either experimental or control conditions. All patients received neuroleptic medication.

Relapse Rates

The definition of relapse was roughly equivalent in the four studies: either the reappearance of schizophrenic symptoms or the exacerbation of symptoms which had stabilized at discharge. Despite the differences in these approaches the results regarding relapse rates were very similar over a 1- or 2-year follow-up period (Fig. 1). After 1 year, the mean relapse rate in the family treatment condition was 11% in contrast to 49% in the control group. After 2 years, the mean difference was even more pronounced: 20% and 72%, respectively. In

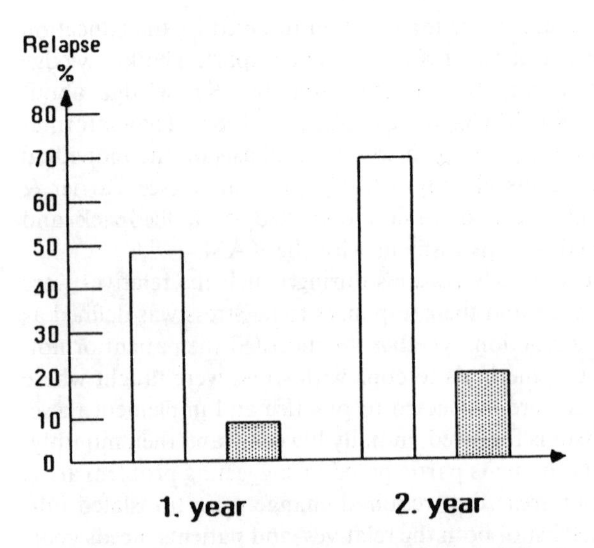

Fig. 1. Relapse rates of schizophrenic patients – comparison of family therapy with normal outpatient care. *Open columns*, normal outpatient care; *shaded columns*, family therapy. (From Anderson et al., 1986; Falloon et al., 1984; Leff et al., 1986; Tarrier et al., 1988)

Tarrier et al.'s study the short educational intervention did not reduce relapse significantly compared to the control group (47% vs. 53%) over 9 months.

Clinical Morbidity

Only Falloon (1986) provided data regarding clinical morbidity. During the first 9 months, patients in the control condition maintained symptom stability about half the time, whereas family management cases remained stable for about 80% of the time. These trends were maintained during the less intensive follow-up phase.

Social Morbidity

Evidence for enhanced social functioning of patients treated with family management comes from the Falloon et al. study (Falloon, 1986). Family management cases were associated with a substantial increase in functional work performance and greater overall social adjustment than cases without family involvement.

Family Functioning

Expressed Emotion. In both the Leff et al. (1986) and the Hogarty et al. (1986) studies the effect of family treatment on the level of EE of the relatives was evaluated. In the Leff et al. study the CFI was administered at admission and at the 9-month follow-up. At admission all relatives had had a high level of EE. A highly significant reduction in criticism was observed in the experimental group, while relatives in the control condition did not change their critical attitude. No significant changes were observed with regard to emotional overinvolvement. In the Hogarty et al. study, the CFI was administered at admission and at 1-year follow-up. All patients at admission lived within high-EE households. Most interestingly, (a) there was no patient relapse in any household which changed from high to low EE, independent of treatment condition; and (b) only the combination of family therapy *and* social skills training prevented relapse in households which stayed high EE (0% relapse; controls = 42%; family treatment: 33%; social skills training: 29%).

These results suggest tentatively that a reduction in the critical attitude of relatives can be achieved by family treatment. However, in nonchanging households, family treatment has to be combined with patients' social skills training to prevent relapse most effectively.

Family Burden. Falloon et al. (1984) assessed the subjective overall burden family members associated with having the index patient living in the household. Relatives in behavioral family care showed a significant and linear reduction in burden over the 2-year follow-up period, while control relatives did not change.

Family Communication. As described earlier the CFI measures the relatives' attitudes towards the patient expressed within the context of an interview with a mental health professional. Evidence is accumulating that these attitudes are also expressed behaviorally when the relative is interacting face to face with the patient. In a series of studies Goldstein and his coworkers assessed the relationship between EE attitudes and direct interactional behavior. The major results showed that a critical attitude is associated with critical behavior during a family interaction task. An attitude of emotional overinvolvement was associated with a high frequency of relatives' intrusiveness towards the patient (see Strachan, Goldstein, & Miklowitz, 1986). These findings have been replicated recently, showing that high-EE families behaved far more negatively and less positively nonverbally during the interaction task than low-EE families. Furthermore high-EE families engaged in long-lasting negative escalation patterns, while low-EE families were able to deescalate (Hahlweg et al., 1987).

Given these findings it seemed necessary to investigate whether family interaction patterns can be changed by family treatments. The Falloon et al. study was specifically designed to test this aspect. On three occasions (at admission, after 3 months, and after 24 months) family members were asked to discuss relevant family problems without the therapist present. These discussions were audiotaped and later transcribed. Results on the 3-month (short-term) changes have recently been published by Doane, Falloon, Goldstein, and Mintz (1985) and Goldstein and Strachan (1986) using the "affective style" (AS) coding system. Relatives in behavioral family care showed a significant reduction in criticism when compared to relatives in the control condition. Also, relatives in family care showed significantly more problem-solving behaviors than control relatives at 3 months.

Hahlweg, Falloon, and Goldstein (1985) analyzed the long-term (2 years) effectiveness of behavioral family care in changing families' communication behaviors using the *Kategoriensystem für partnerschaftliche Interaktion* (KPI, Interaction Coding System; Hahlweg et al., 1984). The KPI was specifically designed to assess families' verbal and nonverbal communication skills and their problem-solving ability. Both relative and patient behavior is coded.

At pretest, families in family care and in the control condition did not differ in any of the variables. At the 2-year follow-up the attendance rates of families were quite different. While 83% of the families in family care attended the diagnostic session, only 56% of the control families were present. As can be seen in Fig. 2, families in family care significantly decreased the amount of criticism and disagreement, while control families did not change. In both conditions families increased their rate of problem-solving statements significantly (Fig. 3). However, families in family care showed a more pronounced increase in problem-solving attempts.

When discussing these results one has to take into account the higher attrition rate of control families. One can speculate that the most difficult/negative families did not attend the 2-year assessment session. One can therefore assume that a lower attrition rate would have yielded even better

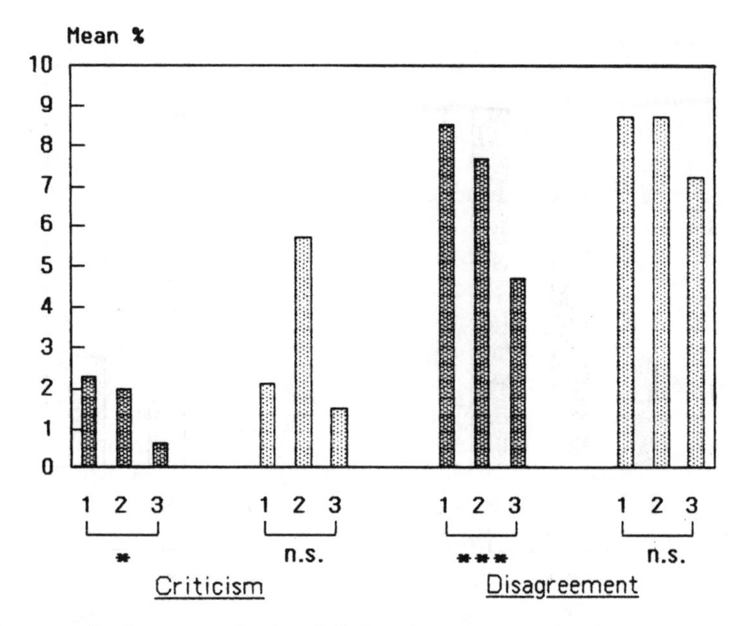

Fig. 2. KPI – changes in family communication. 1, Before therapy; 2, 3-month follow-up; 3, 24-month follow-up; *heavily shaded columns*, behavioral family therapy; *lightly shaded columns*, individual therapy. * $p<0.05$; *** $p<0.001$.

results in favor of family care. When looking at the positive verbal codes, results are less impressive than in the negative domain. This may imply that in the future more emphasis should be put on the training of positive communication behaviors, especially those statements which indicate acceptance of and caring for the schizophrenic family member.

The results indicate that behaviorally oriented family care is successful in bringing about long-lasting changes in family communication, especially in reducing criticism and disagreement and in increasing the problem-solving ability of families with a schizophrenic member, thus reducing family tension and stress – a prerequisite of relapse prevention.

Economic Benefits

A crucial limitation of many new approaches to health services lies in the cost, which often exceeds that of previous approaches and, despite the advantages of improved effectiveness, restricts general implementation. In the Falloon et al. study all direct and indirect costs of community management to patients, families, health, welfare, and community agencies were recorded. The results after 1 year showed that the overall costs of the family approach were approximately 20% less than those of the control condition.

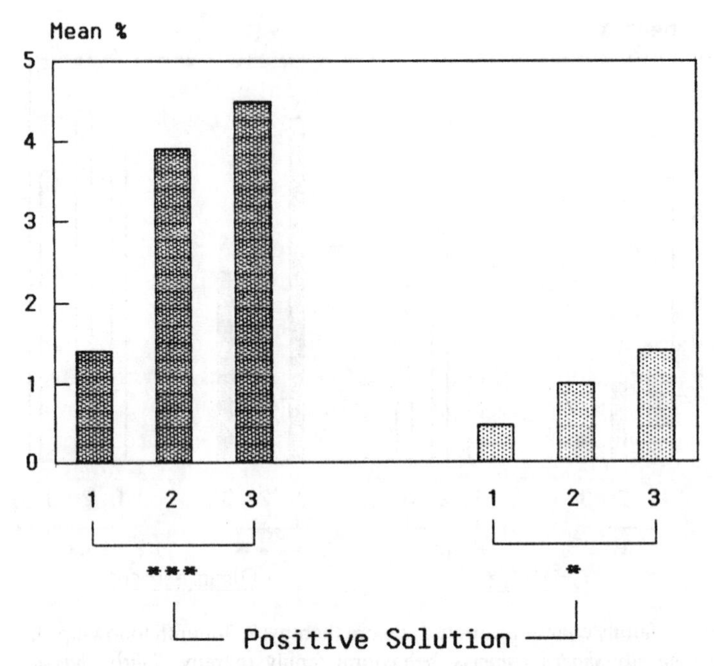

Fig. 3. KPI – changes in family problem-solving: 1, Before therapy; 2, 3-month follow-up; 3, 24-month follow-up; *heavily shaded columns*, behavioral family therapy; *lightly shaded columns*, individual treatment. *$p < 0.05$; ***$p < 0.001$.

Implications of Psychophysiological Results for Family Interventions

Psychophysiological measures, especially electrodermal measures, have proven useful in examining the psychobiological processes that underline the stress-vulnerability interaction (Turpin, Tarrier, & Sturgeon, 1988). However, there is a complex relationship between levels of EE, schizophrenic symptomatology, and electrodermal activity. There is strong evidence that a high-EE relative will provoke higher arousal in the patient than a low-EE relative (Sturgeon, Turpin, Berkowitz, Kuipers, & Leff, 1984; Tarrier & Barrowclough, 1984) and this can be hypothesized as the mechanism of relapse. However, of more importance would be the capability of psychophysiological testing to differentiate between an environmental vulnerability, that is, for example, the increased stress of living with a high-EE relative, and an underlying biological vulnerability. At present there is some evidence to suggest that this may be possible, although it comes only from one longitudinal case study (Tarrier & Barrowclough, 1987). It is hoped that analysis of the extensive psychophysiological data collected in the Salford study will support or refute this suggestion. If there is support for this, then it will be possible to differentiate patients who are at risk principally from environmental factors, such as high-EE relatives. These patients will benefit greatly from environmental (e.g., family) intervention and could remain well for extensive periods of time. Patients at risk from biological factors could benefit from family intervention, but only in as much as it would delay relapse in the short term by removing the extra risk of environmental precipitators.

Conclusions

The past decade has witnessed renewed efforts to support the role of family caregivers in the community rehabilitation of schizophrenic patients. Following the leads provided by studies that have identified the strengths and weaknesses of family support systems, a series of empirically based family treatment approaches has been developed. These methods have differed in format, duration of treatment, and in the specific interventions employed. However, they are based on the vulnerability-stress model and all emphasize more effective problem solving to cope with life stressors, provide information about schizophrenia and medication, and encourage more active family participation in the long-term management of schizophrenia. The results of controlled outcome studies have demonstrated that a substantial reduction in major exacerbations of schizophrenia can be achieved when these interventions are provided in association with optimal neuroleptic drug therapy. Furthermore, it seems that – at least when using a behavioral approach – sustained reduction in the clinical, social, and family morbidity associated with schizophrenia can be achieved. Following family care, long-lasting improvements in family communication have been demonstrated. Overall, these family approaches provide a significant (and cost-effective) advance in the community management of schizophrenia.

Programs for patients not returning to a family after discharge have been discussed by Brenner et al. (this volume) and Liberman et al. (this volume).

Acknowledgment. The authors wish to thank Peter Fiedler, Department of Psychology, University of Heidelberg, FRG, for his helpful comments.

References

Ackermann, N. (1966). *Treating the troubled family.* New York: Baisc Books.

Anderson, C.M., Reiss, D.J., & Hogarty, G.E. (1986). *Schizophrenia and the family.* New York: Guilford.

Barrowclough, C., & Tarrier, N. (1984). Psychosocial interventions with families and their effects on the course of schizophrenia: A review. *Psychological Medicine, 14,* 629–642.

Barrowclough, C., Tarrier, N., Watts, S., Vaughn, C., Bamrah, J.S., & Freeman, H.L. (1987). Assessing the functional value of relatives' reported knowledge about schizophrenia: A preliminary report. *British Journal of Psychiatry, 151,* 1–8.

Bateson, G., Jackson, D.D., Haley, J., & Weakland, J. (1956). Toward a theory of schizophrenia. *Behavioral Science, 1,* 252–264.

Bell, J.E. (1963). A theoretical position for family group therapy. *Family Process, 2,* 1–14.

Berkowitz, R., Kuipers, E., Eberlein-Vries, R., & Leff, J. (1981). Lowering expressed emotion in relatives of schizophrenics. In M.J. Goldstein (Ed.), *New developments in interventions with families of schizophrenics.* San Francisco: Jossey-Bass.

Bowen, M. (1961). The family as the unit of study and treatment. *American Journal of Orthopsychiatry, 31*, 40–60.

Brown, G.W., Birley, J.L.T., & Wing, J.K. (1972). Influence of family life on the course of schizophrenic disorders: A replication. *British Journal of Psychiatry, 121*, 241–258.

Carpenter, W.T., Stephens, J.H., Rey, A.C., Hanlon, T.E., & Heinrichs, D.W. (1982). Early intervention vs. continuous pharmacotherapy of schizophrenia. *Psychopharmacology Bulletin, 18*, 21–23.

Diagnostic and statistical manual of mental disorders, 3rd ed. (DSM-III). (1980). Washington DC: American Psychiatric Association.

Doane, J.A., Falloon, I.R.H., Goldstein, M.J., & Mintz, J. (1985). Parental affective style and the treatment of schizophrenia: Predicting course of illness and social functioning. *Archives of General Psychiatry, 42*, 34–42.

Esterson, A., Cooper, D.G., & Laing, R.D. (1965). Results of family-oriented therapy with hospitalized schizophrenics. *British Medical Journal, 2*, 1462–1465.

Evans, A.S., Bullard, D.M., & Solomon, M.H. (1960). The family as a potential resource in the rehabilitation of the chronic schizophrenic patient. *American Journal of Psychiatry, 117*, 1075–1083.

Falloon, I.R.H. (1986). Behavioral family therapy for schizophrenia: clinical, social, family and economic benefits. In M.J. Goldstein, J. Hand, & K. Hahlweg (Eds.), *Treatment of schizophrenia. Family assessment and intervention* (pp. 171–185). Berlin, Heidelberg, New York: Springer.

Falloon, I.R.H., & Liberman, R.P. (1983). Behavioral family interventions in the management of chronic schizophrenia. In W. R. McFarlane (Ed.). *Family therapy in schizophrenia*. New York: Guilford.

Falloon, I.H.R., Boyd, J.L., McGill, C.W., Razani, J., Moos, H.B., & Gilderman, A.M. (1982). Family management in the prevention of exacerbations of schizophrenia: A controlled study. *New England Journal of Medicine, 306*, 1437–1440.

Falloon, I.R.H., McGill, C.W., & Boyd, J.L. (1984). *Family care of schizophrenia*. New York: Guilford.

Friedman, A.S., Boszomenyi-Nagy, I., Jungreis, S., Lincoln, G., Mitchell, H., Sonne, J., Speck, R.L., & Spivack, G. (1965). *Psychotherapy for the whole family*. New York: Springer.

Goldiamond, I. (1974). Towards a constructional approach to social problems. Ethical and constitutional issues raised by applied behaviour analysis. *Behaviourism, 2*, 1–84.

Goldstein, M.J., & Kopeikin, H.S. (1981). Short- and longterm effects of combining drug and family therapy. In M.J. Goldstein (Ed.), *New developments in interventions with families of schizophrenics*. San Francisco: Jossey-Bass.

Goldstein, M.J., & Strachan, A.M. (1986). The impact of family intervention programs on family communication and the short-term course of schizophrenia. In M.J. Goldstein, J. Hand, & Hahlweg, K. (Eds.), *Treatment of schizophrenia. Family assessment and intervention*. Berlin, Heidelberg, New York: Springer.

Goldstein, M.J., Rodnick, E.H., Evans, J.R., May, P.R.A., & Steinberg, M.R. (1978). Drug and family therapy in the aftercare of acute schizophrenics. *Archieves of General Psychiatry, 35*, 1169–1177.

Goldstein, M.J., Hand, I., & Hahlweg, K. (Eds.), (1986). *Treatment of schizophrenia. Family assessment and intervention*. Berlin, Heidelberg, New York: Springer.

Hahlweg, K., Reisner, L., Kohli, G., Vollmer, M., Schindler, L., & Revenstorf, D. (1984). Development and validity of a new system to analyze interpersonal communication (KPI). In K. Hahlweg & N.S. Jacobson (Eds.), *Marital interaction: Analysis and modification*. New York: Guilford.

Hahlweg, K., Falloon, I.R.H., & Goldstein, M.J. (1985). Changes in schizophrenic families' communication patterns after behavioural family care. Fifteenth European Congress of Behaviour Therapy. August 15, 1985, Munich, FRG.

Hahlweg, K., Nuechterlein, K.H., Goldstein, M.J., Magana, A., Doane, J.A., Snyder, K.S., & Mintz, J. (1987). Parental expressed emotion attitudes and intrafamilial communication behavior. In K. Hahlweg & M.J. Goldstein (Eds.), *Understanding major mental disorder. The contribution of family interaction research*. New York: Family Process Press, pp 156–175.

Haley, J. (1959). The family of the schizophrenic: A model system. *Journal of Nervous and Mental Disease*, *129*, 357–374.

Hogarty, G.E. (1984). Depot neuroleptica: The relevance of psychosocial factors – A United States perspective. *Journal of Clinical Psychiatry*, *45*, 36–42.

Hogarty, G.E., Anderson, C.M., Reiss, D.J., Kornblith, S.J., Greenwald, D.P., Javna, C.D., Madonia, M.J. and the EPICS Schizophrenia Research Group (1986). Family psycho-education, social skills training and maintenance chemotherapy in the aftercare treatment of schizophrenia I. One year effects of a controlled study on relapse and expressed emotion. *Archives of General Psychiatry*. *43*, 633–642.

Hooley, J.M., Orley, J., & Teasdale, J.D. (1986). Levels of expressed emotion and relapse in depressed patients. *British Journal of Psychiatry*, *148*, 642–647.

Jackson, D.D. (1959). Family interaction, family homeostasis and some implications for conjoint family psychotherapy. In J. Masserman (Ed.), *Individual and family dynamics*. New York: Grune and Stratton.

Jackson, D.D., & Weakland, J.H. (1961). Conjoint family therapy: Some consideration on theory, technique and results. *Psychiatry*, *24* (2), Suppl. 30–45.

Jenkins, J.H., Karno, M., de la Selva, A., Santana, F., Telles, C., Lopez, S., & Mintz, J. (1986). Expressed emotion, maintenance pharmacotherapy, and schizophrenic relapse among Mexican-Americans. *Psychopharmacology Bulletin*, *22*, 621–627.

Kane, J.M., Rifkin, A., Woerner, M., Reardon, G., Sarantakos, S., Schiebel, D., & Ramos-Lorenzi, J. (1983). Low dose neuroleptic treatment of outpatient schizophrenics. I. Preliminary results for relapse rates. *Archives of General Psychiatry*, *40*, 893–896.

Laing, R.D., & Esterson, A. (1964). *Sanity, madness and the family*. London: Tavistock.

Langsley, D., Machotka, R., & Flomenhaft, K. (1968). Family crisis therapy. Results and implications. *Family Process*, *7*, 145–156.

Langsley, D., Machotka, R., & Flomenhaft, K. (1971). Avoiding mental hospital admission: A follow-up study. *American Journal of Psychiatry*, *127*, 1391–1394.

Lansky, M.R., Bley, C., McVey, G.G., & Brotman, B. (1978). Multiple family groups as aftercare. *International Journal of Group Psychotherapy*, *28*, 211–224.

Laqueur, H.P. (1972). Mechanism of change in multiple family therapy. In C.J. Sager & H.S. Kaplan (Eds.), *Progress in group and family therapy*. New York: Brunner/Mazel.

Leff, J.P. (1979). Developments in family treatment of schizoprenia. *Psychiatric Quarterly*, *51*, 216–232.

Leff, J.P., & Vaughn, C.E. (1985). *Expressed emotion in families*. New York: Guilford.

Leff, J.P., Kuipers, L., Berkowitz, R., Eberlein-Vries, R., & Sturgeon, D.A. (1986). Controlled trial of social intervention in the families of schizophrenic patients. In M.J. Goldstein, J. Hand., & K. Hahlweg (Eds.), *Treatment of schizophrenia. Family assessment and intervention* (pp. 153–170). Berlin, Heidelberg, New York: Springer.

Lidz, T., Cornelison, A., Fleck, S., & Terry, D. (1957). Intrafamilial environment of schizophrenic patients. *American Journal of Psychiatry*, *114*, 241–248.

McFarlane, W.R. (Ed.). (1983). *Family therapy in schizophrenia*. New York: Guilford.

Miklowitz, D.J., Goldstein, M.J., Nuechterlein, K.H., Snyder, K.S., & Doane, J, (1987). Family factors and the course of bipolar affective disorder. In K. Hahlweg & M.J. Goldstein (Eds.), *Understanding major mental disorder. The contribution of family interaction research* (pp. 195–211). New York: Family Process Press.

Norton, N., Detre, T., & Jarecke, H. (1963). Psychiatric services in general hospitals: A family-oriented redefinition. *Journal of Nervous and Mental Disease*, *136*, 475–484.

Nuechterlein, K.H., Snyder, K.S., Dawson, M.E., Rappe, S., Gitlin, M., & Fogelson, D. (1986). Expressed emotion, fixed-dose fluphenazine decanoate maintenance, and relapse in recent-onset schizophrenia. *Psychopharmacology Bulletin*, *22*, 633–639.

President's Commission on Mental Health (Vol. 2) (1978). Washington, DC: Government Printing Office.

Selvini-Palazzoli, M., Cecchin, A., Prata, G., & Boscolo, L. (1978). *Paradox and counterparadox*. New York: Aronson.

Strachan, A.M., Goldstein, M.J., & Miklowitz, D.J. (1986). Do relatives express emotion? In M.J. Goldstein, I. Hand, & K. Hahlweg (Eds.), *Treatment of schizophrenia. Family assessment and intervention* (pp. 51–58). Berlin, Heidelberg, New York: Springer.

Sturgeon, D., Turpin, G., Berkowitz, R., Kuipers, L., & Leff, J. (1984). Psychophysiological responses of schizophrenic patients to high and low expressed emotion relatives: a follow-up study. *British Journal of Psychiatry*, *145*, 62–69.

Tarrier, N., & Barrowclough, C. (1984). Psychophysiological assessment of expressed emotion in schizophrenia: A case example. *British Journal of Psychiatry*, *145*, 197–203.

Tarrier, N., & Barrowclough, C. (1987). A longitudinal psycho-physiological assessment of a schizophrenic patient in relation to the expressed emotion of his relatives. *Behavioural Psychotherapy*, *15*, 45–47.

Tarrier, N., & Barrowclough, C. (1986). Providing information to relatives about schizophrenia: Some comments. *British Journal of Psychiatry*, *149*, 458–463.

Tarrier, N., Vaughn, C., Lader, M.H., & Leff, J.P. (1979). Bodily reactions to people and events in schizophrenia. *Archives of General Psychiatry*, *36*, 311–315.

Tarrier, N., Barrowclough, C., Vaughn, C., Bamrah, J., Porceddu, K., Watts, S., & Freeman, H. (1988). The community management of schizophrenia. A controlled trial of a behavioural intervention with families to reduce relapse. *British Journal of Psychiatry*, *153*, 532–542.

Turpin, G., Tarrier, N., & Sturgeon, D. (1988). Social psychophysiology and the study of biopsychosocial models of schizophrenia. In H. Wagner (Ed.), *Soical psychophysiology: Perspectives on theory and clinical applications*. (pp. 251–272) New York: Wiley.

Vaughn, C.E., & Leff, J.P. (1976). The influence of family and social factors on the course of psychiatric illness. *British Journal of Psychiatry*, *129*, 125–137.

Subject Index